# EL ALAMEIN
# TO THE RIVER SANGRO

# NORMANDY
# TO THE BALTIC

# EL ALAMEIN
# TO THE RIVER SANGRO

---

# NORMANDY
# TO THE BALTIC

*by*

Field-Marshal
The Viscount Montgomery
of Alamein
K.G., G.C.B., D.S.O.

BARRIE & JENKINS
in association with
THE ARCADIA PRESS
LONDON

EL ALAMEIN TO THE RIVER SANGRO
first published by Hutchinson & Co., Ltd., 1948

NORMANDY TO THE BALTIC
first published by Hutchinson & Co., Ltd., 1947


This Edition published in 1973 by
Barrie & Jenkins Ltd.
24 Highbury Crescent, London N5 1RX
in association with
The Arcadia Press
38 George Street, London W1H 5RE

Second impression 1973

© copyright text Field-Marshal The Viscount
Montgomery of Alamein, K.G., G.C.B., D.S.O.
© copyright maps H.M.S.O.

ISBN 0 214 66901 7

# CONTENTS

# Contents

## PART III

### THE INVASION OF THE MAINLAND OF ITALY AND
### THE ADVANCE TO THE RIVER SANGRO,
### 3 SEPTEMBER–31 DECEMBER 1943

## MAPS

Contents

# BOOK TWO
# *Normandy to the Baltic*

## MAPS

# Contents

## Contents

## DIAGRAMS

## INDEX

# ACKNOWLEDGEMENTS

The publishers wish to thank the following for permission to reproduce the copyright illustrations: The Keystone Press Agency Limited, numbers 16, 17, 18 and 19 in Book One, and number 28 in Book Two; B. T. Batsford Limited, number 29 in Book Two; The Imperial War Museum for all others.

The publishers also wish to express their special thanks to Mr C. D. Hamilton for his invaluable help and advice.

# LIST OF ILLUSTRATIONS

*Illustrations*

# NOTE BY FIELD-MARSHAL MONTGOMERY
## FOR THIS EDITION

———

Since these accounts of my two campaigns were first published, I have been back to Alamein twice and to Normandy on many occasions.

After I had been to the desert for the 25th anniversary of the great turning-point battle of the war I wrote this:

'If it is considered that I was successful in these activities, including Alamein itself, I would attribute it to three basic reasons:

(1) I chose good subordinate generals and trusted them.

(2) I built up a very high class staff, under a brilliant Chief of Staff. My staff was so good that once I had decided on a particular course of action I could confidently hand the whole matter over to General de Guingand to implement, and get on myself with thinking about future operations.

(3) I had a very clear understanding of the importance of the human factor in war and of the need to preserve the lives of those under my command to the greatest extent possible.'

These reflections would sum up the story of these campaigns now published in one volume.


1971                                                    MONTGOMERY OF ALAMEIN

# BOOK ONE

# EL ALAMEIN
# TO THE RIVER SANGRO

# FOREWORD

I am anxious to place on record an authoritative and factual account of the activities of the Eighth Army during the period that I commanded the Army. This period was from 13 August 1942 to 31 December 1943: during which time the Army advanced from Alamein to the Sangro River (in Italy). This book contains the story of those days and I have based it on my personal diary.

The Eighth Army was a very happy family. It went from Alamein to half way up Italy without losing a battle or even a serious action, and without ever withdrawing a yard. As a result it acquired a very high morale; the men had confidence in themselves and in their leaders; they knew they were fine soldiers and they looked it: every man an emperor. It was a wonderful experience to command such an Army in the days of its greatest successes.

Montgomery of Alamein
Field-Marshal.

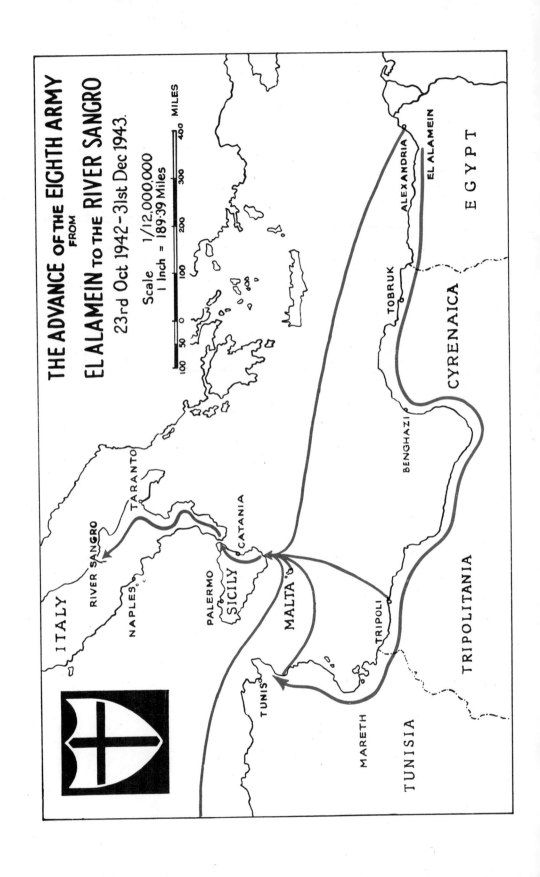

THE ADVANCE OF THE EIGHTH ARMY FROM
EL ALAMEIN TO THE RIVER SANGRO
23rd Oct 1942 – 31st Dec 1943.

Scale 1/12,000,000
1 Inch = 189·39 Miles

0 50 100 200 300 400 MILES

ITALY

RIVER SANGRO

TARANTO

NAPLES

PALERMO

SICILY

CATANIA

MALTA

TUNIS

MARETH

TUNISIA

TRIPOLI

TRIPOLITANIA

BENGHAZI

CYRENAICA

TOBRUK

ALEXANDRIA

EL ALAMEIN

EGYPT

# INTRODUCTION

THIS book tells the story of the Eighth Army's operations in the Mediterranean from El Alamein, 13 August 1942, to the crossing of the River Sangro in Italy, and subsequent operations there until 31 December 1943.

The story concerns primarily the military aspect of the Eighth Army's operations during this period, but the part played by the Royal Navy, and the Royal Air Force in the campaigns in Africa, Sicily, and Italy will not be forgotten.

At all times the Eighth Army was operating with one of its flanks on the sea coast. This fact enabled the Royal Navy to participate in many of our battles and actions, and units of the Fleet were always at hand giving invaluable assistance by bombardment from the sea. Moreover, the progress of the Army was largely governed by the speed with which it could capture and open up ports upon its way; in this matter the Royal Navy played a vital part in assisting our advance. The technique of opening up a port which had been heavily bombed from the air and later deliberately demolished by the enemy in his withdrawal, was developed to a remarkable degree. It has been shown that whatever skill the enemy may employ in his endeavours to prevent the use of a captured port, it can quickly be got working again, and in a short time can be supplying the immense needs of the ground troops and air forces which depend upon it.

A tribute, too, must be paid to the officers and men of the Merchant Navy whose ships brought the material of war from our base to the forward ports. The part they played in our victories was unspectacular; it was nevertheless vital and was accomplished with great heroism and bravery.

The part played by the Royal Air Force in these campaigns was truly tremendous. Mention is constantly made in this story of its operations with the Eighth Army, but in the briefest outline only. It would be difficult for me to pay an adequate tribute to the work and achievements of the Desert Air Force; suffice it to say here that the Desert Air Force and the Eighth Army formed one close, integrated family: collectively they were one great fighting machine, working with a single purpose, and at all times with a single joint plan.

# PART I

THE CAMPAIGN IN NORTH AFRICA
FROM EL ALAMEIN, 13 AUGUST 1942,
TO THE END IN TUNISIA, 12 MAY 1943

# CHAPTER ONE

## *The Situation in the Eighth Army in August 1942*

AT the close of the Axis summer offensive, the battle front in the Western Desert was finally stabilized on a line running approximately north and south from the sea at Tel el Eisa to Qaret el Himeimat: a 35 mile front about 60 miles west of Alexandria.

The Eighth Army defensive positions, known as the El Alamein Line, were constructed astride the gap between the sea and the Qattara Depression, blocking the gateway to the Nile Delta. The original line had been laid out in 1941.

Facing our defences the Axis forces, nominally under Italian command but in fact controlled by Field-Marshal Erwin Rommel, comprised five equivalent German divisions and nine Italian divisions. The German Panzer Army Africa included the German Africa Corps (15 and 21 Panzer Divisions), 90 Light and 164 Infantry Divisions and the Ramcke brigade of parachutists. The Italians were organized in three corps (10, 20 and 21) and included two armoured divisions—Ariete and Littorio.

The Eighth Army front was held by 13 and 30 Corps. The Army disposed six divisions and certain independent armoured and infantry brigades. It was an Imperial force in the truest sense, for it included 9 Australian Division, 5 (later replaced by 4) Indian Division, 2 New Zealand Division, 1 South African Division, and 7 Armoured and 50 Infantry Divisions. There were also Greek and French contingents.

The reverses suffered during the summer of 1942 had left the Eighth Army, in the words of Mr Churchill, 'brave but baffled'. The troops knew that they were worthy of greater things, and indeed the divisions comprised some very fine fighting material. But they had lost confidence in their higher leadership, they lacked a sound battle technique, and they were deficient of equipment and weapons comparable to those of the Germans. It was clear that Rommel was preparing further attacks, and the morale and determination of our troops was undermined by plans for further withdrawals. The 'atmosphere' was wrong.

Such were my impressions when I arrived in the Western Desert and assumed command of the Eighth Army on 13 August 1942.

My mandate was to destroy the Axis forces in North Africa, and it was immediately apparent that the first step necessary was the initiation of a period of reorganization, re-equipment and training. While this was being done, I would have to defeat any attempt by the enemy to break through the Alamein defences, and ensure a firm front behind which a striking force could be prepared for the offensive. On my journey from England, I had decided that the Eighth Army required a reserve corps, well equipped and highly trained. This corps (consisting primarily of armoured divisions) would be trained as the spearhead in our offensives, and would never be used to hold static fronts. The Germans had a reserve formation of this kind—the German Africa Corps—based on two crack Panzer divisions. Our lack of a similar formation in the past had meant that we had never been properly balanced. 'Balance' on the battlefield implies the disposal of available forces in such a way that it is never necessary to react to the enemy's thrusts and moves; a balanced army proceeds relentlessly with its plans in spite of what the enemy may do.

I decided, therefore, that the formation, equipping and training of a reserve corps, strong in armour, must begin at once: as a matter of priority.

### THE NEW DEFENSIVE POLICY AT ALAMEIN

My immediate concern was to ensure that the Alamein Line was securely held. Realizing that the Army might have to withstand a renewed Axis offensive in the immediate future, I ordered at once a new defensive policy.

All existing instructions and plans for further withdrawals were cancelled, and I made it clear that there would be no withdrawal from the Alamein Line; if Rommel attacked, we would fight him where we stood. This change of policy necessitated major alterations in our defences, in particular to give them additional depth, and stocks of ammunition, water and rations had to be increased in the forward areas. These matters were rapidly put in hand. My initial tour of the battle zone convinced me of the vital importance of the Alam Halfa ridge, which I found virtually undefended. It will be seen from the map that this ridge was several miles in the rear of the Alamein Line; it commanded a wide area of desert country, and was essentially one of the keys to the whole defensive system. If the enemy penetrated the Alamein defences in the southern sectors, his subsequent progress would depend on securing this ridge. If it remained in our hands, it would serve either as a base from which to block the enemy's progress to the north towards Ruweisat ridge (the backbone of our defences in the central sector) or alternatively to cut the axis of any hostile thrust attempting to strike east or north-east towards the Nile. I considered a whole division was required to garrison this ridge as a lay-back position, and asked at once for 44 Division to be sent up to me from the Delta, where it had recently arrived from England.

I ordered that divisions should be concentrated and fought as such; this ended the employment of brigade groups, Jock Columns, and the tactical methods which caused divisions to be split up, but to which recourse had been made in the past because of shortage of troops. As part of this policy, I made it clear that armour and artillery develop their maximum effectiveness when employed in mass, and instructions to implement their use in this way were issued.

When I took over command, the Army and Air Headquarters were widely separated, and lacked that close personal relationship which is so essential. I therefore moved my Headquarters to a site adjacent to Air Headquarters, where commanders and staffs could plan and work together as one team.

Lastly, I found a number of higher commanders were tired and in great need of a rest, and I initiated certain changes in order to bring fresh minds to bear on the problem in front of us.

Having established a firm defensive policy, I turned to detailed consideration of the reorganization of the Army, and the formation of the reserve corps—which was to be 10 Corps. During the last weeks of August preparations to this end began to take shape. The reaction within the Eighth Army to the measures I have described was most enthusiastic. The morale of the troops was in the ascendant and their confidence was becoming re-established.

This was the situation when, towards the end of August, it became clear that Rommel intended to attack during the coming full moon.

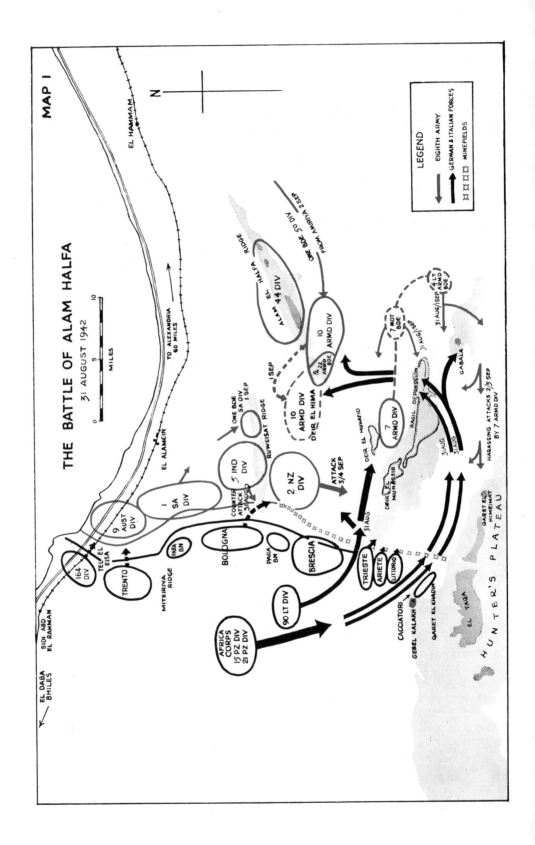

MAP I

THE BATTLE OF ALAM HALFA

31 AUGUST 1942

MILES

0          5          10

TO ALEXANDRIA
60 MILES

LEGEND

EIGHTH ARMY

GERMAN & ITALIAN FORCES

MINEFIELDS

EL HAMMAM

EL ALAMEIN

EL DABA
8 MILES

SIDI ABD
EL RAHMAN

164
DIV

TRENTO

TEL EL
EISA

MITEIRIYA
RIDGE

9
AUST
DIV

I
SA
DIV

5 IND
DIV

COUNTER
ATTACK
31 AUG

ONE BDE
SA DIV
1 SEP

RUWEISAT RIDGE

2 NZ
DIV

ATTACK
3/4 SEP

BOLOGNA

PARA
BN

PARA
BN

BRESCIA

TRIESTE
ARIETE
LITTORIO

CACCIATORI

GEBEL KALAKH

QARET EL KHADIM

DEIR EL
MUNASSIB

DEIR EL MUHAFID

7
ARMD
DIV

RAGIL DEPRESSION

31 AUG

31 AUG

31 AUG

GABALA

HARASSING ATTACKS 2/5 SEP
BY 7 ARMD DIV

QARET EL
HIMEIMAT

EL TAQA

HUNTER'S PLATEAU

AFRICA
CORPS
15 PZ DIV
21 PZ DIV

90 LT DIV

10
ARMD DIV
DEIR EL HIMA

22
ARMD
BDE

1 SEP

7 MOT
BDE

31 AUG/1 SEP

FROM AMIRIYA 2 SEP

ONE BDE 5 TO 10 SEP

ALAM EL
HALFA RIDGE

ALAM
EL
HALFA
44 DIV

10
ARMD DIV

4 LT
ARMD
BDE

31 AUG/1 SEP

# CHAPTER TWO

## *The Battle of Alam Halfa, 31 August 1942*

ON 29 August Rommel announced to his troops that in two or three days they would be in Alexandria, and issued a special order of the day in which he proclaimed that the forthcoming attack would accomplish the 'final annihilation of the enemy'.

His attacks began just after midnight 30/31 August with three simultaneous thrusts. The most northerly attempt was easily repulsed by the Australians and was no more than a raid. In the centre a heavier holding attack, which had lost direction, hit the right of 5 Indian Division, and achieved some initial success. The enemy was ejected from the Ruweisat ridge only after a strong counter attack had been put in at first light on 31 August.

The main thrust was made in the south: between the left flank of the New Zealand Division and Himeimat. Here Rommel employed both 15 and 21 Panzer Divisions, 90 Light Division and 20 Italian Corps which included Ariete and Littorio Armoured Divisions. By 1000 hours 31 August strong tank columns had penetrated our minefields and were moving eastwards between Gaballa and the Ragil Depression. Further north 90 Light Division had some difficulty in crossing the minefields and did not reach Deir el Muhafid until the evening; between the German wings three Italian divisions were operating but, of these, during the whole engagement the Trieste Division alone succeeded in penetrating the mine belts. Our mobile troops of 7 Armoured Division watching the southern flank were forced back in face of this onslaught and, in accordance with their orders, avoided becoming pinned to the ground. 4 Light Armoured Brigade withdrew on Gaballa, and from that area mounted harassing attacks against the flank of the enemy penetration. Further north, 7 Motor Brigade was similarly employed.

My main preoccupation during 31 August was to determine exactly the direction of the enemy thrust line. I hoped that he would move in a tight wheel to the north towards Alam Halfa, and not wide towards El Hammam. Our deception measures had been directed towards that end. During the late afternoon, the enemy armour began to move north-east, in fact directly towards the area for which the Eighth Army layout was designed. A strong wind was blowing and the Royal Air Force was unable to hinder the advance owing to the dust. By about 1700 hours enemy tanks made contact with 22 Armoured Brigade which was in position to the south of the Alam Halfa ridge. 22 Armoured Brigade met this attack on ground of its own choosing, and the enemy was driven off with heavy casualties.

Towards dusk, dust conditions improved and the night bombers took off. Enemy concentrations were pounded throughout the night, and this began a period of intense day and night air action which was a very important factor in our success.

By the morning of 1 September it was clear to me that the enemy axis of advance was directed on the Alam Halfa ridge and thence northwards to the Ruweisat ridge. He was attempting to roll up our line: working from south to north.

Until I was sure of the direction of the main enemy thrust, I had concentrated the bulk of the armour, under Headquarters 10 Armoured Division, to the south of Alam Halfa, where it blocked any attempt to strike north-east and east in order to by-pass our positions and make straight for the Delta. Having established the enemy's intention I was able to switch the armour to the area between the Alam Halfa ridge, held by 44 Division, and the New Zealand positions in the Alamein Line proper. The ground had been reconnoitred in detail by 10 Armoured Division, and when Rommel renewed his attacks northwards I would be well disposed to inflict heavy losses on his Panzer formations. By the middle of the day, I had nearly 400 tanks in the vital area. At the same time Ruweisat ridge was strengthened by the addition of one brigade, which I withdrew from the front of the South African Division. In order to preserve balance, I brought forward a brigade of 50 Division from Amiriya to the area vacated by 10 Armoured Division south of the Alam Halfa feature.

I was now confident of holding the enemy's attacks, and of preventing infiltration behind the main defensive position. I began to consider re-grouping: in order to form reserves and to seize the initiative.

During the morning of 1 September, the enemy had renewed his attacks against 22 Armoured Brigade in position. He achieved nothing and, having again suffered considerable casualties, drew off to the south. He returned to the charge during the afternoon: but the whole of 10 Armoured Division was now firmly established in its new positions, and once more the Panzer formations disengaged with heavy losses.

The relentless pounding of enemy concentrations from the air continued throughout the day.

During the afternoon, I ordered planning to begin for a counter stroke which would give us the initiative. I decided to thin out in 30 Corps sector in the north so as to provide reserves, and to order 13 Corps to prepare to close the gap in our minefields through which the enemy attack had come. The operation would be developed southwards from the New Zealand sector, and proceed methodically and by easy stages.

On 2 September the Axis forces proved reluctant to resume the offensive. They were plainly disconcerted by their failure to draw our armour from its prepared positions. No doubt, too, they were finding the administrative situation difficult. 7 Armoured Division had a good day and intensified its harassing operations north and west of Himeimat, while the Desert Air Force continued to cause great damage and confusion to the enemy.

After visiting the Corps Headquarters, I decided that 13 Corps operations to close the minefield gaps would begin on the night 3/4 September. New Zealand Division would be reinforced for the task by two British infantry brigades. Should the enemy show signs of pulling out, all formations would close in and employ 'jabbing' tactics. I emphasized the importance of destroying soft-skinned vehicles; the more supply lorries we could knock out the greater would be the strain on Rommel's administration. The enemy was known to be short of petrol, and a costly but most effective night bomber raid on Tobruk harbour had done much to aggravate the position. Moreover we had made careful plans to ensure that none of our fuel or supplies fell into his hands.

First light reports on 3 September indicated that the enemy had withdrawn from contact and moved south. His main forces seemed to have edged slightly westwards, leaving the area they vacated strewn with derelict vehicles. I issued very precise instructions at this stage, since it was important to resist any temptation to rush into the attack. The standard of training of the Eighth Army formations was such that I was not prepared to loose them headlong into the enemy; moreover my purpose was to restore the line, and to proceed methodically with my own preparations for the big offensive later on. I therefore ordered that there would be no movement westwards from our main fortified positions in the Alamein Line except by patrols and light forces, and that the attacks to close the gap were to proceed vigorously: but methodically and under careful control. The harassing attacks, particularly those directed against enemy mechanical transport, were to continue with the utmost intensity.

On the afternoon of 3 September three large enemy columns were moving west from the minefield area. The operations of 7 Armoured Division on their southern flank were strengthened and the weight of our air attacks was stepped up to its maximum. On the night 3/4 September the New Zealand Division began to attack southwards as the first stage to closing the gap in the minefields. The reaction was fierce. Bitter fighting took place, and the enemy launched heavy and repeated counter attacks on 4 September to repel our attempts to bottle him in. We did not succeed in cutting him off, but he was forced slowly and relentlessly back throughout 4 and 5 September. At dawn on the following day fighting continued between our two minefield belts, and it was clear that he meant to retain possession of this area and was prepared to fight for it.

At 0700 hours on 7 September I decided to call off the battle, and to leave the enemy in possession of the western edge of our original minefields, organizing fresh positions for the Eighth Army on the eastern edge of them. There were definite advantages in keeping some additional enemy strength on my southern flank.

All energies of the Army could now be directed again to the business of building up our striking force and preparing for the decisive blow.

SOME REFLECTIONS ON THE BATTLE OF ALAM HALFA

The Eighth Army fought as an integrated Army under the direct control of Army Headquarters. Artillery and armour were used in concentrations, and had been so positioned that the enemy armoured thrusts were dealt with quickly and effectively on ground of our own choosing. The initial layout of our forces, together with speedy re-grouping required by the course of the action, had ensured preservation of balance throughout the battlefield. It had thus been unnecessary to conform to Rommel's thrusts, and in our own time we seized the initiative and completed the defeat of the enemy. The tremendous power of the air arm in close co-operation with the land battle was well demonstrated in the operation; the Army and Air Force worked to a combined plan, made possible because the Army and Air Commanders, and their staffs, were working together at one Headquarters.

The victory at Alam Halfa had a profound effect on the Eighth Army. The morale of the soldiers became outstanding. Rommel had been defeated in his purpose, and had suffered severe casualties. The confidence of the troops in the higher command was re-established, and they entered into the preparations for the decisive battle that was to come with tremendous enthusiasm.

I think that this battle has never received the interest or attention it deserves. It was a vital action, because had we lost it, we might well have lost Egypt. In winning it we paved the way for success at El Alamein and the subsequent advance to Tunisia.

An interesting feature of the story of operations against the Germans in North Africa is the recurrence of similar circumstances before the Battle of Mareth, later in the campaign. There, also, success in a defensive battle at Medenine on 6 March paved the way for decisive victory in our subsequent offensive at Mareth on 20 March.

# CHAPTER THREE

## *Preparations for the Battle of El Alamein*

THE Battle of Alam Halfa had interfered with our preparations for the formation of a reserve corps, and had caused us some delay. As soon as the situation had been restored, however, no time was lost in continuing with our plans.

10 Corps (General Lumsden) was to consist of 1 Armoured Division, 10 Armoured Division (including two armoured brigades), and 2 New Zealand Division (with an armoured brigade under command). This Corps was concentrated for training and re-equipment in the rear areas. 2 New Zealand Division was relieved in the line by 44 Division, whose positions at Alam Halfa were taken over by 51 Division, recently arrived from the United Kingdom.

My policy at this stage was to build up the Army on three basic fundamentals: leadership, equipment and training. By early October I was satisfied with the leadership aspect; my subordinate commanders were sound, and I had every confidence in them.

The equipment situation improved rapidly. Sherman tanks, sent to us at the personal instigation of President Roosevelt, started arriving in the Delta from America in August, and were issued to 10 Corps. In the Sherman we had at last a match for the German tanks. We had moreover a great weight of artillery and there was plenty of ammunition.

My great anxiety was that the state of training was still not good, and it was becoming clear that I would have to be very careful to ensure that units and formations were not given tasks which would be beyond their capabilities. I would have to stage-manage the forthcoming battle in such a way that the troops would be able to do what was demanded of them, and I must not be too ambitious in my demands.

During this period of preparation, I was working out the plan for the Battle of Alamein. It was because of shortcomings in the standard of training in the Army, that I had to alter, early in October, the whole conception of how I intended to fight the battle.

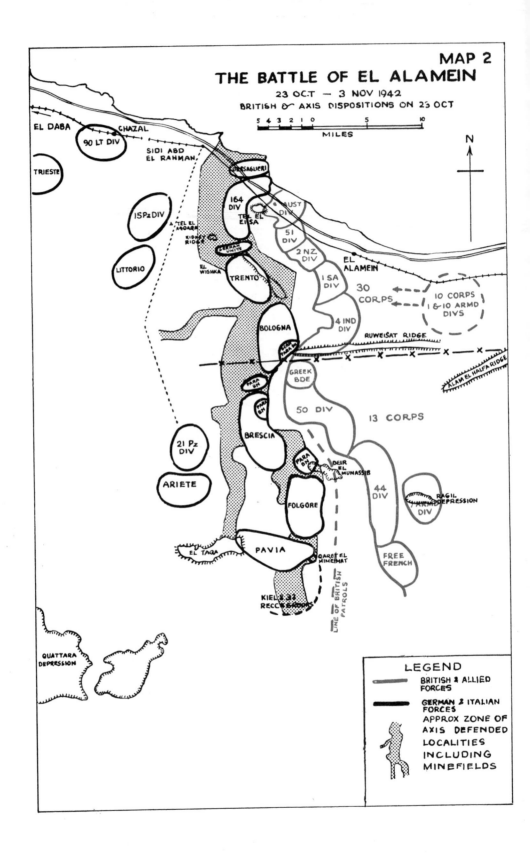

MAP 2

# THE BATTLE OF EL ALAMEIN
23 OCT — 3 NOV 1942
BRITISH & AXIS DISPOSITIONS ON 23 OCT

5 4 3 2 1 0          5          10
MILES

N

EL DABA          GHAZAL

90 LT DIV

SIDI ABD
EL RAHMAN

TRIESTE

BERSAGLIERI

164
DIV          TRUST
DIV

15 Pz DIV          TEL EL
EISA

TEL EL
 AQQARA          51
DIV

KIDNEY
RIDGE          GERMAN
UNITS          2 NZ
DIV

EL WISHKA          TRENTO          1 SA
DIV          EL
ALAMEIN

LITTORIO          30
CORPS          10 CORPS
1 & 10 ARMD
DIVS

4 IND
DIV

BOLOGNA          RUWEISAT RIDGE

RECCE UN
PARA BN          × ─ × ─ × ─ × ─ × ─ × ─ × ─ ×

ALAM EL HALFA RIDGE

PARA BN          GREEK
BDE

PARA
BN          50 DIV          13 CORPS

21 Pz
DIV          BRESCIA

PARA
BN          DEIR
EL MUNASSIB

ARIETE          44
DIV          RAGIL
DEPRESSION
DIV

FOLGORE

EL TAQA          PAVIA          FREE
FRENCH

QARET EL
MINEIMAT

KIEL & 33
RECCE GROUPS          LINE OF BRITISH PATROLS

QUATTARA
DEPRESSION

LEGEND
BRITISH & ALLIED
FORCES
GERMAN & ITALIAN
FORCES
APPROX ZONE OF
AXIS DEFENDED
LOCALITIES
INCLUDING
MINEFIELDS

# CHAPTER FOUR

## *The Battle of El Alamein, 23 October 1942*

### MAJOR CONSIDERATIONS AFFECTING THE PLAN

FULL moon was on 24 October. A full moon was essential for the operation, since there was no open flank, and we had to make gaps in the minefields and to blow a hole through the enemy's defensive system during the night. The earliest therefore that we could mount the offensive was on the night 23/24 October.

The enemy had made good use of the lull after his abortive attack to strengthen and deepen his defences. In the northern sector he had three belts of defended localities and minefields and any attack by us was intended to lose both force and direction within this system itself. In the south, the defences were not so highly organized, but were sited to canalize any penetration we might make. In general the minefields alone extended for some 5,000 to 9,000 yards in depth. The enemy positions were held by one German and five Italian divisions, together with a German parachute brigade; detached German infantry elements were used to stiffen the Italian sectors. In reserve in the north were the 15 Panzer and Italian Littorio Armoured Divisions, and further to the rear, on the coast, was 90 Light Division. In reserve in the south there were 21 Panzer and the Ariete Armoured Divisions. On the Egyptian frontier stood the Pistoia Division.

It was extremely difficult to achieve any form of surprise. It seemed impossible to conceal from the enemy that we meant to launch an attack. At best we could deceive him about the direction of our main thrusts and the date by which we would be ready to begin.

### THE PLAN

In planning the Battle of Alamein the main difficulties confronting us were three: first, the problem of blowing a hole in the enemy positions; secondly, the despatch of a Corps strong in armour through the hole into enemy territory; and lastly, the development of operations so as to destroy the Axis forces.

In September I had been working on the idea of attacking the enemy simultaneously on both flanks—the main attack being made in the north by 30 Corps (General Leese). This operation would force a gap across the enemy's defensive system through which 10 Corps would pass. 10 Corps would position itself on ground of its own choosing *astride the enemy supply routes*; the enemy armour would deploy against it, and be destroyed: probably piecemeal, as I hoped to keep it dispersed as long as possible. The attack of 13 Corps (General Horrocks) in the south would draw off enemy armour to that flank, and thus weaken at least the initial opposition to 10 Corps.

C

As I have mentioned already, early in October I changed the conception of how I would fight the battle, because I was not satisfied that we were capable of achieving success in a plan so ambitious.

It had been generally accepted that the plan in a modern battle should aim first at destroying the enemy's armour, and that once this had been accomplished, the unarmoured portion of his army would be dealt with readily. I decided to reverse this concept and to destroy first the unarmoured formations. While doing this I would hold off the armoured divisions, which would be tackled subsequently. In broad terms, the fighting elements of Rommel's army comprised holding troops (mostly unarmoured) who manned defences and guarded essential areas of ground; and mobile troops (mostly armoured) whose role was offensive. The mobile troops were used to deliver counter attacks during defensive periods, and to form the spearhead of advance in the offensive. If the holding troops could be destroyed, the enemy would be unable to secure ground vital to the action of his armoured forces; these would be denied firm bases from which to manœuvre and within which to refurbish, and their supply routes would lie open to interruption. In these circumstances the armoured forces would be forced to withdraw or perish.

My idea therefore was to aim first at the methodical destruction of the infantry divisions holding the enemy's defensive system. This would be accomplished by means of a 'crumbling' process, carefully organized from a series of firm bases: an operation within the capabilities of my troops. For success, the method depended on holding off the enemy's armour while the 'crumbling' manœuvre was carried out. It was also vital that the 'break-in' battle, designed to gain a foothold in the enemy's defences, should achieve complete success, so that the enemy infantry might be attacked from the flank and rear and its supply routes in the forward area could be cut.

The enemy's armour would obviously not sit still and watch the gradual destruction of the infantry; it would be launched into counter attacks. If I could position my armour beyond the area of the 'crumbling' operations, on ground of its own choosing, the enemy tanks would have to attack in conditions favourable to us, and could be held off. The minefields, particularly those west of the main Axis positions, would restrict the approaches available to those enemy tanks which might try to counter attack our assaulting units while they were dealing with the defending infantry. If the approaches themselves were closed by our own tanks in position, we would be able to proceed relentlessly with our plans.

My orders for the battle, issued on 6 October, provided for three simultaneous attacks.

The main thrust by 30 Corps in the north was to be made on a front of four divisions, with the task of forcing two corridors through the enemy's minefields. 10 Corps was to pass through these corridors.

In the south, 13 Corps was to mount two operations: one into the area east of Gebel Kalakh and Qaret el Khadim, the other further south directed on Himeimat and the Taqa feature.

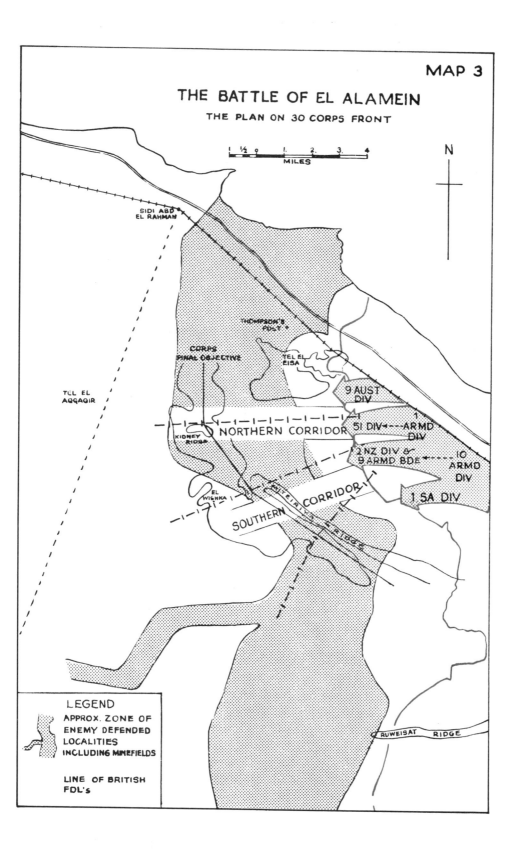

MAP 3

# THE BATTLE OF EL ALAMEIN

### THE PLAN ON 30 CORPS FRONT

MILES

N

SIDI ABD
EL RAHMAN

THOMPSON'S
POST

CORPS
FINAL OBJECTIVE

TEL EL
EISA

TEL EL
AQQAQIR

9 AUST
DIV

KIDNEY
RIDGE

NORTHERN CORRIDOR

51 DIV — ARMD
DIV

2 NZ DIV &
9 ARMD BDE

10
ARMD
DIV

EL
WISHKA

MITEIRIYA RIDGE

SOUTHERN CORRIDOR

1 SA DIV

RUWEISAT RIDGE

## LEGEND

APPROX. ZONE OF
ENEMY DEFENDED
LOCALITIES
INCLUDING MINEFIELDS

LINE OF BRITISH
FDL's

13 and 30 Corps having broken into the enemy's defences were to undertake the methodical destruction of the troops holding the forward positions.

10 Corps had as its ultimate task the destruction of the enemy armour, and was to be manœuvred so as to prevent enemy interference with 30 Corps operations; it would assist, as opportunity offered, in the 'crumbling' process.

The role of 13 Corps was primarily to mislead the enemy into believing that our main thrust was being delivered in the south, and to contain enemy forces there: particularly 21 Panzer Division. 7 Armoured Division was available for the operation, but I ordered that it was to be kept intact on the southern flank, in order to preserve balanced dispositions throughout the front. Whereas everything was to be ready to pass this formation through the minefields and to exploit it in a swing northwards towards Daba, I made it clear that the attack was not to be pressed if heavy casualties were likely to result.

My orders emphasized that it was vital to retain the initiative and to keep up sustained pressure on the enemy. The troops were to take advantage of any weakening and were to avoid any long pauses which might give the enemy time to recover his balance.

The break-in operation was to be facilitated by a very heavy counter-battery plan, the effect of which was to be strengthened by switching the whole of the bomber effort onto the artillery areas as soon as the battle began. I realized that following the break-in, a real dog-fight would ensue. I was confident that our resources were sufficient to withstand the strain which this would impose. The essentials of the battle would be the retention of the initiative, the maintenance of pressure on the enemy, and the preservation of balance so that it would be unnecessary to react to the enemy's thrusts.

The Royal Air Force plan of operations began with the winning of the air battle before the attack opened. Having obtained ascendancy over the German Air Force, the whole of the air effort was to be available to co-operate intimately in the land battle.

THE COVER PLAN

The cover plan for the battle was worked out in August and September. It aimed at misleading the enemy about the direction of the main thrusts and the date of our readiness for the attack.

The basis of 'visual deception' was the preservation of a constant density of vehicles throughout the zone of operations, so that the enemy would be denied the inferences made from the changes disclosed in day-to-day air photographs. By means of pooled transport resources (enlarged by the reduction of divisional holdings) and by the construction of large numbers of dummy lorries, the layout and density of vehicles required for the assault in the northern sector was established on the ground as early as 1 October. During the period of forward concentration of 51 and 2 New Zealand Divisions and 10 Corps, the substitute transport was replaced at night by the operational transport of the divisions concerned. Guns, limbers, and squads of reinforcing artillery units were dealt with in a similar way. The rear areas whence these units and formations came were maintained at their full vehicle quota by the erection of dummies as the real transport moved out. Dumps were concealed by elaborate camouflage and by stacking stores to resemble vehicles. A month before the attack, slit trenches were dug, in which (when the time came) the assaulting infantry could be concealed.

Meanwhile active measures were employed to cause the enemy to believe the main blow would be delivered in the south. A dummy pipeline was started late in September, and progress in the work was timed to indicate its completion by the first week in November; dummy dumps were also made working to a similar date. Headquarters 8 Armoured Division was used to assist, with its wireless network, the notion that armoured forces were moving to the southern flank.

An essential feature of my plan was that every commander in the Army, down to the rank of Lieutenant-Colonel, should know from me personally how I proposed to fight the battle, what issues depended on it, and what were the main difficulties we were likely to encounter. I toured the Army addressing the officers.

On 21 and 22 October, the battle was explained to the troops by their officers.

I was determined that the soldiers should go into battle having been worked up into a great state of enthusiasm, and realizing fully what was expected of them.

Heavy and sustained air attacks against the Axis air forces and land communications reached a crescendo on 22 October. The degree of air superiority thus achieved was such that throughout 23 October our aircraft maintained continuous fighter patrols over enemy landing grounds without interference.

Concentration in the forward assembly areas was completed during the night 22/23 October, and by first light, all formations were dug in and camouflaged. The assaulting infantry spent the day of 23 October unobserved in the slits dug in front of our foremost positions, and it was clear from the absence of shelling of our positions that we would indeed achieve tactical surprise.

The stage was set. During the morning my personal message was read out to all ranks:

"The Battle which is now about to begin will be
one of the decisive battles of history.
It will be the turning point of the war . . . .
The Lord mighty in battle will give us the victory."

With these words the Eighth Army was launched into battle.

[23]

THE 'BREAK-IN'

23–24 October 1942

*Operations 23/24 October*

The night of 23 October was still and clear. At 2140 hours, in the bright moonlight, the Eighth Army artillery opened on located enemy batteries. Over a thousand field and medium guns were employed, and the effect was terrific.

At 2200 hours fire was switched to the enemy's foremost positions, and the assaulting divisions of 13 and 30 Corps advanced to the attack.

In the north, the four divisions of 30 Corps attacked in line. 9 Australian and 51 Divisions, responsible for forcing the northern corridor through the minefields, attacked west from their positions just north of Miteiriya ridge; the New Zealanders and South Africans thrust in a south-south-westerly direction onto the ridge itself, and were to establish the southern corridor. At the same time 4 Indian Division carried out a strong raid against enemy positions on the western end of Ruweisat ridge, and in the extreme north an Australian brigade made a feint attack between Tel el Eisa and the sea.

Heavy fighting continued all night against stiffening resistance, but by 0530 hours most of the final objectives had been reached. The two corridors had been pushed through the main minefield belts and supporting weapons of the infantry were moving forward. 9 Armoured Brigade (2 New Zealand Division) was also reported to be progressing well through the southern corridor.

Behind the divisions of 30 Corps, 1 and 10 Armoured Divisions of 10 Corps crossed their start line at 0200 hours and made for the northern and southern routes respectively. Both formations however got behind schedule. 1 Armoured Division was delayed because a strong enemy locality held up 51 Division. When 10 Armoured Division came up to the Miteiriya ridge, enemy artillery and anti-tank gun fire prohibited its progress. 9 Armoured Brigade of 2 New Zealand Division got forward of the ridge, but met further minefields and also heavy anti-tank gun fire. The armour remained behind the Miteiriya feature and engaged the enemy at long range. 15 Panzer Division delivered a series of minor counter attacks which were beaten off with considerable casualties to the enemy tanks.

Meanwhile in 13 Corps sector to the south, an operation was mounted by 7 Armoured and 44 Divisions with the object of forcing two gaps in the minefields north of Himeimat. At the same time 1 Fighting French Brigade attacked Hunter's Plateau.

The attempt to breach the western field failed after being hung up by scattered mines between the two major belts. 13 Corps therefore resorted to 'crumbling' action between the belts during 24 October and achieved valuable results. The French took their objective, but soft sand delayed their supporting weapons, and they were driven back by a counter attack delivered by the Kiel Group—a German armoured column.

*Situation on 24 October*

In the north we had successfully broken into the enemy positions and secured a

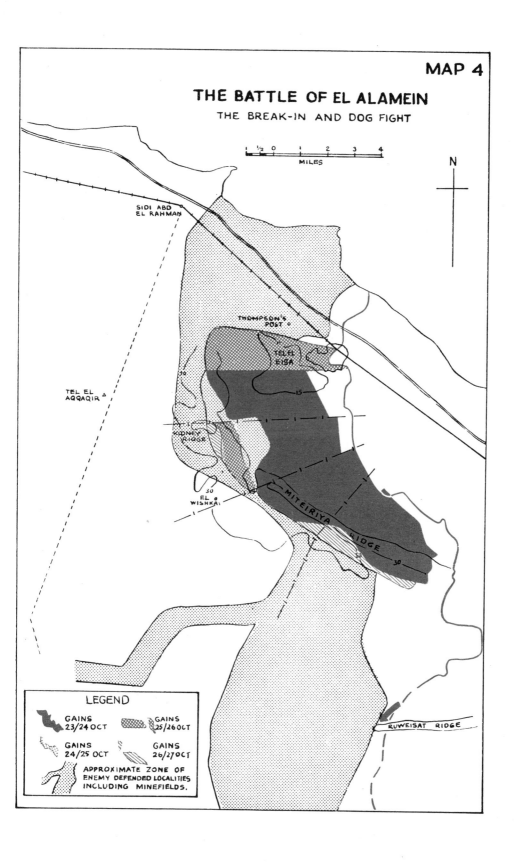

MAP 4

# THE BATTLE OF EL ALAMEIN
## THE BREAK-IN AND DOG FIGHT

MILES

N

SIDI ABD
EL RAHMAN

THOMPSON'S
POST

TEL EL
EISA

TEL EL
AQQAQIR

KIDNEY
RIDGE

EL
WISHKA

MITEIRIYA RIDGE

RUWEISAT RIDGE

LEGEND

GAINS
23/24 OCT

GAINS
25/26 OCT

GAINS
24/25 OCT

GAINS
26/27 OCT

APPROXIMATE ZONE OF
ENEMY DEFENDED LOCALITIES
INCLUDING MINEFIELDS.

good bridgehead. But attempts to pass the armour into the open and to the west of the Axis defensive system had been unsuccessful.

My plan was now to force 1 and 10 Armoured Divisions into the open as quickly as possible, and to commence 'crumbling' operations to the south-west by 2 New Zealand Division. I also ordered a strong raid westwards from the Ruweisat ridge by 30 Corps and completion of the gaps through the southern minefield by 13 Corps.

THE 'DOG-FIGHT'

24–30 October 1942

*Operations 24/25 October*

The attack on the north corridor axis was resumed by 1 Armoured Division and 51 Division at 1500 hours on 24 October. My orders were very firm and produced good results; by 1800 hours 2 Armoured Brigade (1 Armoured Division) had broken out from the western minefield, and was taking up positions beyond.

On the southern corridor axis, 10 Armoured Division supported by 30 Corps artillery, renewed its attack at 2200 hours. During the night reports showed that the operation was not making progress. I feared that my plan for getting this formation through the mine belt was in danger of failure and at 0400 hours, 25 October, I issued orders that it must and would get forward. By 0800 hours, the leading armoured brigade was reported in position, 2,000 yards west of the minefield area, and in touch with 1 Armoured Division on its right. The leading regiment of the other armoured brigade of the division had also cleared the enemy's main position.

Meanwhile 9 Armoured Brigade of 2 New Zealand Division was clear of the corridor, and was operating south-west according to plan.

During 25 October, 15 Panzer Division again made a series of counter attacks, including one near Kidney Ridge in which about 100 tanks were used. Our armour was now in position, and repulsed these attacks with heavy casualties to the enemy.

In the 13 Corps area, 44 Division renewed its efforts to gap the minefields during the night 24/25 October and was successful. A small bridgehead was formed and 4 Light Armoured Brigade was passed through. Scattered mines and an anti-tank gun screen were encountered however, and it was apparent that heavy casualties would be sustained if the attack were pressed home. On the morning of 25 October, I authorized 13 Corps to break off this action, in accordance with my policy of maintaining 7 Armoured Division at effective fighting strength. It was essential to maintain the balance of the Army, and as long as 21 Panzer Division was in the south, I required an armoured division in 13 Corps: and its presence there assisted materially in keeping enemy armour in the south.

On 25 October, 50 Division mounted an attack in the Munassib area. This was not pressed and soon petered out in face of thick wire and anti-personnel mines.

[26]

*Situation on 25 October*

We had now thrust our armour out into positions where it was well placed to meet the enemy tanks and inflict on them heavy casualties. It could function as I had intended, and as long as the enemy attacked us, particularly in isolated and piecemeal fashion, I was well content.

In the south 13 Corps was maintaining the threat well.

My major consideration was now the 'crumbling' process of wearing down the enemy's infantry in the north. It became clear that 2 New Zealand Division's move south-west would be a most costly undertaking, and at midday on 25 October I decided to abandon it and to switch the main 'crumbling' action to the Australian sector. I gave orders for 9 Australian Division to attack north towards the sea, with the object of destroying the German forces in the coastal salient which had been created by our break-in battle. In conjunction with this attack, I provided for operations to be developed westwards by 1 Armoured Division from its position in the bridgehead. If 1 Armoured Division could make progress to the west, the opportunity might come to pass its armoured brigade through to the Rahman track; it could then get behind the enemy holding the salient. In the following days I was constantly considering the problem of establishing armour in the Rahman area, since it was the key to the system of enemy supply routes in rear.

In switching the main 'crumbling' process so radically I hoped to gain surprise and to take a heavy toll of the enemy.

*Operations night 25/26 and 26 October*

The Australian attack on the night 25/26 October was completely successful. The Germans suffered some 300 casualties.

1 Armoured Division, however, failed to make any progress to the west in its operations in the Kidney Ridge sector.

On 26 October, 1 South African Division and 2 New Zealand Division advanced about 1,000 yards, thus gaining more depth in front of the Miteiriya ridge. The same night, 7 Motor Brigade established itself on Kidney Ridge.

*Situation 26 October*

I spent the day in detailed consideration of the situation, and it was from this date onwards that plans were evolved culminating in the final break-out operation which was launched on the night 1/2 November.

My tank state showed over 800 runners, and the ammunition situation was sound. But a note of caution was imposed in my planning. The assaulting divisions had suffered considerable casualties, and there was a lack of replacements for the New Zealand and South African Divisions.

The infantry divisions had, according to plan, carried out slow and methodical improvement of their positions by a series of carefully co-ordinated attacks on narrow fronts with limited objectives. In this they had taken heavy toll of the hostile infantry. 30 Corps was now, however, in need of a short pause for reorganization.

The armoured divisions were forward in positions from which heavy casualties had been caused to the enemy armour.

The momentum of the attack, however, was diminishing and 10 Corps had not broken out into open country. The enemy had withdrawn troops and guns from his forward positions in anticipation of our offensive, and we had therefore found him in greater depth than had been expected. Our break-in area was still ringed by a strong anti-tank gun screen, and attempts to pierce it had been unsuccessful.

By evening on 26 October I had decided to regroup, in order to create fresh reserves for further offensive action. The next phase would be in the north again, as I had been impressed with the results of the Australian attack on the night 25/26 October. If I could get behind the enemy holding the coastal salient, I would annihilate or capture a strong force of Germans and perhaps open up the operation along the coastal axis. The first stage of regrouping was the reversion of 2 New Zealand Division into reserve. Its sector was taken over by 1 South African Division, which was relieved in turn by 4 Indian Division. The latter I placed under 13 Corps.

*Operations 27 and 28 October*

Throughout 27 October the enemy launched heavy armoured counter attacks against Kidney Ridge. These attacks were put in by both 15 and 21 Panzer Divisions, the latter having moved north during the previous night. The enemy was repulsed in all cases, and suffered very heavy losses. 1 Armoured Division alone knocked out nearly fifty German tanks in this engagement.

On 28 October the enemy made a prolonged reconnaissance of Kidney Ridge, probing for soft spots while the two German Panzer Divisions waited in rear. In the evening they began to concentrate for attack, but the Desert Air Force intervened with such effect that the enemy was defeated before he had completed his forming-up.

*Situation on 27 and 28 October*

On 27 October, I developed my plan for breaking out in the northern sector.

I gave orders for 9 Australian Division to launch a heavy attack northwards on the night 28/29 October.

I intended to destroy the enemy coastal salient, and then drive 30 Corps westwards along the road and railway route to Sidi Abd el Rahman. Holding off the enemy armour, our tanks would operate to the south.

The situation in the south was such that I decided that 13 Corps should become primarily defensive. Every endeavour was to be made by means of patrols and artillery action to prolong the enemy's anxiety in this sector, but no further major operations would be staged there. 21 Panzer Division had been contained in the south until the night of 26 October, and our infantry had inflicted heavy casualties on the enemy. 13 Corps had successfully fulfilled its role.

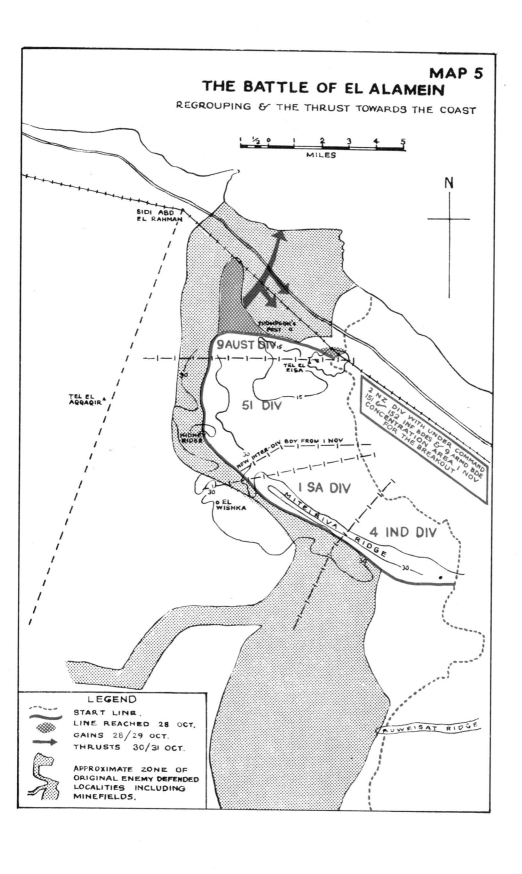

# MAP 5

## THE BATTLE OF EL ALAMEIN

REGROUPING & THE THRUST TOWARDS THE COAST

MILES
1 ½ 0 1 2 3 4 5

N

SIDI ABD
EL RAHMAN

THOMPSON'S
POST Q.

9 AUST DIV 15

TEL EL
EISA

TEL EL
AQQAQIR

51 DIV 15

2 NZ DIV WITH UNDER COMMAND
151 & 152 INF BDES & 9 ARMD BDE
CONCENTRATION AREA 1 NOV
FOR THE BREAKOUT

SYDNEY
RIDGE

INTER-DIV BDY FROM 1 NOV
30
NEW

30

30
EL
WISHKA

I SA DIV

MITEIRIYA RIDGE

4 IND DIV

30
30

RUWEISAT RIDGE

### LEGEND

START LINE.

LINE REACHED 28 OCT.

GAINS 28/29 OCT.

THRUSTS 30/31 OCT.

APPROXIMATE ZONE OF
ORIGINAL ENEMY DEFENDED
LOCALITIES INCLUDING
MINEFIELDS.

I now ordered the second stage of regrouping. 7 Armoured Division (with a brigade of 44 Division), a brigade of 50 Division and the Greek Brigade, were to be sent up to the northern sector from 13 Corps; and, to release troops for the forthcoming Australian attack, a brigade of 51 Division relieved 20 Australian Brigade. 1 Armoured Division needed a pause for reorganization, and since it was clear that the whole German Africa Corps was now facing the northern corridor, I turned the sector over to the defensive, and withdrew 1 Armoured Division and 24 Armoured Brigade into reserve.

New Zealand Division was selected to lead the drive westwards, and since it was low in strength, I arranged for the brigades from 13 Corps to be available to work with it and keep it at operational strength.

In this way re-grouping of the Army was undertaken, and I was soon to have a strong reserve force ready to stage the break-out and to deliver the knock-out blow.

*Operations night 28/29, 29 and 30 October*

The Australian attack on night 28/29 October made good progress and about 200 prisoners were taken. A narrow wedge was driven into the enemy's positions, reaching almost to the road between Sidi Abd el Rahman and Tel el Eisa. On the right of the attack very strong opposition and extensive minefields were encountered round Thompson's Post, which was the bastion of the enemy's coastal salient.

During 29 October, and again early on 30 October, repeated counter attacks by tanks and infantry were hurled against the Australians in the wedge, but they held on and retained the ground won.

*Situation 29 and 30 October*

I learnt during the morning of 29 October that 90 Light Division had moved into the Sidi Abd el Rahman area. This was very significant, for it showed that Rommel was reacting to the threat in the north and had probably guessed my intention of striking west along the road and rail axis.

As a result I modified my plan for the break-out by moving the axis of the westwards drive further to the south, so that the blow would fall mainly on the Italians.

9 Australian Division would resume its threat northwards to the sea on the night 30/31 October. This would prepare the way for the break-out to the west by confirming the enemy's fears in the extreme north. Above all it would probably ensure that 90 Light Division remained about Sidi Abd el Rahman.

On night 31 October/1 November (subsequently postponed 24 hours), 2 New Zealand Division thrusting due west would blow a new gap through the enemy positions just north of the existing northern corridor. Through this gap 10 Corps would pass out into the open desert with 1, 7 and 10 Armoured Divisions and two armoured car regiments. The armoured divisions were to destroy the German Africa Corps and the armoured cars were to operate on the enemy supply routes to intensify the enemy's administrative difficulties—particularly his shortage of petrol. To this operation I gave the name 'Supercharge'.

'Supercharge' was to get us out into the open country and to lead to the disintegration of Rommel's forces in Egypt. We had got to bring the enemy's armour to battle and get astride his lines of communication. 2 New Zealand Division's task involved a penetration of some 6,000 yards on a 4,000 yards front, and I made it clear that should 30 Corps fail to reach its final objectives, *the armoured divisions of 10 Corps were to fight their way through.*

The change of thrust line of 'Supercharge' to the south proved most fortunate. I learnt on 1 November that 21 Panzer Division had joined 90 Light Division in the Rahman area, so that the road and railway axis was very strongly covered. Rommel was playing into my hands, for the bulk of his German forces was now concentrated on the coast, leaving the Italians to hold the more southerly sectors. I could drive a blow between the Germans and Italians and concentrate on destroying the former.

## THE 'BREAK-OUT'

### 31 October–4 November 1942

*Operations 31 October to 3 November*

The thrust north started again on the night 30/31 October as planned. The Australians succeeded in crossing the coast road and pushed forward to the sea and then turned eastwards. The Panzer Grenadiers of 164 Division were thus trapped, and the enemy launched a number of furious counter attacks to free them. Towards evening some German tanks from the west succeeded in joining the defenders of Thompson's Post, and eventually the majority of the Germans fought their way out. But the enemy suffered very severe casualties in this action.

At 0100 hours, 2 November, 'Supercharge' began and the assaulting troops advanced behind a creeping barrage.

151 and 152 Infantry Brigades attacked on the main frontage, under command of 2 New Zealand Division. Subsidiary attacks were staged to extend the base of the salient.

9 Armoured Brigade was to pass through the infantry on its final objective and form a bridgehead beyond the track running south from Sidi Abd el Rahman. 1 and 7 Armoured Divisions (and later 10 Armoured Division) were to debouch from this bridgehead, together with the two armoured car regiments detailed for raids deep in the enemy rear.

The operation achieved great success. The new corridor was established and 9 Armoured Brigade reached the Rahman track just before first light. The Royals swung south-west and reached open country, and were followed later by 4 South African Armoured Car Regiment which had been considerably delayed in breaking out.

As it became light 9 Armoured Brigade ran into a formidable anti-tank gun screen

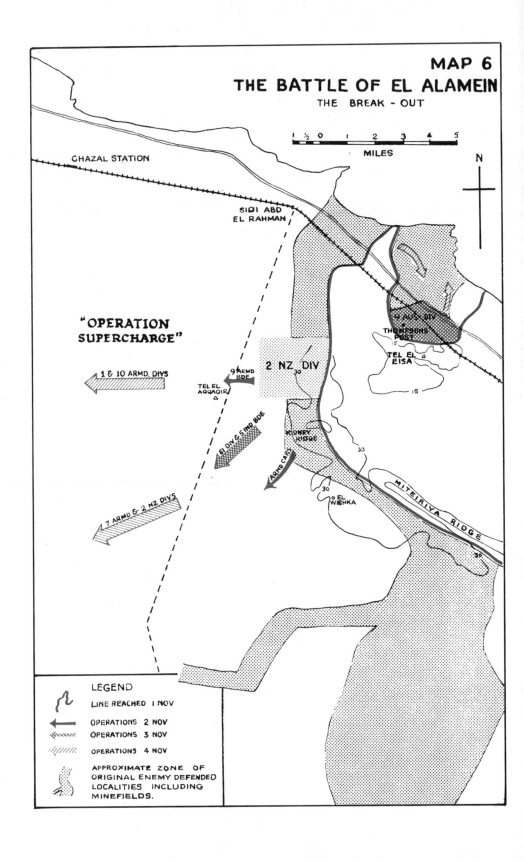

# MAP 6
## THE BATTLE OF EL ALAMEIN
### THE BREAK - OUT

½  0    1    2    3    4    5
MILES

N

GHAZAL STATION

SIDI ABD
EL RAHMAN

"OPERATION
SUPERCHARGE"

1 & 10 ARMD. DIVS

9 ARMD
BDE

2 NZ DIV

9 AUS. DIV
THOMPSON'S
POST

TEL EL
EISA

TEL EL
AQQAQIR

4 EL DIV & 5 IND BDE

KIDNEY
RIDGE

ARMD CARS

7 ARMD & 2 NZ DIVS

EL
WISHKA

MITEIRIYA RIDGE

LEGEND

LINE REACHED 1 NOV

OPERATIONS 2 NOV

OPERATIONS 3 NOV

OPERATIONS 4 NOV

APPROXIMATE ZONE OF
ORIGINAL ENEMY DEFENDED
LOCALITIES INCLUDING
MINEFIELDS.

and during the day suffered over 75 per cent casualties. It hung on tenaciously inflicting losses on the enemy and its action was instrumental in holding the bridge-head. 1 Armoured Division, too, became involved near Tel el Aqqaqir, and a fierce armoured battle ensued in which both sides had losses.

In the afternoon 51 Division extended the salient to the south, and at night 7 Motor Brigade attacked to the west of the Rahman track.

On 3 November, the Desert Air Force reported heavy traffic moving westwards on the coast road, but the enemy anti-tank gun screen held, and 1 Armoured Division was still unable to pierce it.

### Situation 3 November

It was now clear that the enemy contemplated a withdrawal, but would have difficulty in getting his troops away owing to shortage of transport and fuel. And so I expected that he would try and hold me off while his evacuation of the Alamein positions proceeded, but I made plans to complete the break-out and get behind him.

I ordered an attack to the south of Tel el Aqqaqir, with the object of outflanking the anti–tank gun screen which was hemming us in.

### Operations on night 3/4 and 4 November

On the night 3/4 November 51 Division and a brigade from 4 Indian Division launched a very speedily mounted thrust which reached the Rahman track south of Tel el Aqqaqir on a front of over four miles. My intention was to break through the southern sector of the enemy's anti-tank gun screen which was preventing our penetration; the enemy was not in very great depth in the area and once a gap had been made the way would be clear for our armour to pass out into the open desert, out-flanking the stronger resistance to the north. Very great credit is due to the formations which organized this attack in an extremely short time and carried it through success-fully, for by the morning of 4 November the enemy screen had been forced back and reformed facing south-east covering the coast road. The armoured divisions and New Zealanders were set in motion. The Battle of El Alamein had been won. Everywhere the enemy was in full retreat.

### THE PURSUIT FROM EL ALAMEIN

I planned to cut off the retreating enemy by swinging north to cut the coast road at the bottlenecks of Fuka and Matruh. 2 New Zealand Division was ordered to Fuka, and 10 Corps to Matruh.

Meanwhile to the south of the break-out area, 13 Corps formed mobile columns which raced westwards to round up the Italians, four of whose divisions had been left by the Germans without transport and with very little food or water.

The Desert Air Force operated at maximum intensity and took every advantage of the exceptional targets which the fleeing enemy presented.

During 4 November 10 Corps encountered the remnants of the enemy armour south of Ghazal. 2 New Zealand Division by-passed these rearguards to the south, but on 5 November had a sharp engagement near Fuka; during the afternoon 4 Light Armoured Brigade broke through the opposition and swung in to the road.

On 5 November I regrouped for the pursuit. 10 Corps (1 and 7 Armoured and 2 New Zealand Divisions) was to lead the chase. 30 Corps I positioned between Matruh and Alamein, and to 13 Corps I assigned the task of clearing up the battlefield.

By nightfall 6 November, advanced troops were nearing the Matruh–Charing Cross area, where I hoped to cut off a considerable body of the enemy survivors.

Heavy rains interfered with my plans. On 7 November the force was bogged in the desert, with its petrol and supplies held up some miles behind. 1 Armoured Division failed to reach Charing Cross and delay was experienced on the coast in clearing the enemy rearguards at Matruh. The enemy made good use of this respite of some twenty-four hours to retrieve some of his troops and transport, which fled along the coast road, and the long pursuit to the El Agheila position began.

### SOME REFLECTIONS ON THE BATTLE OF EL ALAMEIN

The Axis forces in North Africa had sustained a crushing defeat, and indeed only the rain on 6 and 7 November saved them from complete annihilation. Four crack German divisions and eight Italian divisions had ceased to exist as effective fighting formations.

30,000 prisoners, including nine Generals, were taken.

A great number of enemy tanks had been destroyed, and the quantity of guns, transport, aircraft and stores of all kinds captured or destroyed was immense.

The battle had conformed to the pattern anticipated. The break-in, or battle for position, had given us the tactical advantage; the dog-fight which followed reduced the enemy's strength and resources to a degree which left him unable to withstand the final knock-out blow. The dog-fight demanded rapid re-grouping of forces to create reserves available for switching the axis of operations as the situation required; in this way the initiative was retained, and the battle swung to its desired end.

Tactical surprise was an important factor; the break-in operation achieved it completely, for the enemy had expected our main thrust in the south. In the final thrust again the enemy was deceived; he had prepared for it in the extreme north, and concentrated his German troops to meet it. It was delivered against the Italians, two miles south of the German flank.

The most critical time in the battle was 26 and 27 October. Fighting was intense but the momentum of our attacks was diminishing. It was then that I started drawing divisions into reserve, ready for the final operation. At the time this gave to some the impression that I had decided that we could not break through the enemy and was giving up; but I would say that when you find a commander drawing troops into reserve at a critical moment of the battle, it probably means he is about to win it.

1. 'Donald' was the mascot of the C.M.P.s of the 10th Armoured Division H.Q. He had been 'found' somewhere in the Nile Delta some months before and had been in the desert ever since. 24 October 1942.

2. One of the first pictures taken during the battle shows this group of Italian prisoners captured by the Highland Division. 26 October 1942.

3. German prisoners of the 90th Light Division captured by Australian units are escorted past an appropriate sign.

4. British trucks carrying infantry through a gap in an enemy minefield come under heavy shellfire. 27 October 1942.

5. Something for the troops in the action to dream about! At their barracks British A.T.S. girls enjoy the luxury of their excellent swimming pool.

6. Filling a Crusader tank the hard way with a four-gallon can. Later in the campaign the Allies adopted the 'Jerry-can'.

7.   This amusing sign in the Alamein lines is not so frivolous as it sounds.
27 October 1942.

8.   The realities of war in the desert are brought home in this picture of a dead
Italian lying beside a Breda gun. 29 October 1942.

It was always clear in my mind that once a commander defeated his enemy in battle, everything else would be added unto him. The great hazard at El Alamein was whether the enemy would stand and fight it out. He did; he was decisively defeated; the rest was relatively easy. In the previous desert campaigns, Rommel had never been decisively defeated in battle; he had been forced to withdraw, but not because of decisive defeat. There was now a fundamental difference in the problem of the future conduct of the desert war. To this I will refer again, because it was a basic consideration in my plans to ensure that there would never be another Axis recovery and re-entry into Egypt.

# CHAPTER FIVE

## *The Pursuit to the El Agheila Position*

THERE were three major considerations regarding the pursuit after the Battle of El Alamein.

*First*: the Eighth Army must drive hard to cut off Rommel's remnants; it had been foiled by the rain in the Matruh area, but continued the chase in improving weather on 9 November. The enemy must be given no respite and no opportunity to organize defences to delay us.

*Second*: there was the importance of establishing the Desert Air Force on forward aerodromes. In conjunction with armoured cars, the Air Force could act as our long range hitting weapon, and greatly increase the confusion of the enemy's withdrawal; at the same time fighter cover could be given to the light forces operating in the van of the pursuit. In the broader picture, it was urgent to establish our Air Forces firmly in Cyrenaica, on airfields from which they could dominate the Central Mediterranean, the Libyan ports and Rommel's long lines of communication along the coast to Benghazi and Tripoli. The immediate object was to operate from the fields in the Egyptian frontier area from which Tobruk could be covered. More important was the Martuba group of airfields, in the Jebel el Akdar, whence the Malta convoys could be safely escorted.

*Third*: there was the administrative situation. The pace of the pursuit was fast and the strain on administration became increasingly severe. It was essential for us to get the port of Tobruk as quickly as possible and it was also clear that we should have to be prepared to pause at some stage in Cyrenaica: in order to build up essential stocks of petrol, ammunition and supplies.

I directed the New Zealand Division on Sidi Barrani, and by the evening of 9 November, 4 Light Armoured Brigade had brushed aside the rearguards there and the advance to the frontier continued. Other enemy rearguards were overwhelmed on 10 November, and the next day a surprise attack carried out silently in the dark overran the defenders of Halfaya Pass. Capuzzo, Sollum, and Bardia yielded without resistance, and thus by 11 November the Axis forces had been thrown out of Egypt.

2 New Zealand Division remained in the frontier area to reorganize, while 1 and 7 Armoured Divisions continued the pursuit. Tobruk was entered on 13 November, and after a further brush with the enemy at the Ain el Gazala defile, the Jebel el Akdar was reached. The Martuba airfields were in our hands on 15 November, just in time for aircraft to operate in support of a Malta convoy which sailed from Alexandria the following day.

My next objective was Benghazi. Intelligence reports suggested that the enemy would have great difficulty in getting his stores and material away from the town, and that shortage of petrol and transport might delay the evacuation of his personnel. If therefore we could reach Benghazi quickly, we might round up a considerable number of prisoners; moreover, I wanted to capture the port before the enemy had time to carry out heavy demolitions. I could not continue the pursuit with major forces owing to the maintenance situation and it was essential to wait until supplies had been built up forward. I therefore ordered 10 Corps to send light forces ahead in order to threaten Benghazi from the north and at the same time to cut the main coast road south of it. 4 Light Armoured Brigade operated along the coast road and a force of armoured cars was sent across the desert directed initially on Msus and Antelat. Subsequently the desert column was reinforced by an armoured regiment. Unfortunately heavy rain upset our plans and caused considerable delays to the desert column which gave the enemy some extra time to organize his withdrawal from Benghazi. Eventually the port was captured on 20 November.

My attention meanwhile turned to the Agheila position. The enemy was preparing to turn and face us in the area where twice before our forces had been brought to a halt. He was also digging in at Agedabia, which was the key to the approaches to the Agheila position.

7 Armoured Division quickly developed outflanking movements to the south of Agedabia, and the enemy withdrew by 23 November. He was evidently not strong enough to hold the place and at the same time to man the Agheila defences.

The next task of the Eighth Army was to face up to the enemy, build up the administrative situation while preparing to attack him and then once more drive him back to the west. I brought forward Headquarters 30 Corps to undertake this task. 10 Corps remained in Cyrenaica and I shall discuss its positioning later. 7 Armoured Division passed to command of 30 Corps.

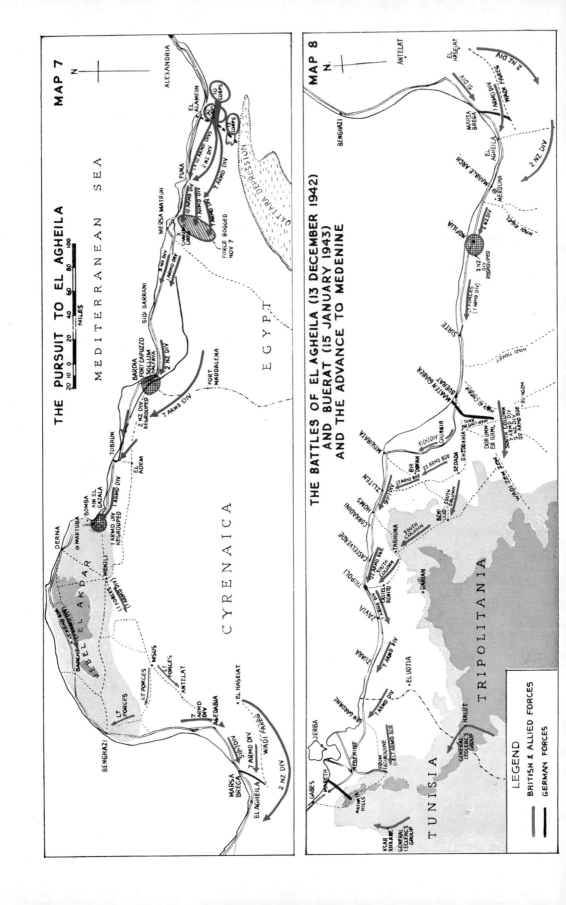

**MAP 7**

THE PURSUIT TO EL AGHEILA

**MAP 8**

THE BATTLES OF EL AGHEILA (13 DECEMBER 1942)
AND BUERAT (15 JANUARY 1943)
AND THE ADVANCE TO MEDENINE

LEGEND

BRITISH & ALLIED FORCES

GERMAN FORCES

## CHAPTER SIX

# *The Actions at El Agheila (13 December 1942) and Buerat (15 January 1943) and the Advance to Tripoli*

### FORCING THE EL AGHEILA POSITION

THE problem was now to turn the enemy out of the El Agheila position as quickly as possible before he had time to perfect the organization of his defences. I wanted to occupy the Agheila bottleneck myself, facing west, and thus ensure that the Axis forces would not hold the gateway to Cyrenaica a third time.

The first consideration was again administration. The bulk of our supplies had to be brought by road from Tobruk until the port of Benghazi could be got working at full pressure, and this task became a matter of urgent priority. At the same time the Royal Air Force demands for daily tonnage of stores were becoming very big and the estimate for these requirements in mid-December reached 1,400 tons per day, so that building up Army stocks for the advance was going to be a slow process. We had to ensure that the Royal Air Force could develop the maximum effort in its many tasks, all of which related directly or indirectly to the problem of removing the Axis forces from Africa, but it meant that I would be unable to start my operations against the Agheila position until mid-December.

My next anxiety was the reinforcement situation. I could not at this stage risk a battle involving heavy casualties. I would have to rely on artillery fire and air bombing, and keep my losses to a minimum.

I toured the forward area at the end of November in order to reconnoitre and make a plan. I was wondering whether, by bluff and manœuvre on the open flank, I could frighten the enemy out of his positions. If it should appear to him that by making a stand to fight he would risk losing his whole force, he might withdraw. This would have suited me, as I could have taken possession of the bottleneck and fought him in the easier country to the west. As I shall explain later, I eventually decided to go all out to annihilate the enemy in his defences.

Meanwhile I worked out the plan of attack.

The Agheila position was naturally very strong. It covered the area of desert between the sea, just west of Marsa Brega and the Wadi Fareg—which formed a difficult obstacle running east and west. In the approaches to the position the 'going' was extremely bad, while for some distance to the south of the Wadi Fareg the ground was unsuitable for manœuvre. A very wide detour would be necessary to outflank the position.

The enemy was known to be working hard at the defences, and he used immense

[39]

quantities of mines to hinder our approach. Tripoli was still receiving heavy traffic and it was estimated that the German forces available in defence now disposed of up to 100 tanks and considerable numbers of anti-tank guns. Although reports during the first week in December indicated that Rommel was sending the Italians west, he showed no sign of evacuating the position. I decided that bluff would not remove him and planned to get behind his German forces and capture them.

My plan depended on finding a suitable route for 2 New Zealand Division to outflank the defensive system. This formation would move wide and cut the coast road well to the west of El Agheila. On the coast I would attack astride the road with 51 Division, and in the centre 7 Armoured Division would operate, with the lorried infantry brigade leading and with the armour positioned in rear. It was essential to conceal the outflanking move from the enemy, as he would be likely to withdraw rather than risk complete encirclement.

I eventually set 14 December as the date of the operation. Heavy artillery and air action against the enemy was to start two days earlier. I issued my orders on 11 December and a policy of large scale raids began at once. The raids were mistaken by the enemy for the main attack and unnerved him; in the early hours of 13 December he started to withdraw under cover of rearguards found by 90 Light Division. In spite of the great caution imposed on our troops by mines and booby traps of all kinds, we succeeded in following up closely, and at the end of the day 51 Division had penetrated the eastern sector of the defences. On the following day 7 Armoured Division took the lead and got into the rearguard just east of El Agheila itself and subsequently reached the causeway of the Marada fork.

The Desert Air Force did great execution on the coast road.

Meanwhile the New Zealand Division's outflanking movement was making fast progress. The Division started from El Haseiat, and passing well to the south of Wadi Fareg, crossed the Marada track about 50 kilometres north of the oasis. It then moved north-west directed on Merduma and the coast road. The line of Wadi Rigel–Merduma was reached on 15 December after a remarkably rapid advance, and it was evident that most of the German armour and the rearguards of 90 Light Division were still to the east. The Germans were in a desperate plight with 7 Armoured Division advancing from the east and 2 New Zealand Division coming in behind. Fighting was intense and confused throughout 16 December. The enemy split up into small scattered groups and struggled through, suffering considerable losses in the process (including some 20 tanks and 500 prisoners) but uncertainty of the going and above all administrative restrictions had limited the size of the outflanking force, so that it was not strong enough to cut off the enemy completely.

The pursuit continued on 17 December, and next day the New Zealanders had a sharp engagement at Nofilia. By 19 December the enemy was withdrawing fast along the coast road, but in view of my administrative situation I was now able to follow up with light forces only.

The battle of El Agheila was at an end. Rommel's forces had been further weakened and I was in possession of the bottleneck which commanded the route into Cyrenaica and Egypt. The enemy had commenced to withdraw when our offensive intentions became clear, but his rearguards were severely mauled in the process. His morale had been further lowered and it was important to follow him up quickly, but the Eighth Army had covered 1,200 miles since 23 October and maintenance was our greatest problem.

### CONSIDERATIONS AFFECTING THE ADVANCE TO THE BUERAT POSITION

When Rommel's forces retreated from El Agheila, his main bodies went back to the area of Buerat, which was the next suitable position on which to oppose our advance: a strong force including tanks remained at Sirte, and the enemy's intention was obviously to prevent Eighth Army from gaining contact with the Buerat position as long as possible.

The tempo of my operations was determined by administrative considerations. Before I could maintain major forces forward of Nofilia I had to build up stocks in the forward area, but 800 tons a day was still being brought by road from Tobruk, and Royal Air Force requirements had increased further with demands for all-weather runways for the heavy bombers. Tremendous efforts were made at Benghazi to improve the port facilities, as once our tonnage requirements could be handled there the transport locked up on the long road run to Tobruk could be switched to the shorter carry forward of Benghazi. Early in January 3,000 tons per day were being handled at Benghazi port and the situation began rapidly to improve.

We were not well placed for forward aerodromes, and the immediate consideration after El Agheila was the establishment of the Royal Air Force at Marble Arch and Merduma with forward squadrons at Nofilia. We also required to take Sirte and start work at once on airfields there, so that the Desert Air Force would be ready to give its customary scale of support in the Buerat battle.

I was also concerned with ensuring the correct balance in the rear areas and, in planning the next phase of our advance, was anxious to bring forward a corps to occupy the El Agheila position when 30 Corps moved on again to the west.

As a result of these considerations I ordered 30 Corps to halt 2 New Zealand Division in the Nofilia area, forward of which 4 Light Armoured Brigade operated alone. My orders provided that a forward base should be established at Sirte whence we would maintain contact with the enemy by means of armoured car patrols only. 7 Armoured Division was to remain about Marble Arch and 51 Division in the Agheila position cleaning up the area.

I decided to plan for the Buerat battle on the basis of ten days' heavy fighting using four divisions, and calculated that the necessary dumping would take some three weeks. I therefore intended to resume the offensive in mid-January.

ADVANCE OF LIGHT FORCES FROM NOFILIA TO BUERAT

Following the engagement at Nofilia on 18 December, the enemy moved westwards with great speed, covered by detachments from his armoured forces.

On 21 December contact was made with strong rearguards at Sirte. Only after outflanking manœuvres by armoured cars and artillery was the enemy compelled to evacuate the place, which we entered on 25 December. Two days later patrols had crossed the Wadi Tamet, and on 28 December they were overlooking the Wadi el Chebir. This implied that the enemy had withdrawn to his main position, which was reported to run from the coast at Maaten Giaber, south-west covering Gheddahia, and along Wadi Umm er Raml towards Bu Ngem.

By 29 December our patrol line was in position west of the enemy defences; Buerat and Bu Ngem were reported clear of enemy.

PLAN FOR THE BATTLE OF BUERAT

The Buerat position was not so strong naturally as Agheila, neither had the enemy had time to construct defences on the scale met previously. The wadis in the area, were, however, serious obstacles, particularly the Wadi Zem Zem. The main weakness of the position was that its southern flank did not rest on any natural obstacle and, by now, it was very apparent that the enemy had become extremely sensitive to out-flanking movements. He was therefore probably uncertain of his ability to hold the Buerat defences and therefore, as soon as he judged that the Eighth Army was resum-ing the offensive, he would begin to withdraw again. This would not have suited me because, primarily for administrative reasons, once I struck at Buerat I intended to drive straight through to Tripoli and open the port. If Rommel pulled back before I was ready I could not follow up, and I did not want him to have time for preparation of other major defences east of Tripoli itself. There was a good defensive position on the high ground from Homs to Tarhuna and beyond, which might prove difficult if developed, and my maintenance situation would not permit any delay in overcoming it.

I had always to take into account the possibility of the enemy withdrawing earlier than I hoped, and my plan was made to cover that eventuality. I estimated that I could resume the offensive on 15 January, and decided that I would not start before then whatever Rommel did, but that once the Army was set in motion, it would go straight to Tripoli. At the same time I gave orders which precluded the enemy suspecting any offensive intentions on my part. Only the armoured cars of 4 Light Armoured Brigade were facing the enemy, and the main bodies of 7 Armoured Division, which was responsible for the front, were to remain east of the Wadi Tamet, some 40 miles behind the line. The battle plan was subsequently worked out with the object of moving main bodies of assaulting formations forward at the last possible moment.

My intention at this stage was that 30 Corps should use four divisions in the assault together with a very strong force of tanks. 50 and 51 Divisions would attack astride the coast road, while 7 Armoured and 2 New Zealand Divisions would deliver the main thrust round the enemy's flank and drive in behind him. 22 Armoured Brigade I intended to keep in Army reserve in the centre, available to reinforce either thrust.

I intended to bring 10 Corps forward to the El Agheila position and subsequently to the Buerat area, so that I should preserve overall balance, and later leapfrog it through 30 Corps for operations west of Tripoli.

On 4 January ground and air reports both indicated that Italian formations were withdrawing from the Buerat position. This conformed to the events at Agheila. There was no sign of the Germans moving, however, and I continued the policy of standing well back and restricting our forward activity to armoured car patrols.

Dumping was going ahead well, when we sustained a major setback due to the weather. A gale raged from 4 to 6 January and created havoc at Benghazi port. Ships broke loose and charged about the harbour; heavy seas breached the breakwater and smashed into the inner harbour. Four ships were sunk, one of which contained 2,000 tons of ammunition, and great damage was done to lighters and tugs. The intake dropped from 3,000 tons per day to 1,000. This created a most awkward situation. We were thrown back on Tobruk and the necessity for a heavy daily lift by road from Cyrenaica to the forward area.

I was still determined to start the drive to Tripoli on 15 January. The enemy must not be given any longer respite, so I decided to modify my plan and accept the risks this would entail.

First, I decided not to bring 10 Corps forward but to take all its transport, both operational and administrative, and employ it in ferrying stores forward from Tobruk. This sacrificed my desire for correct balance, but was not a great risk. We faced a broken enemy, and we knew well that he could not recover sufficiently to launch out to the east again for some considerable time.

Secondly, I reduced the attacking forces of 30 Corps by leaving out 50 Division. This formation I was able to bring up to the Agheila area as custodian of the defensive positions there. The coastal thrust as planned would have had a hard task anyhow, and with only one division now available I ordered that the attack should not be pressed, but should aim at containing the enemy in the sector.

The main risk was in planning to reach Tripoli in ten days from the start of the operation. If I could not get the port in that time, I should be confronted with an extremely grave administrative situation. I decided to accept this risk in view of my great strength in tanks. By stripping 1 Armoured Division (10 Corps) I was able to concentrate 450 tanks for the battle. I was confident that this armoured force would offset the reduction in the number of divisions and, by careful handling, would ensure a speedy drive to the objective.

For the rest my plan of battle remained unchanged. 51 Division would press along the coast road, while 7 Armoured and 2 New Zealand Divisions would outflank the enemy and thrust towards Beni Ulid and Tarhuna. 22 Armoured Brigade would move between the main axes on Bir Dufan, and be ready to switch to either flank as

[43]

required. A comprehensive air plan was drawn up, commencing with the customary domination of the Axis air force and culminating with bombing the enemy positions immediately prior to the attack.

I must mention the very unusual command set-up which was forced upon me in this battle. The plan involved two widely separated thrusts, with an armoured force moving between them under command of Army Headquarters. It was not possible for the one Corps Commander to direct both of these thrusts owing to the distance. The battle was going to require tremendous drive and energy to ensure reaching Tripoli in time, and a superior commander was essential on both flanks. As I had only one Corps Headquarters available for the action, I decided to command the coastal thrust myself from my Tactical Headquarters, leaving General Leese free to concentrate on the outflanking operations. I would move my Headquarters with 22 Armoured Brigade on the central axis.

I took special steps to work up the enthusiasm of the troops before the battle, and to impress upon them the need for firm determination that the attack would not stop until Tripoli was ours.

## THE BATTLE OF BUERAT (15 January 1943) AND THE CAPTURE OF TRIPOLI (23 January 1943)

My final instructions for the Battle of Buerat provided for a due measure of caution to be exercised by the outflanking formations, as I wished to avoid heavy casualties to our tanks. It was necessary first to reconnoitre carefully the enemy anti-tank gun layout before rushing forward, because the defenders were thought to have some two hundred anti-tank guns and about twenty-five 88 millimetre pieces.

7 Armoured and 2 New Zealand Divisions moved off at 0715 hours 15 January. They soon made contact with 15 Panzer Division in the area Dor Umm er Raml, and destroyed fifteen German tanks in the ensuing action. The enemy fell back on the Wadi Zem Zem, and by evening Faschia had been secured and we were on the line of the wadi. On the coastal axis 51 Division attacked at 2230 hours, but was not heavily opposed as it transpired that 90 Light Division had started withdrawing after dusk. By the morning of 16 January our outflanking movement was through the main enemy position and had crossed the Wadi Zem Zem, while 51 Division was advancing on Gheddahia. I now ordered that the advance be conducted with great resolution and the utmost speed; the caution imposed at the start of the operation was cancelled. In the afternoon tanks were encountered again near Sedada, but showed little fight. On the main road, our troops reached Churgia and 22 Armoured Brigade meanwhile advanced on Bir Dufan.

I gave orders on 17 January to 30 Corps to feel for the enemy's southern flank, making as if directed on Garian. Subsequently the thrust was to be developed towards Tripoli from the south as I wanted to play on the enemy's sensitiveness to outflanking movements, hoping he would weaken his Homs sector in order to strengthen the western flank. If the Tarhuna axis proved difficult and if the enemy weakened the Homs area to strengthen it further, I would drive hard from my eastern flank, releasing 22 Armoured Brigade into the plain of Tripoli along the coastal axis.

Steady progress was made on 17 January, but the ground slowed movement in the desert and, on the coast, mines and very skilful demolitions delayed us. By evening the southern column reached Beni Ulid, and on the right, we were only ten miles short of Misurata. Next day the enemy withdrawal continued, but on both flanks we lost contact owing to difficulties of the 'going' and to demolitions.

The advance was becoming sticky, and I was experiencing the first real anxiety I had suffered since assuming command of the Eighth Army. If I did not reach Tripoli within the ten days' time limit imposed by the administrative situation, I might have to face a most difficult decision: I would have to stop the advance and probably fall back to Buerat or even further, in order to maintain the supply of the Army. I was determined, therefore, to accelerate the pace of operations, and to give battle by night as well as by day, in order to break through the Homs–Tarhuna position and secure my objective. I ordered attacks on both axes to be put in by moonlight. I issued very strong instructions regarding the quickening of our efforts, and made clear what I expected of commanders and the troops. On 19 January progress greatly improved; pressure was being developed on Tarhuna and 51 Division entered Homs. I had 22 Armoured Brigade at Zliten, still under my command, waiting for the right moment to release it. The Desert Air Force had a most successful day, and indeed it took a constant and heavy toll of the enemy throughout this action.

I received reports that the Ramcke parachutists had been transferred from the Homs front across to Tarhuna, and this decided me to adopt the plan already contemplated of striking a hard blow on the right flank, and launching 22 Armoured Brigade through to Castelverde and Tripoli.

By the evening of 21 January, 51 Division had forced the enemy back from the hills about Corradini, and 22 Armoured Brigade had been brought up west of Homs. But the pace was still too slow, in spite of my insistence on the urgency of the operation; the difficulty was that the demolitions on the road had been most skilfully related to the ground, so that it was often impossible even for tracked vehicles to by-pass them owing to soft sand and deep ravines.

On 22 January I ordered 22 Armoured Brigade to pass through 51 Division and to force its way forward to Tripoli. By 1400 hours the brigade was held up by rearguards and demolitions west of Castelverde and was unable to get round them; owing to traffic blocks, there was only one company of infantry forward to assist, and I therefore ordered a battalion of 51 Division to ride to the front on Valentine tanks and to attack on arrival. This involved a night attack, and the armour was to follow through by moonlight. Meanwhile progress had been made on the left flank, and the southern column was only seventeen miles from Tripoli. It seemed that the city must now fall, and it was with very great satisfaction that I received reports that it had been entered from the east and south in the early hours of 23 January.

[45]

By dark the enemy were thirty miles west of Tripoli and I ordered the pressure to be continued to Zuara, which was near the Tunisian border. 7 Armoured Division was to follow up. Meanwhile the rest of 30 Corps was grouped round Tripoli, while preparations were made for the next phase of operations.

In three months exactly, we had advanced 1,400 miles and Tripoli, the last Italian colonial city, the prize which had so long eluded the Desert Army, had been captured at last. The damage in the town was not great, but the port was extensively demolished. Quays, wharves and installations were badly destroyed, and the harbour entrance blocked completely. All our energies were concentrated on getting it working again, and indeed this was achieved with remarkable speed and reflected very great credit on the Royal Navy and Army staffs and units concerned. On 3 February the first ship entered the harbour, and a complete convoy was berthed within three days. By 10 February, over 2,000 tons were being handled per day in the port.

The problem now was to build up the maintenance resources of the Army before advancing into Tunisia. Meanwhile I established my Headquarters in a field, four miles outside Tripoli City, and kept my army in the fields and in the desert around it. In Tripoli there were palaces, villas and buildings galore, but I could not have the soldiers getting soft. It was necessary to safeguard their hardness and efficiency for the tasks which lay ahead.

During our stay in Tripoli the Prime Minister, Mr Winston Churchill, paid a visit to the Eighth Army. A ceremonial march past was arranged in the main square, and it was a brave and moving spectacle when he inspected the troops who had fought their long way from Egypt to this fair city.


SOME REFLECTIONS ON THE CAMPAIGN IN EGYPT AND LIBYA

There are some aspects of the conduct of the campaign in Egypt and Libya upon which it is interesting to comment.

Twice our Desert Army had advanced to El Agheila, and twice it had been forced to withdraw into Egypt. This time I was determined to ensure that there could never be any question of another reverse in the Western Desert, and never any possibility of a recurrence of what was then becoming known in the Eighth Army as the 'annual swan' between Egypt and El Agheila. As we approached El Agheila I sensed a feeling of depression, particularly among some of those officers who had participated in our previous offensives and withdrawals; I did not feel depressed at the prospect myself.

I have already mentioned that to me there was a radical difference in the circumstances of the third advance of our Desert Forces to Benghazi and beyond, as compared with previous occasions, because Rommel had been decisively beaten in battle and had been thrown back into Tripolitania as a result of his defeat. Previously he had withdrawn mainly of his own volition, and perhaps primarily for administrative reasons. The full fruits of victory cannot be gathered until the enemy has been defeated in battle. In November and December 1942 the enemy was not in a position to make any effective speedy recovery or to turn to the attack, because he had been beaten and his morale shaken. He was relentlessly pursued westwards. In the engagements after El Alamein, he was quickly set upon and forced to continue his retreat, principally by outflanking manoeuvres which he had been quite unable to withstand.

I did not rely, however, on the effects of Rommel's defeat to ensure that he would not try again to invade Egypt. From the time the pursuit from El Alamein began I gave much thought to the problem. I planned to preserve the strategic balance of the Army by maintaining, in a series of chosen areas, a force which would ensure against the effects of any local failure or surprise being turned to important advantage by the enemy. If then Rommel should succeed in halting our advance and subsequently continue to build up his forces for a renewed attempt on the Nile Delta, I would be able to defeat his purpose.

I decided that the first essential safeguard against another Axis recovery was the positioning of a strong mobile force in the general area to the south-east of the Jebel Akdar, centring on Tmimi and Ain el Gazala. I therefore left 10 Corps in that area, using 7 Armoured Division to continue the pursuit to Agheila. I then brought 30 Corps forward for the Agheila battle. As long as I had 10 Corps poised in the Tmimi area, Rommel could not return to the Egyptian frontier, even if he did find the means to turn and attack us again. 10 Corps blocked the road axis to Tobruk and beyond, and if by-passed to the south would lie on the flank of any overland route the Germans might select across the waterless desert.

Later, when we stood before the Agheila position, my first concern was to acquire its defences for myself. Whoever was established firmly in the Agheila bottleneck held the gateway to Cyrenaica. This was an immensely strong position and, once we could garrison it, there would never again be any question of the Germans returning to the east. For this reason, when Agheila fell my intention was to bring 10 Corps forward to occupy it while 30 Corps advanced to Buerat and subsequently to Tripoli. After forcing the Buerat position, I intended to pull 10 Corps forward to garrison it, while 30 Corps captured Tripoli. I would then leave 30 Corps at Tripoli to reorganize, while 10 Corps 'leapfrogged' through, leading the way into Tunisia. I was prevented from this by the maintenance situation which arose as a result of the storm on 4–6 January, and was obliged to advance leaving only one division on the Agheila position behind me. Admittedly there was little or no risk involved in this, but nevertheless when we went forward from Agheila we were not theoretically 'balanced' in our rear dispositions even though the state of the enemy made it permissible to neglect the full application of this principle.

I was loath to depart from my intentions for 10 Corps at that time; a battle is always fought with more confidence, particularly a mobile battle in the desert, if it is staged in front of a secure base: should the enemy succeed in catching the assaulting formations at a disadvantage, they can reorganize at that base and avoid being overwhelmed and thrown into confusion.

I have elaborated above on my conception of 'balance' in the strategic aspect. It is of equal importance on the battlefield, as has already been apparent in this story.

It is interesting to conjecture why Rommel failed to stand and fight at Agheila. It was the first defensive position at which he had the opportunity to face our advance with any chance of success, yet we turned him out of it with comparative ease. The Agheila position was immensely strong and very heavily mined. If the available German armour had been positioned on its southern flank, north of Marada, it might have been very difficult for me. My outflanking movement was necessarily weak owing to maintenance restrictions, and it was launched into difficult country. My whole force was stretched administratively, relying largely on Tobruk, some 450 miles by road in the rear.

I believe Rommel was unable to fight at Agheila because his own administrative situation was so extended. He was dependent on a road link back to Tripoli, and his losses in transport and shortage of petrol made this distance prohibitive.

Having given up Agheila, it is surprising that he decided to stand at Buerat. The Buerat position was not naturally strong, nor had it been developed into a sound defensive system. Moreover it could readily be outflanked. In rear, covering Tripoli, was an immensely superior defensive position—the escarpment running from Homs on the coast, through Tarhuna and Garian. If the energy expended on Buerat had instead been applied to the Homs–Tarhuna area, I do not think the Eighth Army would have reached Tripoli in January. Not only was this area much more favourable to the defence than Buerat, but my administrative situation would have made it almost impossible for me to follow up even with armoured cars, had the Axis forces gone straight back there from Agheila. They would have had a considerable period of relative immunity from our attentions in which to prepare against a renewal of our offensive. I can think of no sound military reason for Rommel's decision to stop at Buerat. I believe that Mussolini ordered it and that Rommel could not disobey until our advance gave him the excuse. By then it was too late.

The reinforcements made available to Rommel during his withdrawal enabled him to retain the identity of the German formations present at El Alamein. At first sight it seems strange that formations such as 15 and 21 Panzer Divisions continued to oppose us, after their experiences in October and November. The German tank strength began to recover to some extent at Agheila. It was evident that up to the time Tripoli was captured, the Axis Powers made full use of the port to send assistance to their hard-pressed forces. As Rommel subsequently withdrew into Tunisia, he was able to demand for the German Africa Corps its share of resources made available in that theatre. Because of this we continued to meet old opponents right through to the bitter end of the campaign, and it used to be said that Eighth Army would be pursuing '90 Light' till the end of time.

Before continuing the narrative of events, mention may here be made of some of the special problems which confronted us in Tripolitania.

I have frequently referred to the administrative factor from the time we left

El Alamein. The tempo of operations was primarily governed by the speed with which petrol, ammunition, Air Force requirements, and all the necessary stores and materials could be brought forward in sufficient quantities to support the fighting troops. It is important to grasp the distances with which the administrative machine had to contend. From Cairo to Tripoli is 1,600 miles by road; with GHQ at the former and the leading troops at the latter, it was as if GHQ were in London and the leading troops in Moscow, with only one road joining them. After the big storm of 4–6 January, the bulk of our stores was brought from Tobruk to Buerat by road, a distance of 700 miles: equivalent to being disposed at Vienna and drawing stores in London, with only one road available. On arrival in Tripoli, until the port was functioning, all requirements had to come from Benghazi, again about 700 miles by road. I planned to continue at first to maintain the Army by road from Benghazi, so that the intake at Tripoli port could be stored as reserve stocks. As soon as the reserves were adequate for the resumption of the advance in strength, I would close the road link to Benghazi and maintain the Army from Tripoli.

The problem of aerodromes in Tripolitania was an important one. When fighting in Egypt or Cyrenaica there was never any shortage of airfield sites. Both sides had fought over the ground several times, and had constructed many landing grounds, the locations of which were well known. This did not apply in Tripolitania where airfields were scarce and likely to be ploughed up and mined: as in the case of Marble Arch and Merduma. To rehabilitate old sites and construct new ones as the advance continued took time, but until this was done the Desert Air Force was forced to operate from locations in the rear with consequent limitations of range and endurance over the battle-field. I had to ensure, therefore, that due provision was made for airfield construction, and at the same time see that the leading troops did not outrun the air cover. There were very rare occasions when I had to decide between halting the pursuit or continuing without air cover for the leading elements. For example, the importance of reaching Agedabia and the Agheila position quickly was such that I accepted for a short period lack of cover in the forward area, and the enemy air force caused us certain casualties at that stage on the Benghazi–Agedabia road. But in any but special and rare circumstances, I am sure it is unsound to deny the troops fighter protection.

The capture of Tripoli presented us with all the problems of dealing with a large civilian population. I imposed very strict military discipline when we arrived, but was ready to relax it as the situation warranted. The Chief Civil Affairs Officer entered Tripoli with my Headquarters.

CHAPTER SEVEN

# The Advance into Tunisia and the Battles of Medenine (6 March 1943) and of the Mareth Line (20 March 1943)

## THE ADVANCE INTO TUNISIA

As a result of the Anglo-American Conference at Casablanca on 14 January, it had been decided to unify the command of the Allied Forces in North Africa, and General Eisenhower became the Supreme Allied Commander. General Alexander was appointed his Deputy, and Air Marshal Tedder took over command of all the air forces in the Mediterranean. This facilitated the co-ordination of Allied effort, and in particular made possible the concentration of all available air resources when required at any vital point. General Alexander visited me in the middle of February, and it was subsequently agreed by the Supreme Commander that priority should be given to getting the Eighth Army into the open maritime plain of Tunisia towards Sfax and Sousse.

Reverting to the immediate problems confronting us at Tripoli, my object was to push the enemy back to his next defensive position: the Mareth Line. I would have to drive in his covering troops, 'lean' up against his defences and make a plan to pierce them. I had also to secure the necessary centres of communications and lateral roads, and seize the forward airfields: particularly those about Medenine.

Owing to administrative restrictions, I advanced west of Tripoli with 7 Armoured Division only, which then included 4 Light Armoured Brigade. 2 New Zealand and 51 Divisions reorganized in the Tripoli area.

Following the fall of Tripoli on 23 January, the Axis forces continued their withdrawal westwards covered by rearguards of 90 Light and 164 Divisions. On 25 January our troops entered Zavia and two days later were just short of Zuara, while inland El Uotia was reached. At Zuara the enemy stiffened his rearguards and our light forces were much hampered by wet weather and bad 'going'. We did not capture the place until 31 January; on the same day Nalut was reported clear, and by 4 February the last of the Italian Empire was in our hands. Meanwhile reports were being received of enemy activity in the Mareth Line, where the defences were being hurriedly developed and strengthened.

Once across the Tunisian border the enemy resistance stiffened further, and it became apparent that he intended to impose the maximum delay on our approach to his Mareth positions. His first main outpost was Ben Gardane, a fortified village to the south-west of which 15 Panzer Division was located. In order to give confidence and provide balance, I moved 22 Armoured Brigade close behind the front, while 7

Armoured Division prepared to tackle Ben Gardane from the south-east. Unfortunately another spell of heavy rain delayed our plans; from 10 February for several days the desert became a quagmire and made operations impossible, but on 15 February the weather cleared and we entered Ben Gardane without great difficulty the following day.

My next move was to take the important road centres of Medenine and Foum Tatahouine and the airfields at the former place. I decided to bring 51 Division forward, in view of the degree of enemy resistance to our advance, and this formation together with 7 Armoured Division launched an attack on Medenine, which fell on 17 February. The next day Foum Tatahouine was taken. I now had the co-operation of General Leclerc's force in the battle zone; this force had made a remarkable drive across the desert from Lake Chad, and placed itself under my orders. I gave it the task of moving from Nalut along the escarpment to Ksar Rhilane and of subsequently operating eastwards to threaten the enemy's western flank.

I had now secured the key approaches to the Mareth Line, and when ready could close up to it and decide upon my plan.

The port at Tripoli was working well, and soon as much as 3,500 tons were being discharged there in one day—a remarkable achievement. The tank replacement programme was also satisfactory. I hoped to have three armoured brigades and two Valentine regiments up to strength by 20 March, to give me a total of some 550 tanks.

I planned to start operations against the Mareth defences about 20 March. I should require 10 Corps forward for the operation and expected to have 1 Armoured, 4 Indian and 50 Divisions concentrated in the Tripoli area by 16 March.

As planning was beginning for the Mareth battle, events elsewhere in Tunisia were destined to affect the Eighth Army's intentions. On 15 February the enemy launched a strong attack against 2 United States Corps in the Gafsa sector of western Tunisia. The Americans withdrew towards Tebessa, and by 20 February the situation had become very grave. The enemy penetration was threatening to outflank Allied positions to the north, and unless this was halted quickly it seemed 5 British Corps would have to withdraw. General Alexander sent me an urgent request for help, urging me to exert all possible pressure on the enemy on my front in an effort to draw him off the Tebessa drive.

Eighth Army was administratively not ready to operate major forces in southern Tunisia, but this was an occasion when risks had to be taken, and I at once planned to intensify our drive towards the Mareth Line on the coast axis, and also to push Leclerc's force north from Ksar Rhilane. The enemy had weakened his Mareth front in order to strengthen the thrust through Gafsa, and there was always a chance that by forceful and energetic action I might frighten him out of his Mareth position. Though I was weak myself in front, urgent action was necessary if we were to help the Americans.

On 24 February four fighter wings were operating from the Medenine–Ben Gardane area. I ordered 7 Armoured and 51 Divisions to keep up the pressure, the former in the coastal sector, the latter on the main Gabes road. This involved a

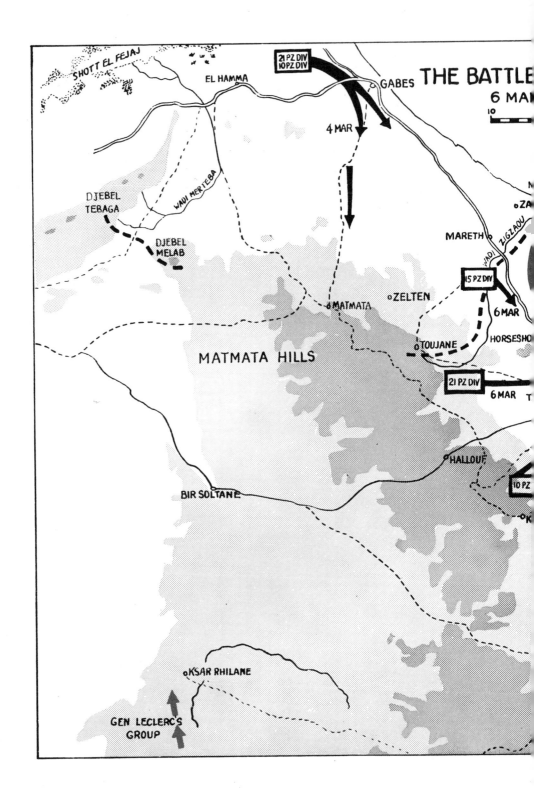

SHOTT EL FEJAJ

EL HAMMA

21 PZ DIV
10 PZ DIV

GABES

THE BATTLE

6 MAR

10

4 MAR

WADI MERTEBA

DJEBEL
TEBAGA

DJEBEL
MELAB

ZA

MARETH

WADI ZIGZAOU

15 PZ DIV

MATMATA

ZELTEN

6 MAR

HORSESHO

MATMATA HILLS

TOUJANE

21 PZ DIV

6 MAR T

HALLOUF

BIR SOLTANE

10 PZ

K

KSAR RHILANE

GEN LECLERC'S
GROUP

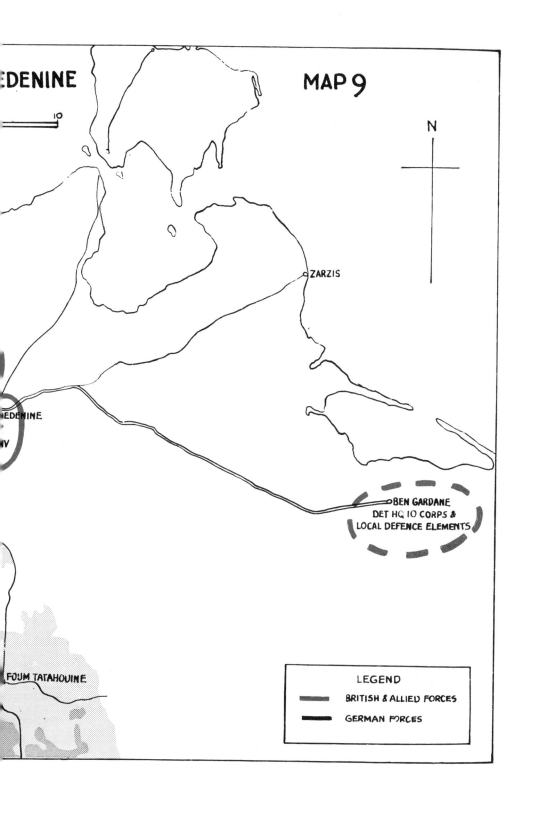

EDENINE

MAP 9

N

⊙ ZARZIS

EDENINE

IV

BEN GARDANE
DET HQ 10 CORPS &
LOCAL DEFENCE ELEMENTS

FOUM TATAHOUINE

LEGEND

BRITISH & ALLIED FORCES

GERMAN FORCES

considerable risk, because if the enemy broke off the Tebessa attack and could regroup quickly against the Eighth Army, I should be in an awkward situation. I had only two divisions forward, with my main administrative area under development at Ben Gardane, and the nearest reserve division (2 New Zealand) was still back near Tripoli.

My leading formations accelerated and strengthened their action against the outer defences of the Mareth Line, and in the last days of February it was clear that this had achieved the desired result. Rommel broke off his attack against the Americans and reports of regrouping of enemy forces began to reach my Headquarters.

On 27 February 15 Panzer Division was located on my front, having been absent during the Tebessa offensive, and 21 Panzer Division was also reported to be moving south again.

It looked indeed as if my anxieties were justified, and that Rommel had decided to strike at the Eighth Army while there was an opportunity of dealing a crushing blow at its leading divisions. He could guess how very stretched we had become, and if he could overwhelm my forward area before I could get more troops forward, and overrun my dumps at Ben Gardane, he could cause a major setback to my plans and gain valuable time for dealing with other sectors of the Allied front in Tunisia.

The enemy tank strength was improving for 'Tiger' tanks were now being reported by First Army and he had 10 Panzer Division in Tunisia. I did not think that Rommel would bring all three armoured divisions against me, but in the event this is what happened.

As soon as the Tebessa thrust was called off by the enemy, the Americans began to advance: out of contact with the Germans who pulled back to their original line. This, together with the reports of 27 February indicating the return of 15 and 21 Panzer Divisions to my front, confirmed the enemy's intentions.

I initiated emergency measures to regain balance and to prepare for an enemy attack. 2 New Zealand Division was ordered to Medenine at once. 8 Armoured Brigade was resting near Tripoli, and had been 'stripped' of its equipment; it was re-equipped with tanks then arriving at Tripoli in readiness for the arrival of 2 Armoured Brigade, and was sent forward. Together with 22 Armoured Brigade and eighty Valentines of 23 Armoured Brigade, I estimated that by 4 March I should have some 400 tanks at the front. By that date, 2 New Zealand Division would have joined 7 Armoured and 51 Divisions. I should then be ready for any move by Rommel, and would be so strong and well positioned that I might give him a rude shock and inflict on him heavy casualties: in fact pave the way for my own offensive against the Mareth Line, in the same manner as the Alam Halfa battle had facilitated the victory at El Alamein.

But I would not be ready until 4 March, and during the period 28 February–3 March the Eighth Army was unbalanced. In driving on to assist the west Tunisian front I had taken serious risks. Rommel had been forced to pull out and was now concentrating against me. The first days of March were an anxious period, during which all the signs of the impending enemy attack were apparent and it remained to be seen whether the enemy could strike before our arrangements to receive him were completed. This was my second period of great anxiety since the advance began.

On 3 March the enemy operated against 51 Division with infantry and tanks in a probing attack which was dealt with very quickly.

During 4 and 5 March, Rommel's intentions were made clear. Air reconnaissance reported heavy movement, including tanks, in the mountains west of Medenine. We began to identify three separate armoured columns, one facing us in the Mareth area (which we knew was 15 Panzer Division), one in the mountains making as if to come upon Medenine from the west and south-west (later identified as 10 Panzer Division), and a third which was also suspected to be in the mountains (and which was 21 Panzer Division).

But Rommel had by now missed his opportunity. My dispositions were complete by the evening of 4 March. In addition to 400 tanks, I had over 500 anti-tank guns in position round Medenine and had brought a nucleus of 10 Corps Headquarters to Ben Gardane to organize local defence of the administrative area there.

We had no wire and no minefields, but the positioning of the infantry and siting of the anti-tank guns, together with the strong reserves of armour, gave our defences great strength, and I was confident that we would repulse the enemy and give him a sharp lesson.

### THE BATTLE OF MEDENINE, 6 March 1943

On 5 March Rommel, by now a sick man, addressed his troops in the mountains overlooking our positions and told them that if they did not take Medenine and force the Eighth Army to withdraw, the days of the Axis forces in North Africa were numbered.

The next day the enemy attack began. When the early morning mist dispersed, a formidable array of tanks bore down upon our positions and it was clear that the main thrust was being made from the west towards the Tadjera feature, immediately north of Medenine, on 7 Armoured Division sector. By 1000 hours all attacks had been held and 21 enemy tanks destroyed. At 1430 hours, 15, 21 and part of 10 Panzer Divisions attacked again with infantry and were speedily beaten off. Our positions remained firm and steady and were not penetrated. There was a total of four main attacks during the day, apart from those which were broken up by concentrations of artillery fire before they had properly developed.

After dark the enemy withdrew: the battle was over. It had been a model defensive engagement and a great triumph for the infantry and the anti-tank gun. Only one squadron of our tanks was actually engaged in the fighting, and we lost no tanks. Fifty-two knocked out enemy tanks were left on the battlefield, and all but seven (dealt with by the tank squadron) had fallen to our anti-tank guns. Without wire or mines our infantry, with strong artillery support, had repulsed an attack by three Panzer divisions and incurred only minor losses in the process. Very great care had been taken in positioning our anti-tank guns, and it should be noted that they were sited to kill tanks at point-blank range: and not to defend the infantry.

### PREPARATIONS FOR THE BATTLE OF THE MARETH LINE

Having disposed of Rommel, I continued my preparations for breaking through the Mareth Line and forcing my way into the maritime plain beyond Gabes.

The Mareth Line was originally constructed by the French to protect Tunisia against attack by the Italians from Libya. The main defences stretched for approximately 22 miles from the sea near Zarat to the Matmata Hills in the west. These hills are very broken and, except for a few tracks running through narrow passes, form a barrier to wheeled transport and give command over the whole western end of the position. At the eastern end of the line, the defences were based on the Wadi Zigzaou, which had been widened and deepened to form a tank obstacle, and which was covered along its whole length by a complicated system of concrete and steel pillboxes and gun emplacements.

Additional work had been done on the line since the Franco-German armistice by Italians under German supervision. Anti-tank ditches, wire and protective minefields had been added, and a switch line was constructed following the Wadi Merteba between Djebel Melab and Djebel Tebaga, to the south-west of El Hamma. The designers of the line had apparently considered it impossible to outflank it west of the Matmata Hills as the ground was extremely difficult, and because any outflanking operation would involve a journey of at least 150 miles over waterless desert before the switch line in front of El Hamma was reached. It was said that the French had tried an exercise in outflanking the line, using a small transport column for the task, and that all the lorries except two broke down owing to the impossibly bad 'going'. The French had therefore contented themselves with employing Arab irregulars to guard the few tracks leading into the Matmata Hills.

In view of our greatly superior transport I was not prepared to accept the French opinion, and as far back as December, when pondering on the problem of the Mareth Line, decided to have the area concerned reconnoitred. At that time I was at Marble Arch and had at my disposal the 'Long Range Desert Group' which was admirably suited to the task. So it was that in January 1943, while in Tripoli, I received a full report on the possibility of finding a way round the Mareth defences, and although it was apparent that very great difficulty would be experienced in crossing the country, it was not impossible, and I was confident that with our vehicles and experience a route could be found which would enable us to outflank the enemy.

An added problem at Mareth was the difficulty in establishing contact with the main defensive system, which was protected by a series of very well sited outpost and covering positions, particularly to the west of the main road running north into Mareth. Moreover, I suspected that I should find another position in rear, covering the bottleneck between the sea and the Shott el Fejaj, and this in fact proved to be the case.

[56]

On the coastal sector the enemy manned the Mareth defences primarily with Italians. 90 Light Division was west of the main road, and in the hills on the western flank 164 Division was located. The armour was in reserve in the rear.

Back in mid-February, before the Axis thrust at Gafsa and its sequel at Medenine, I had started studying the problem of breaching the Mareth Line, and had decided on an outline plan, subject to the normal modifications which subsequent reconnaissance might render desirable. I would attack on the coast with 30 Corps, striking at the Italians holding that area; meanwhile I would send 2 New Zealand Division, heavily reinforced, round the western flank to break in behind the Matmata massif. I would hold 10 Corps in reserve with two armoured divisions and 4 Light Armoured Brigade ready to tackle the Gabes bottleneck. A very great part would be played by the air striking forces in this battle, as we should have call on the combined resources of the Allies in North Africa.

I have mentioned that I planned to launch this operation about 20 March. 10 Corps was due to have concentrated forward by 16 March, and by that time the administrative situation would have become sufficiently strong to support a major offensive operation.

I have explained how Medenine and Foum Tatahouine, the key approaches to the Mareth Line, had been taken in the middle of February, and how operations had continued by 7 Armoured and 51 Divisions driving in the enemy covering troops and thus getting to grips with the main defensive positions.

Following the Battle of Medenine the process was continued.

On the western flank General Leclerc's force was providing an essential screen, which evidently caused the enemy considerable anxiety. On 10 March Rommel suddenly delivered a heavy attack with armoured cars, artillery and aircraft against the French column, apparently intending to destroy it. But Leclerc stood firm and, ably assisted by the Desert Air Force, drove off the attack in which the enemy lost twelve armoured cars, twelve guns and some forty vehicles. This fine performance prevented the enemy reconnoitring towards the New Zealand concentration area.

On night 16/17 March I began operations designed as the immediate preliminaries to the Mareth Battle. I now intended to destroy the last covering positions and also to mislead the enemy about the direction of the main thrust. These operations were completely successful except in the case of the Guards Brigade which attacked the 'Horseshoe' feature, a ring of hills at the south-west end of the Mareth defences, dominating the main road to Mareth. The brigade ran into most intensive minefields; Tellermines, anti-personnel mines and 'S' mines were almost touching in some areas, and it was impossible to get carriers or vehicles forward. Heavy hand-to-hand fighting ensued, and the enemy suffered severe casualties, as did our own troops who were withdrawn at daylight.

Other local operations were carried out on the night 17–18 March, after which everything was ready for the battle. I let the whole front quieten down. General Freyberg's outflanking column, temporarily designated New Zealand Corps, was lying concealed ready to begin its long march round to the west. Minor patrol activity continued on 19 March with the object of drawing the enemy's attention away from the right flank, where my initial blow was to fall.

In my discussion with General Alexander emphasis had been made on the importance of 2 United States Corps attempting to pin down the enemy on the Gafsa sector to prevent reserves being drawn from there to the Mareth Line, and also to re-establish the dumps at Gafsa itself, from which the Eighth Army was to draw when it advanced. 2 United States Corps launched an offensive on 17 March and captured Gafsa, and in the fighting round El Guettar was opposed by 10 Panzer Division and some Italian formations. This American advance was eventually stopped near Maknassy and El Guettar, but assisted our operations above all by containing 10 Panzer Division.

### THE BATTLE OF THE MARETH LINE, 20 March 1943

20 March was a fine clear day, which was particularly welcome as it enabled us to take air photographs to check the enemy battery positions; we had had bad weather for three days during which air photography had been impossible.

My plan, which I explained personally to officers down to the rank of Lieutenant-Colonel throughout the Army, depended on a major attack on the eastern end of the Mareth Line together with a very powerful outflanking movement. I did not think the enemy was strong enough to withstand both blows, and if he concentrated against one then I would succeed in the other. The final objective for the battle I gave as Sfax and ordered that operations would continue without pause until Sfax was secured.

30 Corps was to deliver the coastal attack using 50 Division and 23 Armoured Brigade; these formations would pass through 51 Division which was then holding the eastern sector of the front.

The New Zealand Corps consisting, in addition to 2 New Zealand Division, of 8 Armoured Brigade, Leclerc's force, an armoured car regiment and a medium artillery regiment, was to carry out the turning movement round the enemy's western flank. The Corps was to move towards Nalut, in a wide sweep to the south, reaching the escarpment by way of Wilder's Gap (as we called it), then swinging northwards to pass through Ksar Rhilane to the El Hamma switch line, and so reach its objective: the Gabes area.

10 Corps was to be in Army reserve, and its two armoured divisions were initially sited to guard the central sector between the two major thrusts. The Corps would be ready to exploit success.

A very heavy weight of air support was made available for the operation.

The attack by 50 Division was to commence at 2230 hours on 20 March. The New Zealand Corps was to advance 40 miles to an assembly area during the night 19/20 March, lie concealed all day 20 March, and continue by night marches until discovered by the enemy. In this deception we were unsuccessful for I had reason to believe that the enemy discovered the outflanking move earlier than I had hoped and I directed General Freyberg to continue marching by day throughout 20 March. This

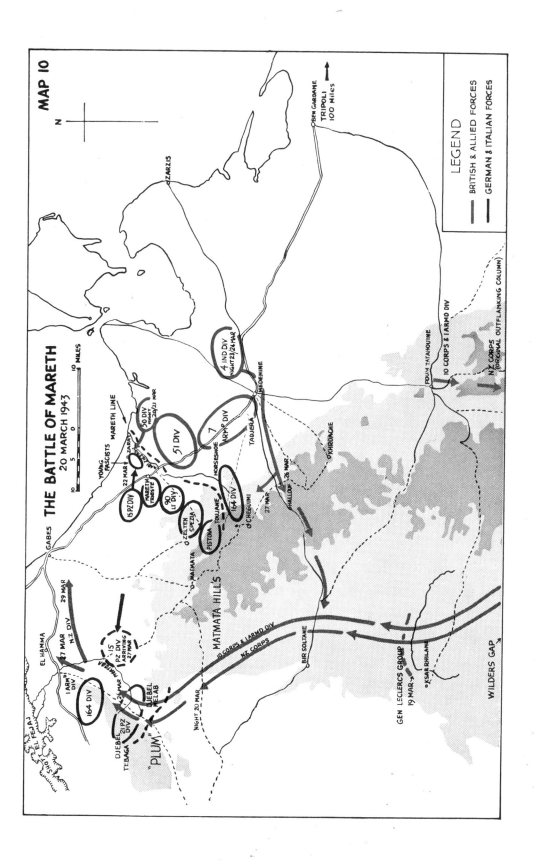

MAP 10

THE BATTLE OF MARETH
20 MARCH 1943

N

10    5    0    5    10 MILES

LEGEND
BRITISH & ALLIED FORCES
GERMAN & ITALIAN FORCES

GABES
EL HAMMA
EL FEJAJ
164 DIV
DJEBEL TEBAGA
21 PZ DIV
"PLUM"
DJEBEL MELAB
26 MAR
NIGHT 20 MAR
NZ DIV
17 MAR
29 MAR
1 ARM'D DIV
15 PZ DIV ARRIVING 27 MAR
MATMATA
28 MAR
10 CORPS & 1 ARM'D DIV
NZ CORPS
BIR SOLTANE
MATMATA HILLS
GEN LECLERC'S GROUP 19 MAR
KSAR RHILANE
WILDER'S GAP

15 PZ DIV
90 LT DIV
22 MAR
MARETH-TOUJANE
ZARAT
YOUNG FASCISTS
MARETH LINE
50 DIV NIGHT 20/21 MAR
51 DIV
ZARZIS
O ZELTEN SPEZIA
PISTOIA
TOUJANE
164 DIV
O CHEGUIMI
HORSESHOE
7 ARM'D DIV
TADJERA
27 MAR
MEDENINE
HALLOUF
26 MAR
O KHROUACHE
FOUM TATAHOUINE
10 CORPS & 1 ARM'D DIV
NZ CORPS (ORIGINAL OUTFLANKING COLUMN)

4 IND DIV NIGHT 23/24 MAR

TRIPOLI 100 MILES
BEN GARDANE

acceleration would, I hoped, distract attention from the coastal sector, and give a greater chance of success to the operations of 50 Division.

The New Zealand Corps pressed on throughout 20 March. It was a great relief to me to hear of its steady progress over the appallingly difficult ground. Very great credit is due to this force of some 27,000 men and 200 tanks in overcoming the truly enormous difficulties of terrain as well as enemy action on the approach march to the El Hamma switch line. Leclerc's force had a stiff task in pushing the enemy off a difficult wadi north of Ksar Rhilane, and a formidable engineering feat then faced the sappers in preparing tracks across the only possible crossing place some 100 yards wide. This and all other difficulties were surmounted so that by last light on 20 March, General Freyberg's troops were only a few miles short of the bottleneck (known to us as 'Plum') between the Djebel Tebaga and Djebel Melab, where the enemy switch line was located.

Preceded by a tremendous barrage of artillery, the attack of 50 Division started according to plan. The assaulting troops crossed the Wadi Zigzaou to capture three major strong points on the northern bank. The wadi proved to be every bit as difficult an obstacle as we had feared; there was a certain amount of water in it, and the banks had been cut away sheer; the enemy's guns and mortars had registered on it accurately, and our troops met intense enfilade fire from the flanks. 50 Division did well in securing its objectives for the strong points were very well found and were protected by wire, minefields and all the adjuncts of well developed static defences. At dawn on 21 March, however, there were still pockets of enemy holding out in some of the defences, and the sappers found extreme difficulty in continuing their work of trying to construct crossing places for infantry carriers, supporting weapons and tanks. A few Valentine tanks did succeed in crossing the wadi, but the going was impossible for wheels. Our tank losses were considerable.

The situation on 21 March on the coastal sector was that we had gained a foothold in the Mareth defences, and the 'dog-fight' was on.

We held all our gains throughout 21 March, and that night there was another heavy artillery programme under cover of which the bridgehead was expanded both laterally and in depth. But the German reserves were now beginning to arrive and fighting increased in intensity. On 22 March we experienced more heavy rain which had a very serious effect on the operation; we had still failed to make a satisfactory crossing over the wadi, and the rain completely spoilt the preliminary work which had by then been done. During the morning it became apparent that 15 Panzer Division was forming up to deliver a counter-attack against our bridgehead, and the Desert Air Force alerted the light bombers in order to deal with this threat. But owing to the rain the aircraft were unable to take off, and during the afternoon the German blow fell. Much of the ground we had gained was recaptured by the enemy because we were not able to withstand his strong force of tanks, for conditions had made it impossible for us to get our own anti-tank guns across the wadi to oppose the German armour. It transpired that the German reinforcements against our bridgehead consisted not only of 15

Panzer Division, but also included a regiment of 90 Light Division and the Ramcke parachutists.

At 0200 hours on the night 22/23 March the full implications of the situation on the coastal sector were evident. The results of the German counter attack were serious but I knew that his reserves were now definitely committed on the eastern flank. I realized that it would be very costly to persist in our attacks there, and I therefore made an immediate decision that I would stop 50 Division's thrust and throw everything into the outflanking movement, planning to deliver the decisive blow on the El Hamma–Gabes axis before Rommel moved his reserves across to oppose it. I would now endeavour to pin down the Germans in the coastal sector, by giving the impression that I was reorganizing for another attack in that area: meanwhile the western flank would be strongly reinforced. I ordered HQ 10 Corps and 1 Armoured Division to move after dark 23 March to join New Zealand Corps, estimating that they would reach their destination on 25 March. They had to move by the same long and difficult detour as the New Zealanders.

I ordered withdrawal from the north side of the Wadi Zigzaou for the night 23/24 March, and this was successfully accomplished under cover of artillery fire.

I also ordered 30 Corps to open up a new thrust in the centre. It seemed clear that 164 Division had moved away from its position at the western end of the Mareth Line proper, and was to oppose the New Zealand Corps in the switch line. There was now, therefore, a good opportunity to open up the road Medenine–Halluf–Bir Soltane through the mountains, which would be an excellent lateral route between my thrust lines, facilitating maintenance and simplifying the switching of forces from one part of the front to another. Moreover, if I could secure the area Toujane–Zelten, and later Matmata, it would be possible to launch 7 Armoured Division through the area to get behind the Mareth positions and cut the Mareth–Gabes road. 4 Indian Division was to undertake this operation and was set in motion after dark 23 March.

As a result of this regrouping, 30 Corps now had on the right 7 Armoured, 50 and 51 Divisions, whose role was to contain the enemy by all possible means, such as raids and artillery fire, to make him prepare for further attacks in the sector. If Rommel did not react to this threat and decided to withdraw troops from the area to reinforce elsewhere, I would be ready to re-open this thrust line. In the centre 4 Indian Division was undertaking a 'short hook' round the Mareth Line, and on the left I had now a very powerful force on El Hamma and Gabes.

My hope was to keep the German reserves involved in the east until my west flank operation got under way. If I could delay the switch of enemy troops for 36 hours, they would be too late to intervene effectively against the outflanking movement. All possible speed was to be employed to mount a 'knock-out' blow by 10 Corps and the New Zealanders, which would burst through the switch line and win the battle.

As HQ 10 Corps (General Horrocks) and 1 Armoured Division were progressing on the long round-about march to join New Zealand Corps, the plan of battle was considered and made ready.

New Zealand Corps was held up at the 'Plum' defile. The Italian troops holding this 6,000 yards bottleneck had been reinforced by Germans, including 21 Panzer Division and 164 Division, and extensive minefields had been laid to strengthen the defences. The enemy had observation over our troops from both sides of the defile, and laborious operations had to be undertaken to secure a foothold on the Djebel Tebaga and on the high ground to the east.

We had now to deliver a lightning attack and break through into the more open country beyond, where the armour would be able to manœuvre and to continue the offensive to Gabes. The possibility of outflanking the switch line by moving round the western end of the Djebel Tebaga was considered, but I decided against it, since it would have placed a complete obstacle between my forces and rendered mutual support impossible. I considered that the answer was to exploit our great air power, and to subject the enemy to such a weight of concentrated and continuous attack from the air, combined with a full scale land offensive, that he would be unable to withstand the onslaught. The Commander of the Desert Air Force agreed to provide the maximum available degree of intimate co-operation on the battlefield and a joint plan was drawn up.

The basic features of this plan were as follows. The enemy positions were to be heavily bombed throughout the night preceding the attack, so that the defenders would get no sleep and become nervy. The following morning and afternoon bombing would continue, reaching maximum intensity about 1500 hours. Heavy concentrations of artillery would follow for an hour, and the attack would then begin, with the sun behind us. (This was the first occasion in the campaign when we could attack from west to east and so take advantage of the afternoon sun, which in setting would tend to blind the defenders.) The ground attack would aim at pushing the armour through the enemy positions on a very narrow front and orders were given that the advance would continue by moonlight in order to effect the maximum penetration before dawn. To assist the progress of the attack, fighter bombers were to maintain continuous operations by relays of squadrons ahead of the artillery concentrations.

The attack was planned for 1600 hours 26 March.

Meanwhile feints were made on 30 Corps front and 7 Armoured Division was moved up close behind the front line to increase the enemy's anxiety. Air activity was also continued in this sector.

4 Indian Division's attack towards Halluf made good progress and it was reported that the lateral road would soon be open.

26 March dawned with a heavy dust storm blowing, which precluded air attacks during the morning but helped to conceal the forming up of 10 Corps and the New Zealanders. Towards afternoon conditions improved and at 1530 hours the light bombers were over the target area, followed by fighter bombers, which carried out a magnificent operation. For two and a half hours squadrons dropped bombs and shot up enemy troops, transport and gun positions; they wrought very great moral and material damage on the enemy.

[62]

The ground attack started according to plan although the last vehicles of 1 Armoured Division arrived only half an hour before the zero hour, after superhuman efforts had been expended in getting the transport across the difficult country.

With considerable artillery support the New Zealanders (with 8 Armoured Brigade) led the attack, and successfully broke into the enemy defences. 1 Armoured Division followed and penetrated to a depth of 6,000 yards, by which time it was pitch dark and the division was forced to halt. As soon as the moon rose the advance was continued, as it was an essential part of the plan to get through the bottleneck over which the enemy had such excellent observation, before first light. This night advance was a great achievement; in the noise and confusion 1 Armoured Division passed straight through the enemy including the whole of 21 Panzer Division and by dawn on 27 March our leading tanks were only a few miles short of El Hamma where they ran into a strong anti-tank gun screen.

Meanwhile the New Zealand Corps was engaged in very stiff 'mopping up'. The Germans fought savagely and desperately and the task of clearing the battlefield was very severe. But the enemy was in a state of confusion difficult to describe; to the east was 1 Armoured Division and to the west New Zealand Corps, and the enemy was caught between them. Surprise achieved by attacking in the afternoon added to the success, as had the unusual stratagem of driving an armoured formation through the enemy rear areas by moonlight.

Rommel's attempts to reinforce the sector failed. He began to switch his reserves too late, so that they were unable to arrive in time to influence the action. Elements of 15 Panzer Division managed to intervene, but they had no time to deliver any concerted attacks. By evening 27 March the defeat of the enemy had been completed, but not before 21 Panzer Division had made two unsuccessful attacks directed against the rear of 1 Armoured Division.

Meanwhile by midday 27 March, 4 Indian Division had opened the road to Halluf and Bir Soltane, and I had transport made ready for one infantry brigade in case I needed some quick reinforcements in the west.

By night 27/28 March the New Zealand Corps, having completed its operation on the battlefield, was now ready for the next task and was directed on Gabes. We were not successful in cutting off the defenders of the main Mareth Line, however, as they evacuated their position on the night 27/28 March, and 30 Corps, which began moving after them at first light on 28 March, was confronted with the usual difficulties of mines, booby traps and demolitions. The same day 10 Corps was delayed in its operations against El Hamma by dust storms.

### SOME REFLECTIONS ON THE BATTLE

The Battle of the Mareth Line was our toughest fight since El Alamein; and whereas the latter was a hard slogging match, at Mareth there had been greater scope for stratagems and subtlety. The defences were exceptionally strong and it was particularly interesting to see how well the covering positions had been sited in order to mislead the attacker in his efforts to contact the main position. The prelude to our victory had been the Battle of Medenine on 6 March; Rommel's abortive attack had failed to interrupt our preparations, and served only to increase the morale of the Eighth Army. The fifty-two tanks which the enemy lost there must have been sorely missed at the switch line on 26 and 27 March! As at El Alamein, Rommel cast in his reserves piecemeal, and when the battle started his armour was spreadeagled—with 10 Panzer Division in the Gafsa sector, 15 Panzer Division soon involved on the coast and 21 Panzer Division arriving in the west to back up the switch line.

The outstanding feature of the battle was the air action in co-operation with the outflanking forces. Several new methods of controlling aircraft working over the battlefield were tried out on this occasion; a Royal Air Force officer observed the battle from a forward observation post, in order to give the pilots (by direct radio link) information about the enemy and our own troops. Our air superiority was virtually complete, and we were never bothered by enemy air action.

We retained the initiative throughout. Even when we lost our gains on the coastal flank, Rommel was kept on the move by the speedy development of the western outflanking movement; having stopped the thrust on the coast, he was not able to switch troops to the El Hamma sector in time to hold us there. The most crucial time in this battle was in the early hours of 23 March, when I made an immediate decision at 0200 hours to switch the whole weight of the attack to the extreme west, discontinuing meanwhile efforts on the coastal axis. Following this decision, the vital considerations were, first, the speed with which the decisive blow could be mounted and delivered and, secondly, the necessity to hold the German reserves on the eastern flank long enough to prevent their assisting the defenders of the switch line west of El Hamma.

As a result of the battle, 15 and 21 Panzer Divisions received a tremendous hammering and 164 Division lost most of its heavy weapons and vehicles. At least three Italian Divisions lost so many prisoners that they were of little fighting value in the future. 2,500 prisoners, mostly Germans, were taken at El Hamma and up to 28 March the total for the battle was 7,000.

# CHAPTER EIGHT

# The Battle of Wadi Akarit (6 April 1943) and the Advance to Enfidaville

### SITUATION AFTER THE BATTLE OF THE MARETH LINE

To the immediate north of the Mareth Line the coastal plain widens between Gabes and El Hamma, but beyond the main road between those places a serious bottleneck is reached, known to us at the time as the Gabes Gap. The gap extends from the coast to the eastern extremity of the system of lakes and marshes called locally Shott el Fejaj and is some 12 to 15 miles wide. Across the gap, a little to the north of its narrowest part, runs the Wadi Akarit, a difficult obstacle to the movement of tanks and vehicles. The north bank of the wadi is dominated by a line of steep sided hills, the main features on the coastal sector being Djebel er Roumana, which extends to within a few miles of the sea, and Djebel Fatnassa.

The Wadi Akarit thus formed an extremely strong natural defensive position and it was to be expected that the enemy would make use of it; in fact, I had always had this possibility in mind when considering the problem of getting to Sfax.

When Rommel evacuated the Mareth defences he gathered his forces for the defence of the Gabes Gap. As usual he held his front chiefly with Italians and his main reserves were 15 Panzer Division and 90 Light Division. My problem was to prevent his settling into this new position and to burst though the gap myself as quickly as possible.

It will be recalled that on 28 March 10 Corps was ordered to send the New Zealanders direct to Gabes and to capture El Hamma. The task of 30 Corps was to advance on the axis of the main Mareth–Gabes road.

On 29 March the enemy withdrew under pressure from El Hamma and 1 Armoured Division was soon north of the town. On the same day Gabes and Oudref fell to the New Zealanders. Contact was now established with the enemy on the line of the Wadi Akarit with the New Zealanders on the right and 1 Armoured Division on the left. 30 Corps was positioned in rear, between Mareth and Gabes. As we probed the new enemy position, it became clear that Rommel was going to attempt a firm stand—an inevitable decision—as he needed time to reorganize his forces after the defeat he had just sustained.

On 30 March I ordered 10 Corps to get close contact with the Akarit defences and to determine whether they could be forced by the Corps with its existing resources. 30 Corps meanwhile was to prepare to deliver a staged attack to gain a bridgehead, in case 10 Corps found the opposition to be very strong. I now abolished the temporary

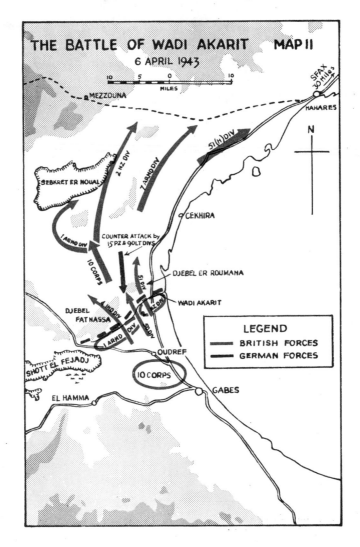

New Zealand Corps, for it had served its purpose admirably and was no longer required.

The next day 10 Corps reported to me that the wadi could be forced by the New Zealand Division but that the operation would probably involve considerable casualties. I did not want to risk this, since the division would be invaluable for the mobile phase which lay ahead. I therefore decided to regroup. 30 Corps took over temporary command of 2 New Zealand Division and also responsibility for the front. It would carry out the attack on the Akarit position with 4 Indian and 51 Divisions, in order to

9.  Rather a macabre sign for one of the many blood banks which moved forward with the advance and saved many Allied lives. 29 October 1942.

10.  The General Priest carries a 105 mm. Howitzer on a self-propelled chassis. It has a high turn of speed and good manœuvrability and proved particularly successful against the German 88 mm. anti-tank guns. 2 November 1942.

11. One of the great pictures of the war. Australians storm a German strong point under cover of a smoke screen.

12. Sherman tanks advance to the front. 5 November 1942.

13. An effective shower except that most of the water was supposed to be saved by the lower tin!

14. After days of action with only water to drink, this Australian takes a long pull at a bottle of beer.

15.　General Montgomery standing in front of his General Grant tank (Monty).
This tank took the General from Alamein to the River Sangro.

secure a bridgehead through which 10 Corps would pass. 10 Corps taking with it the New Zealanders, would be directed on the Mezzouna group of airfields. 30 Corps would advance on the coast road axis to Mahares on a narrow front using 51 Division only; as soon as there was room to manœuvre, 7 Armoured Division would be released for operations to the west of the coast road.

I subsequently decided to increase the assaulting force available for the coming battle; 30 Corps was now to assault with 51, 50 and 4 Indian Divisions, keeping 2 New Zealand Division in a holding role on the front. This was necessary because the strength of the opposition was greater than I at first imagined. The enemy had complete observation over us and the task ahead was formidable. Energetic measures were taken to improve our tank strength, ready for the mobile warfare which was to come, and by 4 April I had nearly 500 tanks available (including the seventy Valentines of 23 Armoured Brigade).

The battle began at 0400 hours 6 April in the dark. Previously our night attacks had always been mounted in moonlight, but I could not wait ten days for the next moon and so decided to change the technique and to attack in the dark; I hoped to gain surprise in this way and indeed was successful. Objectives on the right (51 Division) and left (4 Indian Division) were quickly gained, but 50 Division in the centre had difficulty in the wadi and was delayed until the middle of the day.

The Germans were determined to hold us back and the fighting was bitter. Heavy and determined counter attacks were staged by 15 Panzer and 90 Light Divisions and some localities changed hands several times. My troops fought magnificently, particularly 51 and 4 Indian Divisions, and hung onto the key localities they had taken. The enemy knew that if I could now bring 10 Corps through into the open, he was finished; if I forced him to withdraw he would have no alternative but to go back to the high ground north of Enfidaville: sacrificing the maritime plain and the ports of Sfax and Sousse.

My object was to maintain the momentum of attack. As long as this was done the enemy would be unable to recover, and my superior resources would enable me to continue the pressure until he cracked. I ordered 10 Corps to smash its way out through the front. By noon 6 April it was on the move, headed by 2 New Zealand Division which I had reverted to 10 Corps for the purpose.

By immense endeavours, however, the enemy prevented me from breaking out into the open before dark. But he had exhausted himself; meanwhile I was ready to stage a major 'break-out' action with full scale air and artillery support on 7 April.

Rommel did not wait for the blow to fall but pulled back during the night 6/7 April, and by dawn was in full retreat. The pursuit was taken up according to plan, with 30 Corps on the coastal axis and 10 Corps inland.

Over 7,000 prisoners (mostly Italian), were taken in the battle, and once again Rommel had been defeated and thrown back to the north. He had been surprised by our attack in the darkness, and his troops were overwhelmed by the violence of the 'break-in' operation and by the sustained pressure which followed it.

## THE ADVANCE TO ENFIDAVILLE

By the evening of 7 April, leading troops were on the general line Cekhira–Sebkret er Noual. The countryside was littered with burning vehicles and abandoned equipment, and everywhere parties of Italians were encountered, wandering southwards to give themselves into captivity. On the coastal axis 15 Panzer and 90 Light Divisions provided the enemy rearguards, and intense fighting continued in some areas.

Meanwhile 2 United States Corps in the Gafsa sector was on the move again and on 7 April contact was made between that formation and forward elements of 10 Corps on the Gabes–Gafsa road.

Further north 9 Corps of First Army had started an offensive at the Fondouk Gap and on 9 April, 6 Armoured Division broke through to the east directed on Kairouan.

On 9 April, 30 Corps continued to meet stubborn resistance from enemy rearguards but maintained steady pressure. At last light 22 Armoured Brigade (7 Armoured Division) was but only a few miles short of Sfax, having had a most successful engagement near Agareb against 15 Panzer Division which had been caught ambushed on the move. 10 Corps forged ahead and was directed now on the airfields at Triaga and Fauconnerie. I ordered it subsequently to swing towards the coast at La Hencha to loosen the opposition to 30 Corps.

Sfax was captured on the morning of 10 April. Incidentally, back in Tripoli, I had been promised a Flying Fortress for my own use if I captured Sfax by 15 April. This was soon afterwards generously sent to me by General Eisenhower and for the remainder of the war I had an American aircraft at my disposal.

2 New Zealand Division reached La Hencha and the drive northwards continued. The administrative situation again needed careful watching, as I was still maintaining the army along the single road from Tripoli—now some 300 miles away. It became urgent to get the port of Sfax working.

My orders on 11 April to 10 Corps were to capture Sousse and to join up with First Army at Kairouan, as 6 Armoured Division was now in that area. 1 Armoured Division was halted in the Fauconnerie area. 30 Corps was instructed to move 4 Indian and 50 Divisions north from the Akarit position to join 10 Corps. I decided to hold in reserve Headquarters 30 Corps, with 7 Armoured and 51 Divisions, about Sfax.

Sousse fell on 12 April and by the end of the following day the leading troops of 10 Corps were up against the anti-tank ditch at Enfidaville. Meanwhile we were receiving reports about the enemy positions constructed along the high ground which forms the northern barrier of the maritime plain and reaches almost to the sea just north of Enfidaville. This defensive system became known to Eighth Army as the Enfidaville position.

The Allies were closing in on the Axis forces, and it was now appreciated that the enemy intended to stand on the line Enfidaville–Pont du Fahs–Medjez el Bab–Sedjenane. On 12 April I received word from General Alexander that First Army was to make the main effort in the final phase of the North African Campaign, and that Eighth Army's role would be to exert the maximum pressure on the southern sector of

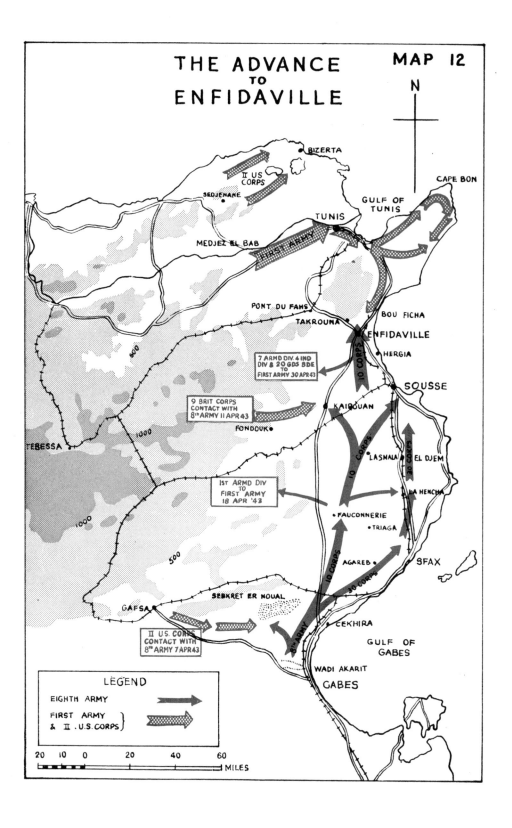

# THE ADVANCE TO ENFIDAVILLE

## MAP 12

N

BIZERTA

CAPE BON

II US CORPS

SEDJENANE

GULF OF TUNIS

TUNIS

FIRST ARMY

MEDJEZ EL BAB

PONT DU FAHS

TAKROUNA

BOU FICHA

ENFIDAVILLE

7 ARMD DIV 4 IND DIV & 20 GDS BDE TO FIRST ARMY 30 APR 43

10 CORPS

HERGLA

SOUSSE

9 BRIT CORPS CONTACT WITH 8TH ARMY 11 APR 43

KAIROUAN

FONDOUK

TEBESSA

1000

1000

500

LASMALA

EL DJEM

10 CORPS

30 CORPS

1ST ARMD DIV TO FIRST ARMY 18 APR '43

LA HENCHA

FAUCONNERIE

TRIAGA

500

SFAX

10 CORPS

AGAREB

30 CORPS

SEBKRET ER NOUAL

GAFSA

II US CORPS CONTACT WITH 8TH ARMY 7 APR 43

CEKHIRA

8TH ARMY

GULF OF GABES

WADI AKARIT

GABES

LEGEND

EIGHTH ARMY

FIRST ARMY & II . U.S. CORPS

20   10   0        20        40        60

MILES

the enemy's front in order to pin down as much of his strength as possible. The plain west of Tunis was the most suitable ground for the deployment of armoured forces and I was asked to send an armoured division and an armoured car regiment to join First Army.

I nominated 1 Armoured Division and the King's Dragoon Guards for this role and in due course they joined 9 Corps.

The Enfidaville position was admirably suited for defence and unless the enemy could be 'bounced' out of it before he had time to organize his defences thoroughly, it was obviously going to be a very difficult undertaking to break through it. The country was generally unsuitable for tanks, except in the very narrow coastal strip, and even there water channels and other obstacles existed. The enemy had excellent observation over our territory to the south; moreover he showed every indication of being prepared to stand and put up a desperate fight.

In these circumstances the decision that the main effort should now be transferred to the Plain of Tunis was a logical one.

I gave orders for 'squaring up' to the Enfidaville position. 10 Corps (now consisting of 7 Armoured, 2 New Zealand, 4 Indian and 50 Divisions) was instructed to endeavour to push the enemy out of the position before he had settled in. The attempt would be made on the coastal axis, and if successful 10 Corps would go on to the next system of defences which were known to exist about Bou-Ficha. If the enemy could not be 'bounced' out, I planned to stage a full scale thrust on the night of 19/20 April.

I intended to retain Headquarters 30 Corps and 51 Division in reserve.

The Desert Air Force meanwhile 'stepped up' to landing grounds in the area Sousse–El Djem–La Smala–Kairouan. This was destined to be its last move in the campaign, since from these fields it could operate throughout the zone remaining to the enemy in Tunisia.

I had from this time to take into account the future role of the Eighth Army when deciding on the grouping and tasks of the various divisions. I had been told in January, when at Tripoli, that the Eighth Army was to form the Imperial component of the combined British and American force destined to invade Sicily, as soon as practicable after the completion of the campaign in North Africa. I was anxious to rest Headquarters 30 Corps and get it prepared for starting on the new task; I should also require 51 Division and either 2 New Zealand or 50 Division for the assault on Sicily, and these formations would have to be refitted and rested before beginning this new enterprise.

By 16 April it was plain that the enemy could not be 'bounced' out of his new defence system and I ordered preparations to be made for a heavy attack using 2 New Zealand and 4 Indian Divisions for the main thrust astride the village of Takrouna, 50 Division for a subsidiary blow on the coast road axis, and 7 Armoured Division for guarding the western flank, linking up on its left with the French 19 Corps.

I called forward 56 Division from Tripoli so that I could relieve 2 New Zealand or 50 Division when the time came for the formation selected to return to Egypt for reorganization.

## THE BATTLE OF ENFIDAVILLE

On the night 19/20 April the attack against the Enfidaville position began. A great weight of artillery support was provided and the customary air programme arranged.

It was quickly apparent that we were going to have difficulty in this task. We were hurling ourselves against a formidable barrier of difficult ground and the defenders were strengthened in their endeavours by the desperate necessity of holding their remaining bridgehead in Africa. Fighting was severe, particularly in Takrouna, but the New Zealanders captured the vital ground we needed. On the right Enfidaville fell and we pushed forward some three miles beyond, while on the left we secured the ground necessary to deny the enemy observation over areas required for the forward deployment of artillery. A series of heavy counter attacks was staged by the enemy on 20 and 21 April, but we retained a firm grip on our gains and advanced another three miles along the coast. The Germans suffered heavy casualties and 800 prisoners were taken in the first two days.

I decided that it was too expensive to continue the thrust in the centre and on 22 April ordered re-grouping of the Army, in order to switch the main thrust line to the coast. At the same time I had to relieve 50 Division, which was now to return to Egypt to prepare for Sicily.

The re-grouping went ahead, but the more I examined the problem now confronting Eighth Army, the more convinced I became that our operations would be extremely costly and had little chance of achieving any decisive success with the resources available. The enemy was located in ideal defensive country and could find a series of excellent positions, one behind the other, from which to oppose us and there was no scope for deploying my armour.

## THE END OF THE NORTH AFRICAN CAMPAIGN

On 30 April General Alexander visited me and we discussed the whole problem of finishing the war in North Africa. Subsequently a major re-grouping between First and Eighth Armies was ordered, with the object of strengthening the projected thrust across the Plain of Tunis to the sea. 7 Armoured and 4 Indian Divisions, 201 Guards Brigade and some medium artillery were switched to First Army and General Horrocks went to command 9 Corps, whose Commander had been wounded.

I was left with 2 New Zealand, 51 and 56 Divisions, a French Division now placed under my command, and two armoured brigades. I decided to hold the front with 56 and 12 French Divisions, to keep 51 Division in reserve (where it might commence training for Sicily) and to employ 2 New Zealand Division with an armoured brigade for an operation on the western flank towards Saouf.

Meanwhile on 6 May First Army launched an attack in great strength from the Medjez el Bab sector, directed on Tunis. Complete success was achieved, and both Tunis and Bizerta fell on 7 May. I was happy to learn that 7 Armoured Division was first into Tunis. Mopping up of the enemy forces continued until 12 May, when the last resistance ceased.

The North Africa Campaign had reached its conclusion and the remaining Axis survivors were lodged in captivity. It had ended in a major disaster for the Germans; all their remaining troops, equipment and stores were captured. Very few personnel were able to get away owing to the effectiveness of the blockade by the Royal Navy and Royal Air Force which closed the escape routes by sea and air. It is idle to speculate why the Axis forces attempted to hold on in North Africa once the Mareth Line and Gabes Gap had been forced. From a purely military point of view there was no justification for their action, but perhaps there were overriding political considerations.

The Eighth Army had travelled 1,850 miles from El Alamein to be in at the death and was now destined to have a short respite. Within two months it was taking part in the opening stage of the first entry into Hitler's 'Fortress of Europe'.

Headquarters and some of the divisions of Eighth Army moved back to the Tripoli area as soon as their task in Tunisia was completed and, before starting on the next enterprise, were honoured by a visit from His Majesty The King—a fitting climax to our campaigning in Africa.

# CHAPTER NINE

## *Administration in the North African Campaign*

WHEN I took over command of the Eighth Army both the staffs of the formations and the troops themselves had already acquired a considerable degree of skill in the rather specialized form of administration necessary in desert warfare. They had learned in the hard school of experience. Two rapid advances to the El Agheila position, succeeded by desperate withdrawals, had led to drastic modifications in previously accepted methods and to the establishment of new procedures for dealing with the conditions obtaining in the desert.

One principle of great value and importance had already been fully accepted, namely that the Staff must exercise a firm control over the administrative plan and watchful co-ordination over its execution. The day had gone when the Head of a Service could say 'The efficiency of my Service is my own concern. Tell me what you want me to do and leave me alone to do it.' It had also been realized that the various administrative installations which are set up to support a formation in battle need centralized control. The Field Maintenance Centre, a sort of administrative township with a headquarters to control it, comprised those installations which were necessary for the support of a Corps. This first made its appearance in the offensive of November 1941 and was by now an established element of administrative organization. The Army Roadhead, which first came into being as such during the Alamein Campaign, was but a development of the same idea.

The Field Maintenance Centre and Army Roadhead represented a departure from previous practice, not only by virtue of their own organization but even more importantly because of the stocks which they held. All textbooks written before the War had assumed that requirements of a force would be met by the despatch of daily pack trains. It was considered neither necessary nor desirable to hold any reserves at a railhead, or forward of it, except in very small amounts necessary to balance deliveries. The campaigns of 1940 and 1941 had shown that this system was not workable in modern conditions of warfare. It was too inflexible. During a rapid advance the demand for petrol rose to staggering levels. By the time that the necessary adjustments had been made in pack train loadings, the need for the petrol had given way to a demand for ammunition because the advance had been stopped and battle was imminent. It is of course true that the holding of large supplies well forward had disadvantages. In spite of every effort made for their destruction, considerable supplies fell into the enemy's hands during the retreat from Gazala to Alamein. As a result of this misfortune an attempt was made to adopt once again the pack train system during the period of static warfare on the Alamein position. The attempt had to be abandoned

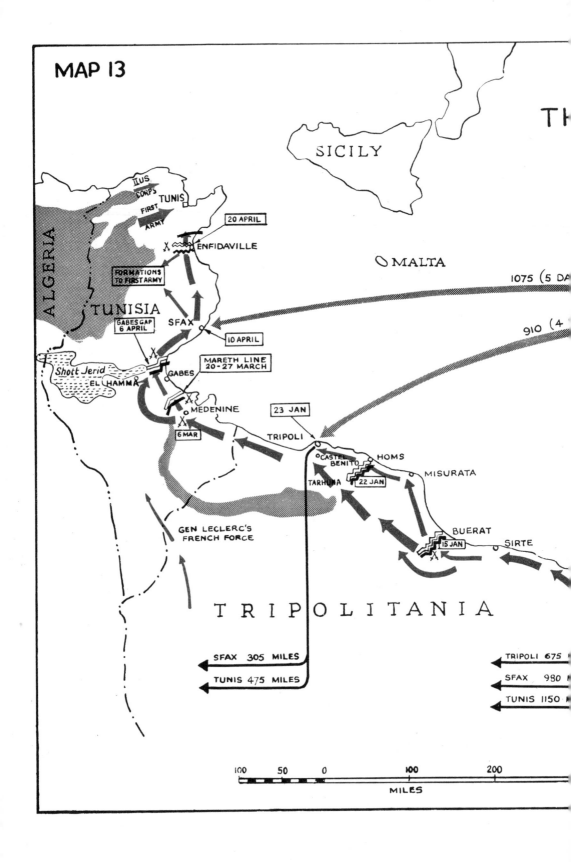

## MAP 13

SICILY

TH

O MALTA

1075 (5 DA

910 (4

**20 APRIL**

IIUS
CORPS
FIRST
ARMY

TUNIS

X ~~~~ ENFIDAVILLE

FORMATIONS
TO FIRST ARMY

ALGERIA

TUNISIA

GABES GAP
6 APRIL

SFAX

**10 APRIL**

**MARETH LINE
20-27 MARCH**

Shott Jerid
EL HAMMA

GABES

X X

X X MEDENINE

**23 JAN**

6 MAR

TRIPOLI

CASTEL
BENITO

HOMS

TARHUNA

**22 JAN**

MISURATA

GEN LECLERC'S
FRENCH FORCE

BUERAT

**15 JAN**

SIRTE

T R I P O L I T A N I A

SFAX    305 MILES

TUNIS   475 MILES

TRIPOLI 675

SFAX    980

TUNIS  1150

100    50    0         100        200

MILES

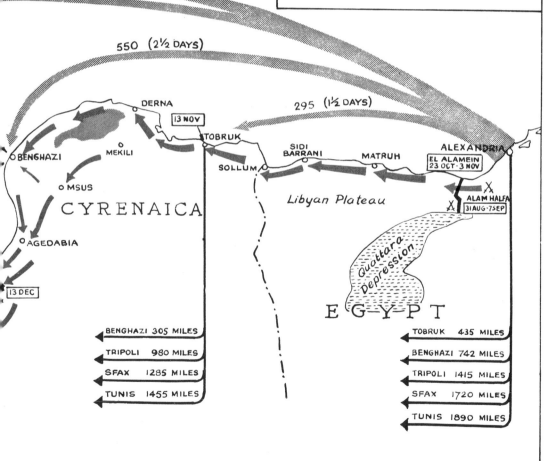

GHTH ARMY
ORTH AFRICA

E & SPACE

## LEGEND

X̄ 6 MAR  MAJOR BATTLES.

EIGHTH ARMY AXIS OF ADVANCE.

SFAX 305 MILES
TUNIS 475 MILES  DISTANCES BY LAND.

295 (1½ DAYS)  DISTANCE IN SEA-MILES FROM ALEXANDRIA TO PRINCIPAL SUPPLY PORTS USED DURING THE CAMPAIGN.

〜〜〜  ENEMY DEFENCE LINES.

⬭  MAIN FEATURES.

550 (2½ DAYS)

295 (1½ DAYS)

DERNA
13 NOV
TOBRUK
BENGHAZI
MEKILI
SOLLUM
SIDI BARRANI
MATRUH
ALEXANDRIA
EL ALAMEIN 23 OCT·3 NOV
MSUS
CYRENAICA
Libyan Plateau
ALAM HALFA 31 AUG·7 SEP
AGEDABIA
Quattara Depression
13 DEC
EGYPT

BENGHAZI 305 MILES
TRIPOLI 980 MILES
SFAX 1285 MILES
TUNIS 1455 MILES

TOBRUK 435 MILES
BENGHAZI 742 MILES
TRIPOLI 1415 MILES
SFAX 1720 MILES
TUNIS 1890 MILES

immediately the advance began. The upshot of this matter is that, if a commander loses his battle, his defeat will be the more serious if he had held reserves forward which fall into the enemy's hands. On the other hand, if he wins his battle, he will not be able to take advantage of victory unless he has such reserves. I have always planned on the assumption of success.

Another lesson which had already been well learnt was the importance of the recovery of armoured vehicles and M.T. The arrangements for this had been brought to a state of efficiency which stood us in excellent stead throughout the advance.

The set-piece battles of Alam Halfa and Alamein presented no unusual or particularly difficult administrative problems. The Army was close to its base, to which it was linked both by rail and road. The pursuit from Alamein to Tripoli and from Tripoli to Tunis, may, on the other hand, be regarded as an administrative campaign of unprecedented interest. It is possible here only to mention some of its outstanding features. Those who are interested in the study of administration in modern warfare should make a detailed examination of it.

I must first pay tribute to those who were responsible for administrative planning at GHQ Middle East Forces. The build-up of the fighting troops which enabled me to win the victory of El Alamein would have been of no avail unless it had been accompanied by an intelligent reinforcement on a large scale of our administrative resources. It would have been of no avail because I should have been unable to reap the fruits of victory. It was a good example of the foresight which is the essence of a successful administration in war.

The keynote of my administrative arrangements throughout the pursuit was austerity. Even with the generous resources provided, the task of administration was immense. Administrative considerations dictated, throughout, the strength of the force which could be deployed at any given time. It follows from this that everything which accompanied the leading troops had to be very carefully scrutinized. We could afford no luxuries. To carry forward more equipment or more men than were absolutely necessary for the battle meant a subtraction from our fighting strength. It was equally essential that the administrative organization itself should be pruned to the limit. In order that it may do itself justice, there is always a tendency for an administrative service to provide for all contingencies. This we could not afford. I must mention particularly the use of fighting troops for work on essential administrative tasks. Infantry were used to help in the discharge of ships at Benghazi, Tripoli and at the small coves between these two places where we landed supplies from craft. By using reserve formations for this purpose we avoided the necessity of bringing forward a corresponding number of pioneer companies. It is most important in such circumstances to explain both to officers and men why they are being used for a task for which otherwise they would have little relish. They must not become discouraged and lose efficiency. The scale of reserves was kept to a minimum throughout, with the result that on isolated occasions certain units were short. This is inevitable in such conditions. If *all* troops had had *all* that they needed *all* the time, it would have been proof that administration had over-insured. In particular the amount of ammunition allowed for each battle was calculated to a nicety with the result that when the action had been fought very little remained on the ground. I think it most important to emphasize this matter of austerity because in subsequent campaigns, when conditions were entirely different, we were able to be more lavish and our troops became accustomed to having everything of which they felt a need. If the British Army has to fight another war, I feel sure that at the outset it will have to operate under an austere regime of administration and not under the relatively comfortable conditions which obtained during the latter phase of this War.

A feature of our administrative arrangements during this campaign, which may fairly be regarded as new, was the organization of what may be termed the 'administrative assault force'. While preparations for the attack at Alamein were being made there was being formed simultaneously a force of administrative units drawn from all three Services. A Commander and staff were appointed to co-ordinate their movements and activities. The role of this force was to advance close on the heels of the fighting troops and to take over as quickly as possible ports and other places of administrative importance and to organize them rapidly for the reception and distribution of supplies. Several references have been made in previous chapters to the work done in opening and developing harbours. This is a combined operation in which all three Services play an essential part and must work together. The three most important members of the administrative assault force were the Area Commander, the Naval Officer in Charge and the Air Officer responsible for fighter defence. These three with their staffs and services lived together during the planning stage and moved forward together on a co-ordinated plan. Special priority tables were worked out to ensure that they should get forward and reach their objective at the earliest possible moment. The name 'Golden List' was applied to these tables and remained in use in subsequent campaigns. The position of each unit on the 'Golden List' was very carefully worked out by the administrative staff. It is possible to keep the same administrative assault force in the van throughout the advance. Alternatively, more than one such force can be organized and the leap-frog principle adopted. The former system, by producing a team of very highly trained and experienced men, ensures that the organization of administration at the most forward point is carried out as rapidly as possible. On the other hand, due to the fact that the spearhead is constantly on the move, the organization of the port or administrative area suffers more at a later stage and the leap-frog principle has an advantage in this respect.

From Alamein to Tunis the advance of the Eighth Army was carried out by well defined bounds. There is always a tendency, natural and indeed laudable, on the part of keen commanders to edge forward as far as possible at all times. When administration is strained this tendency must be checked; it prevents the accumulation of reserves and this means that the mounting of a powerful attack becomes impossible.

The problem of the division of administrative control first came into prominence during this campaign. During the early stage of the advance, the administrative staff of

Eighth Army had control of the railhead or port on which the Army was mainly based and of the entire area in front of it. GHQ Middle East Forces assumed control progressively in rear. Rear Army Headquarters had necessarily to be located near the main railhead or port. This meant a separation in distance which sometimes exceeded 200 miles between Rear Army Headquarters and Main Army Headquarters, at which latter place the chief administrative officer was located. When we reached Tripoli I felt that some alteration in this arrangement was necessary. GHQ Middle East Forces could not assume responsibility for Tripoli because it was too far away and there was no communication other than wireless. Moreover, it was undesirable that it should do so because of the vital dependence of my operational plans on the functioning of the port and its depots. To meet this situation I organized a special staff under a Major-General which not only took charge of the local administration of the Tripoli Area, but, working in very close contact with the Army staff, also became responsible for the formulation of demands on GHQ Middle East Forces. This was the first attempt to solve a problem which repeated itself in Sicily and Italy.

# PART II

## THE INVASION AND CAPTURE OF SICILY

### 10 JULY–17 AUGUST 1943

# CHAPTER TEN

## Planning the Invasion of Sicily

### THE EVOLUTION OF THE PLAN

As the first stage in the policy of striking at the 'underbelly' of Axis Europe, the British and American Governments authorized the invasion of Sicily. The operation was to follow the North African campaign as quickly as conditions permitted, and it was decided that both United States and Empire troops, under the supreme command of General Eisenhower, would take part.

Under the Supreme Commander the Service chiefs appointed were Admiral Cunningham, General Alexander and Air Marshal Tedder. The forces were to be organized in two commands, the Western (United States) and Eastern (British) Naval and Military Task Forces; Allied air resources remained centralized. The Eighth Army formed the military component of the Eastern Task Force, in which my Service colleagues were Admiral Ramsay and Air Vice-Marshal Park (later Air Vice-Marshal Broadhurst).

Late in January 1943, orders to plan and mount Operation 'Husky', as the invasion was called, were received in North Africa, and a planning staff (initially known as Force 141 and later expanded on the Army side into HQ 15 Army Group) was set up in Algiers to commence work on the problem.

It will be noticed that at this time the Tunisian campaign had not yet entered into its last phases. Eighth Army had recently captured Tripoli and First Army was operating in the mountains of western Tunisia, so that the commanders and troops destined to undertake this great combined operation were fully committed in the immediate battle. As a result there were serious delays in planning 'Husky' and in fact the preparation of the expedition was beset with tremendous difficulties at all levels of command throughout the period available for the task.

Before dealing with the development of detailed planning in the Eastern Task Force, I will discuss the evolution of the plan of invasion, for this was a matter which took considerable time and was brought to finality only after much discussion and delay.

Although I knew in January that Eighth Army was to take part in 'Husky', it was not until 23 April that I had an opportunity of leaving the battle in Tunisia for a few days (while my formations were regrouping before Enfidaville) in order to make a detailed study of the proposed outline plan. The original version had been produced by joint Allied planning staffs and with certain modifications was under discussion at Force 141. A series of planning staffs was concerned with the examination of the plan, but had to function without the customary and essential guidance of the commanders directly

[81]

responsible for carrying out the operation. This system of 'absentee landlords' led to all the obvious disadvantages.

After examination I came to the conclusion that the existing plan was unsound, and immediately submitted my views to General Alexander. The plan proposed was that Sicily should be invaded simultaneously in two distinct areas: by the Western Task Force in the north-west corner of the island, and by the Eastern Task Force in the south-east on a frontage between the Gulf of Catania and the Gulf of Gela. For the assault the Americans were to have shipping and craft for three divisions with some armoured troops, with another equivalent division available to discharge immediately behind the assault; Eighth Army would have four assaulting divisions, with a tank brigade in 'floating reserve'. An airborne division was available for each task force.

The most important immediate objectives were ports and airfields. Ports were essential quickly as there was no available experience of maintenance over beaches, which was viewed with the greatest mistrust. The distance of Sicily from our available airfields made it essential, moreover, to establish the air forces in the island urgently, or the Axis air force would be able to interfere with our landings and sea routes, perhaps with disastrous results. These considerations were covered by the proposed plan, which provided (in the case of the Eastern Task Force) for the early capture of two groups of airfields (the Catania group and the Comiso–Gela group) and the ports in the south-east of the island—Catania, Augusta and Siracusa.

But—and to my mind this was the vital point—the proposed plan was based on the existing enemy garrison in Sicily in early 1943 and assumed that the Axis powers would not reinforce the island before our invasion. To spread four divisions, with a relatively slow build-up of forces behind them, between the Gulf of Catania and Gela obviously implied negligible resistance to our assault and a decision on the part of the enemy not to send reinforcements from Italy to oppose us.

I had seen the fierce resistance that the Germans and Italians were showing in Tunisia and considered that it was essential to prepare to meet strong enemy reaction in Sicily. By the time we launched the invasion there was no reason to suppose that the island garrison would not be reinforced; moreover the Axis powers could send troops across the Straits of Messina more quickly than we could hope to build up our forces across the sea. To assume negligible resistance to our enterprise and to disperse our assaulting divisions, therefore, appeared to me fundamentally unsound and the first point upon which I made strong representations was that the formations of the Eastern Task Force must land within supporting distance of each other. A suitable area could then be secured as a firm base from which to develop further operations. This conclusion led me to propose an alternative plan.

The essentials of the problem from the Army's point of view were that a bridgehead had to be seized, the choice of which was limited to those areas of the island which were within fighter range of our aerodromes; its size was dependent on the available forces, which had to be landed concentrated and prepared for hard fighting. Within the bridgehead it was essential to secure the port and airfield facilities without which the combined operation would inevitably collapse. Applied to 'Husky', these factors led to the conclusion that the best area for putting the Eighth Army ashore was in the Gulf of Noto and astride the Pachino peninsula. This would limit the frontage of assault to suit our resources and a suitable firm base could be developed from the beaches across the south-east portion of the island; Siracusa could be captured rapidly and operations swung northwards to secure Augusta and Catania. But this possibility did not satisfy one essential requirement: the seizure of an adequate number of airfields. The air forces were insistent that the Comiso–Gela group must be included in the initial bridgehead: not only in order to deny the fields to the enemy, but also to enable our own squadrons to deploy in sufficient strength to dominate the enemy air force and assist in the development of our operations.

Here then was an impasse, nor was there an alternative area of assault for the Eastern Task Force which could satisfy the demands of·all three Services. If the proposed bridgehead were shifted north to include Catania and its airfields, we should overshoot the zone of fighter cover; if moved westwards to include Comiso and Gela there was no immediate prospect of capturing ports: and with its existing resources the Army was unable to accept the degree of dispersion which would embrace both the ports and airfields required.

I therefore recommended that the Eastern Task Force should be allotted two more assaulting divisions, with adequate build-up resources, to enable us to assault on a frontage from the Gulf of Noto to Gela inclusive.

On 2 May I attended a conference at Algiers and put forward my views. The outcome was a decision by the Supreme Commander to shift the assault of the American Seventh Army from the north-west corner of the island to the Gulf of Gela. This implied that the two task forces would land side by side within mutual supporting distance and would secure a bridgehead which included all the vital requirements of the Navy, and Air Forces. I heard of General Eisenhower's decision on 3 May and from that date detailed planning was able to progress on a firm basis.

I based my outline plan on having available 10, 13 and 30 Corps. Briefly my intention was as follows:

13 Corps would land in the Gulf of Noto south of Siracusa with two divisions. Its task would be to secure the high ground overlooking the beaches, then wheel north to capture successively Siracusa, Augusta and Catania. The Corps would be assisted by a seaborne commando operation and by airborne landings. Astride the Pachino peninsula 30 Corps would assault with two divisions and secure a firm base from which it would join up with the American forces to the north-west, and operate to the north in order to take over the 13 Corps beachhead. In this way units of 13 Corps would be released for the capture of Siracusa and the other ports.

I decided to hold 10 Corps in reserve in the Tripoli area.

SOME PLANNING DIFFICULTIES CONFRONTING THE EASTERN TASK FORCE

I have mentioned that the preparations for this operation were carried out in extremely difficult conditions. The Eastern Task Force planning headquarters was in Cairo. In April I started sending members of Eighth Army staff from Tunisia to Cairo and gradually assembled there a nucleus from the various branches. Not until 16 May was HQ Eighth Army proper released from Tunisia.

Releasing troops from the battle in order that they could reorganize and commence training for combined operations had proved very difficult, but it will be recalled that I had kept HQ 30 Corps and 51 Division in reserve during the final phase in Tunisia and that 50 Division had been relieved by 56 Division before the end of the North African campaign. Meanwhile HQ 13 Corps (General Dempsey) was in the Delta, having been out of the line since El Alamein.

Thus it will be evident that circumstances prevented a 'tidy' start being made on preparations for the 'Husky' venture.

The mounting of the Eastern Task Force was primarily the responsibility of GHQ Middle East, but part of the force was mounted in Tunisia and one division in England. The detailed planning was done by Task Force Headquarters and 13 Corps in Cairo; 30 Corps completed its planning in Tunisia; 10 Corps was at Tripoli; and our immediate superior headquarters was at Algiers.

The troops destined to take part were even more dispersed. 1 Canadian Division, located in England, was to join the assault direct from home ports. 51 and 78 Divisions were to embark in Tunisia, where 1 Airborne Division was based inland at Kairouan. In the Tripoli area I had 7 Armoured and 56 Divisions. In the Middle East, destined to embark at Alexandria, the Canal ports and at Haifa were 5 and 50 Divisions together with 231 Infantry Brigade (which had formerly been in Malta).

The detailed order of battle was a nightmare because it was not known until the end of the North African campaign which divisions would in fact emerge in sufficient strength and condition to be ready for Sicily in the time available. The planning of the assault was subject to the availability of various types of assault craft and ships, a factor which constantly changed up to the very last minute: with the inevitable repercussions on the planning of the units and formations concerned. Not the least of the difficulties arose from relatively minor matters such as the difference between the War Establishment tables in England, the Middle East and North Africa, which resulted in seemingly endless misunderstandings, when staff work was being handled over such immense distances.

In the wider aspect of planning for the whole Task Force, the main difficulty was the separation of the Navy and Army staffs from their Air Force counterpart. The air forces were represented in Cairo by a liaison staff provided from North Africa, but the Air Force Command immediately concerned with our activities was in Malta: very busily involved with air operations for which Malta was a key base. It was therefore impossible to plan in close contact with the actual air staff with which the battle was to be conducted at the Task Force level. A further complication which affected the Army was that as soon as units of our tactical air component were established in Sicily, they were to come under command of a different Air Force headquarters.

Between the Royal Navy and the Army there were no such complications, for the two staffs worked together in close harmony in the same building in Cairo.

During the preparatory period formations and units carried out intensive training and special courses were arranged at the available Combined Operations centres. Formations reorganized, absorbed their quotas of reinforcements and were re-equipped while staffs worked feverishly at the mass of detailed preparation which an invasion demands. Perhaps the most difficult problem which faced the subordinate formations of the Army arose from continually varying estimates of availability of craft and shipping. For example, every time an assault craft is added to, or still worse, subtracted from, the allotment made to a unit, the loading tables and probably the detailed tactical plan have to be revised, and the alteration may have repercussions on the next higher formation as well as on subordinate sub-units. Moreover, the availability of the various types of special assault craft was very limited, so that the scope for organization of assaulting units and tactical grouping in craft was greatly restricted. Yet another complication was the time which units and formations would be at sea before the landing operation began; troops cannot be packed into landing craft for long periods, when such craft are designed to carry them relatively short distances.

I will not elaborate on these difficulties, for I have given sufficient instances to make it clear that the planning and mounting of Operation 'Husky' presented a formidable task.

THE OVERALL PLAN

During May and June the detailed plan took shape. The Supreme Commander's orders gave as his intention the seizure of Sicily. The operation was to be conducted in five phases; first, the preparatory measures by Naval and Air Forces to neutralize enemy naval efforts and to gain air supremacy; second, the seaborne assault, assisted by airborne landings, with the object of seizing airfields and the ports of Siracusa and Licata; third, the establishment of a firm base from which to conduct operations for the capture of the ports of Augusta and Catania and the airfields in the Plain of Catania; fourth, the capture of these ports and airfields; finally, the reduction of the island.

Eighth Army's task was to assault between Siracusa and Pozzallo to capture the port of Siracusa and the airfield at Pachino. We were then to advance to the general line Siracusa–Palazzolo–Ragusa, making contact at Ragusa with Seventh United States Army. Subsequently we were to secure Augusta and Catania and the group of airfields in the Plain of Catania, then complete the capture of the island in conjunction with the Americans. General Patton's Seventh Army was to assault between Capo Scaramia and Licata with the object of capturing the port of Licata and the group of airfields which included Ponte Olivo, Biscari and Comiso. Seventh Army was to ensure the defence of the airfields and subsequently was to protect the left flank of Eighth Army from any enemy threats developed from the west of the island.

Intelligence regarding the layout of the Axis defences in Sicily was gradually collected and it eventually became apparent that the garrison consisted of two German armoured divisions—the 'Hermann Goering' and the 'Sicily'—and five Italian field divisions. (Shortly before our invasion the 'Sicily' Division was renamed 15 Panzer Grenadier Division.) In addition to these formations, a series of Italian coastal divisions, six in number, was disposed round the coast. The layout of the enemy's dispositions in general indicated that he considered the south-east and east to be the most likely area of assault, but that he did not dismiss the possibility of landings in the west. It was evident that he wished to safeguard against any threat to Licata and the airfield group to the north-east of it and also to Catania and its associated aerodromes. The long coastline abounded in suitable assault beaches and it was to be presumed that the coastal defence screen was designed to delay hostile landings, reliance being placed on strong counter attacks to push any invader back into the sea. On Eighth Army's sector 206 Coastal Division was strung out over nearly sixty miles of coast from Capo Campolato to Licata and was known to be poorly equipped and low in morale. I did not therefore anticipate any great difficulty in the initial assault, but appreciated that counter attacks might develop soon after and that increasingly severe opposition would be encountered in the advance towards Catania. Both the Hermann Goering and 15 Panzer Grenadier Divisions were facing the south-east corner of the island, but were split into battle groups which were very dispersed and, in view of the poor roads, it was likely to be many hours before they could concentrate. The Italian formations were also very scattered.

The estimated rate of enemy reinforcements to the island was potentially $1\frac{1}{2}$ to 2 divisions a week, but I considered this unlikely owing to maintenance limitations: which I felt would severely limit his build-up.

The defences of the assault beaches, though continuous, did not appear strong. There were short belts of barbed wire, machine gun posts and a few pillboxes, while the artillery strength in the coastal sectors appeared to be negligible. The fighting value of the Italian troops was open to question, as none of them had been in action elsewhere and there was no reason to believe that they were above the average. But as I have already mentioned, the Italian troops fought desperately in the closing stages of the Tunisian campaign and it was reasonable to assume that they would show even more spirit in the defence of their homeland.

As is well known, the general topography of Sicily is very mountainous and movement off the roads and tracks is seldom possible. In the beach areas there was a narrow coastal plain, but behind this the mountains rose steeply and the road network was very indifferent. It was apparent that the campaign in Sicily was going to depend largely on the domination of main road and track centres and the story of the operations will show that these invariably became our main objectives.

## THE EIGHTH ARMY PLAN

13 Corps was to assault immediately south of Siracusa. Its operation was planned to begin with the drop of 1 Air Landing Brigade Group west of Siracusa between 2210 and 2230 hours on 9 July in order to capture a very important bridge over the Anapo River called Ponte Grande, together with the coastal batteries north of the river and the seaplane base nearby. Commando troops were to land from the sea four hours later and capture a main coastal battery at Capo Murro di Porco. The main assault of 13 Corps would then be made by 5 Division on a two brigade front and 50 Division on a one brigade front. The former was to capture Cassibile and subsequently advance on Siracusa in co-operation with the airborne troops. 50 Division was to capture Avola and protect the Corps bridgehead from the west and south-west. The protection of the bridgehead involved securing a firm footing on the plateau some two and a half miles inland which completely dominates the coastal road between Noto and Cassibile. In the second phase 5 and 50 Divisions were to secure bridgeheads over the Simeto River and capture Catania, being relieved for this task by 30 Corps, which was to take over the initial 13 Corps beachhead.

30 Corps plan provided for a landing by 231 Infantry Brigade Group south of Marzamemi with the task of developing a beachhead to protect the Corps right flank; patrols were to be pushed out as rapidly as possible to gain contact with 13 Corps near Avola. 51 Division was to land in the centre on a frontage of four battalions astride the south-eastern point of the Pachino peninsula, with the immediate object of capturing the town of Pachino. On the left of 51 Division, 1 Canadian Division was to establish a beachhead protecting the Corps left flank and was made responsible for capturing the Pachino landing ground. The seizure of this airfield and its immediate rehabilitation was considered a primary Corps task and, although allotted to 1 Canadian Division, orders provided for its capture by whichever formation in the Corps made the most rapid progress.

30 Corps first main objective was the road Noto–Rosolini Spaccaforna. After its capture, 51 Division was to be prepared to relieve 50 Division (13 Corps) at Avola. The second main Corps objective was the high ground covering the convergence of road routes in the area Palazzolo–Ragusa. At the latter place 1 Canadian Division was to make contact with 2 United States Corps. The main thrust line of 30 Corps was then to be along the road axis Palazzolo–Vizzini.

Naval supporting ships were to assist the initial landings and our subsequent advances on the coastal sector. A comprehensive plan of air support was also drawn up.

## FINAL PREPARATION FOR THE ASSAULT

On 3 July I arrived in Malta to find the whole of the Eighth Army staff installed there for the start of the invasion.

My first aim was to see Air Vice-Marshal Park in order to get from him the complete air picture. Only at this late stage were we able to make close contact with the Air Force authority responsible on our front for the assault phase. The enemy long-range bombers had been pushed well back, but there was still a formidable hostile fighter strength in Sicily and in spite of all our efforts the enemy fighters were refusing combat. But the Allied air forces were dealing with the enemy in no uncertain way and it was not likely that his air forces would cause us any great trouble.

According to my normal custom I issued a personal message to the troops, which was read out to them when they embarked. The stage was set for the operation which was to carry Eighth Army across the sea and ultimately into the mainland of Europe. The soldiers were very enthusiastic and soberly confident of the issue and so was I, although I suffered from no delusions about the serious fighting which lay ahead.

# CHAPTER ELEVEN

## The Assault on Sicily, the Extension of the Bridgehead and the Advance to the Plain of Catania, 10–21 July 1943

### THE ASSAULT

DURING 9 July the convoys of the Seventh United States and Eighth Armies closed towards their rendezvous areas east and west of Malta. During the day the wind rose sharply in the central Mediterranean and the naval assault formations were formed up in a heavy sea, prior to the approach to the Sicilian coast where landings were due to commence in the early hours of 10 July. The swell threatened to make the beaching of assault craft and the landing of troops a hazardous undertaking and many of the men were suffering from sea sickness. During the night the invasion convoys reached the transport areas from which assault craft were to be launched, but at this time the wind began to slacken so that there was a fair hope that the gale would subside before the troops landed.

It was an anxious time, but the risk of attempting to postpone the assault until the weather became more favourable was greater than the hazard of continuing with the plan. In the event the convoys were up to schedule and reached their correct stations punctually. I would like here to pay tribute to the work of the Royal Navy in this operation. It was beyond all praise. The entire naval arrangements for landing the expedition in Sicily were brilliant.

Meanwhile in the early evening of 9 July formations of airborne forces took off from Tunisia. Unfortunately their operation did not go as planned; there was a high wind, a number of gliders fell into the sea and a large proportion of the troops landed wide of the objective. Only a very small force, therefore, reached the Ponte Grande, which was nevertheless held with remarkable heroism for nearly eighteen hours.

The seaborne assault was an outstanding success. It was greatly facilitated by the failure of the enemy air force seriously to oppose it and because, as a result of the gale, the enemy garrison, already wearied by false alerts and scares, had relaxed its vigilance. The first waves of our assault achieved complete tactical surprise and the enemy's confusion and disorganization were such that he was unable to offer any co-ordinated opposition. Some of the beaches came under sporadic fire from coastal batteries and artillery inland, but little damage was done and the guns were soon silenced; the naval supporting gunfire was admirable. By first light successful landings had been made on all our beaches.

Resistance in 30 Corps sector was very light and by 0730 hours 10 July, the rehabilitation of the Pachino airfield, which had been ploughed up, was in progress;

soon after midday the strip was ready for use. By early afternoon the town of Pachino was reported clear and by the end of the day the whole of the peninsula was in our hands and a thousand prisoners had been taken. Progress was slower at first in 13 Corps sector owing to the heavy seas and a certain amount of enemy shelling, but by 1000 hours we had captured Cassibile and Casanuova and gained a footing in Avola and Noto. By the early evening 5 Division was firmly established on the plateau overlooking Cassibile and on its left 50 Division held the southern end of the same plateau north-west of Noto. On the right of 13 Corps, 5 Division reached Ponte Grande in the afternoon and succeeded in rescuing the survivors of the airborne party who had removed the charges from the bridge. As a result our troops were able to march on Siracusa without delay and captured the town undamaged.

The first day of this great amphibious enterprise had been eminently successful. All our initial objectives had been secured without enemy counter attacks or indeed serious opposition. None of the German battle groups had been able to intervene against Eighth Army and even the Italian division located near Siracusa had failed to oppose us. We had got ashore with very few casualties and the landing of troops and stores over the beaches had continued throughout the day with marked success in spite of a heavy surf. We had secured a firm foothold in the Island.

### THE ADVANCE TO THE PLAIN OF CATANIA AND ENNA

On 11 July the main thrusts were initiated by 13 Corps towards Augusta and by 30 Corps on the axis Palazzolo–Vizzini. Throughout the day the discharge of ships and craft at Siracusa and on the beaches continued satisfactorily and there was every reason to believe that our build-up of reserves, vehicles and weapons would proceed satisfactorily.

The first major enemy counter attack fell on the American sector and was delivered towards Gela by a force of about sixty German tanks. After making some progress they received a tremendous hammering and the enemy eventually lost forty-three tanks. Meanwhile contact was made between the Canadians and the right American corps in the Ragusa area.

I took my Tactical Headquarters over from Malta during the morning of 11 July and spent the day visiting the front. I was confirmed in my view that the battle of Sicily would be primarily a matter of securing the main centres of road communication. Movement off the roads and tracks in the hilly country was very difficult and often impossible, so that if the nodal points were gained it was clear that the enemy would be unable to operate.

By the end of 12 July we were firmly in possession of the south-east of the Island. 13 Corps had some trouble in securing Augusta owing to German tank counter attacks which were eventually beaten off with naval and air co-operation. The port was entered during the night 12/13 July. Two intrepid destroyers of the Royal Navy had sailed into the harbour before the troops arrived in the town! Meanwhile 30 Corps was established on the general line Sortini–Palazzolo–Ragusa–Scicli. The operations were very exhausting for the troops, for we had not yet got any troop-carrying transport ashore, and long marches in the hot sun were most tiring. But I ordered all efforts to be made to maintain the pressure, as it was essential to take every advantage of the disorganized state of the enemy before he sorted himself out. Once left by the Germans, the Italian troops showed little fight and either surrendered after token resistance, demobilized themselves, or fled to the north. The German forces had not yet become properly concentrated or co-ordinated and, although their rearguards began to stiffen on 12 July, we were not seriously held up.

My orders on 12 July were for the advance to continue on the two axes, 13 Corps along the coast towards Catania and the north, 30 Corps to Caltagirone, Enna and Leonforte. The Americans were advancing well, and it seemed to me that if they got established at Caltanissetta, Canicatti and Agrigento we should be in a position to develop operations to cut off all the enemy in western Sicily.

Progress was slower on 13 July. It was very hot and the troops were getting tired, but 30 Corps made progress towards Vizzini. There was a danger of overlapping between the two armies in the area Vizzini–Caltagirone, but this was put right by orders from 15 Army Group which made the road axis through those places to Piazza Armerina and Enna inclusive to Eighth Army. On the 13 Corps flank I decided that we should make a great effort to break through into the Plain of Catania from the Lentini area and ordered a major attack for the night 13/14 July. A parachute brigade and a commando were made available for the operation, in which the main problems were to force the bottleneck through the difficult country between Carlentini and Lentini and to secure two bridges: one north of the Lentini ridge and the other, the Primasole, over the River Simeto.

The plan was to land the parachute brigade during the night near Primasole bridge with orders to capture it and establish a small bridgehead on the north bank. Contact was then to be made with the commando whose task, having landed west of Agnone, was to secure the other bridge. The main thrust, directed on Catania, was to be delivered by 50 Division with an armoured brigade leading. Naval support for the air and sea landings was arranged.

The first stages of the attack were successful and both bridges fell into our hands intact. The airborne operation was accomplished by a small part of the brigade, since only half the parachutists' aircraft dropped troops over the target and only a proportion of the gliders landed in the correct area. But the charges were removed from the bridge and the paratroops hung on until darkness on 14 July, by which time they had with-stood a series of counter attacks by tanks and infantry and were becoming hard pressed. The commando meanwhile removed the charges from its bridge, but was subsequently forced to withdraw. The main body was held up in most difficult country by very strong enemy forces covering Carlentini and not until the afternoon of 14 July, when some of our tanks succeeded in working round the enemy's east flank, was our infantry able to continue the advance through Lentini. In the early hours of 15 July contact

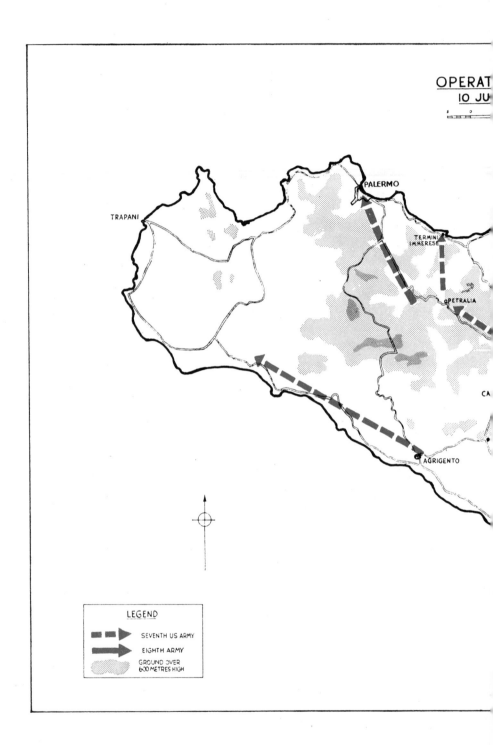

OPERAT
10 JU

TRAPANI

PALERMO

TERMINI
IMMERESE

PETRALIA

CA

AGRIGENTO

LEGEND

SEVENTH US ARMY

EIGHTH ARMY

GROUND OVER
600 METRES HIGH

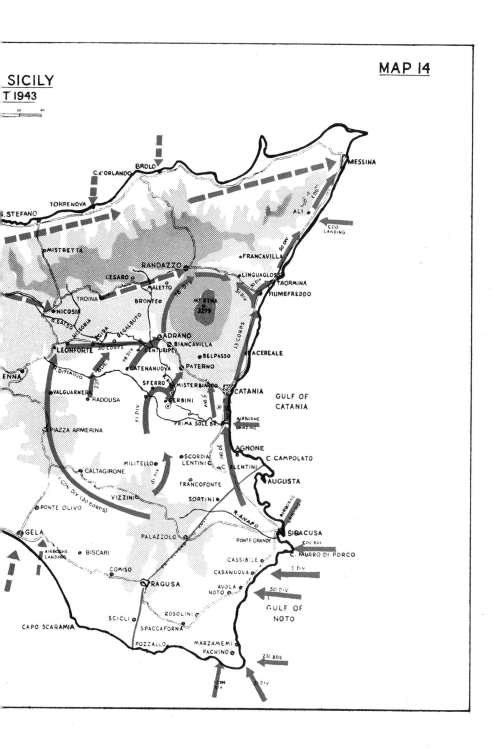

## SICILY
T 1943

MAP 14

STEFANO
TORRENOVA
C.d'ORLANDO
BROLO
MESSINA
ALI
CDO LANDING
MISTRETTA
FRANCAVILLA
RANDAZZO
LINGUAGLOSS
TAORMINA
CESARO
MALETTO
FIUMEFREDDO
TROINA
BRONTE
MT ETNA 3279
NICOSIA
R.SALSO
NISSORIA
AGIRA
REGALBUTO
ADRANO
LEONFORTE
CENTURIPE
BIANCAVILLA
ACEREALE
CATENANUOVA
BELPASSO
ENNA
DITTAINO
PATERNO
VALGUARNERA
SFERRO
RADDUSA
GERBINI
MISTERBIANCO
CATANIA
GULF OF CATANIA
PIAZZA ARMERINA
PRIMA SOLE BR.
AIRBORNE LANDING
AGNONE
MILITELLO
SCORDIA LENTINI
C.CAMPOLATO
CALTAGIRONE
C.LENTINI
FRANCOFONTE
AUGUSTA
VIZZINI
SORTINI
PONTE OLIVO
R.ANAPO
SIRACUSA
GELA
PALAZZOLO
PONTE GRANDE
AIRBORNE LANDING
BISCARI
C. MURRO DI PORCO
COMISO
CASSIBILE
CASANUOVA
RAGUSA
AVOLA NOTO
SCICLI
ROSOLINI
GULF OF NOTO
CAPO SCARAMIA
SPACCAFORNA
POZZALLO
MARZAMEMI
PACHINO
231 BDE

13 CORPS
30 CORPS
231 BDE
51 DIV
1 CDN DIV (30 CORPS)
5 DIV
50 DIV

[93]

was made with the parachute brigade which had withdrawn to a ridge overlooking the plain and the Primasole bridge: which was still intact.

The enemy's rearguard action had given him time to organize firm resistance north of the Simeto and the fate of the vital bridge hung in the balance for several days. In attacks on 15 July we got some infantry and tanks temporarily across the bridge, but heavy counter attacks prevented tanks from remaining north of the river, and attempts to cross upstream were unsuccessful. By evening the bridge was still in dispute.

On 16 July before dawn a shallow bridgehead was at last established over the Simeto and by the end of the following day we were firmly over the river, with anti-tank guns and tanks in support of the infantry, holding a bridgehead some 3,000 yards deep. In spite of all the enemy's efforts to regain it, the bridge remained intact. We had now sufficient depth north of the river to mount a full scale attack towards Catania and on the night 17/18 July 50 Division launched a strong thrust northwards. Hostile resistance was firm and determined and fierce counter attacks were put in by the enemy so that little was achieved.

On my western flank 30 Corps continued to progress against stiffening opposition provided by elements of the Panzer divisions together with some paratroops. The enemy was endeavouring to hold routes open for the German troops in the west, and as the country inland became more mountainous and rugged, so the task of the at-tackers became more difficult. 51 Division leading the 30 Corps advance was held up at Vizzini on 13 July and the town was not in our hands until the afternoon of the next day.

Meanwhile my two main thrusts were diverging and I decided that I needed a strong pivot between them in order to preserve balance. Since 51 Division was now very tired, I ordered 30 Corps to bring 1 Canadian Division into the lead, leaving 51 Division in reserve with the task of clearing up the area Scordia–Francofonte Militello.

After the fall of Vizzini, the Canadians advanced rapidly through Caltagirone to Piazza Armerina, which fell during the night 16/17 July. Operations were then developed towards Valguarnera and Leonforte with the object of cutting the Enna–Catania road at Leonforte and tackling Enna (which was known to be in a state of defence) from the east.

On 16 July, I ordered 30 Corps to advance 51 Division towards Paterno in order to assist the operations of 13 Corps. By the end of 17 July the Division had crossed the Simeto river and was within 10 miles of Paterno, facing strong enemy positions.

The opposition was beginning to crystallize. The bulk of Hermann Goering Division was now in the Catania Plain, and reinforcements from 1 Parachute Division had been flown in from Italy on successive nights until a total of about six battalions were in the line. Two German fortress battalions were also identified having been rushed over from the mainland.

## COMMENCEMENT OF THE LEFT HOOK TOWARDS MOUNT ETNA

It had been decided on 15 July by 15 Army Group that the Seventh United States

Army should develop operations northwards from Caltanissetta to Caterina and Petralia. Meanwhile with the outer flank of Eighth Army thus secured, I could thrust to Leonforte and thence eastwards on Adrano and get round the northern side of Etna. From Petralia the Americans could operate to cut the north coastal road and thus complete the isolation of the west of the Island; my thrust should get behind the enemy in the Catania area and drive a wedge between the Hermann Goering Division in the Catania Plain and 15 Panzer Grenadier Division which was getting into position on its western flank.

During 17 and 18 July the enemy's plan of action became clear. He was with-drawing the German forces into the north-east of the Island, pivoting on Catania, and was determined to hold the city and to deny us the airfields south of it. Indeed the airfields in the Plain of Catania were the greatest prize in the Island, for as soon as our Air Forces could become established on them we would not only derive greater strength for the battle, but would be able to develop air operations further afield with greater intensity. In defending Catania the enemy was greatly assisted by the ground, which was admirably suited to defence; his positions in the plain were backed by the foothills of Mount Etna which gave him excellent observation. Meanwhile on the western flank he was now developing a heavy scale of demolitions, which were skilfully related to the mountainous country and were beginning to slow down the speed of operations.

Following 50 Division's attack on the night 17/18 July, 5 Division was brought round on to its left flank and on the afternoon of 18 July began thrusting towards Misterbianco, in an effort to broaden the front of our attacks on Catania and get round the core of enemy resistance there. I was now therefore operating four divisional thrusts. 13 Corps had 50 Division on the coast directed on Catania and 5 Division on its left making for Misterbianco. In 30 Corps, 51 Division was thrusting towards Paterno while 1 Canadian Division was directed on Leonforte and Adrano.

The four thrusts continued on 19 July. Progress in 13 Corps continued to be slow, but our artillery fire and steady pressure were taking effect and the enemy's casualties were extremely heavy. 5 Division crossed the Simeto and drew level with the 50 Division bridgehead, but was unable to get further until a proper crossing place had been constructed to facilitate moving supporting weapons to the north bank. 51 Division established a bridgehead over the Dittaino River at Sferro and on 20 July captured most of the Gerbini airfield, but on the following day was thrown back by a strong enemy counter attack to positions south of the aerodrome. 1 Canadian Division, after some delay north of Valguarnera on 19 July, advanced to within a few miles of Leonforte on the following day. 231 Infantry Brigade was brought up to fill the gap between 1 Canadian and 51 Divisions and having captured Raddusa reached the Dittaino River bridge (on the road from Raddusa to Agira). On 19 July the brigade approached to within three miles of Agira itself but, as it was known to be strongly held by the enemy, 30 Corps decided not to press attacks there until Leonforte had been taken and the Agira position could be threatened from the west by the Canadians.

Fierce fighting for Leonforte continued during 21 July but the town was finally surrounded and entered that night.

Meanwhile Seventh United States Army was thrusting northwards and on 22 July cut the north coast road near Termini, while, by the same time, a series of thrusts directed north-west and west led to the capture of Palermo and the clearance of the whole of western Sicily. Many thousands of Italian prisoners were taken.

# CHAPTER TWELVE

# The Completion of the Capture of Sicily

## PREPARATIONS FOR BREAKING THE GERMAN DEFENCE OF NORTH-EAST SICILY

Now that the conquest of Western Sicily had been completed, the Allied resources were concentrated on forcing the enemy out of the north-east corner of the island. It was clear that he intended to impose the maximum delay on our efforts to evict him and evidence of the arrival of further reinforcements began to be received on 20 July, when elements of 29 Panzer Grenadier Division were identified by 30 Corps. Apart from political considerations, it appeared that the Germans had three main military reasons for striving to retain their bridgehead in Sicily. The immediate purpose was to deny us, for as long as possible, use of the airfields in the Catania Plain from which we could strike with increasing weight at the heart of Italy. Secondly, it was necessary to delay us in Sicily while the German defence of Italy was organized, since it was increasingly obvious that no reliance could be placed on the Italians even in the defence of their own country. Finally, the escape route to the mainland had to be held open for the time when fighting in Sicily could not be prolonged. We had therefore to face fierce and protracted resistance.

The topography of north-east Sicily greatly favoured the enemy. It was possible for him to organize a series of very strong delaying positions all the way to Messina and there was no opportunity of exploiting in mass our superiority in armoured forces. In the weeks ahead we were daily planning to land forces from the sea behind the enemy and indeed, success was achieved in this way, but beaches were scarce and generally unsuitable for the deployment of any but minor forces. Moreover, the availability of landing craft was greatly restricted, since they were being overhauled in preparation for the invasion of the Italian mainland. In the air, our mounting offensive was achieving outstanding success and not only were we virtually unhindered by enemy aircraft, but we were able to keep up a relentless pounding of the hostile troops and of communication.

The enemy ultimately employed four German divisions in the Island: 29 Panzer Grenadier Division on the northern sector of his defences, 15 Panzer Grenadier Division in the centre, and Hermann Goering Division in the east. 1 Parachute Division did not operate independently, but provided detachments at various key points. Remnants of three Italian divisions remained fighting with the Germans.

Our own troops had been constantly engaged since the landing and were beginning to show definite signs of fatigue owing to the intense July heat and continual marching over the mountainous country. On 20 July I ordered 78 Division to be brought over from Sousse, in order to increase my offensive power, since all my available divisions in Sicily were now deployed in the line.

On 21 July I decided that it was necessary to shift the main weight of the Eighth Army offensive to the left flank. It was by then quite clear that the enemy was going to hold Catania to the last and to persist with the direct advance on that axis would result in heavy casualties which I could not afford. A better approach would be to pass round the north of Mount Etna and come in behind him. I would give 78 Division to 30 Corps in order to capture first Centuripe and then Adrano and afterwards swing north to Bronte and Randazzo. Meanwhile it was essential to provide more aerodromes for the Royal Air Force, in order to increase the weight of air attack on the enemy: our object being to isolate Sicily from the mainland, smash the key road centres to the island and demoralize the hostile troops.

I therefore ordered that 13 Corps front and 51 Division of 30 Corps should revert to the defensive, maintaining aggressive patrol activity and raids in order to pin the opposing enemy formations in their existing positions. The left flank of 30 Corps was to be my main thrust and the target date for the full scale drive on the enemy was fixed as 1 August, by which time I hoped to have 78 Division ready for action. In the meantime, I directed 30 Corps to continue operations on the axes Leonforte-Agira-Regalbuto and Catenanuova-Centuripe in order to get within striking distance of Adrano which I reasoned was the key to the Mount Etna position.

On my left, Seventh United States Army was regrouping for the drive on Messina and Army Group orders provided for the development of two divisional thrusts (the maximum strength which could be maintained in the sector) along the roads Nicosia-Troina-Randazzo and Termini Immerese-San Stefano-Capo d'Orlando. 1 August was set as the target date for these drives to develop from the line Nicosia-Mistretta-San Stefano.

### THE ADVANCE EAST FROM LEONFORTE

After the fall of Leonforte the enemy continued to resist 30 Corps advance fiercely. 1 Canadian Division was held up east of the town and again in front of Nissoria, which was cleared on 24 July. Meanwhile 231 Infantry Brigade was attacking towards Agira from the south but, having succeeded in cutting the main road east of the town, was forced to withdraw in face of strong counter-attacks. Very heavy fighting continued round Agira until 28 July, when it fell into our hands.

Meanwhile 78 Division was brought into the line in the Catenanuova area and together with a Canadian brigade launched an attack on the town on the night 29/30 July. After fierce fighting Catenanuova was cleared early in the morning and a further attack the following night cleared the high ground to the north and north-east, thus providing us with an adequate bridgehead from which to launch an operation against Centuripe. This place, built on a very high mountain mass and reached by a single road which twists and turns up the steep side of the feature, presented an extremely difficult objective. However, during the night 1/2 August leading troops of 78 Division entered the town, but they were forced to withdraw at first light when the enemy was found to be in the houses in considerable strength. An attack to dislodge the Germans was mounted the following day and eventually on the morning of 3 August, we took full possession of the town, the enemy having fallen back across the Salso river.

The storming of Centuripe was a fine achievement and reflected the greatest credit on 78 Division, for its capture was the essential preliminary to the battle of Adrano. With Centuripe in our possession the fall of Adrano was a certainty. We now dominated the approaches to a key point in the enemy's Etna position. Its fall would mean that the end of the campaign in Sicily could not be long delayed.

Following the fall of Agira 231 Infantry Brigade led the west flank advance towards Regalbuto. Road blocks impeded progress but no serious resistance was met until the morning of 30 July on the outskirts of Regalbuto itself. Operations on the night 30/31 July were only partially successful owing to strong enemy counter attacks and, after severe fighting throughout 31 July, our troops were still a mile west of the objective. The Canadian Division was brought up from Agira and after more hard fighting during 1 August the town was entered late in the afternoon and occupied in force the following morning, by which time the leading troops were three miles to the east.

During the development of operations on the western flank, 13 Corps continued its activities in order to pin down enemy forces on its front. In the centre sector I had ordered 13 Corps on 22 July, to take over the front of the right hand brigade of 30 Corps in order to provide additional resources for the main thrust. The front of 5 Division was increased accordingly. I anticipated that the enemy might attack towards Sferro as a natural reaction to my advance on the Adrano axis and on 29 July ordered reinforcements of two infantry battalions (provided from Beach Bricks) and a regiment of Canadian tanks to be sent to the left of 5 Division. 51 Division continued to maintain balance between the two Corps.

At the end of the month we made a most interesting capture of a map of enemy dispositions which clearly showed that Adrano was indeed the key to the German Etna position, confirming that it was correct to launch the main Eighth Army thrust towards that place, for once we could smash the Adrano hinge the Etna position would disintegrate.

At this stage I was considering the regrouping necessary for carrying the war on to the mainland of Italy. There were two separate Corps operations under consideration for the invasion of the 'toe' by Eighth Army. 10 Corps was waiting in the Tripoli area. I had already discussed with the Commander, General Horrocks, its possible role in Calabria. I now turned to the grouping of 13 Corps and decided that it would be used for the direct crossing of the Straits of Messina. For this purpose 1 Canadian and 5 Divisions would be required in the assault, while 78 Division would be held available as the immediate reserve. Once the war in Sicily was over it would be necessary to rest 50 and 51 Divisions which had been fighting hard since El Alamein, and it was therefore my intention to finish the 'Husky' operation with 30 Corps (consisting of 50, 51 and 78 Divisions) as soon as the two thrusts around Mount Etna met in the north. This would enable me to rest and refit 1 Canadian and 5 Divisions during the last phase in Sicily.

### THE FALL OF CATANIA AND RANDAZZO

On 4 August I gave orders to the Corps concerning the future conduct of operations. 30 Corps was to continue the drive on Adrano. In 13 Corps, 50 Division was to be ready to seize Catania when the opportunity came and 5 Division, after taking Misterbianco, was to be directed on Belpasso. I stipulated that 13 Corps would maintain an infantry brigade with a tank regiment on the Sferro–Paterno axis where it was essential to provide a firm link. After the fall of Adrano 30 Corps was to revert 1 Canadian Division to reserve and, following the capture of Belpasso, 13 Corps was to place 5 Division in reserve. These formations could then commence planning and refitting for the invasion of Italy. Subsequent operations would be conducted east of Mount Etna by 13 Corps with 50 Division and on the west by 30 Corps directed on Randazzo with 51 and 78 Divisions. When the two corps met north of the mountain, 30 Corps would take command of 50 Division and complete the 'Husky' operation, Headquarters 13 Corps coming out of the line in preparation for the attack on the mainland.

The advance of 30 Corps beyond Centuripe and Regalbuto directly threatened the main enemy Etna position and was beginning to endanger the troops holding up 13 Corps in the Catania area. It became clear on 3 August that the enemy had commenced thinning out in the Catania sector with the object of withdrawing the bulk of the German forces to the north. 5 Division attacked on the night 3/4 August on a two brigade front and by the following afternoon an advance of about four miles had been made. In the immediate coastal sector extensive demolitions and mines considerably hindered movement and on the 50 Division front a fierce rearguard action was fought in the southern outskirts of Catania, astride the main coast road. During 5 August, however, advances were made throughout the 13 Corps front and Catania, Misterbianco and Paterno were captured. East of Mount Etna the main enemy force withdrew to new positions on a narrow front north of Acireale.

Meanwhile 30 Corps closed in on Adrano which was relentlessly pounded from the air. 78 Division crossed the Salso river astride the Centuripe–Adrano road during the night 4/5 August while 1 Canadian Division made another crossing on its left. The attack was pressed in face of strong resistance and on 6 August 78 Division reached the southern outskirts of Adrano, while patrols by-passed it and got close to the Bronte road north of the town. During the night 6/7 August the enemy withdrew and 78 Division took possession of the place and, on the following morning, turned north to follow up the enemy towards Bronte. The advance was now very slow owing to mines and demolitions and the extreme difficulty of deploying off the very indifferent road which ran through extensive lava belts and terraced cultivation.

On the right of 30 Corps 51 Division operated towards Biancavilla which was captured on 6 August.

With the fall of Adrano the main defence line across north-eastern Sicily was broken and the enemy was now in retreat on all sectors. But it was extremely difficult to follow him up closely and he continued to impede our progress with widespread and skilful demolitions. The Air Force, however, were able to inflict heavy damage and casualties on the retreating columns. Aerial reconnaissance now began to reveal increasing traffic across the Straits of Messina, from which we inferred that the enemy was beginning to send back to the mainland his rearguard installations and equipment. It became a matter of first importance for our naval and air forces to prevent this evacuation.

At dawn 8 August, 78 Division entered Bronte and to the east of Mount Etna 50 Division was fighting some eight miles north of Catania. Meanwhile United States forces had had a fierce battle round Troina ending with its capture on 6 August, and two days later entered Cesaro, whence operations were continued along the main road towards Randazzo.

At this time I was moving my Tactical Headquarters with 30 Corps, intending to switch to the 13 Corps axis when we got east of Randazzo.

North of Bronte progress continued to be very slow. South of Maletto the enemy was encountered in some strength and it was not until 12 August that the town itself and the high ground in its vicinity were captured. The following day Seventh United States Army attacked Randazzo.

Returning to the eastern flank, I had decided on 9 August to modify my orders to 13 Corps concerning the advance on a single divisional front east of Mount Etna. My original idea was to get 5 Division in reserve to prepare for the invasion of Italy. Had the advance to Randazzo been quicker the threat to cut off the forces east of the mountain would have developed earlier and enabled 13 Corps to advance without undue difficulty. When it became apparent however that the Randazzo operation was going to take time, indeed that the enemy was reinforcing that sector from his coastal axis, it became essential for 13 Corps to drive hard along the coast and I ordered it to bring 5 Division forward into the line again so as to operate on a two divisional front. I wanted to get firm control of the triangle Francavilla–Taormina–Fiumefreddo and, if it was going to be difficult to get round the west side of Etna, I would force my way round the east; for it was obviously vital to cut the southern approach to Messina as quickly as possible. On 11 August I decided on further regrouping, because the target date for landing in the toe of Italy was now advanced to 1 September. I therefore ordered that 51 Division should relieve 5 Division and that Headquarters 30 Corps should take over the responsibilities of Headquarters 13 Corps on 13 August. I could no longer delay getting the invasion force for Italy into reserve.

### THE FINAL PHASE IN SICILY

The Americans captured Randazzo on 13 August, at which time 78 Division was fighting strongly to the south of the town. The fall of Randazzo presaged the final elimination of the enemy from Sicily, but progress from now on was still inevitably slow as the Allied forces had to follow up along coastal roads from which deployment was almost impossible.

On 14 August the enemy had broken contact at all points on the Eighth Army front and on the following day 50 Division occupied Taormina. 51 Division secured Linguaglossa and 78 Division cleared the lateral road from Randazzo to the coast.

During this time, on the north coast road Seventh United States Army had progressed east of Capo d'Orlando, having carried out two amphibious operations between Torrenova and Brolo in order to cut off the retreating enemy and accelerate the speed of advance.

I gave orders for a landing in front of 30 Corps on the night 15/16 August, which was successfully accomplished by a commando with some tanks at Ali, but the enemy had already withdrawn north of the area before the landing was made. Owing to demolitions on the Corniche road the force was unable to advance either to the north or south and a party moved inland on foot, seeking a route across country to Messina.

American troops entered Messina on the night of 16 August, while enemy batteries on the Calabrian peninsula intermittently shelled the town. On the following morning elements of the commando which had landed at Ali joined the Americans.

The fall of Messina marked the end of the Sicilian campaign which had cost the Germans 24,000 killed.

Eighth Army now looked out across the lovely straits of Messina towards the 'toe' of Italy, while it prepared to carry the war into the mainland of Europe. The Sicilian campaign had lasted thirty-eight days and had involved fierce and continuous fighting in most difficult country at the hottest season of the year. For a second time the Germans had been pushed back into the sea and we now stood at the gates of the 'Fortress of Europe'.

### REFLECTIONS ON THE SICILIAN CAMPAIGN

Axis strategy in Sicily had been faulty to a degree. The Allies had achieved complete tactical surprise in the landing and we had caught the German forces very dispersed. Failure of the Italian troops to show any serious opposition, combined with the action of the Air Forces in hindering the use of the indifferent road network, had imposed great delay on the concentration of the German formations and we had become very firmly established in the Island before the opposition crystallized against us. The subsequent development of the campaign had been quite straightforward from our point of view and, considering the extremely difficult nature of the country, had been brought to a close very speedily.

The hardest fought battle in the campaign was at Primasole bridge; it may have seemed curious that, having won that battle, I switched my main axis of operations from the coastal plain leading to Catania across to the inland route leading to Adrano. Yet to persist in the thrust toward Catania would have meant very heavy casualties and I was by no means convinced that success would follow this expenditure of life. Furthermore, I did not wish to blunt the weapon when it was clear that much hard fighting lay ahead on the mainland of Europe. The object could be achieved with less loss of life by operating on the Adrano axis, with the added advantage that on that flank we would be in close touch with our American Allies.

The Eighth Army had been born, trained and grown to manhood in the North African deserts and it was a source of great satisfaction to me that it adapted itself so readily to the very difficult conditions existing in Sicily. This confirmed my view that once a fighting machine has been trained thoroughly in the basic principles of warfare, it will have no great difficulty in operating successfully in whatever conditions of climate and terrain it may have to face. It is of course essential that commanders on all levels should be versatile and mentally robust and that they should not adhere rigidly to preconceived tactical methods.

# CHAPTER THIRTEEN

## *Administration in the Sicily Campaign*

ALTHOUGH the campaign in Sicily lasted thirty-eight-days only, the administrative problems involved both in mounting the expedition and during the campaign itself were of great interest. For the staffs and troops of Eighth Army this operation marked the opening of a new phase in the war and for the first time we tackled a combined operation involving a large scale assault on a hostile and defended coast. The experience gained in Sicily was to prove most valuable in solving the administrative problems of the subsequent campaigns in Italy and Normandy.

The preparation of a large scale combined operation provides an immense task of calculation and organization for the administrative staff. I have already shown that the planning for the Sicily operation was started before the campaign in North Africa had been brought to an end. The unusual complexity of the problem may therefore be well imagined.

The invasion of Sicily was the first occasion in this war in which large forces had been maintained over open beaches for a considerable period. In the Eighth Army we planned to capture the port of Siracusa as quickly as possible after the assault and in fact it was in our hands within 48 hours. This enabled us to reduce the period of beach maintenance considerably, although we continued to land personnel and stores over the beaches astride the Pachino peninsula for some time. The Seventh United States Army, on the other hand, depended upon beach maintenance for a much longer period. During the planning stage there were many who expressed the gravest doubts as to the wisdom of depending upon beach maintenance, but there was no alternative to the acceptance of the risks involved once the decision had been made to land the Eastern and Western Task Forces side by side. In the event experience in Sicily showed that large forces can be maintained for long periods over open beaches, given adequate resources in landing craft and specialized equipment and reasonably favourable conditions of tide and weather.

An essential difference between the Sicilian campaign and that which Eighth Army had fought in North Africa, was that maintenance had to be carried out over indifferent roads through enclosed country. In the desert there was no limit to the number of vehicles which could move along the desert tracks, but in Sicily the roads were narrow, steep and tortuous and traffic control assumed greater importance than ever before. Special measures were devised to control the movement of convoys, to limit the number and class of vehicles on the roads and to deal with the problem of civilian traffic. This experience again stood us in good stead in subsequent campaigns.

The bridging problem came to the fore in Sicily as a result of the wide scale of demolitions practised by the enemy. Fortunately plans for the provision of bridging equipment had been made on a generous scale and large quantities of Bailey bridging were landed at an early date.

Another major problem in Sicily arose from the prevalence of malaria. This had been foreseen, but despite all possible precautions the casualties from malaria exceeded those incurred in battle. The disease was particularly rampant in the Plain of Catania.

Yet another aspect of the arrangements for the Sicilian campaign, which provided invaluable experience for the future, was the evolution of a special inter-Service staff machinery for controlling the loading and despatch of convoys subsequent to the assault. A plan is, of course, essential for the loading of the follow-up and build-up convoys, but this has to be made before the operation and in the event elasticity is essential to ensure that supporting troops, reserves, reinforcements and stores are called forward in the order required by the operational situation. This inter-Service staff was originally called 'Ferry Control'. In the North West European campaign the name was changed to 'Build Up Control'.

The maintenance plan to support the operations of Eighth Army in Sicily was worked out at Allied Force Headquarters in North Africa. After the initial period scheduled supply convoys were arranged from the United Kingdom and the Middle East, while ordnance stores were provided from the depots in North Africa. There was a division of responsibility, particularly between North Africa and Headquarters Middle East Forces, but a smooth system of working was quickly established. There was no intention to set up base depots or workshops in Sicily as the campaign was too short to justify their establishment. It is not possible, however, to keep the maintenance of a modern army at concert pitch unless it is in close contact with its base, and difficulties arose which increased considerably during the initial stages of the Italian campaign.

In speaking of the maintenance arrangements made for the final phase in North Africa I mentioned the question of administrative control. This matter became very prominent in Sicily. The special administrative headquarters which I had set up in Tripoli to look after my lines of communication and to provide for my requirements had carried out these functions satisfactorily. The Headquarters itself formed part of the Eighth Army administrative machine, and I was therefore anxious to carry it with me so that it could perform the same function in Sicily. This was eventually done, the headquarters being called 'Fortbase'. Headquarters 15 Army Group had only a small administrative staff in Sicily, designed to ensure co-ordination between the two armies, to control the ferry service and to provide the Army Group Commander with administrative advice. While this arrangement worked satisfactorily in Sicily it became very difficult to operate in Italy and eventually had to be changed.

# PART III

THE INVASION OF THE MAINLAND OF ITALY

AND

THE ADVANCE TO THE RIVER SANGRO

3 SEPTEMBER–31 DECEMBER 1943

# CHAPTER FOURTEEN

## Planning the Invasion of Italy

### THE EVOLUTION OF THE PLAN

I HAVE already mentioned that there were originally two separate operations under consideration for the invasion of Italy by the Eighth Army. The first was known as Operation 'Buttress', which provided for a landing in the area of Gioia Taur on the north coast of the 'toe', and the other was called Operation 'Baytown' in which the plan was to make a direct crossing of the Straits of Messina.

Towards the end of July 1943 a third plan (Operation 'Avalanche') designed for a landing near Naples began to receive consideration. It was immediately apparent that our resources in craft and shipping would not permit three different assault landing operations. By 17 August, when the Sicilian campaign finished, it had been decided that 'Buttress' would not take place, but that the Italian mainland would be invaded across the Straits of Messina by Eighth Army and subsequently in the Bay of Salerno by Fifth United States Army. 10 Corps was placed under command of Fifth Army and I was therefore left with 13 and 30 Corps for Operation 'Baytown'. The target date for my operation was 30/31 August, and 'Avalanche' was to follow on 10 September. It has been seen that planning for biting off the 'toe' of Italy had been going on for some time within the Eighth Army and that, before the end of the war in Sicily, I had withdrawn formations into reserve so that they could refit and prepare themselves for the next phase of our operations.

I set in motion the preparations for invading Italy with maximum speed, as it was essential to follow up the enemy as quickly as possible before he had time to improve his arrangements for our reception on the far side of the Straits. 30 Corps artillery began concentrating in the Messina area in order to commence the preparatory bombardment of the enemy defences and to support the assault when the time came. Intensive work was carried out on the roads and railways in Sicily in order to improve the administrative axes which we would require in the island and the formations of 13 Corps began detailed planning for carrying out the assault landing.

The object given to me for Operation 'Baytown' was as follows:—

"Your task is to secure a bridgehead on the 'toe' of Italy to enable our Naval forces to operate through the Straits of Messina. In the event of the enemy withdrawing from the 'toe' you will follow him up with such force as you can make available, bearing in mind that the greater the extent to which you can engage enemy forces in the southern 'toe' of Italy, the more assistance you will be giving to 'Avalanche'."

The preparation of the operation proved by no means a simple and straightforward matter and my chief difficulties arose over the question of availability of naval craft for the assault and subsequent build-up of my forces on the mainland. 'Avalanche' was given priority of resources since it was a larger operation than 'Baytown' and involved a much longer sea passage. The initial interpretation of this priority reduced the craft available for Eighth Army to an assault lift for some four equivalent battalions, with a very slow build-up. Available intelligence on the other hand made it necessary to prepare for a landing which would be opposed by German troops. 29 Panzer Grenadier Division was known to be defending the Straits together with Italian troops and 26 Panzer Division had been located behind it. In these circumstances it seemed to me that to reduce the assaulting forces to the strength of a major raid would be to risk disaster and I made urgent requests for additional resources.

In order to achieve the object of the operation, I considered it necessary to assault on a frontage of two divisions, with tanks, and to secure the Catanzaro 'neck' as the first main objective. This 'neck' formed the narrowest part of south-western Italy, between the Gulf of Squillace and the Gulf of S. Eufemia, and, if firmly occupied, would give us a proper footing on the Italian mainland and open the Straits for the Navy.

On 23 August a conference of the Commanders-in-Chief was held at Algiers where I explained my plan. This was accepted and the necessary additional resources were allotted to the Eighth Army.

By this time it was too late to launch Operation 'Baytown' at the end of August as had originally been planned, and eventually the target date was set for the night 2/3 September. It was at this conference that I heard some details concerning negotiations which were being carried on with the Italian Government about armistice terms. It was planned that following the Eighth Army's invasion of the mainland and immediately preceding Operation 'Avalanche', the Italian Government would broadcast concurrently with the Allies acceptance of armistice terms and would give instructions that all Italian resistance would cease. It was hoped that this action would so undermine the position of the Germans in Italy that they would be forced to withdraw from the country. But there were in Italy at this time some fifteen German divisions and it remained to be seen what their reaction would be. I considered it very unwise to assume that the Allied task in invading the Italian mainland would be an easy one or that the Italian armistice would necessarily presage the collapse of German resistance in Italy. On my own front I sent small parties across the Straits to land at various points in an attempt to find out the exact situation regarding the opposition and the attitude of the Italians. On the night 27/28 August a party landed at Bova Marina and found the place deserted; a prisoner brought back said that the Italian population had fled into the hills and that Italian soldiers were deserting and joining the civilians. I followed this up with other small parties sent to various places, but nearly all of them failed to return. I therefore decided that Operation 'Baytown' would have to go forward as a properly staged assault and that we could not afford to take risks nor make hasty assumptions for which we had no tangible proof.

### THE OUTLINE PLAN

I originally envisaged using 13 Corps for the assault. 30 Corps would support the landings from Sicily and subsequently take over the Reggio area, in order to release 13 Corps for the advance inland. This project I abandoned, owing to shortage of craft and the consequent slow rate of build-up which would have resulted in great administrative problems. I decided to use initially 13 Corps only and my orders provided for an assault on a two division front immediately north of Reggio, 1 Canadian Division on the right and 5 Division on the left. 30 Corps artillery positioned round Messina would support the assault together with a heavy weight of air attack. The main objective was the Catanzaro 'neck' and I decided that the main thrust would be made by 5 Division along the north coast road axis, while 1 Canadian Division would advance along the road San Stefano–Delianuova–Cittanova. Two commandos and 231 Infantry Brigade Group were to be held at Riposto in Sicily ready for mounting seaborne hooks along the north coast of the 'toe' as required. There were insufficient bridging resources to develop operations along the south coastal road axis and I therefore instructed 13 Corps to establish a block south of Reggio in order to secure the southern flank against enemy interference.

By 26 August the deployment of 30 Corps artillery had been completed. It included eighty medium guns and forty-eight American heavy guns lent by Seventh United States Army.

# CHAPTER FIFTEEN

## *The Assault on Calabria, the Advance to the Catanzaro 'Neck' and Development of Operations to Potenza, 3–19 September 1943*

### THE ASSAULT

AT 0430 hours on 3 September, under cover of air action and artillery bombardment, the leading troops of 13 Corps landed on the beaches between Reggio and Villa San Giovanni. The Italian coastal troops and their supporting artillery surrendered after firing a few shots and the only German fire reported was spasmodic long range shelling from guns sited inland. These were quickly silenced by air attack. Early in the morning Reggio was captured, together with the airfield immediately to the south and San Giovanni was in our hands at 1130 hours. During the day there was no contact with German troops and by evening 1 Canadian Division had reached San Stefano and 5 Division was in Scilla. The beaches and roads were not mined, the inhabitants proved friendly and it was gratifying to find that the port of Reggio was not greatly damaged.

I ordered a landing on the north coast for the night 3/4 September at Bagnara which was successfully carried out by commando units; they succeeded in getting behind the German forces which were now opposing our advance along the coast road. Contact between the commandos and 5 Division was soon established in Bagnara, although owing to the heavy demolitions only troops on foot were able to enter the town.

It is necessary to realize throughout the story of our operations in Italy the important part which demolitions played in the campaign. The roads in Calabria and southern Italy proper twist and turn in the mountainous country and are admirable feats of engineering; they abound in bridges, viaducts, culverts and even tunnels and thus offer unlimited scope to military engineers for demolitions and road blocks of every conceivable kind. The Germans took the fullest advantage of this fact and our advance throughout was barred and delayed by demolitions on the widest possible scale: carried out both on the rail and road axes. On the railways, not content with the destruction of bridges, the enemy frequently resorted to the systematic blowing of each individual rail, together with ploughing up the sleepers and railway bed by means of a machine specially made for the purpose. These demolitions were skilfully sited with respect to the difficult country so that it was normally almost impossible to circumvent them. Our progress in Italy demands a great tribute to the sappers for their speed in constructing usable routes and to the resourcefulness of the troops who managed to forge ahead in spite of the frequency with which they met obstacles.

### THE ADVANCE TO CATANZARO

On the axis of 1 Canadian Division progress was slow owing to road blocks, but by the end of 4 September the road running south to Melito had been cut. The subsequent advance proved so difficult that on 6 September I ordered 13 Corps to switch the Canadians to the south coast road and to proceed along it directed on Catanzaro. Prior to this, patrols had pushed south from Reggio to Bova Marina and it became clear that the enemy had completely evacuated the southern part of the 'toe'. The advance of 5 Division along the north coast road was held up north of Bagnara on 5 September by enemy rearguards. General Dempsey intended to put 231 Infantry Brigade Group ashore that night at Gioia but owing to a storm this operation was cancelled; however, 5 Division secured the place by noon 6 September. I ordered 13 Corps to advance 5 Division with 231 Infantry Brigade under command on Nicastro.

On the night 7/8 September a successful landing operation was carried out at Pizzo by 231 Infantry Brigade, which got behind the enemy rearguards and destroyed some transport. On both coast axes the advance continued to the line Catanzaro–Nicastro, which was reached by 10 September. Extensive reconnaissance was then pushed forward by both divisions with the particular object of reporting the situation at the port of Crotone and the airfields situated nearby. At the Catanzaro 'neck' it was necessary for me to have a short pause, for we had advanced 100 miles in seven days and were getting very strung out. Maintenance difficulties were beginning to appear owing to the delays imposed upon transport echelons on the heavily damaged roads. Moreover, the rate of our build-up was not providing us with the number of L of C units and transport columns we required in order to continue at this pace.

### THE ITALIAN ARMISTICE AND THE LANDING AT SALERNO

At 1800 hours 8 September the armistice with Italy was announced. In the previous two years the main objects of Allied strategy in the Mediterranean had been to clear North Africa of Axis forces and to knock Italy out of the war. Both had now been accomplished.

At the same time we were involved in operations in Italy on two separate fronts. In the early hours of 9 September, Fifth U.S. Army landed in the Gulf of Salerno and began operations which had as their immediate object the capture of Naples; on the Eighth Army front by 10 September we had secured the line of the Catanzaro 'neck' and were preparing for further advances to assist the Salerno landing by pinning down the German forces in Calabria.

My next objects were to secure the port of Crotone in order to ease the maintenance situation, and to establish the Desert Air Force on the Crotone group of airfields. I therefore ordered 13 Corps to move 5 Division forward to the line Spezzano–Belvedere on 14 September, followed in about two days by the Canadian Division which was to be directed to the area Carati–Savelli–San Giovanni. These moves would establish my leading troops in the Castrovillari 'neck' and cover our interests in the Crotone area.

After midnight on 10 September I received a message from General Alexander concerning Operation 'Avalanche'. He emphasized the importance of maintaining the pressure against the Germans on my front to prevent their reinforcing the opposition to Fifth Army. At the same time he told me of the intention to land troops at Taranto, where by 15 September we were due to have eight thousand men put ashore from naval ships. Eighth Army was administratively very stretched at this time but I had to take every justifiable risk in order that my front could give assistance to Fifth Army operations.

### THE PLAN OF ADVANCE TO POTENZA

My object was now to get forward as quickly as possible in order to pin down the enemy and to initiate without delay a threat to the southern flank of the Germans opposing the Salerno bridgehead.

The problem was to achieve these results at a time when administratively it was quite impossible for me to move major forces forward until additional resources, including transport companies and rearguard units and installations, had been provided. The shortage of craft and shipping available to the Eighth Army made the build-up relatively very slow; we were being kept at a minimum owing to other demands of higher priority.

I decided that there were three measures immediately possible. First, I ordered light forces to be despatched north of the Catanzaro 'neck' at once, with instructions to operate as far ahead as possible. Secondly, I accelerated the provision of resources for the establishment of the Desert Air Force in the Crotone area, whence air action could be developed against the Germans opposing the Salerno bridgehead and against any enemy column which might be switched from my front to the north. The action of the air, together with my light forces, would quickly make apparent to the enemy that we were pressing forward and cause him to fear for the safety of his southern flank. This threat would be accentuated by the landings at Taranto, where leading elements of 1 Airborne Division arrived on 9 September. Thirdly, I required to open Crotone port as quickly as possible to ease the administrative situation by eliminating the long and slow carry by road from Reggio.

Events developed quickly on 11 September. Crotone port was secured and found to be undamaged, meanwhile light forces reached the general line Castrovillari–Belvedere before dark. By taking considerable administrative risks I planned to concentrate all 5 Division in to the Castrovillari 'neck' by 15 September and to order the Canadian Division forward to the area Rossano–Spezzano by 17 September. At the same time I drove the forward elements further north to the limit of their supplies.

### THE TARANTO BRIDGEHEAD

On 13 September I was asked by 15 Army Group to take command of the Taranto bridgehead as soon as it could be arranged.

The landing at Taranto was one of a number of plans which had been considered in connection with the anticipated change of front of the Italian forces, for the original conception of the Italian armistice was that they would turn against the Germans and assist in evicting them from the country. When this suggestion was put to me early in September I expressed doubts about the ability of the Italians seriously to influence events in the way it was hoped, and gave as my opinion that it would be unwise to count initially on effective fighting support from the proposed co-belligerents. It seemed to me dangerous, particularly in view of our shortage of shipping and resources, to make a series of weak landings in Italy on the assumption that the Italian forces would rally and fight with them. Such a course might involve us in very dangerous commitments which we would be unable to support.

Ultimately only the Taranto operation was carried out. 1 Airborne Division on 9 September began unopposed landings from naval ships, with the object of securing the port, airfields and installations in the area. Our troops were without supporting artillery and had very little transport, but the German garrison in south-east Italy, 1 Parachute Division, strung out between Foggia and Taranto, was only 8,000 strong.

A weak perimeter was established round Taranto and beyond it patrols were sent to a depth of about 40 miles to locate the German forces and contact the Italian garrisons. There were minor clashes with the enemy, but no serious opposition was encountered, as the Germans withdrew to the north and formed a perimeter line covering Altamura–Matera–Ginosa.

It was planned to follow up the Airborne Division by Headquarters 5 Corps and 8 Indian Division, which were to be sent from Egypt.

I agreed to accept responsibility for the Taranto bridgehead at once. This step enabled me to authorize certain adjustments of craft allocation to be made between the sea routes to Crotone and Taranto in order to accelerate the arrival of certain essential stores at Crotone and thus to assist the speed of 13 Corps advance towards the Salerno battle area. At the same time, after consultation with General Allfrey (commanding 5 Corps) I ordered the despatch of elements of 78 Division from Sicily to the Taranto front, including the divisional reconnaissance regiment and a field artillery regiment. These units were later followed by the rest of the Division.

### THE CAPTURE OF POTENZA AND AULETTA

During the period 13–15 September, the situation at Salerno remained serious and we continued our efforts to solve our maintenance difficulties in order to speed up the advance. 5 Division was to commence concentrating in the Belvedere area on 14 September, but I ordered 13 Corps to push a brigade ahead to Sapri, from which light forces could operate to the north. From Sapri I would be able directly to threaten the German forces opposing the southern flank of Fifth Army bridgehead.

The enemy resistance to our advance was not strong during this phase and the main difficulty operationally continued to be the extensive demolitions, which demanded ever-increasing resources in engineers and engineering material.

On 15 September additional craft for ferry work and extra transport companies were put at my disposal by Army Group and I was able to plan a further speed up of operations. I instructed 13 Corps to send detachments of 5 Division north along the road Sapri–Agropoli to endeavour to contact the right flank of Fifth United States Army. At the same time I sent to General Clark to tell him of this move. By 16 September I planned to have my leading troops on the western flank up to the line Sapri–Lagonegro while bringing 1 Canadian Division into the Castrovillari area. With the extra maintenance resources now available I decided to order the advance of main bodies to the general line Potenza–Auletta to commence on 17 September. This still involved considerable administrative risks, but they had to be accepted.

Leading elements of Eighth Army were now operating at great distances in advance of the main bodies and the threat to the Germans opposing Fifth United States Army had developed well. On 16 September contact was made between troops of 5 Division and American patrols near Vallo and at the same time Canadian reconnaissance elements met patrols sent out from the Taranto bridgehead. The enemy rearguards of 26 Panzer Division withdrew north through Lagonegro. The enemy was swinging back the southern sector of his line facing the Salerno front and on 17 September the withdrawal of enemy forces continued to the north. The immediate crisis at Salerno had passed and the bridgehead there was now to be steadily strengthened and developed.

By 19 September leading troops of 5 Division reached Auletta while the Canadians secured Potenza after driving out the German garrison belonging to 1 Parachute Division.

Eighth Army had advanced nearly 300 miles in seventeen days. The country favoured the German rearguards who were by now well practised in demolitions. The task of our sappers was enormous. Moreover, considerable administrative risks had been taken, but we had been ordered to make all haste and I think we made faster time than the enemy had bargained for. We may perhaps never know fully what effect the news of our approach had upon the enemy forces pinning down the Allied bridgehead at Salerno. On their own admission, however, the Germans felt unable to continue that enterprise in face of the growing threat from the south and began to disengage.

Meanwhile in the Taranto sector, Tactical Headquarters 5 Corps had already landed, and leading units of 78 Division were due shortly to arrive at Bari.

# CHAPTER SIXTEEN

# The Development of Allied Strategy in Italy and the Advance of Eighth Army to the River Sangro

THE GENERAL SITUATION IN ITALY ON 20 September 1943

THE pattern of Allied strategy in Italy was now beginning to emerge. A bridgehead had been secured at Salerno and from Taranto we were forming a firm base which was rapidly growing in strength. Between these two pivots and in contact with them, 13 Corps was becoming established in the Potenza–Auletta area.

The Italian armistice had not seriously prejudiced the German position in Italy. Very firm measures were taken by the enemy to prevent the Italian Army endangering his hold on the country and a new Fascist regime was instituted in the German zone to supplant the Badoglio Government and to ensure retention of dictatorial powers over the population and available resources. The enemy's intentions in Italy were not entirely clear at this stage, except that he was determined to deny us the port of Naples as long as possible. In the central and eastern sectors of the front he was continuing a policy of withdrawal pivoting on the high ground north of Salerno and leaving behind him demolitions on the widest scale.

The scope of the Allied plan of campaign had developed considerably since the original landings at Reggio. As a result of the opposition at Salerno, Eighth Army had been brought up to the Potenza area at great speed, far indeed from the original objectives necessary to secure the Straits of Messina. In addition, landings had been made at Taranto, which were now linked with Eighth Army, so that a wide front had been established across southern Italy. There was however no hope of the sudden collapse of German resistance and, for the time being, the co-belligerency of Italy seemed unlikely to affect the situation militarily.

The problem now, therefore, was to build up a firm front and secure the Foggia airfields and the port of Naples. The airfields round Foggia represented the most valuable objective in southern Italy, for their acquisition would give us bases from which our strategic air forces could carry the bombing offensive to industrial plants in Austria and to the oilfields in Roumania, both of which were then beyond the regular range of escorted attack.

In the development of Eighth Army's operations into the Plain of Foggia the major factor was administration. It was clearly necessary to switch my administrative axis from Calabria to the ports in south-east Italy, of which the most important were Taranto, Brindisi and Bari. This was a major undertaking requiring considerable time and the allocation of the necessary resources. Taranto was largely occupied

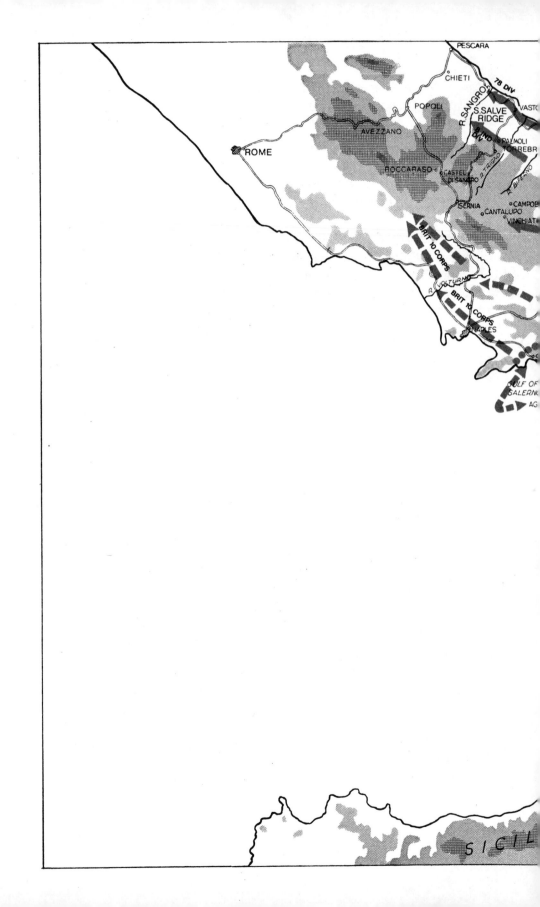

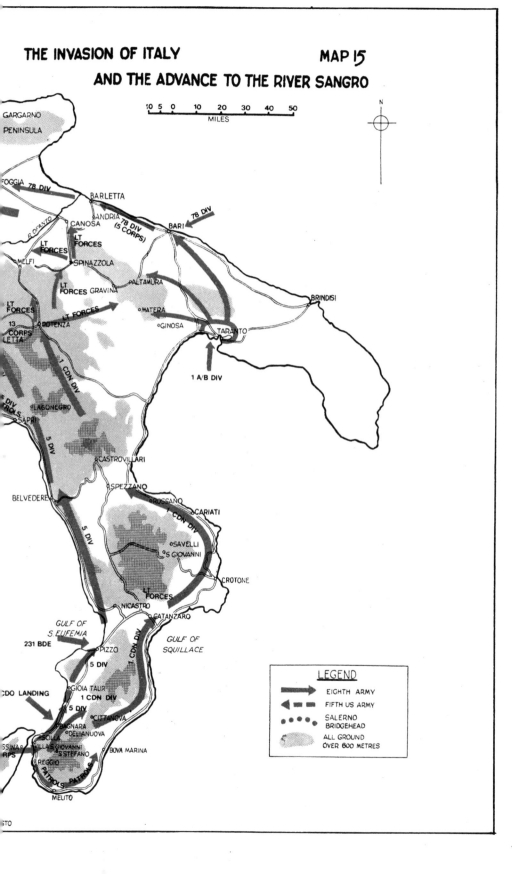

# THE INVASION OF ITALY
## AND THE ADVANCE TO THE RIVER SANGRO

MAP 15

10 5 0   10   20   30   40   50
MILES

N

GARGARNO PENINSULA

FOGGIA   78 DIV

BARLETTA

SANDRIA   78 DIV (5 CORPS)

CANOSA

78 DIV

BARI

R. OFANTO

MELFI

LT FORCES

LT FORCES

SPINAZZOLA

BRINDISI

LT FORCES   GRAVINA

PALTAMURA

LT FORCES

MATERA

LT FORCES

13 CORPS LETTA

POTENZA

GINOSA

TARANTO

1 A/B DIV

1 CDN DIV

S DIV TROLS

LAGONEGRO

SAPRI

5 DIV

CASTROVILLARI

SPEZZANO

BELVEDERE

ROSSANO

CARIATI

1 CDN DIV

5 DIV

SAVELLI

S GIOVANNI

CROTONE

LT FORCES

NICASTRO

GULF OF S. EUFEMIA

CATANZARO

231 BDE

PIZZO

GULF OF SQUILLACE

5 DIV

5 CDN DIV

GIOIA TAUR

1 CDN DIV

CDO LANDING

5 DIV

CITTANOVA

BAGNARA

DELIANUOVA

SSINA RPS

SCILLA

VILLA S.GIOVANNI

S STEFANO

BOVA MARINA

REGGIO

PATROLS   PATROLS

MELITO

STO

### LEGEND

| | |
|---|---|
| ➡ | EIGHTH ARMY |
| ◀- - | FIFTH US ARMY |
| •••• | SALERNO BRIDGEHEAD |
| ▨ | ALL GROUND OVER 600 METRES |

with troop convoys and Brindisi could not be opened before 27 September. It became apparent that I would not be able to operate my main forces north of the line Bari–Altamura–Potenza before 1 October.

The second major problem now confronting me was the regrouping of my forces in order to transfer the main weight of the Army to the east flank. I could not do this until the Salerno front was definitely secure, so I consulted General Clark on 24 September, when he agreed that my regrouping could start at once.

My plan was to advance on Foggia with 13 Corps, consisting of 1 Canadian and 78 Divisions, 4 Armoured and 1 Canadian Tank Brigades. 78 Division, as it arrived by sea, was to concentrate in the Bari area. 5 Division would initially be under command of 13 Corps but would remain in the Potenza area as the pivot of manœuvre and link between 13 Corps and Fifth United States Army. When 13 Corps reached the general line Barletta–Melfi, 5 Division would change to command of 5 Corps, which I intended initially to leave in reserve in the Taranto area with 8 Indian and 1 Airborne Divisions. Subsequently 5 Corps would be stepped forward in rear of 13 Corps to protect the left flank.

Regrouping began on 25 September, but meanwhile light forces were operating well ahead of their main bodies, although there was no way of avoiding the delay imposed by the change of administrative axis and the necessity to establish stocks of all kinds in the new base area. Even by waiting until 1 October before advancing beyond Bari, I could not avoid a further pause on the line Termoli–Campobasso–Vinchiaturo, since there were no reserve stocks in the country and the whole administrative machine required time to build up and adjust itself to the new plan of operations. The switch of base to the Taranto area and development of major operations along the east coast of Italy had not been envisaged, and advance arrangements had not been made to install the necessary resources now so much in demand.

### OPERATIONS BY LIGHT FORCES
#### BETWEEN 20 September AND 1 October

My orders to 13 Corps on reaching the Potenza–Auletta line provided for the despatch of light forces and reconnaissance elements to clear up any remaining enemy south of the line Altamura–Gravina–Potenza, then to push forward to Spinazzola and Melfi. Meanwhile 5 Corps was to continue aggressive patrolling northwards along the coast axis. The enemy covering Altamura withdrew under the combined pressure of 1 Airborne and 1 Canadian Divisions on 23 September, and our patrols pushed north through Spinazzola and reached Canosa three days later. In the coastal sector, elements of 78 Division together with some detachments of 4 Armoured Brigade landed at Bari on 22/23 September, and at once moved north to make contact with enemy rearguards at Barletta and Andria. Resistance was quickly overcome and patrols reached the Ofanto River on 24 September. After some delay due to demolitions, the advance was resumed through Foggia, which had been abandoned by the enemy on 27 September. By 1 October the Gargarno peninsula had been reported clear, but there were indications that the enemy was preparing to stand and fight in the hills north and west of the Foggia Plain.

### THE ADVANCE TO TERMOLI

On 1 October 13 Corps crossed the general line Barletta–Canosa, directed initially on the lateral road Termoli–Vinchiaturo. Once established firmly on this important lateral route, Eighth Army would recover the Plain of Foggia and its airfields and our immediate objective would be secured. At the Termoli line I would in any case be compelled to halt for maintenance reasons but my orders were to continue the advance as quickly as possible to secure the lateral road Pescara–Popoli–Avezzano, in order to outflank Rome. The capture of Rome, though of little military importance, was stated to be of great political significance and the city now became the next main Allied objective.

My orders to 13 Corps were that the advance to the Termoli line would be conducted on a two divisional front, 78 Division following the axis of the main coast road, while 1 Canadian Division advanced into the mountains to Vinchiaturo. Once established at Vinchiaturo the Canadians would be able to operate westwards towards Naples in co-operation with Fifth Army if by then the city had not fallen. 5 Corps was instructed to move behind 13 Corps ready to protect its west flank and rear—a necessary precaution as firm contact between Fifth and Eighth Armies was not easy to maintain in the high mountains. The positioning of 5 Corps was very important, as preservation of balance depended upon it. I laid down that as 13 Corps went forward 5 Division should be advanced to the Foggia area and that 4 Armoured Brigade (which was to pass to command of 5 Corps on reaching Termoli) should be positioned astride the Foggia–Naples lateral road. The Airborne Division was to stay in the general area Barletta–Andria–Canosa, while 8 Indian Division was located between Bari and Barletta.

The Desert Air Force planned to move up to the Foggia area as soon as possible.

The advance of 13 Corps started well. The enemy was known to have positions on the line of the River Biferno covering the small port of Termoli and, since the country greatly favoured the defence, plans were made to secure Termoli quickly by landings on the coast behind the enemy. On the night 2/3 October commando forces landed near the town, with the object of securing it in advance of the 78 Division thrust along the coast road. Complete surprise was achieved and the commandos secured the port and linked up with the bridgehead which was successfully established over the Biferno. Initial success was followed up by landing a brigade of 78 Division in the Termoli bridgehead on the following night.

The enemy reaction, however, was very speedy. 16 Panzer Division was rushed over from the front opposing Fifth Army, arrived during the night 3/4 October and during the next three days launched a number of strong attacks against both the

Termoli bridgehead and our forces which had crossed the river south of the town. On 5 October the enemy was fighting in Termoli itself and the flooded river prevented the passage of our tanks to assist in the battle, but by the end of the following day the bridgehead over the Biferno was firm. By 7 October the situation in the Termoli bridgehead had been restored, following the landing there of an additional brigade of 78 Division.

The enemy disengaged and fell back to positions covering the River Trigno, which were held by 16 Panzer Division (by now very depleted), and elements from 26 Panzer and 1 Parachute Divisions. As anticipated, delays were imposed by maintenance considerations and we were unable to follow up in strength until the administrative situation had been improved.

Meanwhile the Canadians were experiencing strong opposition in the difficult mountainous country and progress was slow. By 3 October they were only some 15 miles from Vinchiaturo, but the capture of the village took several days. This thrust was now diverging from the line of advance of 78 Division and I decided to bring forward another division to fill the gap between the two axes. This decision involved regrouping, for the front was becoming too wide for one corps to control and I ordered 5 Corps to take over the coastal sector with 78 Division, while 13 Corps was instructed to operate inland on a front of two divisions—1 Canadian and 5 Divisions.

2 New Zealand Division was due to be concentrated in the Taranto area by 15 November and this I decided to hold initially in Army reserve.

By 11 October, Eighth Army was established at Termoli and Vinchiaturo and the Foggia airfields were safeguarded; my forces were regrouping and once again major operations awaited the administrative adjustments which were being made in the rear areas.

## THE SITUATION IN EIGHTH ARMY ON REACHING THE TERMOLI–VINCHIATURO LINE

Having secured the Foggia airfields, Eighth Army was given the task of advancing to the 'Rome Line', which was the name given to the lateral road Pescara–Avezzano–Rome. There were two major factors confronting me in planning the development of my operations: administrative considerations and the weather.

I have explained already that our advance from Reggio was continually delayed by maintenance difficulties. Administration had not been able to keep pace with operational planning and this was now to have serious consequences, for the winter weather was beginning. Obviously our difficulties were going to be greatly increased when winter conditions set in, because the 'leg' of Italy is essentially ideal defensive country and when climatic conditions operated in the enemy's favour, it might become almost impregnable. The Adriatic winter is severe; seaborne operations would be uncertain; on land progress would become impossible off the main roads owing to snow and mud; mountain torrents subject to violent fluctuations would create great bridging difficulties and flying would be constantly restricted by low cloud and mist.

Rome was the immediate Allied objective and it was increasingly certain that unless we could secure the city very rapidly, weather would undoubtedly impose long delays on our plans. At the same time, our difficulties were immeasurably increased by a change in the enemy's conduct of the campaign, for it became apparent from his resistance at Salerno, Vinchiaturo and Termoli that his withdrawal policy had been superseded. The Allied advance along the whole front was now being solidly contested and reports showed that the German forces in Italy were being reinforced and had reached a total of some twenty-four divisions.

### RESUMPTION OF THE ADVANCE FROM THE TERMOLI–VINCHIATURO LINE

During the middle of October our preparations were proceeding for the resumption of the advance in strength. At the same time on Fifth Army front the River Volturno had been crossed but the enemy resistance continued to be very strong and further reinforcement of the front opposite Eighth Army had also been established. We had now four German divisions facing us—16 and 26 Panzer, 29 Panzer Grenadier and 1 Parachute Divisions grouped together as 76 Panzer Corps.

After the fall of Termoli operations on a limited scale continued with the object of squaring up to the defences on the River Trigno, but I had to wait until 21 October before commencing really strong efforts to get into close contact with the enemy positions. My outline plan for breaching the Trigno defences was based on diversionary operations on the western flank, followed by a strong thrust up the coast. In order to focus the enemy's attention inland I intended that 13 Corps should deliver a strong attack on the axis Vinchiaturo–Isernia prior to the 5 Corps operations on the river, and set a target date of 28 October for the thrust. On the night 30/31 October 5 Corps would attack across the Trigno with 8 Indian and 78 Divisions. Providing the weather held, I did not anticipate great difficulty in crossing the river, but further north the enemy was preparing a major defensive system based on the River Sangro. I therefore gave orders that once the 5 Corps operation started it would be carried through to the Sangro position, as we should probably need a pause there in order to study the opposition and launch a full scale attack. At the same time I ordered 2 New Zealand Division forward to the Foggia area to preserve balance in my dispositions and to provide a safeguard for the Foggia airfields.

During the pause energetic patrolling on 5 Corps front achieved considerable local success and on the night 22/23 October 78 Division got a battalion across the Trigno River. On the south bank the ground descended steeply to end in a bluff which made crossing operations difficult; on the north bank there was a plain some two miles wide leading to the San Salvo ridge along which the main enemy positions were disposed. Preliminary operations aimed at establishing forces in the plain, but from this time forward the offensive on all sectors began to be affected seriously by heavy and continuous rain. Efforts to increase the 78 Division bridgehead over the Trigno on 27 and 28 October were foiled by the mud and wet, while 13 Corps attack towards Isernia had to be postponed. Eventually 5 Division of 13 Corps started off in the pouring rain on the night 29/30 October and, in spite of the weather, difficult country and demolitions, succeeded in capturing Cantalupo on 31 October. Progress on this flank met increasing difficulties and the enemy resistance appeared to have been further strengthened; his tactics were now based on fortifying the very strongly built mountain villages which became formidable to capture; and when forced to withdraw, he destroyed existing accommodation in the villages so that the attacking troops would find little shelter in them.

After a number of postponements because of the downpour, 5 Corps launched the main thrust across the river on the night 2/3 November. A heavy artillery programme and naval gunfire supported the assault and good progress was made during the night in spite of firm resistance. During 3 November heavy fighting went on, particularly round San Salvo station where our troops were counter attacked by enemy tanks. Operations continued on the second night, during which an interesting incident occurred when an infantry battalion advanced into a German tank leaguer; intense confusion followed, but as a result the German armour in the sector withdrew a considerable distance. On the morning of 4 November the enemy was found to have started pulling back on the whole 5 Corps front. Troops of 78 Division passed through Vasto on the following day and continued the advance towards the Sangro. On their left 8 Indian Division took Palmoli and reached the lateral road to Vasto and had soon cleared down to the area of Torrebruna. By then 13 Corps, after considerable delays due mainly to demolitions, had captured Isernia. I was careful to ensure that no gap occurred between the two Corps thrusts and gave orders that reconnaissance troops were to be used for patrolling between the main axes of advance.

By 8 November 78 Division was on the high ground overlooking the River Sangro on a two brigade front, with 8 Indian Division coming up on its left. Preparations for tackling the Sangro position were now initiated.

REFLECTIONS ON THE SITUATION AS WE APPROACHED THE SANGRO

The conduct of operations was still suffering from the frustration due to lack of resources, which made it impossible to develop the desired strength and speed of action. The possibility of the Allies' securing Rome quickly was now remote. The build-up of our forces in Italy was being retarded by the withdrawal of craft and shipping in preparation for the North West European campaign and, since there were insufficient Allied resources to fight two major campaigns, it was no longer to be expected that spectacular results could be achieved in Italy quickly. This factor, combined with the enormous difficulties of campaigning in ideally defensive country in severe winter conditions, together with the strengthening of the enemy opposition, argued that from a strictly military point of view the continuance of the offensive during the winter would be unjustified. It was considered, however, desirable for other reasons that we should get Rome: but the problem of securing this objective was becoming increasingly formidable. At the beginning of November Eighth Army still had many of its units in Africa and it was becoming clear that we should not reach the Pescara Line with four infantry divisions only: I required at least one more. My troops were getting very tired and my formations had suffered considerable casualties since the landings at Reggio. In particular the officer situation in the infantry had become acute.

# CHAPTER SEVENTEEN

## The Battle of the River Sangro, 28 November 1943

### PRELIMINARY OPERATIONS

IN conformity with his policy of holding the Allied advance, the enemy on our front had undertaken the construction of the 'Winter Line', a very strong natural position based on the River Sangro and strengthened by defence works. The Sangro was in flood, the level of water being subject to wide variation according to the amount of rain falling in the mountains, but with very great difficulty it could be forded at certain periods. On the south bank of the river there is an escarpment. On the north a low lying plain extends to a steep sided ridge along which the main enemy positions were located, and to which I shall refer in this narrative as the Sangro Ridge. The main bastions of the enemy defensive system on the ridge were the two villages of Mozzagrogna and Fossacesia.

I had of course been considering the methods of tackling the Sangro position while we were on the River Trigno. The time factor made it important for me to manœuvre the Army during the advance from the Trigno to the Sangro in a way which would ensure minimum delay in getting to grips with the problem of piercing the 'Winter Line'; we were running what was to prove a losing race with the winter weather.

There were three alternatives for the Sangro battle. First, to attack on the left flank with 13 Corps astride Castel di Sangro on the two roads leading north to the Pescara–Avezzano lateral. Here we should be faced with difficulties in the high mountains, where the roads are liable to be blocked by snowdrifts; at best only one division could operate on each road and they would not be mutually supporting because of lack of lateral communications across the high central massif. In short, a powerful offensive on the left flank was hardly possible in the winter months, for apart from the operational limitations there would be great maintenance problems and the conditions of cloud and mist in the mountains would virtually preclude the use of our air power.

Secondly, there was the possibility of an attack in the central sector of 5 Corps front astride the roads from Atessa to Casoli and Castel Frentano. It would have been difficult if not impossible, however, to mount a major attack on this axis because of the extremely poor communications south of the river. But it gave quick access to the lateral road to the west from San Vito, which ran behind the Sangro River, and would therefore be useful for establishing a threat to the enemy's defences.

Thirdly, on the coastal axis a possible thrust line was through Fossacesia to Lanciano and San Vito thence northwards to Pescara and Chieti. An attack on this axis would have a good main road and could be prepared and mounted quickly with full artillery support. In the coastal plain the air forces would operate in the best available conditions and warships too could co-operate from the sea.

I therefore decided to deliver a strong blow on the coastal sector with 8 Indian and 78 Divisions with the object of breaking into the enemy defences on the Sangro Ridge on a narrow front. The troops were then to work outwards from the area of penetration. In order to increase the power of the offensive I decided to bring 2 New Zealand Division up on the left of 5 Corps to mount a strong threat along the road axis running north from Atessa. If operations went well this division could be pushed through to an area west of Chieti on the Rome lateral, ready to turn west directed on Popoli and Avezzano. If it were in any way possible to get this division to Avezzano the problem of helping Fifth Army forward towards Rome would be simplified. Meanwhile 5 Corps would advance along the main coast road to Pescara and Chieti with the ultimate object of establishing a bridgehead north of the Pescara River.

At a conference held at Army Group Headquarters on 8 November, I explained my plan for piercing the 'Winter Line' and my proposal for the subsequent development of operations. It was agreed that Fifth United States Army would continue pressure on its front so as to pin down the enemy and assist the development of the Eighth Army's plan to establish our troops in the Avezzano area.

### ORDERS FOR THE ATTACK ON THE WINTER LINE

My detailed orders for the attack over the River Sangro were based on achieving surprise by deceiving the enemy as to the direction of my main thrust. I intended to continue attempts to divert the enemy's attention to my western flank so I now ordered 13 Corps to operate strongly to secure the area Castel Alfedena and later Roccaraso. At the same time I asked Fifth United States Army to co-operate by increasing its activity on my western flank. These operations were to commence at once and would have the effect of breaking into the southern end of the Sangro position. Meanwhile 5 Corps was to close up to the Sangro line and prepare to launch the main attack which would be delivered by 8 Indian and 78 Divisions together with 4 Armoured Brigade.

My plan involved relieving 8 Indian Division on the left sector of 5 Corps front by 2 New Zealand Division, then concentrating the former behind 78 Division ready for the assault on a very narrow front. These moves had to be kept from the Germans and with this object a brigade of 8 Indian Division was to remain on the New Zealand front until the last minute. The target date for the attack by 5 Corps was 20 November and the first main objective was the general line Ortona–Lanciano.

Thenceforward the weather rapidly deteriorated. Heavy rain frequently continued for two days, only to be followed by one or two further days of drizzle and mist. Snow was falling in the mountains and the state of the roads and country became wet and very muddy. At least 48 hours' dry weather was necessary before the country became passable after a wet spell and in these circumstances the plan was subjected to continual postponements. Eventually it became necessary to modify the plan itself.

During the period 9–15 November 78 Division succeeded in crossing the river and in establishing a small bridgehead on the north bank from which battle patrols operated forward to the escarpment. Our identifications showed that the Germans opposing 78 Division belonged to 65 Infantry Division, which had horse transport. Behind it was 15 Panzer Grenadier Division, believed to be very weak in tanks. All we needed therefore was a spell of fine weather in order to exploit our superiority over the enemy, but the rain was persistent and the level of the Sangro repeatedly varied by as much as six or seven feet in a day as a result of downpours in the mountains. The mud and slush became truly appalling.

I had to postpone the date of the attack, and decided that I should have to modify the scope of my plan. In the prevailing weather conditions it did not seem feasible to launch a major breakthrough operation which would carry us straight to the Pescara line. As a first phase we could not hope to do more than take quick advantage of a dry spell to secure the Sangro Ridge. Once the enemy was denied observation over the river, bridging could be started, roads and tracks built up and the general movement problem across the valley properly organized. We would then be able to continue our advance northwards. In short, the weather forced me to adopt a policy of advancing by short methodical stages between which communications could be established and demolitions and obstacles overcome.

I ordered 5 Corps to build up the strength of the bridgehead in the river plain, preparatory to attacking the ridge. This involved sacrificing some of the measures taken to achieve surprise and I therefore ordered 2 New Zealand Division to get patrols across the Sangro, in order to increase the pressure on the enemy and to broaden the front.

In accordance with my new policy five battalions were established on the north bank of the river by 22 November, but further rain then brought us again to a complete standstill.

It looked as if we would have an indefinite time to wait before an operation could be launched which involved the use of large numbers of tanks, and I came to the conclusion that I would have to devise further modifications to the plan in order to make it independent of tanks and of weather. I instructed 5 Corps to reorganize the bridgehead on a two divisional basis, bringing 8 Indian Division up on the left of 78 Division and to plan the capture of the Sangro River by a series of very limited operations each supported by the whole Corps artillery. Before dawn on 26 November an attack would be mounted to secure the enemy localities halfway up the ridge towards San Maria. Two days later a further attack would be delivered against San Maria and Mozzagrogna, and subsequently 78 Division would operate from San

Maria in a north-easterly direction towards Fossacesia in order to clear the ridge. If the mud and wet precluded tank attacks, these thrusts were within the capability of the infantry alone and were to be carried through with fierce determination.

By 24 November I had a very firm bridgehead north of the River Sangro about 2,000 yards deep on a frontage of 10,000 yards. This was a very fine performance on the part of the infantry and sappers. Meanwhile, New Zealand patrols were active across the river in their sector and the south bank had been cleared of enemy throughout its length. In connection with 5 Corps attack on 28 November, the New Zealand Division was ordered to launch an assault across the river at the same time on a two brigade front. Meanwhile 13 Corps operations on the western flank continued and on 24 November Castel Alfedena was taken and held in face of strong counter attacks.

### BATTLE OF THE RIVER SANGRO

By 27 November all was ready for the battle. It was a fine dry day and 100 tanks of 4 Armoured Brigade, many carriers and much transport were got across to the north bank. Throughout the day the enemy positions were heavily bombed. On the New Zealand sector our troops closed up to the river and worked hard on improving communications to the front. If the weather held it was probable that armoured units would be able to accompany the infantry in their attacks along the ridge and this would, of course, accelerate the rolling up of the hostile defences from the flanks and rear. Very heavy artillery support was available and, weather permitting, a great weight of air power. I anticipated that once we got onto the ridge and captured Mozzagrogna and San Maria, we should have a 'dog-fight' which might well last two days before we completed the capture of 5 Corps objectives.

The weather on 28 November was fine and the assault began at 2130 hours. 8 Indian Division captured Mozzagrogna quickly, but demolitions prevented tanks and supporting weapons getting forward and ground had to be sacrificed in face of a German counter attack at dawn. On the left, 2 New Zealand Division went well and secured its initial objectives, together with a good bridgehead over the river by first light 29 November. Throughout the day heavy fighting continued round Mozzagrogna where the enemy was using tanks and flame-throwers, but during the night 28/29 November the village was captured and 4 Armoured Brigade got through the place by midday. Tanks and infantry, having got onto the ridge, began to turn outwards in order to clear it and experienced intense fighting, but our progress was greatly facilitated by the magnificent scale of air support. It was clear towards the end of 29 November that we had broken into the enemy's 'Winter Line', and I ordered 5 Corps to continue operations on 30 November in two directions: 78 Division was to clear Fossacesia and then move north-west towards San Vito; 8 Indian Division was to operate from Mozzagrogna along the ridge towards Castel Frentano. It was important to give the enemy no let-up as the full brunt of our attack had fallen on 65 Infantry Division: which had received a great hammering and was now very unsteady.

[129]

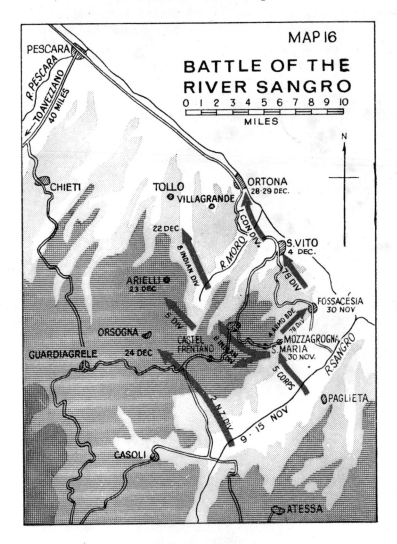

During 30 November 4 Armoured Brigade took Fossacesia supported by a heavy artillery barrage and 8 Indian Division, after beating off a counter attack by 26 Panzer Division at Mozzagrogna, worked along the ridge and captured the high ground overlooking Castel Frentano. Meanwhile the New Zealanders, having overcome great difficulties in establishing a river crossing and approaches to it, were expanding their bridgehead. By dark the whole ridge overlooking the River Sangro, which was the backbone of the 'Winter Line', was in our hands, and the 5 Corps and New Zealand bridgeheads had linked up to form one deep penetration of the enemy defensive system. 1,000 prisoners and much equipment were captured.

16. A Sherman tank leaves a landing craft in the Sicily landings.

17. This fuel dump near Cesaro gives some idea of the vast amount of materials which were transported to Sicily to support the Allied invasion.

18. This Italian coastal gun-battery was part of the enemy defences which were deployed along parts of the Sicilian coast to prevent further Allied landings while the enemy troops withdrew to the mainland.

19. Highlanders unload parcels of cigarettes sent as a present from General Montgomery to the men of the Eighth Army.

My orders on 1 December provided for the establishment of a firm base on the vital Sangro Ridge, while limited thrusts were launched on the two flanks. I instructed 5 Corps not to send main bodies beyond the line of the lateral road San Vito–Lanciano until communications across the Sangro had been made storm-proof and flood-proof. 78 Division with 4 Armoured Brigade was to secure San Vito and send light forces ahead towards Ortona. 8 Indian Division with the Canadian Tank Brigade (which I now brought forward) was to form the firm base on the ridge. I also ordered 2 New Zealand Division to push forward to secure Castel Frentano, Guardiagrele and Orsogna. In order to cover the gap between the New Zealanders and 13 Corps, I ordered forward a Parachute brigade with a regiment of airborne artillery, which was to operate under command of the New Zealand Division. The layout of the front was now well organized, but we needed good weather to exploit our victory. My object was to push one division along the coast road to Ortona and later on if possible to Pescara, while a second progressed on the inland axis towards Chieti. 78 Division was now very tired and I gave orders for its relief by 1 Canadian Division which was to be brought across from 13 Corps. 13 Corps now could have little but a holding role, for which only one division was required in the line, and 78 Division, after relief, would go into reserve in 13 Corps area. By 4 December 5 Corps had captured San Vito and Lanciano but was held up on the line of the River Moro, and 2 New Zealand Division had faced up to Orsogna and Guardiagrele. Operations were now again delayed by rain, but by 6 December the high level bridge across the River Sangro at Paglieta had been completed.

The enemy resistance was very determined along the whole front. Our moves were subject to strong and repeated counter attacks, particularly in the New Zealand sector where, in addition to 26 Panzer Division and some parachute battalions, 65 Infantry Division had been brought back into the line after a brief respite. 5 Corps was now opposed by 90 Panzer Grenadier Division, which had started arriving on our front on 1 December. Away on the left flank 13 Corps was opposed by one parachute division only, and since any offensive in the mountains was out of the question, I decided to regroup my divisions with the object of strengthening the right flank further. I therefore ordered Headquarters 13 Corps with 5 Division to come across to the coastal sector, leaving 78 Division to hold the mountain flank directly under Army command. I proposed to continue my drive to the north on a frontage of two Corps: on the right 5 Corps with 1 Canadian and 8 Indian Divisions and on the left 13 Corps with 2 New Zealand and 5 Divisions.

By 10 December 1 Canadian Division had secured a bridgehead over the River Moro and pushed on towards Ortona, in spite of numerous counter attacks in which very heavy casualties were inflicted on the enemy. The Desert Air Force was doing splendid work and co-operation from warships was also proving most valuable. I instructed 5 Corps to swing 8 Indian Division up towards Tollo on the left flank of the Canadians and accelerated the leading brigade of 5 Division now moving round to the coastal sector with 13 Corps, so that I could order it into the line between 2

New Zealand and 8 Indian Divisions. The opposition at Orsogna and Guardiagrele was still very sticky for the two villages had been converted into major strong points, and their location on dominating ground made them very difficult of approach. The ground floors and cellars of the houses had been strengthened and in them the enemy garrison withstood repeated air attacks.

### THE DEVELOPMENT OF OPERATIONS NORTH OF THE RIVER SANGRO

My long term policy remained to secure the Pescara–Chieti lateral and then to develop operations towards Rome. My plan involved driving forward on a front of two Corps with the object of establishing a bridgehead over the Pescara River with 1 Canadian Division on the right and 5 Division on the left. 8 Indian Division would pass into reserve between Pescara and Chieti while the New Zealanders, having advanced through Guardiagrele to Chieti, would turn south-west to Avezzano. Owing to the difficulty of the Guardiagrele–Chieti road axis, I intended to advance 5 Corps ahead of 13 Corps in order to threaten the communications of the enemy troops in the general area of Orsogna. This would facilitate the progress of 13 Corps and the New Zealanders.

Meanwhile, the enemy was known to be sending further reinforcements to the Eighth Army front and we heard of the expected arrival of 334 Infantry Division from Genoa. This was the third division which the Germans had sent to reinforce his eastern flank since the beginning of the Sangro battle, the others being 90 PG Division from Venice and 26 Panzer Division from the Fifth United States Army front.

5 Corps operations against Ortona continued relentlessly against desperate enemy resistance. The Canadians got into the outskirts of the town on 20 December, but it took a week to clear it owing to the remarkably tenacious fighting of the German paratroop garrison. The Canadian troops were quite magnificent and in the end outfought the Germans.

Meanwhile 8 Indian Division continued its operations towards Tollo and succeeded in taking Villa Grandi on 22 December.

In 13 Corps, the plan to assault Orsogna was eventually dropped as it would have proved very costly. Instead, operations were developed to outflank the enemy's defences to the north and by 24 December the New Zealanders had captured the high ground to the north-east of the town. Between 2 New Zealand and 8 Indian Divisions, 5 Division captured Arielli on 23 December.

This was the general situation on the front of Eighth Army at the close of 1943 when I was ordered to hand over my command and return to fresh tasks in England.

### SOME REFLECTIONS ON THE CAMPAIGN IN ITALY

The original Allied object in invading Italy was to knock that country out of the war. This was achieved very soon after our leading troops had landed on the mainland.

Following the Armistice there had been a hope that to evict the Germans from Italy with the aid of the Italian Army would be a speedy matter. Events proved this impossible and we became involved in a major campaign lacking a pre-determined plan of action. The result was that the administrative machine became unable to keep pace with the constantly widening scope of our operational commitments. We were therefore unable to exploit our advantages in September and October, when operationally a speedy advance to the 'Rome Line' seemed still a very feasible proposition. If then we had had the resources to allow us to maintain pressure on the enemy, our superiority in armour and in the air might have enabled us to roll the enemy back to the 'Rome Line' before the winter began.

By the time the Allies had secured Naples and the Foggia airfields the bad weather was upon us. If the capture of Rome was then considered an urgent necessity, it could have been ensured only by the allocation of sufficient resources to build up the Armies and their immediately associated Air Forces to a strength adequate for the task. By then, however, other considerations were involved; craft and shipping were removed in preparation for the Western European front, and local import facilities were restricted by the demands of the Strategic Air Forces which were being established at Foggia. We could not do everything at once.

The tempo of the land operations in Italy therefore decreased and the capture of Rome became increasingly difficult. In three months the Allies had captured Sicily, knocked Italy out of the war, locked up the Italian fleet in Malta and secured Naples and the Foggia airfields. These were spectacular gains. Thereafter it was necessary to reduce the resources made available for the land forces. And, since this coincided with increased enemy resistance and the advent of winter, we could no longer hope for quick results.

# CHAPTER EIGHTEEN

## Administration in the Campaign in Italy

THROUGHOUT Part III I have had to say repeatedly that my operations were hampered by administrative difficulties. In the immediately preceding paragraphs, in which I gave my reflections on the campaign, I indicated the reason. We became involved in a major campaign without having made in advance the administrative plans and arrangements necessary to sustain the impetus of our operations.

It may be of interest to explain rather more fully what this lack of previous planning involved.

Sound administrative arrangements had been made to maintain the Eighth Army, with its two Corps in Sicily. When Operation 'Baytown' was launched on 3 September across the Straits of Messina, the administrative build-up was incomplete; a proportion of the units and supplies intended to complete it was subsequently delivered but others were diverted to the 'Avalanche' operation at Salerno. The complete priority awarded to the Fifth United States Army absorbed such reserves of administrative resources as were immediately available in the Mediterranean. The operation launched at Taranto by 5 Corps was prepared at short notice and the scale of administrative support allotted to it was of the slenderest: reliance in the first instance being placed on assistance from the Italians both as to supplies and transport.

The effect of these circumstances was that a reinforced Eighth Army had to be supported in Italy by something less than the administrative resources which had been provided for its operations in Sicily. But stores and transport collected in Sicily could not be suddenly spirited into Italy. Rail communications did not exist. Roads were long and heavily demolished and the ferry at Messina could handle only a small volume of traffic.

The further stores convoys which were scheduled for Sicily were diverted to the 'heel' ports of Italy, but these ships had been loaded in bulk on the assumption that their cargoes would be used to stock up the depots in Sicily where a small balanced stock had already been accumulated. Their arrival in the 'heel' ports did not help the situation very materially; the Eighth Army, having just based itself on Taranto and Brindisi wanted certain things only, and wanted them badly. The capacity of the ports was strictly limited and they were faced with the problem of discharging large quantities of stores, useless for the moment, in order to extract the vital stores which were needed so badly.

The switch of my administrative axis from Calabria to the 'heel' ports was, from an administrative point of view, the crisis of the campaign. It must be remembered that I 'drove' the Eighth Army forward into the Potenza area at great speed in order to assist the operation at Salerno. In doing so I had been fully warned by my staff that I was taking big administrative risks. The advice was sound, just as I consider that my decision to ignore it was sound. The risks were real and, although I succeeded in my tactical objective to relieve the enemy pressure on the Fifth United States Army, I paid the penalty of finding that my own reserves were exhausted and that a flow of supplies to replenish them was not forthcoming. Had all this been foreseen, adequate supplies might already have arrived in the 'heel' ports and my administrative situation could have been re-adjusted. But there was no pre-determined plan and a crisis occurred; it could not quickly be overcome and right up to the end of my operations in Italy its effects continued to be felt: though in an ever lessening degree.

Our administrative difficulties were not confined to shortage of ordinary supplies such as rations and petrol. Equally important was the difficulty in maintaining the efficiency of our transport. In describing the Sicilian campaign I have mentioned that it had been decided, and rightly, not to establish in Sicily base workshops or base ordnance depots. Soon after the campaign on the Italian mainland had been started it was decided to establish advanced ordnance depots at Naples and Bari. Owing to the time which it takes to set up depots of this description, the benefit from them was hardly felt during my period of command in Italy. This was a circumstance which could not have been avoided given the conditions in which the Italian campaign was launched. With regard to base workshops it was planned that the repair of engine assemblies should continue to be done in the base workshops in Egypt. There was grave difficulty about moving these workshops, not the least of which was that they employed a very large number of local artisans. The distances, however, that separated my troops from these workshops in Egypt was such that a satisfactory turn-round could not be established whereby unserviceable assemblies could be promptly replaced. For these reasons my transport resources became progressively weaker just at the time when I had most need of them.

A new feature in the Italian campaign was the heavy rate of ammunition expenditure. Experience gained in the desert proved rather deceptive in this respect. The Sicilian campaign had not lasted long enough to bring the matter of ammunition expenditure into prominence. The Battle of the Sangro was the first real warning given to us that in close and easily defended country we could expect a need for ammunition on a scale far higher than that to which we had been accustomed.

The capture of the Foggia airfields immediately gave rise to heavy demands for supplies for the Strategic Air Force. The obvious point of entry for these supplies was Bari. In these circumstances the three 'heel' ports between them could not meet the combined demands of Eighth Army and the Air Force. There was surplus port capacity available at Naples where the United States Engineers had accomplished a remarkable achievement in repairing the very heavy damage. The extent, however, to which Naples could be used immediately to satisfy my requirements was limited. In the first place it involved a diversion of shipping which can seldom be accomplished without some loss of time. Secondly, the only rail communication available between the Bay of Naples and the Adriatic was a difficult single line track via Potenza and Taranto.

The plan which had been made for the development of the port of Naples aimed at using it for the Fifth United States Army consisting of one United States Corps and one British Corps. The fact that British as well as American supplies had to be handled at Naples, and that supplies for the United States Air Corps as well as for the British Eighth Army had to be handled in the 'heel' ports, demanded a close co-ordination between the administrative arrangements of the two Allies. Headquarters Fortbase, which had been responsible for organizing my rear administration in Sicily, was set up in Taranto at the end of September to fill the same role on behalf of Eighth Army in Italy. The Peninsula Base Section, which fulfilled the corresponding role for the American troops in the Fifth United States Army, was established about the same time in Naples. It was urgently necessary to co-ordinate the working of these two staffs. The decision taken was to close down Headquarters Fortbase, to transfer the staff to Naples and to reconstitute it there on a strengthened basis as an advanced administrative echelon of Allied Force Headquarters. Its responsibilities for local administration on the Lines of Communication were transferred to a District Headquarters under its command. This advanced administrative echelon was then given authority to co-ordinate on the spot all administrative arrangements, British and United States, in Italy. In particular it was given power to control the acceptance of cargoes at all ports, to allocate rail capacity and to lay down priorities for railway repairs. The officer in charge of this advanced echelon Headquarters was also appointed as administrative staff officer to General Alexander, who simultaneously dispensed with his own administrative staff. This change in organization was beneficial and its effects were quickly felt in the Eighth Army. A further change was made in December when the command of this administrative staff passed to Headquarters 15 Army Group, so that it became in name, as well as in fact, the administrative portion of 15 Army Group staff. This revision to a more normal arrangement was completed when General Alexander concentrated his Headquarters, both operational and administrative, at Caserta in January 1944.

I have mentioned these various changes which took place in the administrative organization in rear of Eighth Army partly because they had a very definite effect on my maintenance position, and partly because they concern the problem to which I have been referring in previous chapters: namely the problem of administrative control. The American method of solving this problem is a straightforward one. The Army Commander controls administration within his own area. The lines of communication in rear are controlled by the Services of Supply. I think that our own system is more flexible, but for that very reason it sometimes tends to become complicated. An administrative organization should be simple. It should normally ensure that the commander of a formation has control of an area extending back to the point at which his supplies are mainly delivered. Normally, in the case of an

Army, this is a group of railheads but it may, as in the desert, be a port. In the case of an Army Group, the Army Group Commander will normally control a series of ports at which his supplies are delivered from overseas. If more than one Army Group is involved a GHQ must be set up to control the Base Depots and ports from which they are fed. The administrative responsibilities of the Army Group are then confined to the allotment of priorities between the demands of the various Armies, in order to ensure that available supplies are utilized in the manner which best fits the operational plan of the Army Group Commander. These are the broad principles, in my opinion, which should decide the answer to the problem of administrative control. I agree that there should be flexibility in their application, but two conditions must always be observed. The first is that every administrative organization must be simple. The second is that every operational commander must have a degree of control over the administrative plan corresponding to the scope of his responsibilities for the operational plan.

# CHAPTER NINETEEN

## *My Farewell to the Eighth Army*

TOWARDS the end of December I was appointed to command Twenty-First Army Group which was then preparing in England for the invasion of Western Europe. On 31 December I handed over to my successor, Lieutenant-General Sir Oliver Leese, and took off from the Sangro airstrip for home. Before leaving I issued a farewell message to all ranks of the Eighth Army, which is reproduced in this book, and I think I can here say little more than is expressed there about my feelings at relinquishing command of this great family of fighting men.

I spent 1 January 1944 at Marrakech with the Prime Minister. Before I left for England that night, Mr. Churchill wrote the following in my autograph book:

"The immortal march of the Eighth Army from the gates of Cairo along the African shore, through Sicily, has now carried its ever victorious soldiers far into Italy towards the gates of Rome. The scene  changes and vastly expands. A great task accomplished gives place to a greater, in which the same unfailing spirit will win for all true men a full and glorious reward.

WINSTON S. CHURCHILL."

# EIGHTH ARMY

## PERSONAL MESSAGE FROM THE ARMY COMMANDER

### To be read out to all troops

1. I have to tell you, with great regret, that the time has come for me to leave the Eighth Army. I have been ordered to take command of the British Armies in England that are to operate under General Eisenhower—the Supreme Commander.

2. It is difficult to express to you adequately what this parting means to me. I am leaving officers and men who have been my comrades during months of hard and victorious fighting, and whose courage and devotion to duty always filled me with admiration. I feel I have many friends among the soldiery of this great Army. I do not know if you will miss me; but I will miss you more than I can say, and especially will I miss the personal contacts, and the cheerful greetings we exchanged together when we passed each other on the road.

3. In all the battles we have fought together we have not had one single failure; we have been successful in everything we have undertaken.

I know that this has been due to the devotion to duty and whole-hearted co-operation of every officer and man, rather than to anything I may have been able to do myself.

But the result has been a mutual confidence between you and me, and mutual confidence between a Commander and his troops is a pearl of very great price.

4. I am also very sad at parting from the Desert Air Force. This magnificent air striking force has fought with the Eighth Army throughout the whole of its victorious progress; every soldier in this Army is proud to acknowledge that the support of this strong and powerful air force has been a battle-winning factor of the first import-ance. We owe the Allied Air Forces in general, and the Desert Air Force in particular, a very great debt of gratitude.

5. What can I say to you as I go away?

When the heart is full it is not easy to speak. But I would say this to you:

"YOU have made this Army what it is. YOU have made its name a household word all over the world. YOU must uphold its good name and its traditions.

"And I would ask you to give to my successor the same loyal and devoted service that you have never failed to give to me."

6. And so I say GOOD-BYE to you all.

May we meet again soon; and may we serve together again as comrades in arms in the final stages of this war.

ITALY  
*1 January 1944*

B. L. MONTGOMERY  
General, Eighth Army

[139]

BOOK TWO

# NORMANDY
# TO THE BALTIC

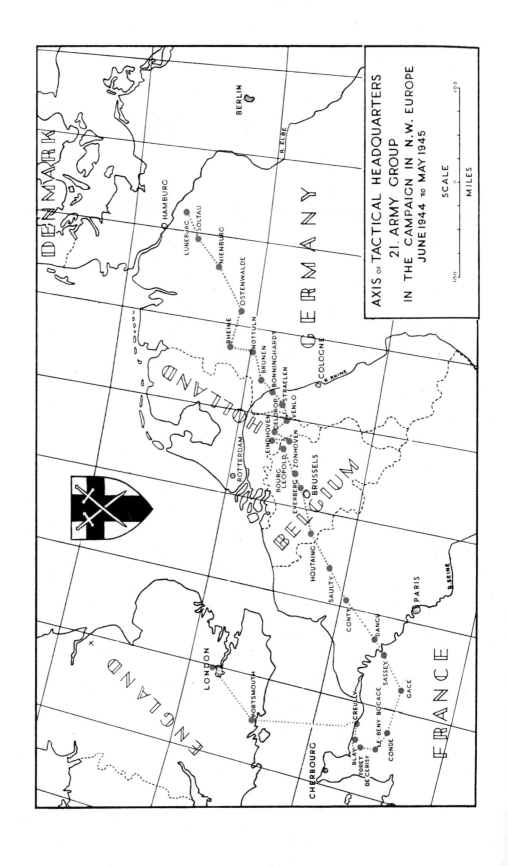

AXIS OF TACTICAL HEADQUARTERS
21. ARMY GROUP
IN THE CAMPAIGN IN N.W. EUROPE
JUNE 1944 TO MAY 1945

SCALE

MILES

DENMARK

BERLIN

R. ELBE

GERMANY

HAMBURG

LUNEBURG
SOLTAU

NIENBURG

OSTENWALDE

RHEINE

NOTTULN

BRUNEN
BONNINGHARDT

COLOGNE
R. RHINE

CELDROP
STRAELEN
VENLO

EINDHOVEN

HOLLAND

ROURG
LEOPOLD
EVERBERG
ZONHOVEN

BRUSSELS

ROTTERDAM

BELGIUM

HOUTAINC

SAULTY

PARIS

R. SEINE

CONTY

DANCU

ENGLAND

LONDON

PORTSMOUTH

CREULLY

SASSEY

GACE

CHERBOURG

BLAY
FORET
DE CERISY

LE BENY BOCAGE

CONDE

FRANCE

# FOREWORD

W E are still too close to the event to attempt a critical analysis of the campaign in North-West Europe from June 1944 to May 1945 and my object is therefore to present a factual account of the part played by 21 Army Group in the conquest of Germany while the details are still fresh in my mind. The subject matter is based on my personal papers, and I have been careful to relate the changing circumstances of the campaign as they appeared to me at the time. I hope the value of this story will lie in recording the factors and reasoning which gave rise to the more important operational plans and decisions within 21 Army Group.

A great Allied team went into battle in North-West Europe in June 1944 under the supreme command of General Eisenhower. The efficiency of the team to which we all belonged can best be judged by the results it achieved. When Allies work together there are bound to be different points of view, and when these occur it is essential that they are thrashed out fully and frankly; but once a final decision is given, it is the duty of all members of the team to carry out that decision loyally. The Allied team worked in this spirit, and by its team work achieved overwhelming victory.

In June 1945, when the German war was over and Supreme Headquarters was being dissolved, I wrote to General Eisenhower and thanked him for all that he had done for the British armies: and for myself; I said that I wanted him to know that I, a British General, had been proud to serve under American command. Ike, as I like to call him, wrote me this very charming letter:

### General Eisenhower's letter of 8 June, 1945

*Dear Monty,*

*Your note to me, written on the 7th, is one of the finest things I have ever received. I am intensely gratified that you feel as you do. In the aftermath of this Allied effort enduring friendships and feelings of mutual respect among higher commanders will have a most beneficial effect. The team must continue to exist in spirit.*

*Your own high place among leaders of your country is firmly fixed, and it has never been easy for me to disagree with what I knew to be your real convictions. But, it will always be a great privilege to bear evidence to the fact that whenever decision was made, regardless of your personal opinion, your loyalty and efficiency in execution were to be counted upon with certainty.*

*I hope that you realise how deeply appreciative I am of your letter and the spirit that prompted you to write it, as well as of the tremendous help and assistance that you have been to me and to this whole Allied Force since it was first formed. In whatever years are left to both of us, possibly we may occasionally meet, not only to reminisce, but to exemplify the spirit of comradeship that I trust will exist between our two countries for all time.*

*With warm personal regards,*

*As ever*

*IKE.*

*Foreword*

There were a number of occasions during the campaign when American troops served under my command. I first saw Americans in battle in Sicily and formed a very high opinion of their fighting qualities; in the campaign in North-West Europe I saw them constantly and got to know them well. The American is a brave fighting man, steady under fire, and he has that tenacity in battle which stamps the first class soldier. I have formed a very great affection and admiration for the fighting men of the United States and I am proud to number many friends amongst the General Officers of the American Army.

I take this opportunity to pay tribute to the various Allied contingents which served under my command. Belgians, Czechs, Dutch, French, Poles and other nationals were included in 21 Army Group; they all played their part with distinction and earned our admiration. We shall not forget, moreover, the truly tremendous welcome and hospitality that we received in the liberated countries on our long march into Germany.

*Montgomery of Alamein*
*Field-Marshal.*

GERMANY                                    C-in-C
*April 1946*                    British Army of the Rhine

[144]

# INTRODUCTION

## I

THIS is an account of the part played by 21 Army Group in the Campaign in North-West Europe from June 1944 to May 1945.

Modern operations of war are essentially the concern not of one Service but of all three working in close co-operation, and it is neither possible nor desirable to isolate the purely military aspect of the story; on the other hand it is not within the scope of this book to make more than brief reference to the work and achievements of the Allied Navies and Air Forces in the Campaign.

The Navies ensured that our requirements reached us safely from across the seven seas, and fought in close companionship with us: not only in the assault, but in all our battles along the seaboard of North-West Europe. The participation of the Air Forces in the land battles was invaluable and often decisive; never before have land forces operated with the co-operation of such tremendous deployment of air power.

There has been a closer comradeship between the three Services in this war than was ever achieved before, and with it the soldiers have gained a deep respect and admiration for the heroism and fighting skill of the sailors and airmen.

The narrative contains only brief references to our great Russian ally, but it will never be forgotten that the Russians throughout bore the greatest weight of the enemy onslaught on land. There was a close interdependence between the Allied fronts, and the mighty development of Marshal Stalin's strategy in the east was the complement to the Anglo-American offensives in the south and west.

In conclusion, I wish to pay tribute to the splendid fighting spirit, heroism and endurance of the ordinary soldier of the British Commonwealth of Nations. Once again he has indeed proved himself second to none. And if I were asked what is the greatest single factor which contributed to his success, I would say morale. I call morale the greatest single factor in war. A high morale is based on discipline, self-respect and confidence of the soldier in his commanders, in his weapons, and in himself. Without high morale, no success can be achieved—however good may be the strategic or tactical plan, or anything else. High morale is a pearl of very great price. And a sure way to obtain it is by success in battle.

## II

It is certain that this campaign received a degree of publicity in the world press and radio unparalleled in the history of war. Modern means of communication made it possible for the observers at the front to report events on the battlefield by wireless and in the newspapers of the world, within a few hours of their occurrence. The experiences and impressions described by these War Correspondents have profound effects, not only on the morale of the home country, but also upon the actual fighting soldiers, who listen to broadcasts and who rapidly receive copies of their home newspapers. The relationships of the Commander and his staff with War Correspondents have therefore become a matter of first importance; the Commander must study the requirements of the Correspondents accredited to him and must be well informed on the whole subject of war reporting.

The main problem from the military Commander's point of view which arises from the requirements of the Press in war is the conflict between the necessity for security on the one hand, and on the other hand the desire to ensure that the War Correspondents are kept as fully as possible in the military picture. It is vital that as soon as security conditions allow, the Press and Wireless should be permitted to report events—both failures as well as successes—in the fullest possible way. But the dictates of security must sometimes leave War Correspondents with an acute sense of frustration and dissatisfaction. It has therefore been my policy to take them as much as possible into my confidence at all times, and I am happy to record that the loyalty and integrity of the Correspondents accredited to 21 Army Group were always of the very highest order.

In the public interest the Press obviously has the right to criticize events at the front, but the problem is to ensure that its criticism is based on sound premise, because there are bound to be occasions during a campaign when 'events are not what they seem'. It is no reflection on a Commander's confidence in his Correspondents to say that there are some military secrets which he cannot divulge to them, and this particularly applies to his long term projects for operations; it frequently happens that a long term plan is not even divulged to all the members of the Commander's executive staff, since there is no justification for burdening more individuals than necessary with vital secrets. This point is well exemplified when a Commander is fighting a battle for position, in which he is attempting to pursue a policy of attrition, or wearing down the enemy strength, and forcing the enemy into a position favourable for launching a decisive blow. Such a stage may take some time, and while it is proceeding the visible day-to-day results from an observer's point of view may appear disappointing; unless the observer knows exactly the object behind the operations, and can be told the degree to which the stage is being set, he may well misinterpret the situation, and express disappointment at the apparent lack of results. If he does, he can undermine the confidence of the soldiers in their leader and affect adversely their morale.

The fact is that the Press requires daily reports for its public, whereas a Commander is largely concerned with events which may be weeks or even months ahead. How then can we prevent misunderstandings in the minds of the War Correspondents? This is a problem which demands our closest study.

21 Army Group was served by a very fine body of representatives of the Press and Radio, and I always regarded them as an integral part of my staff. The relations

between them and the headquarters and formations of the Army Group were excellent, and they became indeed a part of the big family. It is a great tribute to them all, and the Public Relations Service, that such a great degree of co-operation and friendship was achieved, and that the tremendous influence which they have was exerted in accordance with the highest principles of truth and loyalty.

# CHAPTER ONE

## *The Second Front*

THE great design for the return of Allied Forces to North-West Europe had its beginnings at Dunkirk. From that time, in spite of the many setbacks which we endured during the early war years, the resolution remained that one day our forces would go back to France and the Low Countries to avenge the defeats of 1940.

In December 1941 President Roosevelt and Mr Churchill agreed upon the complete unification of the war effort of the countries they represented, and thereafter the United States and British forces were deployed under the direction of the Combined Chiefs of Staff. Soon after, the conception of a mighty cross-Channel assault against the Fortress of Europe began to receive consideration, for in April 1942 it was jointly decided that such an enterprise would constitute the principal Anglo-American effort for the defeat of the German forces.

In the spring of 1942 the Red Army was slowly falling back before the German onslaught, and joint conferences were held in London with the object of determining means of relieving pressure on the Soviets. In July Admiral King and General Marshall visited the British Chiefs of Staff in an urgent endeavour to find some way of distracting German forces from the Eastern Front. It was a dark hour; our resources were so meagre and our commitments so widespread, that a solution was difficult to determine. The possibility of attacking Western Europe was examined, but the strength of the enemy, and our own lack of equipment and of all the special adjuncts required for such an operation, made its successful accomplishment out of the question at this time.

It was eventually decided that the only operation that could be undertaken with a fair prospect of success was an assault landing in North Africa. This was far from Germany, but was calculated to divert at least some German energies from Russia, and would also materially improve the critical situation in the Middle East.

When the North African project was approved, it was accepted that the cost in joint resources would mean not only that any hope of an operation in Western Europe in 1942 would have to be abandoned, but also that it would be impossible to complete the assembly of forces in England for a major cross-Channel assault in 1943.

It has since been learned that the German plan at that time was to attempt the defeat of Britain by aerial bombardment and by destruction of her forces in the Middle East. Hitler's main project was to break through Stalingrad and Egypt and join the two salients in the Middle East. The heroic defence of Stalingrad and the crushing defeat Rommel sustained at El Alamein dislocated the German pincer movement. The development of operations in North Africa together with the advance of the

Eighth Army, and the Soviet offensive from the Volga, proved to be the turning points in the war: the Axis was forced on to the strategic defensive.

When Mr Churchill and President Roosevelt met at Casablanca in January 1943 it was apparent that the African campaign was destined to achieve decisive success, and the development of operations after the Tunisian campaign was discussed.

Again the most desirable course of action would have been to close with the enemy in Western Europe. But again the Allied war potential had not yet been developed sufficiently to produce and sustain the resources required for such a gigantic undertaking, and once again the opening of the so-called 'Second Front' had to be postponed. Axis control of the Mediterranean islands and southern coast of Europe still forced our shipping into the 12,000 mile detour round the Cape; time was required to develop the vast mobilization in the United States, to ferry men and material across the Atlantic to England, to complete the defeat of the submarine, to develop the strategic air offensive over Germany, and to manufacture and assemble the truly enormous mass of material which the invasion of Western Europe demanded.

It was therefore decided that the next step would be to knock Italy out of the war, lock up the Italian fleet and open the Mediterranean. This would result in a great saving in shipping, would cause diversion of German forces, and would give us a footing in 'Fortress Europe' together with airfields of great strategic importance.

At the same time, it was resolved at Casablanca to resume the concentration of forces and material in the United Kingdom, and to commence detailed planning for the cross-Channel project. A joint Anglo-American staff was instituted, under the leadership of a Chief of Staff to the Supreme Commander (designate); and taking the initial letters of his appointment, the organization was christened 'Cossac'. Cossac was directed by the Combined Chiefs of Staff to make preparations for the return of Allied Forces to Western Europe, in the event of a sudden weakening of Germany to the extent that landings could be made in the face of light or negligible resistance, and at the same time to make plans for a major seaborne assault as early as possible in 1944.

In preparation for the operation, the Allied Commanders decided to undertake the great strategic bombardment of Germany, which aimed at inducing a creeping paralysis throughout the country by smashing its industrial and economic capacity; by the middle of 1943 the air assault by Bomber Command and Eighth United States Air Force was in full swing and producing important results.

At the Washington Conference in May 1943 the conception of a full scale invasion of the Fortress of Europe was confirmed, and the code name 'Overlord' was formally accepted for the operation. The spring of 1944 was then designated as the target date.

By August 1943 Cossac had produced a tentative plan which was considered at the Quebec Conference, and, although at that time Mr Churchill suggested an increase in the forces it was proposed to employ in the assault, approval was given for implementing the project as far as it was possible before the appointment of a Supreme Commander.

This brief summary of the history of 'Overlord' brings us to the close of 1943.

During the long period of consideration given to the invasion of Western Europe, a number of long term projects were initiated which played an important part in the success which the operation achieved. The design and production of artificial harbours, the preparation of cross-Channel pipe lines for fuel supply, the evolution of the technique for assaulting defended beaches and the collection and collation of an immense volume of geographical and geological data concerning the 'invasion coast' and its hinterland, were some of the tasks undertaken many months and even years before D-day, the first day of operation 'Overlord'.

It has been shown why the opening of the 'Second Front' did not take place earlier than 1944. By the late spring of 1944, however, the progress of the German forces had been halted in all theatres; in the Battle of the Atlantic the submarine was defeated; the Battle of the Air was paralysing Germany; and as a result of our operations in the Mediterranean, the short sea route had been reopened and the enemy had been forced to make considerable dispersion of his forces in southern Europe.

The stage was properly set for launching the greatest amphibious operation in military history.

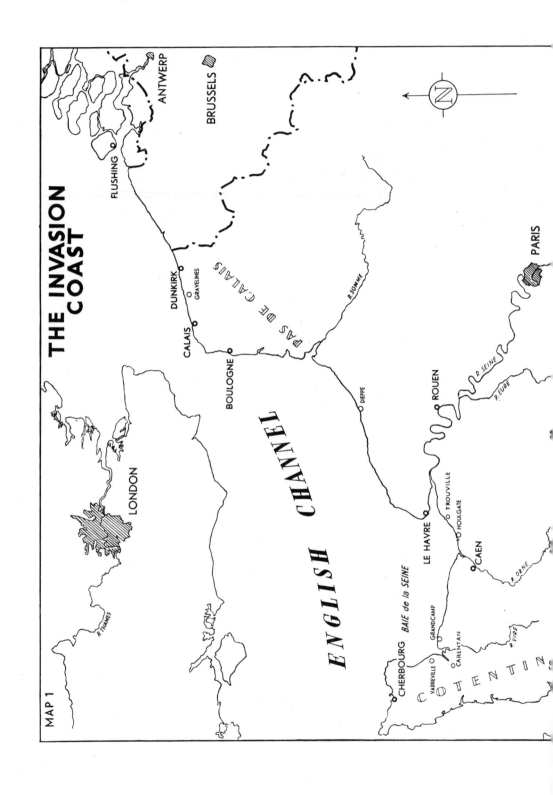

MAP 1

THE INVASION COAST

ENGLISH CHANNEL

PAS DE CALAIS

BAIE de la SEINE

COTENTIN

LONDON
R. THAMES

FLUSHING
ANTWERP
BRUSSELS
DUNKIRK
GRAVELINES
CALAIS
BOULOGNE
R. SOMME
DIEPPE
ROUEN
R. SEINE
R. EURE
PARIS
LE HAVRE
TROUVILLE
HOULGATE
CAEN
R. ORNE
CHERBOURG
GRANDCAMP
VARREVILLE
CARENTAN
R. VIRE

CHAPTER TWO

## The Appointment of the Higher Command for Operation 'Overlord' and the Evolution of the Revised Outline Plan

AT the end of 1943 President Roosevelt and Mr Churchill met in Cairo and subsequently went to Teheran to confer with Marshal Stalin. Following these meetings the announcement was made of the appointment of General Eisenhower as Supreme Allied Commander for 'Overlord', and in due course I was appointed Commander-in-Chief of 21 Army Group: which comprised the British and Canadian forces in the United Kingdom destined to take part in the operation.

On 1 January 1944 I handed over command of the Eighth Army and started my journey to England from the Sangro River airstrip in Italy. It was arranged that I should stop at Marrakech to visit Mr Churchill who was recuperating there from his recent attack of pneumonia. With him I found General Eisenhower. I was shown for the first time a copy of the Cossac plan for the invasion of France, and the Prime Minister asked for my comments. In the short time available I did no more than express the opinion that the initial assaulting forces were too weak for the task of breaking through the German coastal defences, and that the proposed frontage of assault was too narrow, having in mind the necessity to plan for rapid expansion of the bridgehead and for the speedy reception of the follow-up forces and subsequent build-up.

It was decided that on my arrival in England I should examine the Cossac plan in detail, together with the Naval and Air Commanders-in-Chief, with a view to recommending any changes or modifications considered necessary to ensure the success of the operation. The Supreme Commander was on his way to the United States, but his Chief of Staff, General Bedell Smith, came to London bearing a letter which instructed me to act on General Eisenhower's behalf during his absence.

The Commander-in-Chief of the Allied Naval Expeditionary Force was Admiral Sir Bertram Ramsay and of the Allied Expeditionary Air Force, Air Chief Marshal Sir Trafford Leigh-Mallory. There was no parallel appointment of Commander-in-Chief of the Allied land forces, but General Eisenhower decided that I should act in that capacity for the assault, and subsequently until the stage was reached in the development of our operations when a complete American Army Group could be deployed on the Continent. The assault was an operation requiring a single co-ordinated plan of action under one commander; I therefore became the overall land force commander responsible to the Supreme Commander for planning and executing the military aspect of the assault and subsequent capture of the lodgement area.

[153]

I arrived in England on 2 January 1944, and immediately started a detailed study of the Cossac plan. I formulated my views on the measures required to convert the project into a practical proposition with reasonable chances of success, and discussed them at length with Admiral Ramsay and Air Chief Marshal Leigh-Mallory. By 21 January, when the Supreme Commander held the first conference following his return from the United States, we were in agreement on a Revised Outline Plan, which General Eisenhower accepted.

The object of Operation 'Overlord' was 'to mount and carry out an operation, with forces and equipment established in the United Kingdom and with target date 1 May 1944, to secure a lodgement on the Continent from which further offensive operations could be developed. The lodgement area must contain sufficient port facilities to maintain a force of some twenty-six to thirty divisions and enable that force to be augmented by follow-up shipments from the United States or elsewhere of additional divisions and supporting units at the rate of three to five divisions per month'.

The first problem was to decide where to deliver the assault. The Allied forces had got to smash into the German 'Atlantic Wall' defences, gain a firm foothold and then secure port facilities, in order to build up sufficient strength and resources to carry the war into Germany.

The Cossac plan selected the area between Grandcamp and Caen, in the Baie de la Seine, for the assault. This area was known by the code name 'Neptune', to differentiate it from other possible sectors in which 'Overlord' might have been launched. The choice was made after exhaustive inter-service study of the 'invasion coast', which, by the factor of aircraft range for fighter cover from home bases, was limited to the sector between Flushing and Cherbourg. Consideration of the beach areas suitable for combined operations revealed that those offering the best conditions for passing vehicles and stores inland were, firstly, in the Pas de Calais area (between Gravelines and the River Somme) and secondly, in the Baie de la Seine (between the River Orne and the base of the Cotentin Peninsula).

The Pas de Calais area involved a shorter distance from home bases, and thus would have enabled us to develop optimum air support and would have given a quicker turn round for shipping; but the strongest enemy defences along the whole coast existed in this sector, which was also a focal area for hostile fighter aircraft disposed for defence. The Caen area was relatively lightly defended and afforded the great advantage of a coastline sheltered from prevailing winds.

The hinterland of the Baie de la Seine provided good terrain for airfield construction (especially south-east of Caen) and offered the choice of developing operations to secure the Seine ports or the Cherbourg–Brittany group. From the Pas de Calais the rapid seizure of adequate port facilities would have been more difficult, as the alternatives were the Channel ports proper, including Antwerp—which could be reached only after crossing a series of major river and canal obstacles—or the Seine ports, which lay some 150 miles to the south-west of the most suitable beach areas.

Obviously the development of the full Allied potential depended on securing ports;

the overriding consideration in the plan of operations once a bridgehead had been established, was the speed with which ports could be captured and opened for our shipping. Accordingly the Cossac plan recommended initially the seizure of Cherbourg and subsequently of the ports in the Brittany peninsula, including Nantes. The lodgement area therefore was to cover the Cotentin and Brittany peninsulas, and, in order to develop airfields, the area south-east of Caen. With these factors in mind, and in view of the need for space to assemble the forces required for the invasion of Germany, it was considered that the eastern flank of the lodgement area should be carried to the line of the River Eure and lower Seine, while the southern boundary was to follow the line of the Loire.

Until ports had been captured, reliance was to be placed on creating artificially sheltered berths by sinking specially built caissons and cargo ships in the Baie de la Seine, the projects for which went by the name of Mulberry (artificial harbours) and Gooseberry (breakwaters). The Cossac plan dismissed the possibility of the early capture of Cherbourg by assaulting the Cotentin peninsula, on the grounds that it would be easy for the enemy to block the base of the peninsula, and thus prevent further expansion of the bridgehead; the alternative of including beaches on the eastern side of the peninsula, as part of the frontage of assault, was also dismissed, as it was feared that the Carentan estuary and marshy country surrounding it would split our forces and render them liable to defeat in detail.

The operational plan of assault and subsequent development of operations was based on conjectural dispositions of enemy mobile reserve formations, on the basis of the maximum number regarded as acceptable if the project were to have a reasonable chance of success. Counting the coastal crust, it was assumed that we should encounter five enemy divisions on D-day, and that another seven would arrive in the beachhead area by D + 5. Of these twelve, five would be Panzer divisions.

The invasion forces were assumed to be provided with sufficient landing ships and craft to lift three assault divisions and two follow-up divisions, while two further divisions would be afloat on D-day in ships. The anticipated air lift for airborne forces was two-thirds of one division.

The plan therefore provided for an assault on a frontage of one corps of three divisions, and, assuming optimum weather conditions, the build-up by D + 5 was planned to ensure some nine divisions with a proportion of armour being available, exclusive of airborne troops. However, a study of weather conditions in the Channel in May over a number of years indicated that up to one day in four might be unsuitable for beach working. The effect of this might reduce our forces available on D + 5 to only seven divisions. Subsequent build-up was to be at the rate of one division per day (again assuming favourable weather) and the bridgehead was to be developed to the general line Trouville–Alençon–Mont St Michel by D + 14, by which time it was hoped to have completed the reduction of Cherbourg. Later staff studies indicated that this timing was probably very optimistic. Meanwhile the Cossac plan made certain reservations; the total number of enemy first line divisions immediately available in western Europe to reinforce Normandy was not to exceed twelve, and not more than an additional fifteen divisions should be moved into France from other theatres during the first two months after D-day.

The Cossac plan emphasized the vital necessity of reducing the effectiveness of the German Air Forces before undertaking the operation and also the reliance which had to be placed on the untried expedient of establishing artificially sheltered waters: since it would be necessary to rely on building up and maintaining our forces over the beaches for an appreciable period.

This was the plan which I first saw at Marrakech.

My immediate reaction was that to deliver a seaborne assault by one corps of only three divisions against the German Atlantic Wall as then constituted could hardly be considered a sound operation of war.

While accepting the suitability of the Baie de la Seine for the assault, I considered that the operation required to be mounted in greater strength and on a wider front. It was vital to secure an adequate bridgehead at the outset, so that operations could be developed from a firm and sufficiently spacious base; in any event the area we could hope to seize and hold in the first days of the invasion would become very congested. Experience in amphibious operations had shown me that if build-up arrangements and expansion from the landing beaches are to proceed smoothly, each corps and army to be employed in forming and developing the initial bridgehead must be allotted its own sector in the assault; it is unsound to aim at passing follow-up and build-up divisions of one corps through beachheads established by another, because confusion inevitably results together with delay in deployment at the vital time. Moreover the relatively narrow front of assault proposed in the Cossac plan appeared to me to give the enemy the opportunity of 'roping off' our forces quickly in a shallow covering position, in which the beaches would be under continuous artillery fire. An increased frontage would make it more difficult for the enemy to discover the extent of our operation and delay him in deciding the direction of our main axes of advance inland; at the same time we should have greater opportunity for finding and exploiting soft spots, and greater chances of locating adequate exit routes from the beaches for our transport. The latter problem was complicated by the coastal inundations which canalized the beach exits through a number of small villages.

Recognizing the vital importance of securing Cherbourg quickly, I felt that we should get a foothold in the Cotentin peninsula in the initial operation. The river lines and flooded marshy areas at the base of the peninsula might well enable the enemy to seal off our western flank even with minor forces, and thus render the capture of Cherbourg a difficult and lengthy operation. I therefore recommended increasing the frontage of assault to the west, to embrace beaches on the eastern side of the Cotentin peninsula, between Varreville and the Carentan estuary. If necessary the link-up across the estuary could be facilitated by the employment of airborne forces.

East of the River Orne, invading forces would come within range of the formidable coast defence batteries located in the Havre area and between Havre and Houlgate, and I therefore recommended that the invasion front should extend from the Varreville area to the River Orne. This frontage amounted to some fifty miles.

In deciding the degree to which the assault could be strengthened, the main factor was availability of craft and shipping, but in order to cover the front and facilitate organizing the operation on a frontage of two armies, I recommended invading on a five-divisional frontage, with two divisions in the immediate follow-up, and using at least two, and if possible three, airborne divisions: to be dropped prior to the actual seaborne assault.

It was desirable to acquire additional sea lift not only for the assault, but also for the subsequent build-up. As I saw the problem, we had to ensure that there would be adequate forces to withstand immediate counter attacks on D-day, and we also had to 'build-up' sufficiently rapidly to meet the first major co-ordinated counter attack: which I appreciated might develop on D + 4. Once we had established a footing on the Continent in spite of hostile attempts to hurl us back into the sea, the enemy would concentrate to deliver a properly staged thrust at some selected area. The Cossac plan envisaged five or six mobile enemy divisions being in action against the beachhead by D + 3, and it was essential that our own build-up should ensure that we had comparable forces ashore and ready for action on that day: bearing in mind that the assault divisions would by then be very tired and probably depleted.

The problem was whether the naval and air forces would be able to fall in with these revisions to the Cossac plan, and above all whether the additional craft and shipping could be found to make them possible. Air Chief Marshal Leigh-Mallory agreed to the modifications and from the point of view of the Air Forces there appeared to be no insoluble difficulties. But Admiral Ramsay showed that grave problems confronted the Allied Navies in the revised plan. The additional naval resources, assuming provision of craft, would create serious congestion of shipping on the south coast of England, affording a good target for hostile air action or rocket activity; the standard of training of the extra crews required would not be as high as that of the naval forces already organized for the invasion; the wider area of assault would increase the mine-sweeping commitment, as extra cross-Channel lanes would be required; and an increased naval bombarding commitment would be incurred for neutralizing the enemy coast defence batteries. The basic problem was provision of the necessary assault craft to transport the larger invasion force; this would have to be obtained from the Pacific, from the Mediterranean, from current production in Britain and the United States, or from a combination of these sources. If the target date could be extended to 31 May (instead of 1 May) craft production of an additional month would be available and the extra time would give the opportunity for improving the training of additional assault craft crews. Admiral Ramsay therefore favoured a revised target date.

On examination it was found that, even with an additional month's production, there would still be insufficient craft for the undertaking and it was thereupon suggested that additional resources should be made available for 'Overlord' from the

Mediterranean. To go back some time, an operation called 'Anvil' had been under consideration in the Mediterranean since the Casablanca Conference, having as its object the mounting of an assault on southern France, which was to link closely with the timing of the invasion of north-west Europe. The 'Anvil' assault was planned on a frontage of three—or at worst two—divisions and a corresponding proportion of available landing ships and craft had been allocated to the Central Mediterranean theatre.

The Supreme Commander regarded 'Anvil' as an important contribution to 'Overlord', for it was to contain enemy forces in southern France; but he advised the Combined Chiefs of Staff that he regarded 'Overlord' as first priority, and that if insufficient naval resources were available for both operations he considered 'Anvil' should be postponed or reduced to a one-division assault: to be delivered when enemy weakness justified its implementation.

The major factors affecting the provision of craft for 'Overlord' were thus the question of extending the target date and the postponement or reduction in scope of Operation 'Anvil'.

Apart from naval considerations, the advance of the target date to 31 May afforded a longer period for the strategic bombing offensive on Germany: for the effective completion of the programme for reducing the enemy's railway potential, and for destroying the major bridges on his communications in western Europe. Moreover it appeared likely that weather conditions at the end of May would be more likely to favour the mounting of a large-scale Russian offensive which would assist 'Overlord'; and in the Mediterranean the situation might be sufficiently resolved to exclude the necessity for 'Anvil', in that our forces in Italy might have drawn the available German reserve divisions in southern Europe into that country. The Supreme Commander was averse to any postponement if it could be avoided but, when there appeared to be no alternative, he recommended to the Combined Chiefs of Staff that 'Overlord' should be mounted with a target date not later than 31 May. The Combined Chiefs of Staff agreed to this on 1 February, and at the time General Eisenhower made the reservation to them that the exact date of assault be left open pending detailed study of moonlight and tidal conditions prevailing during the first week of June.

The decision to provide extra craft for 'Overlord' at the expense of 'Anvil' was not taken immediately, but eventually the Combined Chiefs of Staff agreed to General Eisenhower's recommendations and confirmed that the additional craft required would be found from the Mediterranean. 'Anvil' was postponed and indeed did not finally take place until August 1944.

I have already mentioned that the Cossac plan assumed an air lift for only two-thirds of an airborne division; this lift was to be used on D-day for a descent on Caen. It was evident that airborne forces could play an extremely important role in the assault, and it seemed unfortunate that such a small lift should be at our disposal when there would be three or four airborne divisions available for operations on D-day. Extension of the invasion frontage to the base of the Cotentin peninsula resulted in increased commitments for airborne forces, as they were required on the western flank to ensure the capture of the causeways leading across the inundations behind the assault beaches. The Supreme Commander strongly supported the need for additional air lift and, as a result of his recommendations, the availability of transport aircraft and gliders was materially increased. The extension of the target date helped in this matter, for the extra time made it possible to concentrate more aircraft and to train additional crews.

I will discuss my plan for the development of operations in a later chapter. The task was, as in the Cossac plan, to secure Cherbourg and the Brittany group of ports, and to establish the lodgement area.

At the conference on 21 January, General Eisenhower approved the revisions to the Cossac plan and recommended their adoption to the Combined Chiefs of Staff. As time was already short for completion of all the detailed staff work required for such a great undertaking, he ordered that planning be undertaken at once on the basis of the revised plan.

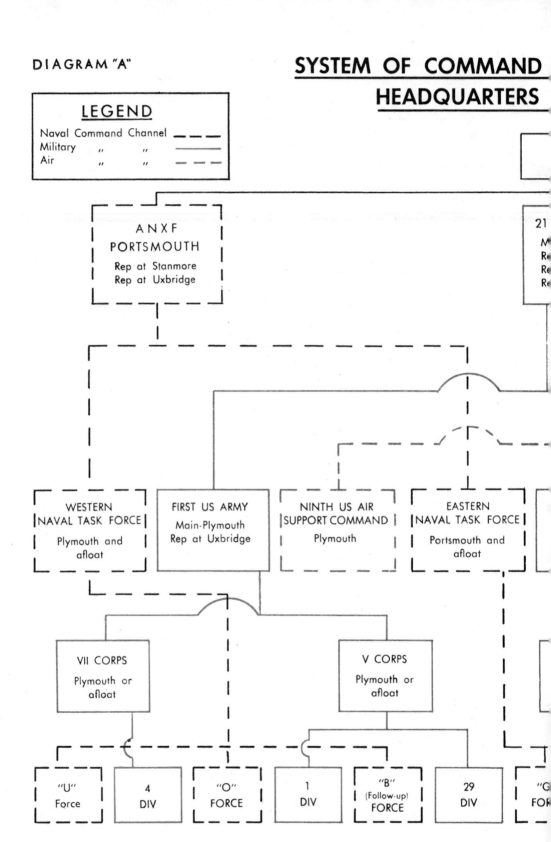

# OCATION OF PRINCIPAL
# ASSAULT PHASE

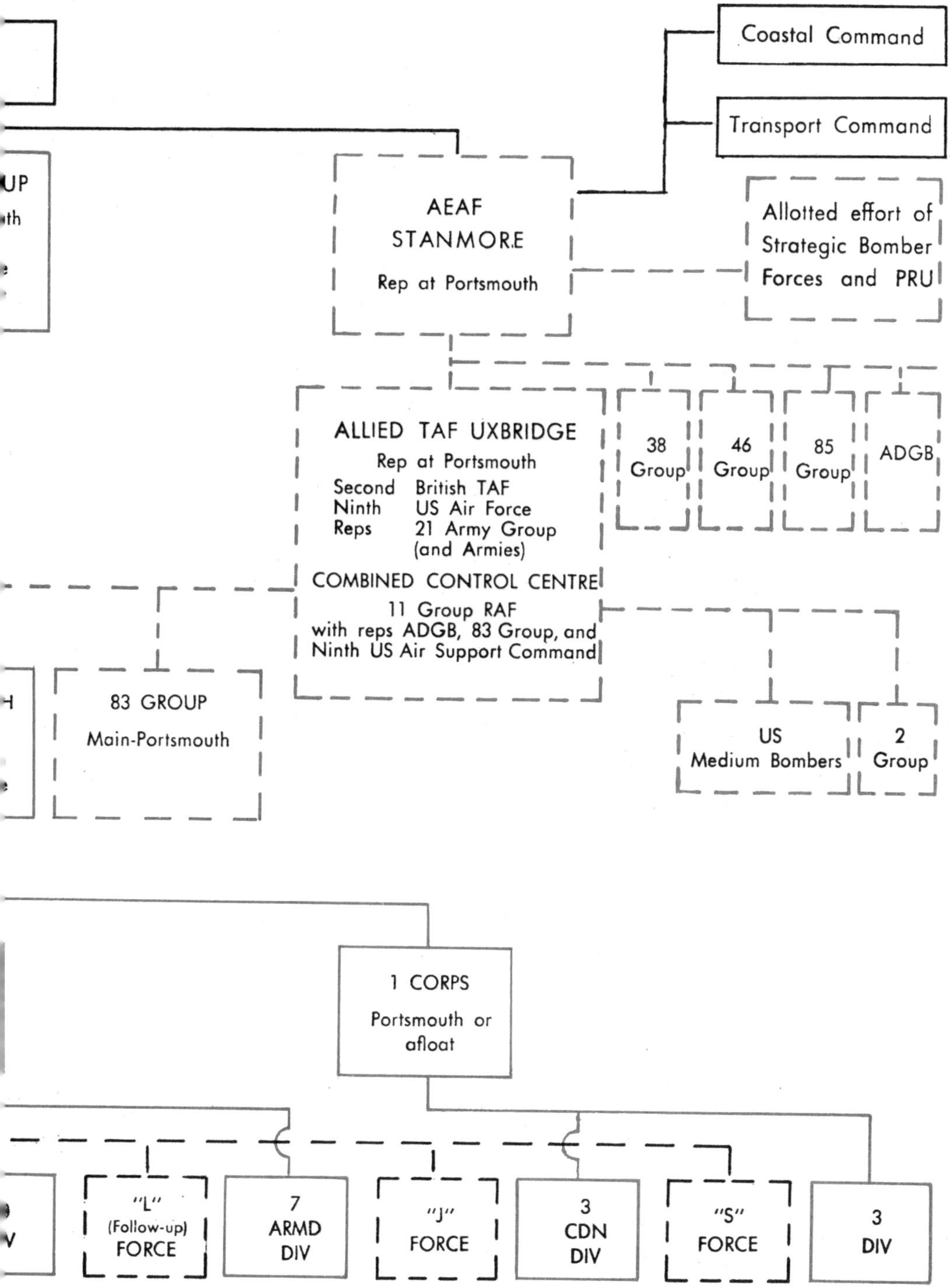
Coastal Command
Transport Command
AEAF
STANMORE
Rep at Portsmouth
Allotted effort of
Strategic Bomber
Forces and PRU
ALLIED TAF UXBRIDGE
Rep at Portsmouth
Second British TAF
Ninth US Air Force
Reps 21 Army Group
(and Armies)
COMBINED CONTROL CENTRE
11 Group RAF
with reps ADGB, 83 Group, and
Ninth US Air Support Command
38
Group
46
Group
85
Group
ADGB
83 GROUP
Main-Portsmouth
US
Medium Bombers
2
Group
1 CORPS
Portsmouth or
afloat
"L"
(Follow-up)
FORCE
7
ARMD
DIV
"J"
FORCE
3
CDN
DIV
"S"
FORCE
3
DIV

# CHAPTER THREE

## *The Inter-Service Organization for 'Overlord' and the Order of Battle of the Invasion Forces*

GENERAL EISENHOWER set up his headquarters, called Supreme Headquarters, Allied Expeditionary Force (SHAEF), at Bushey Park. My own headquarters was located at St Paul's School in West Kensington, while the Allied Naval and Air Forces headquarters were both at Norfolk House in St James's Square.

Admiral Ramsay, Air Chief Marshal Leigh-Mallory and myself were jointly charged with planning and executing the assault and initial development of the lodgement area. Our respective staffs were closely associated in the production of the detailed plans and directives which guided the planning of our subordinate formations. On 1 February we presented for the Supreme Commander's approval an 'Initial Joint Plan', which provided the basis for planning the operation. Subsequently the Armies, with their associated naval and air force authorities, produced detailed plans of action, and the whole planning period culminated in the 'Presentation of the Plans' Exercise, staged in London on 7 April 1944, when commanders of the three Services explained their intentions and examination was made of the whole project. Subsequently the joint Commanders-in-Chief presented their final plans to the Supreme Commander.

My orders provided for an assault on a frontage of two armies, First United States Army on the right, employing two divisions, and Second British Army on the left, with three divisions. This arrangement of forces placed the American troops on the Atlantic flank, as they would ultimately be maintained direct from the United States. In conformity with this organization, the associated naval forces were organized into the Western Task Force working with First United States Army and the Eastern Task Force which was allied to Second British Army. These Task Forces were in turn divided into seven forces, one for each of the assault and follow-up divisions. The Eastern Naval Task Force comprised Forces S, G and J, with Force L as its follow-up; the Western Naval Task Force had Forces O and U in the assault, and Force B in the follow-up. The lettering of these Force designations corresponded (in the assault echelons) to the code-marking of the beach areas they were to attack.

Ninth United States Air Force planned with First United States Army, while Second British Army worked with Second Tactical Air Force, RAF.

The troops under my operational control comprised 21 Army Group and First United States Army (General Omar N. Bradley). The outline Order of Battle is shown in the following chart, from which it will be seen that 21 Army Group comprised First Canadian Army (Lieutenant-General Crerar), Second British Army (Lieutenant-

1. Invasion craft as seen from the French coast on D-day. 6 June 1944.

2. Bren carriers of the 50th Division landing on D-day. 6 June 1944.

3. Some enemy defences that failed: these wooden posts set in concrete were topped with Tellermines and were just submerged at high tide. The Allied landings were near low tide and the obstacles were clearly visible.

4. Vehicles leaving an L.S.T. 7 June 1944.

General Dempsey), the British Airborne Troops (Lieutenant-General Browning), and the various Allied contingents. Attached to First United States Army were the American 82 and 101 Airborne Divisions.

It was General Eisenhower's intention to assume direct command of the land forces on the Continent when the growing build-up of the American forces had led to the deployment of an American Army Group in the field. No definite period was stipulated for this, but Headquarters Twelve United States Army Group were formed in London and prepared to take command of First and Third United States Armies at the appropriate time. Meanwhile I became responsible for co-ordinating the planning of Twelfth United States Army Group with a view to ensuring that there would be no interruption in the general conduct of operations when it took the field. Within the scope of this co-ordination were included plans made by Twelfth United States Army Group for introducing Third United States Army into the Continent.

In view of my responsibility towards United States forces I arranged with General Bradley for a proportion of American officers to join Headquarters 21 Army Group, to assist in the detailed planning, to ensure smooth and efficient liaison with the United States formations, to advise on the framing of orders and instructions having in mind the difference between the organization and staff procedure of the two Armies, and to take their share in the staff work of the operation until the American Army Group became operational. On the General Staff side the staffs were integrated, but the difference in the administrative systems of the two Armies proved so great that it was found preferable to attach a self-contained American administrative echelon to 21 Army Group. The American Brigadier-General in charge was appointed deputy to my Chief Administrative Officer (CAO) and the two staffs worked side by side so that their planning marched in step. Under the general co-ordination of 21 Army Group, First United States Army was responsible for its own detailed administrative planning, while longer term projects were handled by Twelfth United States Army Group. These arrangements proved eminently satisfactory and I would like to pay tribute to the knowledge, efficiency and adaptability of the American officers who served with 21 Army Group staff.

I made a number of changes in 21 Army Group staff proper in order to introduce officers who had already had considerable experience in the field. I brought back from Italy a number of senior staff officers, including my Chief of Staff, Major-General de Guingand.

During the later planning stages some difficulties arose over the so-called 'levels' of command between the army and air forces authorities. As long as 21 Army Group was responsible for overall direction of the land battle, the appropriate air headquarters with which planning was conducted was Allied Expeditionary Air Forces; but when two Army Groups were later deployed under SHAEF, Headquarters Second Tactical Air Force was to become our associated air command. Longer term planning therefore suffered delays because co-ordination with two separate air force authorities was required.

# OUTLINE ORDER OF BATTLE - 21

**21 ARMY**

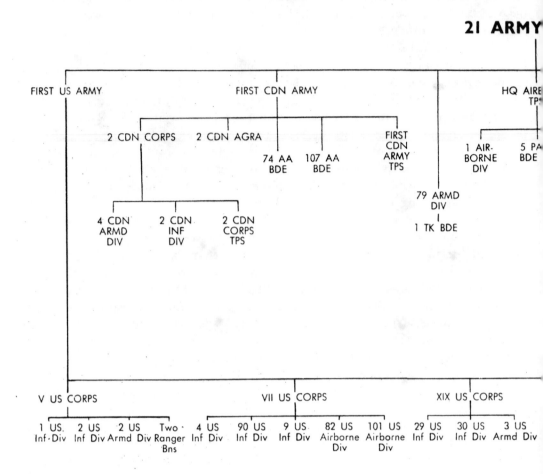

FIRST US ARMY

FIRST CDN ARMY

HQ AIRE
TP?

2 CDN CORPS — 2 CDN AGRA

74 AA BDE — 107 AA BDE

FIRST CDN ARMY TPS

1 AIR-BORNE DIV — 5 PA
BDE

79 ARMD DIV
|
1 TK BDE

4 CDN ARMD DIV — 2 CDN INF DIV — 2 CDN CORPS TPS

V US CORPS

1 US. Inf·Div — 2 US Inf Div — 2 US Armd Div — Two Ranger Bns

VII US CORPS

4 US Inf Div — 90 US Inf Div — 9 US Inf Div — 82 US Airborne Div — 101 US Airborne Div

XIX US CORPS

29 US Inf Div — 30 US Inf Div — 3 US Armd Div

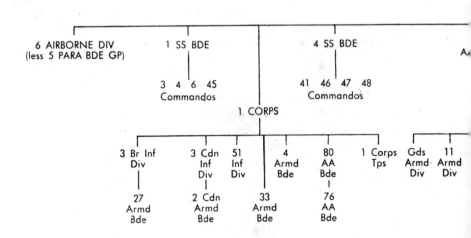

6 AIRBORNE DIV
(less 5 PARA BDE GP)

1 SS BDE

3  4  6  45
Commandos

4 SS BDE

41  46  47  48
Commandos

1 CORPS

3 Br Inf Div
|
27 Armd Bde

3 Cdn Inf Div
|
2 Cdn Armd Bde

51 Inf Div

4 Armd Bde
|
33 Armd Bde

80 AA Bde
|
76 AA Bde

1 Corps Tps

Gds Armd Div — 11 Armd Div

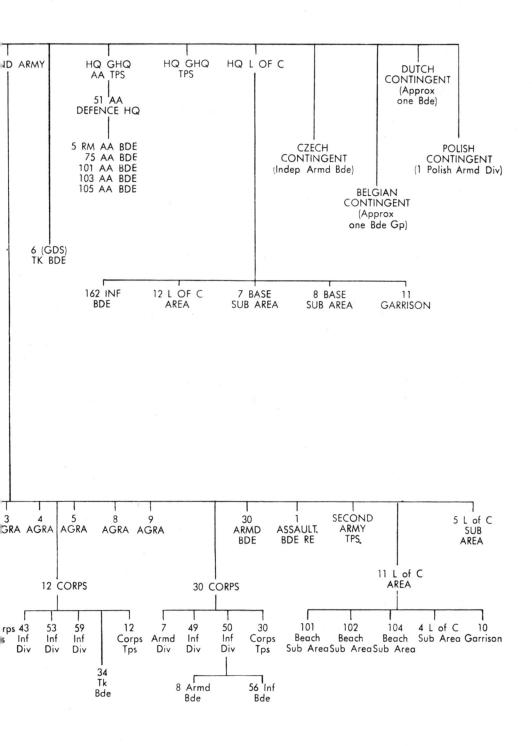

ND ARMY

HQ GHQ
AA TPS

51 AA
DEFENCE HQ

5 RM AA BDE
75 AA BDE
101 AA BDE
103 AA BDE
105 AA BDE

HQ GHQ
TPS

HQ L OF C

DUTCH
CONTINGENT
(Approx
one Bde)

CZECH
CONTINGENT
(Indep Armd Bde)

POLISH
CONTINGENT
(1 Polish Armd Div)

BELGIAN
CONTINGENT
(Approx
one Bde Gp)

6 (GDS)
TK BDE

162 INF
BDE

12 L OF C
AREA

7 BASE
SUB AREA

8 BASE
SUB AREA

11
GARRISON

3
GRA AGRA

4
AGRA

5
AGRA

8
AGRA

9
AGRA

30
ARMD
BDE

1
ASSAULT.
BDE RE

SECOND
ARMY
TPS.

5 L of C
SUB
AREA

12 CORPS

30 CORPS

11 L of C
AREA

rps 43
Inf
Div

53
Inf
Div

59
Inf
Div

12
Corps
Tps

7
Armd
Div

49
Inf
Div

50
Inf
Div

30
Corps
Tps

101
Beach
Sub Area

102
Beach
Sub Area

104
Beach
Sub Area

4 L of C
Sub Area

10
Garrison

34
Tk
Bde

8 Armd
Bde

56 Inf
Bde

It should be remembered that the highly complex Anglo-American organization set up for launching 'Overlord' had little more than five months for the completion of its task, from the time the higher command was finally settled. Events have amply shown that a splendid spirit of co-operation was established between the British and American services, and that under General Eisenhower a strong, loyal team was quickly brought into being, while the various components of the great invasion force were welded into a fine fighting machine.

CHAPTER FOUR

# The Plan

THE Initial Plan has been mentioned as forming the basis for the detailed planning of Operation 'Overlord'. For my part, I will show that the basic principles of my plan for delivering the assault and for the subsequent development of operations were decided upon early in the planning stage, and these were never altered or modified but were carried through relentlessly to a successful conclusion. In matters of detail, however, the plan was subject to seemingly endless alterations and amendments which continued until the last moment before D-day. This was inevitable because, to take a primary example, the situation concerning the enemy forces in western Europe and the strength and organization of the Atlantic Wall defences were developing through the planning period. Again, uncertainty about the precise availability by types of the various landing craft persisted for a considerable period and had repercussions on the detailed planning of all subordinate formations: down to the actual assaulting units.

In describing the plan I shall indicate the final D-day version, and the factors which were known to us at that time, though in some matters it may be of interest to describe the changing circumstances which made amendments to the plan necessary.

### BASIC CONCEPTION OF THE ARMY PLAN

The intention for Operation 'Overlord' was to assault, simultaneously, beaches on the Normandy coast immediately north of the Carentan estuary and between the Carentan estuary and the River Orne, with the object of securing as a base for further operations a lodgement area which was to include airfield sites, the port of Cherbourg and the ports of Brittany.

To achieve this task I decided upon the plan of the land battle and subsequently explained it myself to the General Officers of the Field Armies in London on 7 April 1944.

Once ashore and firmly established, my plan was to threaten to break out of the initial bridgehead on the eastern flank—that is, in the Caen sector. I intended by means of this threat to draw the main enemy reserves into that sector, to fight them there and keep them there, using the British and Canadian armies for the purpose. Having got the main enemy reserves committed on the eastern flank, my plan was to make the break-out on the western flank, using for this task the American armies under General Bradley, and to pivot the whole front on Caen. The American break-out thrust was to be delivered southwards down to the Loire and then to be developed eastwards in a wide sweep up to the Seine about Paris. This movement was designed

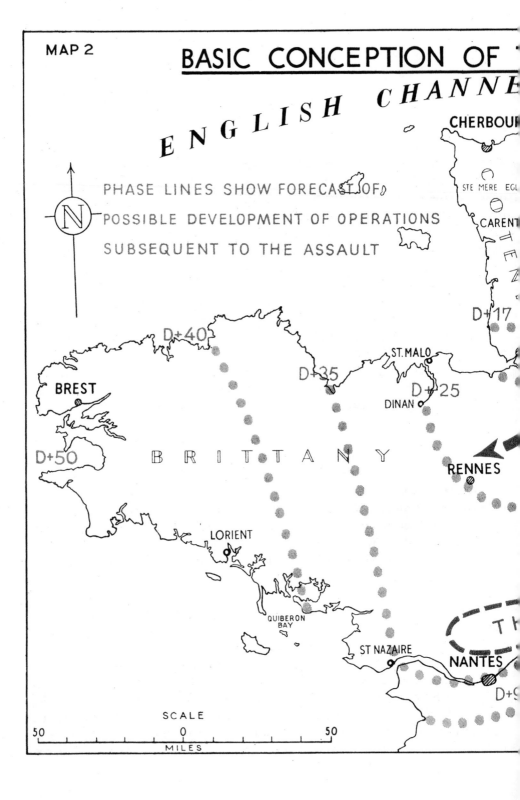

MAP 2

BASIC CONCEPTION OF T

ENGLISH CHANNE

CHERBOUR

PHASE LINES SHOW FORECAST OF

POSSIBLE DEVELOPMENT OF OPERATIONS

SUBSEQUENT TO THE ASSAULT

STE MERE EGL

CARENT

D+17

D+40

ST.MALO

D+35

D+25

BREST

DINAN

D+50

B R I T T A N Y

RENNES

LORIENT

QUIBERON
BAY

T

ST NAZAIRE

NANTES

D+9

SCALE

50          0          50

MILES

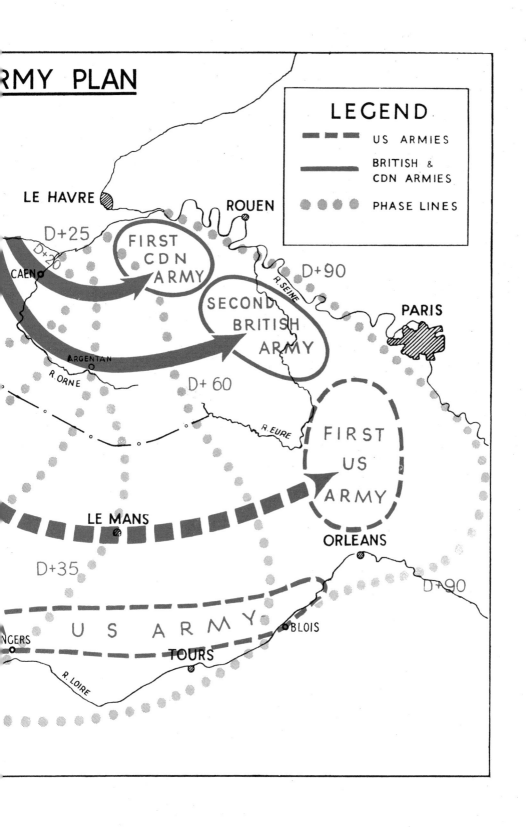

# RMY PLAN

**LEGEND**

- – – – US ARMIES
- —— BRITISH & CDN ARMIES
- •••• PHASE LINES

LE HAVRE

ROUEN

D+25

D+20

CAEN

FIRST CDN ARMY

D+90

R. SEINE

SECOND BRITISH ARMY

PARIS

ARGENTAN

R. ORNE

D+60

R. EURE

FIRST US ARMY

LE MANS

ORLEANS

D+35

D+90

US ARMY

BLOIS

NGERS

TOURS

R. LOIRE

to cut off all the enemy forces south of the Seine, over which river the bridges were to be destroyed by air action.

This strategy was evolved from consideration primarily of the layout of enemy reserve formations in western Europe, the run of rail and road communications leading to Normandy and the immediate task of the operation: which was to secure ports. The capture of the Cotentin and Brittany peninsulas and the opening of the ports located in them meant that we required to make rapid territorial gains in the west; on the eastern flank, acquisition of ground was not so pressing providing the air force requirements for airfield construction could be met. This pointed to the need for breaking out on the American front. If in turn the expansion in the west were to proceed rapidly, we had to draw the enemy weight from that flank and in this we were greatly assisted by the immense strategic importance of Caen.

The city of Caen was a vital road and rail communication centre through which the main routes from the east and south-east passed. Since the bulk of the enemy mobile reserves was located north of the Seine they would have to approach Normandy from the east and might be expected to converge on Caen. Hence if a major threat to the enemy containing forces could be developed and sustained in the Caen sector, his reserves would tend to become initially committed there.

It was to be expected that the enemy would react strongly to an advance on Caen; such a course would indicate to him our intentions to break through the Caen bottle-neck in order to exploit our armoured resources in the more open country to the south-east. This direction would moreover give us the shortest approach to the Seine ports and Paris.

These arguments convinced me that strong and persistent offensive action in the Caen sector would achieve our object of drawing the enemy mobile reserves on to our eastern flank.

This was my original conception of the manner in which the Battle of Normandy was to be developed. From the start it formed the basis of all our planning and was the aim of our operations from the time of the assault to the final victory in Normandy. I never once had cause or reason to alter my plan. In order to understand the Battle of Normandy, it is essential that this fact should be clearly appreciated.

The German commander in France and the Low Countries was Field-Marshal von Rundstedt; his title was Commander-in-Chief West. Under his command were two Army Groups: the larger, comprising more than two-thirds of the operational troops available, was Army Group 'B', commanded by Field-Marshal Rommel, which consisted of Seventh Army (Normandy and Brittany), Fifteenth Army (Pas de Calais and Flanders) and 88 Corps (Holland). Rommel was appointed to this command in February 1944 at the direct instance of Hitler. It was his first operational command since he had left Tunisia, nearly a year previously.

Army Group 'G', commanded by Blaskowitz, had the First and Nineteenth Armies, stationed on the Biscay coast and in the Riviera respectively.

There was a third headquarters in France of Army Group status, called Panzer

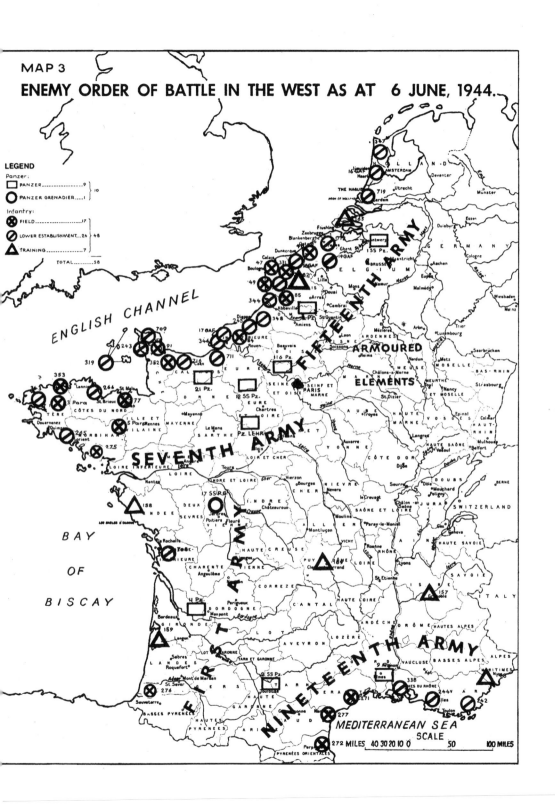

MAP 3

# ENEMY ORDER OF BATTLE IN THE WEST AS AT 6 JUNE, 1944.

Group West under General Schweppenburg. It was responsible for the administration and training of the Panzer formations while they were operationally under command of the other Army Groups. It was originally intended to command them in battle. This system later led to some confusion in the handling of the enemy armour.

These Army Groups at D-day comprised some sixty divisions, or about one quarter of the field force of the German Army. From the end of 1943 their strength was conserved, and even increased, in anticipation of the Second Front, and in spite of losses in Italy and Russia. The only formation which left the theatre in 1944 was an SS Corps, which was despatched to Russia in April, but returned to Normandy within two months.

There was considerable variation in the quality of the German divisions in the west. The equipment, training and morale of the SS and Panzer divisions was of the highest order; the infantry formations varied from low quality static coast defence troops to fully established field formations of normal German type.

For several years the Germans had been developing the coastal defence organization, which was known collectively as the 'Atlantic Wall'. The enemy assumed that an invader would have to secure a port either in the initial assault, or very quickly afterwards, in order to land the heaviest types of equipment and organize maintenance and supply. Port areas were therefore given first priority for defence, and by 1944 had become virtually impregnable to seaward assault. After the ports, attention was turned to the Pas de Calais which bordered the narrowest part of the Channel and was considered the most likely area we would choose for the assault.

Elsewhere defences were on a less organized scale, for by the beginning of 1944 the enemy had not had the resources or transport to put the whole coast line in a uniform state of defence. From March 1944, however, there was a most noticeable intensification of the defences in Normandy, following a tour of inspection by Rommel.

The coastal defence of the Baie de la Seine was based on a system of linear defences, arranged in strong points which were manned chiefly by static coastal troops of low category. The gun positions and localities were protected by concrete and armour from naval gunfire and air attack, and extensive use had been made of minefields, wire entanglements and obstacles to strengthen the layout. Extensive flooding of the low-lying areas in the coastal belt had been effected particularly in the marshy country round the Carentan estuary. Existing sea walls had been strengthened and prolonged to form anti-tank obstacles behind the beaches, which themselves were extensively mined. On the beaches and extending over varying distances below high water mark were belts of under-water obstacles, the purpose of which was to halt and impale landing craft and to destroy or cripple them by means of explosive charges attached to the individual obstacles; types of under-water obstacles included 'Element C' with Tellermines on the forward face, the ramp type wooden obstacle with Tellermines at the top of the ramp, wooden posts with Tellermines attached, steel hedgehogs and steel tetrahedra.

The enemy artillery defence consisted of long range coast artillery and field artillery.

The former was sited well forward, covering in particular the entrances to Cherbourg, the Carentan estuary and the Seine. Heavy gun batteries located in the Cherbourg area and round Le Havre almost overlapped in range and presented the gravest danger to the approach of all large vessels to the transport area off the Normandy beaches. Behind the coast artillery, some two or three miles inland, field and medium artillery units of the divisions occupying the coastal sectors were sited; the task of these guns was to bring fire to bear on craft approaching the beaches and on to the beaches themselves. In all there were some thirty-two located battery positions capable of firing on the assault beach areas.

After Rommel's inspection there was an acceleration in the construction of under-water obstacles and these were developed at increasing distances below high water mark; the number of coastal batteries increased and the construction of casemates and overhead cover was undertaken on a wider scale. Flooding became more extensive. Anti air-landing obstacles commenced to appear on our air photographs in the most suitable dropping and landing areas; they consisted of vertical poles and stakes, and in some cases were fitted with booby traps.

The enemy dispositions in the west up to D-day are shown on the map. They reflect the conflict of opinion between Rommel and von Rundstedt on the manner in which invading forces should be dealt with. Rommel, who was no strategist, favoured a plan for the total repulse of an invader on the beaches; his theory was to aim at halting the hostile forces in the immediate beach area by concentrating a great volume of fire on the beaches themselves and to seaward of them; he advocated thickening up the beach defences and the positioning of all available reserves near the coast. Von Rundstedt on the other hand, favoured the 'crust–cushion–hammer' plan; this implied a 'crust' of infantry manning the coast line, with a 'cushion' of infantry divisions in tactical reserve close in rear, and a 'hammer' of armoured forces in strategic reserve further inland. The cushion was designed to contain enemy forces which penetrated the crust, and the hammer was available for launching decisive counter attacks as required. These differing theories led to a compromise; the armoured reserves were generally kept well back, but the majority of the infantry divisions was committed to strengthening the crust. The result was that, in the event, the Panzer divisions were forced to engage us prematurely and were unable to concentrate to deliver a co-ordinated blow: until it was too late.

In the Neptune sector we anticipated an enemy garrison of three coast defence divisions supported by four reserve divisions, of which one was of the Panzer type. In the last weeks before D-day, however, we had indications that some redistribution of enemy forces was taking place in France, but in the event our appreciation of the resistance proved substantially correct.

The estimated rate of enemy build-up and the probable development of his defensive strategy were constantly reviewed during the planning period. The speed of con-centration of enemy reserves was largely dependent on the success of our air operations designed to reduce his mobility, together with the effect of sabotage activities of the

French Resistance organization. Events showed that we achieved a degree of success in this direction far greater than we had hoped. At this stage of the planning, it was estimated that the enemy could concentrate up to twenty divisions (including eight Panzer divisions), in the Normandy area by D+6. This contrasted with the earlier Cossac estimate of twelve divisions. By D+20, under the worst conditions for ourselves, we might expect opposition from some twenty-five to thirty divisions, of which nine or ten would be armoured formations. We had to anticipate the possibility of the enemy having up to fifty divisions in action by D+60.

We appreciated that the Germans would be alerted in the Neptune area on the night D—1 as our seaborne forces approached the Normandy coast, and that by the end of D-day the enemy would himself have appreciated that 'Overlord' was a major operation delivered in strength. In accordance with his policy of defeating us on the beaches, it was to be expected that he would summon initially the nearest available armoured and motorized divisions to oppose us, and that in the first stages we should have to meet immediate counter attacks designed to push us back into the sea. Having failed in his purpose we appreciated that the enemy would concentrate his forces for major co-ordinated counter attacks in selected areas; these might develop about D+4 or D+5, by when it was estimated that he might have in action against us some six Panzer divisions. By D+8 it was reasonable to suppose that, having failed to dislodge us from the beaches, the enemy would begin to adopt a policy of attempting to cordon off our forces and prevent expansion of the bridgehead. For this he would require to bring up infantry in order to relieve his armoured formations, which would then be concentrated for a full-out counter stroke. We had to expect, then, an initial concentration against the bridgehead of armoured and motorized divisions, followed by the arrival of infantry formations.

There were encouraging factors in the Intelligence appreciations in April and May. Whereas in January 1944 it had been appreciated that within two months of the start of 'Overlord' the enemy would be able to move as many as fifteen divisions into western Europe from other theatres, the corresponding estimate in April was six, as a result of the mounting successes of the Soviet forces on the Eastern Front and of events in Italy. By D-day the Allies had captured Rome and Kesselring's forces in Italy were in retreat, while in Russia the Crimea had been cleared and the Germans were nervously predicting an all-out Russian offensive. Identifications on the Eastern Front and in Italy received in the immediate pre-D-day period gave an increasingly encouraging picture of absorption of German armour on fronts other than our own.

## TOPOGRAPHY

The inundations behind the selected beach areas, and particularly in the Varreville sector at the base of the Cotentin peninsula, created a grave problem in ensuring the creation of adequate exits from the beach areas to the hinterland. In the Varreville sector it was of the utmost importance for us to secure the causeways across the flooded areas if we were to avoid being pinned by relatively minor enemy forces to the very narrow beach strip. In the Vierville–Caen sector beach exits tended to canalize through small coastal villages, which were in a state of defence and had been provided with extensive obstacles. They would require speedy clearance by our assaulting troops. The system of water lines, inundations and marshes behind the Carentan estuary was extensive and there were few available routes crossing these barriers; the seizure of these routes intact was of the utmost importance.

The hinterland behind the beaches generally favoured defensive tactics and was on the whole unsuitable for the deployment of armoured forces.

Apart from the open rolling plain to the south-east of Caen, the area was covered to a depth of up to forty miles inland by 'bocage'—pasture land divided by unusually high hedges, banks and ditches into many small fields and meadows. In such conditions, observation was extremely limited, and movement off the road defiles was very restricted: not only for wheeled transport, but often for tanks. On the other hand it was ideal infantry country; there was excellent concealment for snipers and patrols, while defensive positions dug into the banks were well protected from tanks and artillery.

The Normandy highlands ran from south-east to north-west across the invasion frontage, at a depth of up to twenty-five miles inland. The country was broken and irregular in parts, with steep hills and narrow valleys. The dominating feature of the northern ridge was Mont Pinçon, some eighteen miles south-west of Caen.

### PRELIMINARY OPERATIONS

In the broad strategic sense, preparations for the invasion of north-west Europe began at sea and in the air many months before D-day. Winning the Battle of the Atlantic was essential to ensure the passage of the vast volume of personnel and stores from America and Canada to the battle front. The strategic air offensive against Germany had a vital effect on the war by strangling the whole economic structure of the country.

We are here concerned, however, with the more directly military aspect of preparatory air operations which paved the way for the assault on Normandy.

An essential preliminary to the assault was the reduction of the German Air Force to the degree required to ensure mastery in the air over our seaborne forces in the Channel and over the beaches on the invasion coast. The next army requirement was the interdiction of rail and road communications, with the object of delaying the movement of enemy troops and supplies to the battle area. We also wanted to mislead the enemy about the sector selected for the assault and, lastly, to pave the way for our actual landing operation by pre-D-day air attacks against coast defences and installations. Other preliminary air tasks of direct importance to the army were the flying of reconnaissance missions over a wide area, and the prevention of enemy reconnaissance over our centres of concentration and embarkation.

So admirably were these commitments carried out by the Air Forces that we were afforded immunity from enemy air reconnaissance during the vital period, a factor

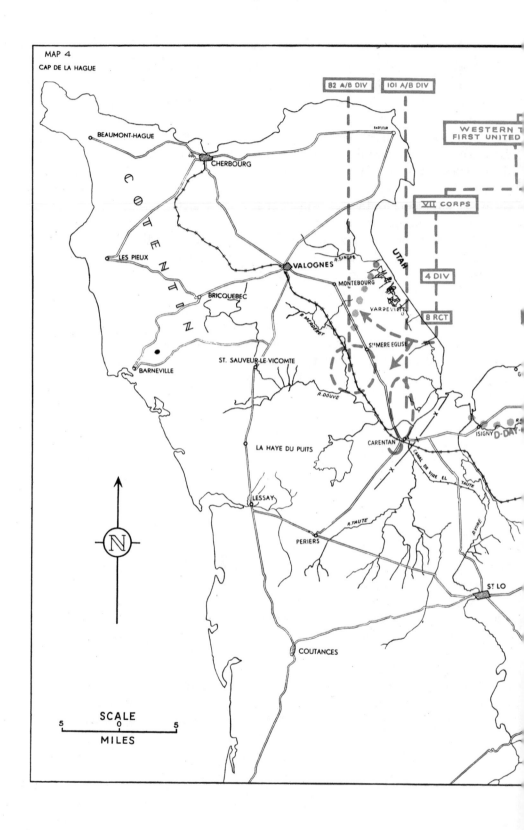

MAP 4

CAP DE LA HAGUE

82 A/B DIV    101 A/B DIV

WESTERN T
FIRST UNITED

BEAUMONT-HAGUE

BARFLEUR

CHERBOURG

VII CORPS

C O T E N T I N

LES PIEUX

R. SINOPE

UTAH

VALOGNES

4 DIV

MONTEBOURG

BRICQUEBEC

VARREVILLE

8 RCT

R. MERDERET

ST. SAUVEUR-LE-VICOMTE

STᵐᴱMERE EGLISE

BARNEVILLE

R. DOUVE

ISIGNY  D-DAY

LA HAYE DU PUITS

CARENTAN

CANAL DE VIRE EL

TAUTE

LESSAY

R. TAUTE

R. VIRE

N

PERIERS

ST LO

SCALE
5    0    5

MILES

COUTANCES

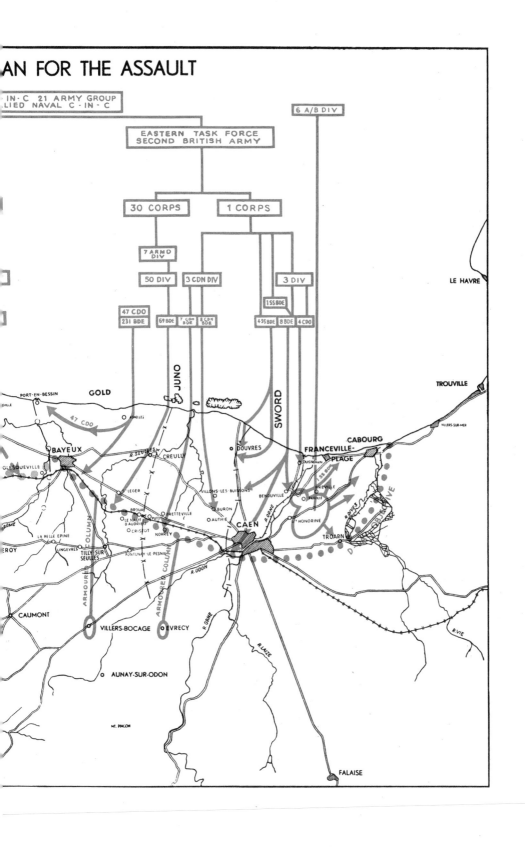

# AN FOR THE ASSAULT

EASTERN TASK FORCE
SECOND BRITISH ARMY

6 A/B DIV

30 CORPS

1 CORPS

7 ARMD DIV

50 DIV

3 CDN DIV

3 DIV

1 SS BDE

47 CDO
231 BDE

69 BDE

7 CDN BDE

8 CDN BDE

4 SS BDE

8 BDE

4 CDO

GOLD

JUNO

SWORD

LE HAVRE

TROUVILLE

PORT-EN-BESSIN

VILLERS-SUR-MER

47 CDO

BAYEUX

R SEULLES

CREULLY

DOUVRES

CABOURG

FRANCEVILLE-PLAGE

OUISTREHAM

GLESQUEVILLE

ST LEGER

VILLONS-LES-BUISSONS

BENDUVILLE

RANVILLE

VALLE

BROUAY

PUTOT

BRETTEVILLE

BURON

BREVILLE

ROME

LE HAUT D'AUDRIEU

CRISBOT

AUTHIE

R ORNE

HONORINE

CAEN

TROARN

LA BELLE EPINE

NORREY

EROY

LINGEVRES

TILLY SUR SEULLES

FONTENAY-LE-PESNIL

R ODON

ARMOURED COLUMN

ARMOURED COLUMN

CAUMONT

VILLERS-BOCAGE

EVRECY

R ORNE

R LAIZE

R VIE

AUNAY-SUR-ODON

MT. PINCON

FALAISE

of first importance in the design for achieving tactical surprise in our assault operation; moreover, not one single attack was carried out by the German Air Force on the assault forces during the sea passage or at any time on the beaches during D-day.

The interdiction of rail communications was effected as a result of a detailed plan for destroying the servicing and repair facilities which were essential for the operation of railways in northern and western France, the Low Countries and western Germany. In full operation by D−60, the programme brought attacks closer to the Neptune area as time grew shorter, and the result was a shortage of locomotives and stock, repair facilities and coal over a wide area, while seventy-four bridges and tunnels on routes leading to the battle area were impassable on D-day. Reports on 7 June showed that all railway bridges over the Seine between Paris and the sea were impassable, and also those on the lower section of the Loire. Road bridges were also attacked with most successful results; the thirteen bridges between Paris and the Channel, and the five main road bridges between Orleans and Nantes, were either destroyed or damaged.

Attacks prior to D-day on coast defence batteries in the Neptune area were worked into an overall plan of action against the whole length of the invasion coast, in order to mislead the enemy about our intentions. These operations retarded the construction of overhead cover for major batteries covering the Baie de la Seine, and at the same time served to increase the enemy's fears that we were intending to assault in the Pas de Calais: astride Cap Gris Nez. This was a matter of first importance in our plans.

Preliminary naval operations included sweeps against enemy U-boats, R-boats and E-boats, and minelaying designed to afford protection to the sea passage across the Channel.

### THE ASSAULT

The overall plan of assault was designed to concentrate the full weight of the available resources of all three Services in getting the assaulting troops ashore and in assisting them in their task of breaking through the Atlantic Wall.

First United States Army was to assault astride the Carentan estuary with one regimental combat team between Varreville and the estuary (Utah beach), and two regimental combat teams between Vierville and Colleville (Omaha beach). The initial tasks were to capture Cherbourg as quickly as possible and to develop operations southwards towards St Lô in conformity with the advance of Second British Army.

Second British Army assault was to be delivered with five brigades between Asnelles and Ouistreham (Gold, Juno and Sword beaches), with the initial task of developing the bridgehead south of the line St Lô–Caen and south-east of Caen, in order to secure airfield sites and to protect the eastern flank of First United States Army while the latter was capturing Cherbourg.

The inter-army boundary made Port-en-Bessin, and the line of the River Drôme to Englesqueville, inclusive to Second British Army.

5. Allied troops examine the remains of a German blockhouse on the Normandy beachhead.

6. Cromwell tanks pass along a French road after the landings. 7 June 1944.

7. Shattered buildings at Hermanville sur Mer destroyed during the fighting for the beaches. In the foreground men of the 13/18th Hussars are constructing shelters. 7 June 1944.

8. Commando troops passing through the streets of Delivrande near Caen. 8 June 1944.

9. General Montgomery at his first press conference since D-day at Port en Bessin. 11 June 1944.

10. A Sherman tank proceeds inland through the shattered streets of Reviers. 11 June 1944.

11.  Churchill and General Montgomery walking along the seashore of the bridgehead. 12 June 1944.

12.  King George VI arrives at General Sir Bernard Montgomery's H.Q. 16 June 1944.

During the night preceding D-day, while the naval assault forces made the sea passage, the programme of intensive air action against the enemy defences was to begin with operations by Bomber Command, while airborne forces were to be dropped on the flanks of the invasion area. At H-hour, supported by naval bombardment and air action and by the guns, rockets and mortars of close support craft, the leading wave of troops was to disembark and force its way ashore.

The total initial lift in the assault and follow-up naval forces was of the order of 130,000 personnel and 20,000 vehicles, all of which were to be landed on the first three tides. In addition to the basic eight assaulting brigades/regimental combat teams, a variety of attached troops were required in the assault including special assault engineers, amphibious tanks, and other detachments which varied for the different beaches according to the specific 'menu' (*i.e.*, composition of the assault wave) decided upon by the subordinate formations. The total forces to be carried in the initial lift consisted of the essential combat elements (with minimum transport) of:

First United States Army:
> Three infantry divisions
> Five tank battalions
> Two Ranger battalions
> Corps and Army troops
> Naval and Air Force detachments.

Second British Army:
> Four infantry divisions (less two brigade groups)
> Three assault tank brigades
> One armoured brigade
> Two SS brigades (Commandos)
> Corps and Army troops
> Naval and Air Force detachments.

Priority of air lift was given to American airborne forces owing to the vital tasks of securing the beach exits and facilitating deployment from the Utah beach. Main bodies of both 82 and 101 United States Airborne Divisions were to land in the general area of Ste Mère Eglise on the night D−1/D, the latter to assist the seaborne assault on the Utah sector and the former to guard the landward flank and prevent the movement of enemy reserves into the Cotentin peninsula. The remaining air lift was allotted to Second British Army for 6 Airborne Division (less one brigade) which was to land before H-hour east of Caen, with the tasks of seizing the crossings over the Orne at Benouville and Ranville and, in conjunction with Commando troops, of dominating the area to the east of Caen in order to delay the movement of enemy forces towards the town.

American Ranger units were to land in the assault on the west of Omaha beach and had the task of attacking enemy defences on the east side of the Carentan estuary.

DIAGRAM "C"

THE ASS

DIAGRAM SHOWING ESSENTIAL ELEMENTS

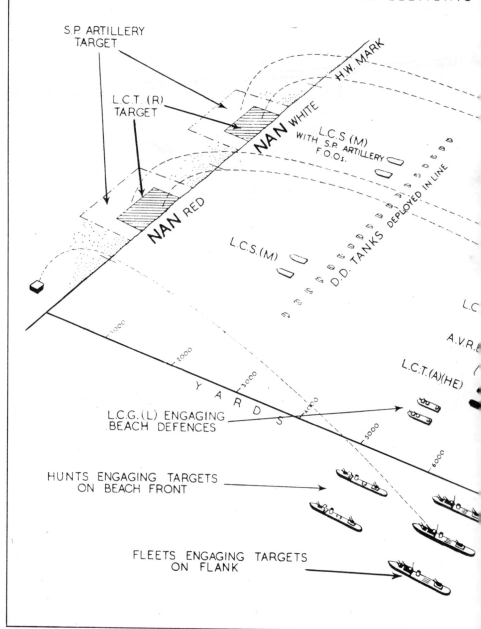

S.P. ARTILLERY
TARGET

L.C.T. (R)
TARGET

H.W. MARK

NAN WHITE

L.C.S. (M)
WITH S.P. ARTILLERY
F.O.Os.

NAN RED

L.C.S.(M)

D.D. TANKS DEPLOYED IN LINE

L.C

A.V.R.

L.C.T.(A)(HE)

1000

2000

3000

Y
A
R
D
S

4000

5000

6000

L.C.G. (L) ENGAGING
BEACH DEFENCES

HUNTS ENGAGING TARGETS
ON BEACH FRONT

FLEETS ENGAGING TARGETS
ON FLANK

**GLOSSARY:** **FLEETS**—*Class of Destroyer.* **HUNTS**—*Class of Destroyer.*
**L.C.A.**—*Landing Craft, Assault.* **M.L.**—*Motor Launch.*
**L.C.T.(R)**—*Landing Craft, Tank (Rocket).*
**L.C.F.**—*Landing Craft, Flak.*
**L.C.A.(HR)**—*Landing Craft, Assault (Hedgerow) used to
explode enemy minefields.*

RIGADE GROUP APPROACHING THE BEACH

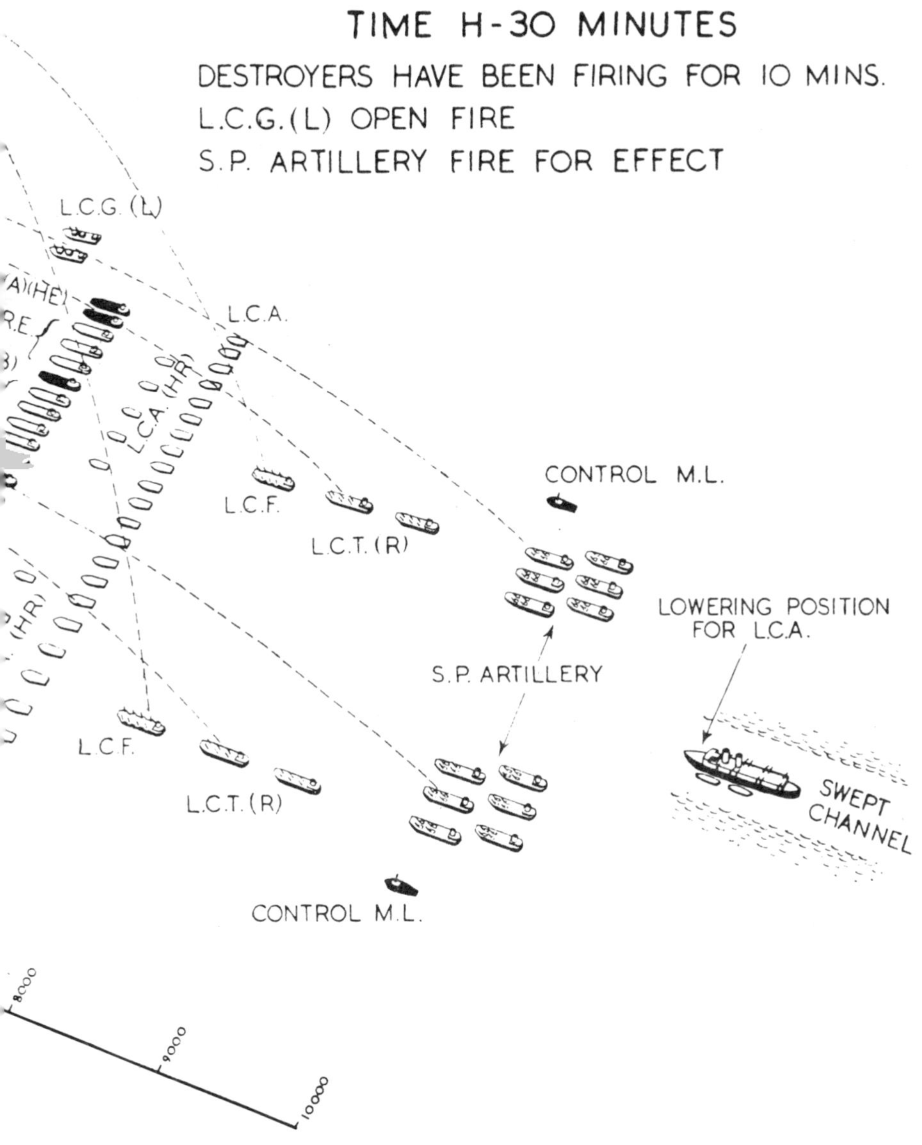

## TIME H-30 MINUTES

DESTROYERS HAVE BEEN FIRING FOR 10 MINS.
L.C.G.(L) OPEN FIRE
S.P. ARTILLERY FIRE FOR EFFECT

L.C.G. (L)

A)(HE)

R.E.

L.C.A.

L.C.A. (HR)

CONTROL M.L.

L.C.F.

L.C.T. (R)

LOWERING POSITION
FOR L.C.A.

S.P. ARTILLERY

L.C.F.

(HR)

L.C.T. (R)

SWEPT
CHANNEL

CONTROL M.L.

8000

9000

10000

C.T.(A)(HE)—*Landing Craft, Tank (Armoured) (High Explosive).*

V.R.E.—*Assault Vehicle, Royal Engineers.*

C.T.(CB)—*Landing Craft, Tank (Concrete Buster).*

D. Tanks—*Duplex Drive Tanks, fitted with flotation device.*

C.S.(M)—*Landing Craft, Support (Medium).*

C.G.(L)—*Landing Craft, Gun (Large).*

One British brigade of two Commandos was to link the assaults on the Juno and Sword sectors. A second Commando brigade was to land behind the assaulting division on the Sword sector and while one Commando dealt with Ouistreham, the remainder of the brigade was to cross the Orne at Benouville and attack the enemy coast defences east of the river up to Cabourg inclusive.

### The assault technique

Prolonged study and numerous experiments had been devoted to the development of the technique of assaulting a defended beach. As a result, various types of specialized military equipment were available by D-day, including assault engineer tanks, tank-carried bridges for crossing anti-tank ditches, mat-laying tanks for covering soft clay patches of the beaches, ramp tanks over which other vehicles could scale sea walls, flail tanks for mine clearance, and amphibious assault tanks. These devices were integrated into the specially trained assault teams which led the invasion forces.

The development of under-water obstacles on the invasion coast has already been mentioned, and it was necessary to include in the assault some teams of sappers trained in clearance of this type of obstruction. These obstacles also affected the decision on the tidal conditions required at the time of commencing the assault because the engineers could not work on demolishing them until they were uncovered by the tide.

### The selection of D-day and H-hour

The determination of H-hour, defined as the time at which the leading wave of assault craft should hit the beach, and of D-day for the assault, was made only after a prolonged and intensive study of the various factors affecting them.

In the first place it was jointly decided that H-hour should be in daylight and that there should be moonlight during the preceding night. From the naval point of view a daylight assault facilitated station keeping and deployment of the vast armada of ships and craft employed, and also the accurate location of the beaches. Moreover, in order to provide accurate naval gunfire and air bombardment against the enemy defences immediately before H-hour, a period of daylight was necessary for observation. These advantages were considered to outweigh the drawbacks of allowing the enemy time to engage by observed fire our ships and craft before the assault began, and of making our troops advance to the attack in daylight; we had such preponderance of naval and air resources that we counted on stunning the defenders with the weight of our bombing and shellfire. The moonlight preceding H-hour was preferred for facilitating naval movements and the approach of airborne forces.

Having decided on a daylight assault, it was in the Army's interest to fix H-hour as early after first light as possible, so that the defenders would have the minimum time for observation of our movements, and in order to conserve as many hours of daylight as possible for landing the follow-up on the second tide before nightfall. There would be a period before sunrise when aircraft spotting for naval guns, and heavy bombers observing above the target area, would be able to see sufficient for their purpose before the visibility became clear for defenders at sea level. The crux of the problem was to decide upon the minimum time required for effective engagement of shore targets by the naval guns and for delivery of the bomb loads by our air formations; eventually the period from nautical twilight (the first sign of morning light) to forty minutes later was accepted as sufficient for our needs.

Tidal conditions had now to be considered. The timing of H-hour had to be related to the height of the tide for naval reasons and because of the necessity to deal with under-water obstacles: which were sited to offer maximum interference at high water and which could not be demolished by sappers unless exposed by the tide.

The obstacles could most easily have been dealt with if the troops had landed at low water, but at low tide the landing craft would have grounded so far from the shore that assaulting infantry would have had to cross a wide stretch of exposed beach before closing with the defences; moreover the beach surfaces in some cases were so uneven that troops wading ashore from the low tide mark would have dropped into hollows deeper than the height of a man before reaching dry land. Again, it was desirable to have as many hours as possible of rising tide upon which to land the supporting arms and enable the landing craft to retract; but the flow of the tide until about three hours before high water, and from three hours after, was so fast that there would have been insufficient time to discharge the landing craft before they became completely grounded.

From a consideration of these factors it was decided that the best conditions would obtain if H-hour were fixed forty minutes after nautical twilight on a day when at this time the tide was three hours before high water mark. These conditions could not be obtained on all beaches simultaneously, because the flow of the tide up the English Channel resulted in high water occurring in the Utah area about forty minutes earlier than in Sword area. This fact, together with the difference in positioning of under-water obstacles on the various beaches, and complications due to the rock outcrop on Juno beach, led to the decision that a separate H-hour should be fixed for each beach. This inevitable compromise resulted in the right-hand beaches having the bare minimum period for observed fire prior to the assault, whereas the left-hand beaches had considerably more than had been deemed essential. On the day ultimately selected H-hour varied between 0630 for the Western Task Force to 0745 on the east sector of Juno area.

The selection of H-hour to fill these many requirements restricted the days suitable to three in every fortnight or, with moonlight, to three in every month. I have already explained that, while the target date was set for 31 May, the Supreme Commander had specified at the time that tidal and other conditions might cause D-day to be selected during the first week in June—in fact 5 June was determined as the first of a three-day period suitable for the operation. Elaborate arrangements were made for weather forecasting, and for a machinery of postponement should this become necessary; but it should be noted that, had the weather been unsuitable in the first three-day period, a postponement of at least a fortnight, and more probably a month in order to have moonlight conditions, would have been inevitable.

## *The Joint Fire Plan*

The purpose of the Joint Fire Plan was to allocate tasks to the resources of the three Services with the object of assisting the Army to get ashore. The chief requirements were to destroy or neutralize the enemy coast artillery batteries which might interfere with the approach of the naval convoys or bring fire to bear on the anchorages, and to neutralize the enemy strong points and defended localities that were sited for the immediate defence of our assault beaches.

It has been shown that preliminary air attacks were delivered against enemy coast defence batteries in the preliminary operations prior to D-day. The Fire Plan was to begin on the night preceding the assault, when the heavy bombers of Bomber Command were to attack in great strength the ten most important batteries: the operation was to be timed as late as would be consistent with the return of the aircraft to England by daylight. Following the Bomber Command operations attacks were planned by medium bombers, using special navigational devices, on a further six coast defence targets; this phase was to begin at civil twilight and about the same time bombardment was to start from assault craft carrying various types of armament. Shortly afterwards, naval gunfire directed by spotting aircraft was timed to commence, and about half-an-hour before H-hour the heavy bombers of the Eighth United States Air Force and medium bombers of the Ninth United States Air Force were to begin action against coast defence artillery and enemy beach defences and localities. Included in the naval assault forces was a variety of specially fitted craft carrying 4.7 inch guns, 4-inch mortars, barrages of 5-inch rockets, Centaur tanks fitted with 75 millimetre howitzers, 17-pounder anti-tank guns, as well as ordinary self-propelled field guns of the assaulting divisional artilleries which were to be embarked in tank landing craft and to work as regimental fire units.

The Fire Plan aimed at building up the supporting fire to a tremendous crescendo which would reach its climax at the latest possible moment before the leading troops waded ashore, in order to give the defenders the minimum time to recover before being set upon. The heavy air bombardment was timed to continue on the beach frontages to within ten minutes of H-hour, and from this time fighters and fighter-bombers were to take up the air offensive, and in particular undertake the task of neutralizing the enemy field batteries located inland. Air support tentacles were to accompany the assaulting troops, and fighter bomber squadrons were to be at hand to answer calls for close support, while the medium and heavy bombers returned to their bases to refuel and re-arm in readiness for further missions. No fewer than 171 Allied fighter squadrons were to be employed in the overall assault phase, and in the event the Allied air forces flew some 11,000 sorties on D-day.

### DIRECT AIR SUPPORT ARRANGEMENTS

The joint army and air forces organization for direct air support becomes a complicated machinery in major amphibious operations. Special arrangements are necessary to cover the period before the army and air force headquarters and control staffs are set up on the far shore and the air formations arrive overseas.

For the assault, the problem was complicated by the location of Headquarters Allied Tactical Air Forces at Uxbridge, while the Naval and Army Group Headquarters were at Portsmouth during the assault phase. It thus became necessary to set up the army component of Air Support Control at Uxbridge, together with a special intelligence staff which was charged with supplying the air staff with information concerning the progress of operations. The Anglo-American army staff at Uxbridge was controlled from my main headquarters at Portsmouth, and worked in matters of immediate air support on general directives, which defined the military plan and priorities for the application of the available direct support air effort. Under the conditions of the initial stage of amphibious operations it will invariably be necessary to move the focus of control of army/air operations back to Army Group level, because of the necessary centralization imposed on the Air Forces and because the normal point of control (Army Headquarters) has no Air Force counterpart with it and no air formations within reach or communication.

Special assault tentacles were allotted to all assaulting brigades and were to provide the initial means for requesting air support, pending the landing of the normal detachments. These tentacles worked to Uxbridge, while on the same network were included Divisional and Corps headquarters ships as well as Army and Army Group headquarters. Army headquarters were to monitor calls for support, but the responsibility for their submission to the Tactical Air Forces rested with the Army Group detachment at Uxbridge.

In order to provide means of immediate response to calls for air assistance during the assault, some squadrons were airborne within wireless range of divisional headquarters ships in anticipation of requests for direct support.

Requests for pre-arranged air support during the assault phase were co-ordinated at main Army Group headquarters and submitted to the air forces through the Uxbridge staff. The latter also co-ordinated the bomblines and ensured that all concerned were kept informed.

### THE COVER PLAN

The Cover Plan employed in connection with these operations formed part of the co-ordinated Allied deception measures which embraced all the European battle fronts.

It was clearly impossible to hide from the enemy the preparations being made in the United Kingdom and, as D-day approached, the concentrations of shipping and craft in southern England would indicate our intentions to strike across the Channel.

The Cover Plan therefore aimed at misleading the enemy about the area of attack, and at persuading him that we should not be ready to launch the assault until about six weeks after the actual date for D-day.

Prior to D-day the plan was to indicate to the enemy that the assault was to be delivered in the Pas de Calais, astride Cap Gris Nez. After D-day our object was to show that the 'Neptune' assault was a preliminary and diversionary operation designed to draw German reserves away from the Pas de Calais and Belgium and that our main attack was still to be delivered in the Pas de Calais.

Our air action prior to D-day was carefully controlled in order to indicate the Pas de Calais as the intended area of assault. Whatever bombing effort was expanded in the 'Neptune' area, twice the amount was delivered in the Pas de Calais, where coast defence guns, enemy defended localities and installations were the targets. Large numbers of dummy landing craft were assembled in ports in south-east England where dummy hard standings, full scale embarkation signposting and other visible signs of preparation were made obvious. American and Canadian troops were moved into the Dover–Folkestone area to lend credence to the idea.

These deception measures continued, as planned, after D-day and events were to show that they achieved outstanding results and in fact played a vital part in our successes in Normandy.

### DIVERSIONARY OPERATIONS

In connection partly with the main operation and partly with the Cover Plan, a series of diversionary operations was mounted.

The plan provided for two diversions which were carried out by specially equipped naval craft and aeroplanes, one in the Straits of Dover and the other near Cap d'Antifer. In both operations radio counter measures were employed to give the same appearance to enemy radar as that given by the real naval invasion forces. It is now known that these diversions were successful and were instrumental in enabling our forces to continue far towards the enemy coast before their true position could be determined.

Dummy paratroops were dropped in three main areas in order to confuse the enemy about the destination of our airborne forces and cause delay and temporary dispersion of hostile forces employed in clarifying the situation.

Plans were made for ensuring as far as possible the co-operation of the French Resistance Movement in our operations. Arms and equipment had been delivered by air to the French over a long period and a network of wireless communications had been set up. Arrangements were made to pass instructions and guidance concerning sabotage to the Resistance leaders and to alert their organizations as soon as the invasion began.

A considerable number of our own Special Air Service troops were dropped in France with sabotage missions designed to delay the movement of enemy reserves. In many cases these troops linked up with Resistance personnel who afforded them ready assistance.

## THE BUILD-UP

The general principles upon which the build-up of our forces and material was planned were, first, the provision of the maximum number of fighting formations on the Continent in the first few days and, secondly, the introduction into the build-up system as quickly as possible of the maximum degree of flexibility: so that changes in priority of troops, administrative echelons, transport and stores could be made as the situation demanded.

By the end of D-day it was planned that, including airborne forces, the Allies would have eight divisions ashore together with Commandos, Ranger battalions and some fourteen tank regiments. By D+6 the total forces would rise to some thirteen divisions, exclusive of airborne formations, with five British armoured brigades and a proportionate number of American tank units. Between twenty-three and twenty-four basic divisions were due in Normandy by D+20. Comparison with the estimated enemy strength was difficult to make; some types of enemy division were organized on a considerably smaller establishment than our own; some were under conversion from training organizations and were known to be deficient of equipment. Our own build-up moreover, included a considerable proportion of fighting units classed as corps and army troops and which, therefore, were not apparent in the divisional figures of the build-up table.

Planned build-up tables are inevitably suspect; it was impossible to estimate the delaying effect on the enemy build-up of our air action, or the success our Cover Plan arrangements would achieve in causing a dispersion of German resources. In our own estimates, the effect of weather on cross-Channel movement and beach working was a major imponderable.

In order to make our build-up plans flexible, a special inter-Service staff was organized called 'Build-Up Control' (BUCO). This body was formed, as a result of Mediterranean experience, to organize the loading and despatch of craft and ships from home ports, and was the agency by which changes in priority were effected.

It is of interest to record that in order to fit the assault forces into the available craft and shipping, British divisions were limited to 1,450 vehicles in the initial lift, the corresponding figure for armoured brigades being 320. No formation was to be made up in excess of 75 per cent of its War Establishment in transport until after D+14. Similar limitations were imposed on the American units.

## PLANNED DEVELOPMENT OF OPERATIONS

I have already outlined my broad strategic plan for the development of operations designed to secure the lodgement area.

Once the troops were ashore it was necessary for them to 'crack about'; the need for sustained energy and drive was paramount, as we had to link our beachheads and penetrate quickly inland before the enemy opposition crystallized. I gave orders that the leading formations should by-pass major enemy centres of resistance in order to 'peg out claims' inland. I emphasized to commanders on all levels that determined leadership would be necessary to withstand the strain of the first few days, to retain the initiative and to make sure that there would be no setbacks.

In the planning stages of a major operation it is customary to issue for the guidance of subordinate commanders and staffs, an estimate of the progress of operations. Such an estimate normally takes the form of a series of 'phase lines' drawn on an operational map to indicate the positions to be reached by leading troops at intervals of a few days. The phase line map for the operations is shown in the form it was produced in April 1944 (see map No. 2). I was not altogether happy about this phase line map, because the imponderable factors in an operation of the magnitude of 'Overlord' make such forecasting so very academic. While I had in my mind the necessity to reach the Seine and the Loire by D + 90, the interim estimates of progress could not, I felt, have any great degree of reality. The predictions were particularly complicated by two major divergent requirements. On the one hand the general strategic plan was to make the break-out on the western flank pivoting the front on the Caen area, where the bulk of enemy reserves were to be engaged; on the other hand the Air Forces insisted on the importance of capturing quickly the good airfield country south-east of Caen. Though I have never failed in my operations to exert my utmost endeavour to meet the requirements of the Air Forces, in planning these operations the overriding requirement was to gain territory in the west. For this reason, while accepting an estimate for seizing the open country beyond Caen at a relatively early date after the landing, I had to make it clear that progress in that sector would be dependent on the successful development of the main strategic plan.

### ADMINISTRATION

The administrative problem facing the British forces was essentially different from that of the Americans. The operational plan demanded the very rapid development of lines of communication behind the American forces, and the administrative requirements for opening up railways and roads from Cherbourg and the Brittany ports were very large. There was no parallel problem foreseen on the British flank.

The limiting factor in the build-up of operational forces appeared likely to be the rate at which maintenance resources could be landed. The problem therefore was to develop the capacity of the beaches to the maximum degree. Since there would be no port facilities at all until Cherbourg was captured and opened, and since in any case Cherbourg would not be able to do more than relieve some of the burden of beach maintenance, it was planned to erect two artificial harbours, together with a number of breakwaters, in the Baie de la Seine. The components which made up these artificial harbours were to be towed across the Channel in special lanes through the minefields, and although the estimated time required for their construction was from fourteen to forty-two days, it was provided that as far as possible use would be made of the shelter of the outer breakwaters once they had been completed. The subsidiary breakwaters were to be formed by sinking sixty block ships in groups of twelve at suitable sites along the coast.

The British forces were to be maintained over the beaches until such time as sufficient ports were captured and developed, and it was assumed that beach maintenance could cease on the opening of the Seine ports. In the United States sector it was planned to open Cherbourg and subsequently the main ports of the Brittany peninsula, and in this way to dispense gradually with the necessity for beach working.

Special establishments were created for operating the British beaches, comprising Beach Bricks, Beach Groups and Beach Sub-Areas. These special units and headquarters were formed on an inter-Service basis and included detachments of the various arms. In this way the individual beaches were worked by self-contained organizations.

It was planned to maintain Second British Army for the first few days from Beach Maintenance Areas and subsequently from two army roadheads, one of which was ultimately to be handed over to First Canadian Army; a Rear Maintenance Area was to be established as soon as conditions permitted. In view of the damage caused by our bombing, it was considered necessary to be independent of railways for the first three months of the operation; the lines of communication were therefore to be entirely road operated for this period.

The administrative planning for the operations was based on the expectancy of reasonable weather conditions during June, July and August. Some allowance was made in planning the rate of administrative build-up for days when the beaches would be working at low capacity; but the risk had always to be faced that any serious or prolonged break in the weather, particularly during the first two weeks, might have a grave effect on the maintenance of the forces and therefore on their operational capabilities.

### CIVIL AFFAIRS

Civil affairs planning initially aimed at ensuring that the civil population did not impede troop movements, at preparing for the organization of local labour and transport, and at setting up the necessary machinery for the control and use of local resources and for the replacement of unacceptable local officials. It was anticipated that there would be a large number of refugees and civilian wounded, and special composite detachments of Civil Affairs personnel were organized in readiness to deal with the problem, while arrangements were made for food and medical supplies for the inhabitants of the bridgehead to be phased in from D+1 onwards.

### REFLECTIONS ON THE PLANNING PERIOD

In retrospect, the major drawback of the inter-Service planning organization on the Army Group level prior to D-day was the lack of a single joint Service commander. Experience indicated that the speed and efficiency of planning the initial phases of the operation might have been greatly improved had there been some set-up on the Army Group level analogous to the United States Task Force system, with a Task Force

Commander. It must be realized that the commanders of this operation were appointed only five months before D-day, and however much preliminary work may be done on a plan, no finality can be reached until the commander responsible has taken up his appointment.

Had the Task Force system been adopted, I realize that considerable changes in the command set-up of the Naval and Air Forces would have been necessary; but the fact remains that the system employed in 'Overlord' led to delays caused by the necessity for briefing and holding conferences between the high-ranking commanders on various levels. In particular, the fact that the Allied Air Forces were divided into commands held by parallel commanders-in-chief reacted on the speed of military planning because it frequently took long periods and many lengthy meetings in order to finalize, in a co-ordinated form, the plan of the various Air Forces in support of the land operation.

In considering the time available for planning, it was regrettable that the command set-up and appointment of the commanders were so much delayed. The responsibility and importance of the task laid upon the commanders and staff, and the truly formidable amount of detailed work for such a gigantic undertaking, would imply that no effort should have been spared to ensure that those concerned had time to discharge their functions under reasonable conditions. In the event, by D-day, when they should have been fit and fresh for the start of the great adventure, in many cases the staffs were bordering on a state of exhaustion.

From the military point of view, the most difficult single factor during the period of planning was the delay in deciding the higher headquarters organization of the Allied Air Forces. This delay was not a purely Air Force concern, and planning in the Army suffered commensurate delays, because speedy solution of inter-Service problems could not be made until the various Allied Air Force headquarters and responsibilities had been clarified.

The detailed composition of the Naval assault forces, which was determined by the availability of the various types of landing ships and craft, was not finalized until relatively late in the planning period. Since every alteration in allocation of craft calls for changes in the landing tables, and often even in local assault plans, the constant amendments imposed a tremendous burden of work on the Army staffs at all levels.

It was fully realized during the planning period how very dependent we were going to be upon the weather and every reasonable allowance was made for the effect that adverse conditions in the Channel might have upon the project. In making such allowances we assumed an average run of weather conditions, which were deduced from a study of the twenty preceding years. In the event, the development of our operations had to be made in spite of unprecedented weather conditions throughout the summer and autumn. This fact must be borne in mind when the story of our campaign in France and the Low Countries is studied, because it had a deterrent effect on our planning; indeed, at one period soon after D-day it was the major cause of a serious reduction in the tempo of our operations.

*The Plan*

There was one matter connected with the detailed planning which may be worthy of comment. In the first days of the invasion it was of primary importance to ensure that nothing was carried over to the Continent unless it was vital to the conduct of operations. With this in view, repeated and detailed examination was made at all levels in the chain of command, of the Order of Battle and Troop Lists of personnel, vehicles and stores loading in the first few days, and particularly in the initial lift of craft and shipping. I believe as a result that our only major over-insurance was in the matter of anti-aircraft protection.

The early requirements of the anti-aircraft organization were worked out by an inter-Service committee which based its recommendations on the appreciation of the probable strength and capabilities of the German Air Force at the time of the invasion. There is no doubt that there could have been nothing more calculated to upset the establishment and working of our beachheads than hostile enemy air activity against them, and on these grounds it is understandable if the appreciation of the enemy air reaction to the landing erred on the gloomy side. The fact remains that the artillery state in the early days showed that anti-aircraft guns represented an appreciable percentage of the total number of pieces ashore.

In general, events were to prove that the overall planning for the assault was sound and that in spite of the magnitude of the task and the shortage of time for its completion no essential detail had been overlooked. The plan proved capable of implementation and workable in practice.

# CHAPTER FIVE

## *Forging the Weapon*

REFERENCE to the Order of Battle of 21 Army Group shows that the bulk of forces available for Operation 'Overlord' was lacking in battle experience. These formations had spent a long period energetically training in England, but inevitably some of their notions and doctrines had become theoretical. During the planning period, therefore, I set about the task of putting across to the troops under my command a sound battle technique. This process was facilitated by the fact that I had 7 Armoured, 50 and 51 Divisions and two Armoured Brigades who had had considerable service in the Eighth Army; by exchanging officers between these formations and those less experienced I endeavoured to spread our available experience as much as possible. I also held a conference of all General Officers in the Army Group as early as I could arrange it, to explain to them my views on the major points of battle technique. I moreover decided to make certain changes amongst the commanders of formations in England, again with the object of making good as far as possible the inevitable lack of battle experience I found so prevalent.

Time for these tasks was short, and I found it necessary to give firm guidance and quick decisions in order to ensure that the formations would be properly launched when the time came. In this I received every possible support from the War Office. The relationship between the War Office and 21 Army Group developed on the basis of complete understanding, confidence and team work and, in a letter of appreciation that I wrote to the War Office just prior to D-day, I thanked the staff there for its unfailing co-operation, and acknowledged that our efforts and successes would owe much to the teamwork existing between the two organizations.

The process of forging the weapon for the task which lay ahead occupied much of my time right up to D-day. I was determined to gain the confidence of the fighting troops, and to inspire them with confidence in themselves and in their ability to achieve the task which lay ahead of them. I aimed to build up their morale to the highest possible state so that they would sweep all before them in this great adventure. I travelled throughout England in order to visit each individual formation under my operational control—both British and American. In these essentially informal visits, I gave a talk to the officers and men on the subject of the war and of the job we were undertaking, and in this way established a personal link between them and myself.

In preparing an army in the home country for a great operation, there are many important factors which go to build up its morale which differ from those affecting an army based overseas. 'Overlord' was to be one of our greatest national military undertakings, and the essential background to the morale of the soldiers was public confidence in the Army, and in its ability to achieve results. It was a case of the whole nation becoming partner in the battle, and of the preparation of an inspired Army drawing strength from an inspired people. I did all I could to play my part in the 'Salute the Soldier' campaign and in other measures which were designed to achieve this high and vitally important degree of morale and sense of duty. At the invitation of the Ministry of Supply I also visited a number of factories to tell the workers on the home front about the Army, and to assist in the fostering of that spirit of a single team striving together with a single purpose.

The British troops and their Canadian and American colleagues went into this battle inspired to the highest purpose, confident of the wholehearted backing of their homelands and possessed of a tremendous morale.

In a final tour of the formations I spoke to all officers down to and including the rank of Lieutenant-Colonel. In these talks I emphasized again the major points of battle doctrine, and reviewed the latest Intelligence on the enemy situation. I took the opportunity to wish the senior officers Godspeed in the great task we were about to undertake.

As had become my normal practice, I held an exercise attended by all the General Officers of the First and Third United States, First Canadian and Second British Armies, in order to recapitulate to them my plan of operations, to hear from them an outline of formation planning, and to study with them certain hypothetical situations which might arise once the operation had begun. This exercise was held in London on 7 and 8 April and was extremely valuable. The conference was attended by the British Chiefs of Staff; the Prime Minister also visited it and gave a short talk on the importance to all the Allies of the successful outcome of the forthcoming operation.

In these various ways what I term 'forging the weapon' was accomplished, and as D-day drew nearer I had no qualms or doubts about the successful showing that this mighty force would make on the Normandy beaches.

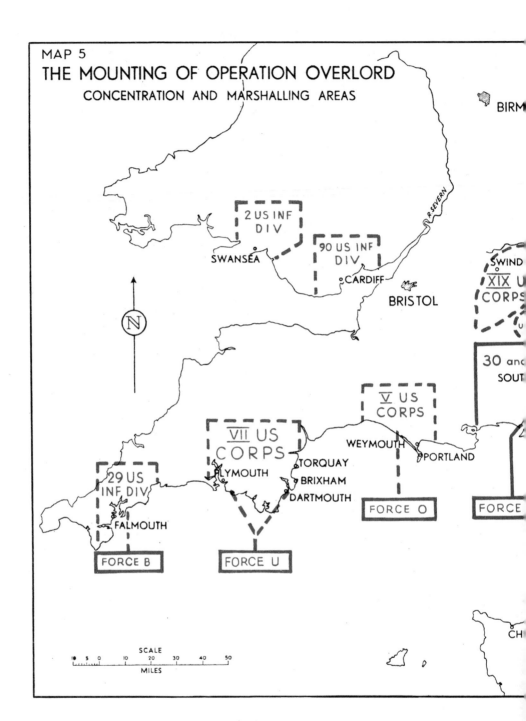

MAP 5

# THE MOUNTING OF OPERATION OVERLORD
## CONCENTRATION AND MARSHALLING AREAS

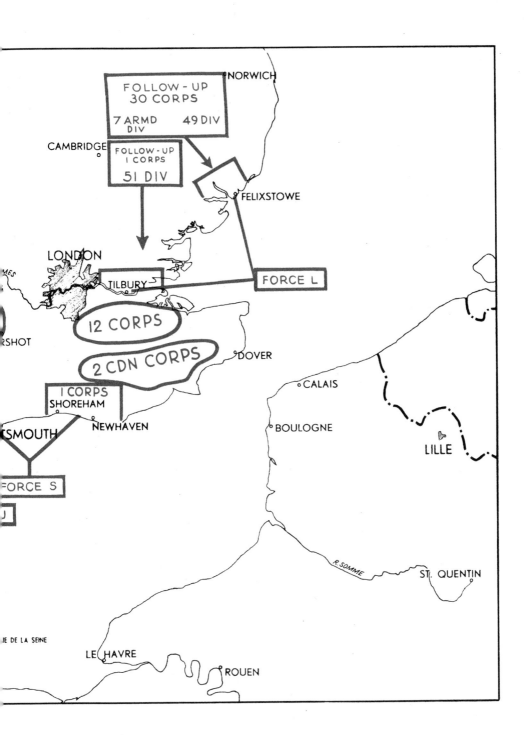

NORWICH

FOLLOW - UP
30 CORPS

7 ARMD    49 DIV
DIV

CAMBRIDGE

FOLLOW - UP
I CORPS

51 DIV

FELIXSTOWE

LONDON

TILBURY

FORCE L

12 CORPS

2 CDN CORPS

DOVER

RSHOT

CALAIS

I CORPS
SHOREHAM

NEWHAVEN

BOULOGNE

LILLE

SMOUTH

FORCE S

R SOMME

ST. QUENTIN

IE DE LA SEINE

LE HAVRE

ROUEN

[195]

# CHAPTER SIX

## *The Mounting of Operation 'Overlord'*

THE mounting of an amphibious operation may be defined as the process of concentrating the troops taking part into suitable areas, from which they move to marshalling areas, whence in turn they are called forward to the points of embarkation. The process is one of great complexity, particularly when concerning an operation of the magnitude of 'Overlord', in which over 20,000 vehicles and 176,000 personnel were to be landed on the far shore in the first two days. Formations and units had to be concentrated with relation to their appropriate marshalling areas and embarkation points, which extended from Felixstowe to Plymouth and South Wales; during the mounting the final stages of waterproofing vehicles and equipment had to be completed to enable them to disembark from landing craft and wade ashore; the assault troops had to be packed up for the operation, and therefore during the last stages 'hotel' servicing had to be arranged for them by other units, which, in many cases, themselves had subsequently to prepare for embarkation; 'residues', in other words the portions of units which were not necessary in the initial phases had to be separated from their parent formations and subsequently despatched overseas to rejoin them; marshalling areas and embarkation points had to be laid out in great detail, often in very confined areas; a highly complicated security system had to be organized and implemented to prevent leakage of information, and in particular to ensure that once the troops had been briefed about the role they were to play, they would be denied contact with the outside world. Special map depots had to be established near the marshalling areas so that maps could be issued at the last possible moment; an immense number of other details had to be worked out including such matters as issuing French currency without prejudice to security and the sealing of NAAFI and welfare personnel working among troops who had been briefed as to their destination. Other measures of security were the suspension of certain diplomatic privileges to foreign nationals during the last days before the operation and the establishment, well in advance of D-day, of a visitors ban for civilians throughout the coastal belt of southern England.

The main basis of the mounting plan was the distribution of the naval forces in the various sectors of our southern coast. The three British naval assault forces were distributed respectively at Felixstowe and Tilbury, at Shoreham, Newhaven and Portsmouth, and at Portsmouth and Southampton. United States forces embarked at Weymouth and Portland, at Torquay, Brixham and Dartmouth, and at Plymouth. Follow-up forces which were loaded prior to D-day sailed from the Thames and Plymouth, and other United States forces loaded in South Wales. In order to position the invasion forces in appropriate areas, the plan of 'shuffling round' in the available accommodation involved moves of troops throughout the United Kingdom.

Great credit is due to the War Office and ETOUSA staffs and to the Movement Staffs, British railways and transport organizations who together achieved successfully this enormous feat of organization.

An additional complication to the mounting plan arose from the possibility of postponement. Many of the troops had to be loaded before D-day in very cramped conditions, and the decision whether the operation would start, or be postponed by reason of adverse weather, had obviously to be left to the last possible moment. The procedure for postponement therefore involved in some cases disembarkation of troops; in the event of such disembarkation, arrangements had to be made for temporary accommodation and feeding, for which special camps had to be set up in some sectors. In the event a postponement was made, proving it to have been fortunate indeed that detailed plans for the eventuality had been perfected.

A short period before D-day an exercise called 'Fabius' was held to test the embarkation machinery. The scope of the exercise included moving and embarking many thousands of troops, and as far as possible the complete organization was put to the test. This exercise proved of the greatest value, as it provided invaluable lessons and experience for the actual operation.

About a month before D-day the various higher headquarters of the invasion forces moved to their operational stations. Considerable thought was given to deciding the various locations, the main factor being the provision of adequate communications. It was unfortunate but inevitable that, because of the communications system, the Air Force had to be split off from the Navy and Army Group Headquarters, and took up its location in the Stanmore–Uxbridge area, while Admiral Ramsay and myself set up with our staffs just outside Portsmouth. Portsmouth was the nerve centre of communications to the embarkation areas, and from my point of view was well placed as a jumping off point for my own Tactical Headquarters which I intended to take over to Normandy as early as events permitted.

At Portsmouth, together with Admiral Ramsay, I was to be in close touch with the headquarters ships of the assaulting formations, and it was therefore obviously the best place for me to be at H-hour. From the Air Forces point of view the centre of communication for all Air Force formations and airfields was at Uxbridge and, since there was no satisfactory alternative, the Air Forces Headquarters were located there. The Supreme Commander moved an echelon of his headquarters near us outside Portsmouth.

CHAPTER SEVEN

# The Battle of Normandy: 1. The Assault

### THE DECISION TO LAUNCH THE OPERATION

ON the morning of 4 June 1944 General Eisenhower and his subordinate commanders met to consider the meteorological forecast for 5 June.

The forecast was so unpropitious that the Supreme Commander ordered a postponement of twenty-four hours. By the time this decision was made, part of the American assault force had already put out into the Channel, but so heavy were the seas that the craft were compelled to turn about and seek shelter. By the morning of 5 June conditions in the Channel showed little improvement, but the forecast for the following day carried a gleam of hope. An interval of fair conditions was anticipated, beginning late on 5 June and lasting until the next morning, with a drop in the wind and broken clouds not lower than 3,000 feet. Towards evening on 6 June, however, a return to high winds and rough seas was predicted, and these conditions were then likely to continue for an indefinite period.

It has been shown that the latest possible date for the invasion in early June which gave the required tidal conditions was 7 June. But a second postponement of twenty-four hours was impracticable, for the naval bombardment forces had already sailed from their northern bases three days before and an additional day's steaming would have made it necessary to put back into port to refuel, thus upsetting the whole schedule of the operation. The Supreme Commander was therefore faced with the alternatives of taking the risks involved in an assault in the bad weather on 6 June, or of putting off the operation for four weeks, when the tide and moon conditions would again be favourable. Such a postponement would not only have been most harmful to the morale of the troops, but might well have prejudiced secrecy and the possibility of gaining tactical surprise. At 0400 hours on 5 June the decision was made: the invasion of France would take place on 6 June.

### THE START OF THE GREAT ENTERPRISE

As they started out for the coast of Fortress Europe, my personal message was read out to all troops:

'. . . On the eve of this great adventure I send my best wishes to every soldier in the Allied team. To us is given the honour of striking a blow for freedom which will live in history; and in the better days that lie ahead men will speak with pride of our doings. We have a great and a righteous cause.

[198]

'Let us pray that "The Lord Mighty in Battle" will go forth with our armies, and that His special providence will aid us in the struggle.

'I want every soldier to know that I have complete confidence in the successful outcome of the operations that we are now about to begin.

'With stout hearts, and with enthusiasm for the contest, let us go forward to victory. . . .'

With these words, the Allied assaulting divisions were launched into battle.

### THE AIRBORNE LANDINGS

At 0200 hours 6 June, a 'coup de main' party of 6 Airborne Division was dropped near Benouville to seize the bridges over the Canal de Caen and the River Orne. Of the six gliders used, four landed with extreme accuracy. Surprise was complete, both bridges were captured intact and a close bridgehead was established. Half an hour later, 3 and 5 Parachute Brigades began to drop east of the Orne. The position at the bridges was reinforced and another of the original objectives—a coastal battery near Merville—was quickly assaulted and overrun. Later the task of blowing the bridges over the River Dives and its tributaries at Varaville, Bures and Troarn was successfully completed, though not before considerable opposition had been overcome.

On the whole, the drop of 6 Airborne Division was more scattered than had been planned, but one repercussion of this was that the enemy was misled about the area and extent of the landings. Enemy counter action began to develop at 0500 hours and strong attacks were delivered against the Orne bridgehead. These were effectively driven off and the division held all its gains in spite of increasing opposition: thus securing the left flank of the Allied beachheads.

101 United States Airborne Division began dropping south-east of Ste Mère Eglise at about 0130 hours. The division was dropped over a large area and had difficulty in assembling for action, but quickly seized the two villages of Pouppeville and St Martin-de-Varreville, behind the Utah beaches. 82 United States Airborne Division landed west of the Carentan–Cherbourg main road from 0230 hours onwards. The division was very widely dispersed astride the River Merderet, but set about its tasks of seizing the town of Ste Mère Eglise and of protecting the inland flanks of 101 Airborne Division.

Cloud and atmospheric conditions had been largely responsible for the scattered nature of the landings, but the airborne divisions succeeded in their mission. They achieved surprise and caused great confusion by cutting enemy communications and disorganizing the German defence, and above all they succeeded in capturing the causeways across the inundated areas behind the Utah beaches.

While the airborne landings were in progress, over 1,100 aircraft of Bomber Command commenced the air offensive as planned. Nearly 6,000 tons of bombs had been dropped on the coast batteries by dawn.

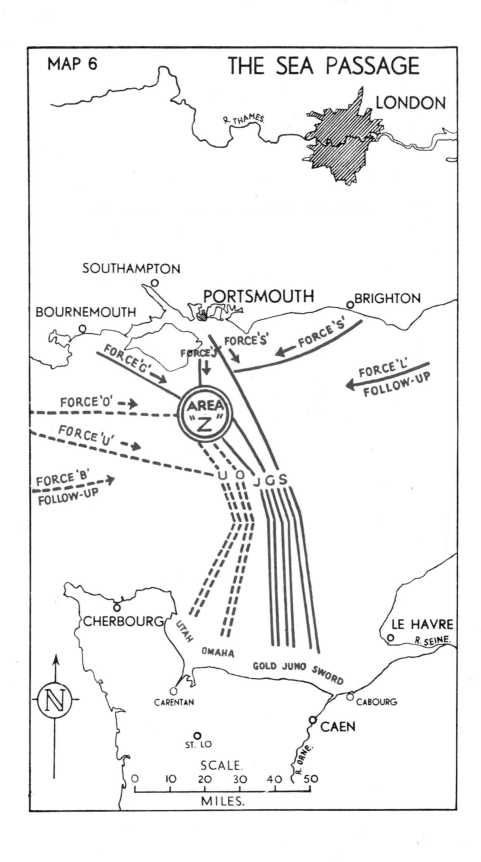

MAP 6      THE SEA PASSAGE

## THE SEA PASSAGE

Meanwhile, the Allied sea armada drew in towards the coast of France, preceded by its flotillas of minesweepers. The passage from the assembly area south of the Isle of Wight had, in the words of Admiral Ramsay's report, an 'air of unreality' owing to the complete absence of any form of enemy reaction. No U-boats were encountered, as the bad weather had drawn the enemy surface patrol craft into port; the German radar system was upset as a result of our air attacks and other counter measures, and no reconnaissance aircraft were observed. Not until the leading ships had reached their lowering positions, some seven to eleven miles offshore, and the naval bombardment squadrons had opened fire on the shore defences, was there any appreciable enemy activity.

During the sea passage heavy seas were running in the Channel, with waves as high as five or six feet, and the wind was strong and gusty; it was an outstanding feat on the part of the naval forces that in spite of this every main essential of the plan was carried out as intended.

The cloud conditions were not very favourable for bombing when over 1,300 heavy day bombers of the Eighth United States Air Force, and eight medium divisions of the Ninth United States Air Force, swept over the target area. Meanwhile the heavy ships of the naval bombardment squadrons opened on the coast defence batteries, while gradually the destroyers and the great number and variety of supporting craft successively came into action as the assault craft ran into the beaches and the troops stormed ashore. Despite the massive air and naval bombardment, the coastal defences in general were not as effectively destroyed as had been hoped, but the enemy opposition was effectively neutralized for the vital period of the assault; field works behind the beaches were largely eliminated, wire entanglements were broken down and some of the mine-fields set off, and the defenders were thoroughly shaken by the weight of our fire. The enemy's communications network was paralysed and his radar system thrown into con-fusion, with the result that during the period of the landings the enemy High Command remained in ignorance of the true extent, strength and objectives of the assault.

The high seas and heavy surf created considerable difficulties in getting the troops ashore. In spite of the outstanding seamanship of the naval crews, landing craft were hurled on to the beaches by the waves and many of the smaller ones were swamped before touching down. The onshore wind had swept the tide up the beaches as much as half-an-hour ahead of schedule, and the under-water obstacles were thus awash sooner than had been anticipated. This made the work of the obstacle clearance parties largely ineffective, so that subsequent waves of assault craft suffered considerable casualties by fouling uncleared obstacles. Numbers of troops were swept off their feet in the water as they waded ashore, and as a result of sea sickness many were very exhausted on reaching dry land. It was moreover impossible on some beaches to 'swim in' the amphibious tanks, upon which we relied to give the infantry fire support in their task of clearing the beach exits.

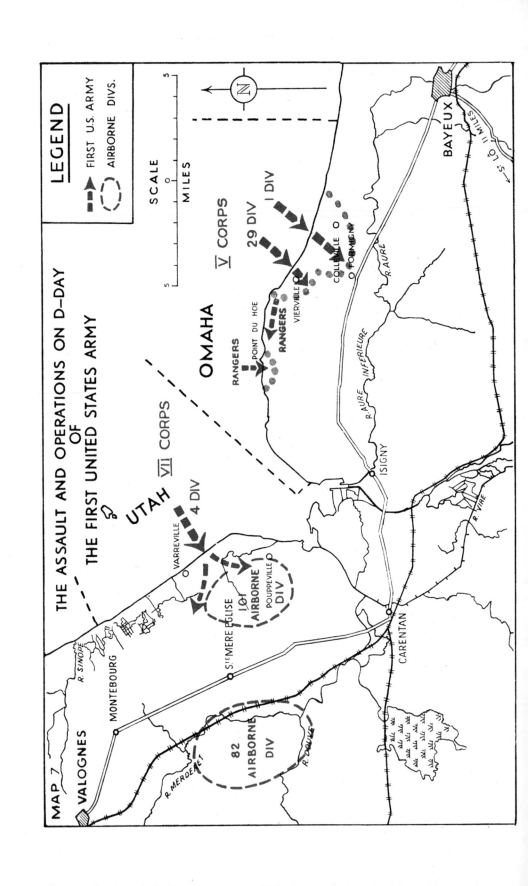

MAP 7

THE ASSAULT AND OPERATIONS ON D-DAY
OF
THE FIRST UNITED STATES ARMY

LEGEND

FIRST U.S. ARMY
AIRBORNE DIVS.

SCALE

5                    5
MILES

N

VALOGNES

MONTEBOURG

R. SINOPE

UTAH   VII CORPS

4 DIV

VARREVILLE

Ste MERE EGLISE

101 AIRBORNE DIV

POUPPEVILLE

82 AIRBORNE DIV

R. MERDERET

R. DOUVE

CARENTAN

R. VIRE

ISIGNY

OMAHA

RANGERS

POINT DU HOE

RANGERS

VIERVILLE

COLLEVILLE

FORMIGNY

29 DIV

1 DIV

V CORPS

R. AURE INFERIEURE

R. AURE

BAYEUX

ST. LÔ, 11 MILES

But the assault was on; more and more troops stormed ashore; the Allies had set foot again in France, and this time they had come to stay.

### THE ASSAULT BY FIRST UNITED STATES ARMY

On Utah beach, 4 Infantry Division led the assault of VII United States Corps, on a front of one regimental combat team. The landing was made approximately on time, though the assault waves touched down some thousand yards south of the planned position. The error in beach finding was due to the coastline being obscured by the haze of the air bombardment, but it turned out to be a fortunate error since the obstacles were fewer where the troops actually went ashore than in the sector originally planned. The progress of the assault was greatly assisted by thirty amphibious tanks, launched five thousand yards offshore, which arrived on the beach with the loss of one only. Casualties were not excessive, and movement ashore proceeded well; a second regimental combat team was soon disembarked, and a beachhead was secured on a four thousand yard front. During the day in some places the troops penetrated up to ten thousand yards, having crossed the inundated area behind the beaches and made contact successfully with 101 Airborne Division.

On Omaha beach, H-hour for the assault had been fixed at 0645 hours. The plan of V United States Corps was to assault on a broad front with two regimental combat teams, one from each of 29 and 1 United States Divisions. The former was to capture initially Vierville-sur-Mer, while the latter was to secure Colleville-sur-Mer, some three miles to the east.

The leading wave touched the shore at 0634 hours, but the heavy seas and density of under-water obstacles caused considerable losses to amphibious tanks and landing craft. Owing to poor visibility the air bombing in this sector had been largely ineffective and the naval guns were hampered by the configuration of the ground which made observation difficult. On Omaha beach the enemy coastal defence troops in the area had only recently been augmented by a German field formation (352 Infantry Division), which was holding a stand-to exercise on the coast and manning the defences as our assault began. The American troops therefore ran straight into an enemy division deployed for action. Deprived of the planned degree of support from amphibious tanks and naval craft, the attacking formations suffered severe casualties and were pinned to the beaches. The Ranger battalions who landed on the right flank of the assault also suffered heavy casualties and for some hours the position at Omaha hung in the balance. With extreme gallantry, however, the American infantry regrouped, and supported by follow-up regimental combat teams, stormed the enemy positions and succeeded in gaining a foothold. By nightfall V United States Corps had secured a beachhead about a mile in depth on the line Vierville–Colleville, and some forward elements were already pushing towards the high ground near Formigny, some two miles inland.

### THE ASSAULT BY SECOND BRITISH ARMY

Second British Army assaulted on the right in the Gold sector with 50 Division of 30 Corps. In the centre sector, designated Juno, was 3 Canadian Division,

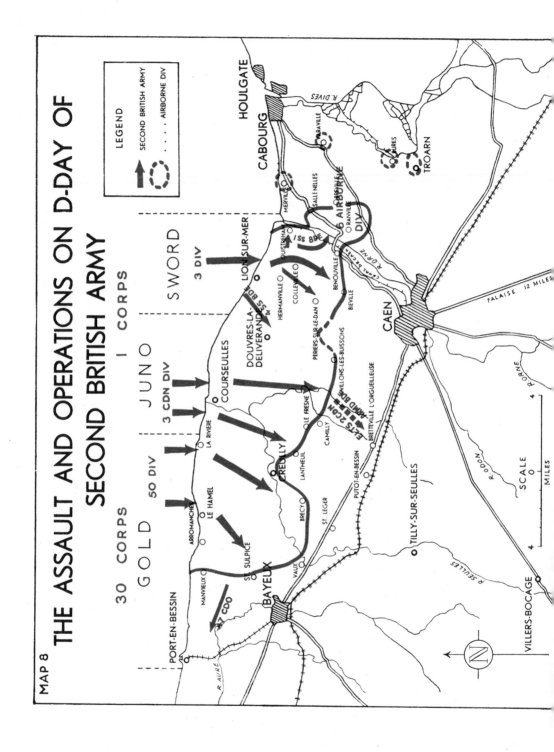

MAP 8

# THE ASSAULT AND OPERATIONS ON D-DAY OF SECOND BRITISH ARMY

LEGEND

SECOND BRITISH ARMY

. . . . . AIRBORNE DIV

30 CORPS    I CORPS

GOLD    50 DIV    JUNO    3 CDN DIV    SWORD    3 DIV

PORT-EN-BESSIN

ARROMANCHES

LE HAMEL

MANVIEUX

ST. SULPICE

47 CDO

VAUX

BAYEUX

LA RIVIERE

COURSEULLES

DOUVERS-LA-DELIVERANDE

LION-SUR-MER

HERMANVILLE

COLLEVILLE

OUISTREHAM

MERVILLE

SALLENELLES

I SS BDE

6 AIRBORNE DIV

RANVILLE

BENOUVILLE

BIEVILLE

PERIERS-SUR-LE-DAN

CREULLY

LANTHEUIL

CAMILLY

LE FRESNE

BRECY

ST. LEGER

SECQUEVILLE

REVIERS

SEULLES-LES-BUISSONS

BRETTEVILLE L'ORGUEILLEUSE

ELTS 2 CDN ARMD BDE

PUTOT-EN-BESSIN

TILLY-SUR-SEULLES

CAEN

CANAL DE CAEN

R. ORNE

R. DIVES

CABOURG

HOULGATE

VARAVILLE

DURES

TROARN

FALAISE 12 MILES

R. ORNE

R. ODON

SCALE

MILES

VILLERS-BOCAGE

R. SEULLES

R. AURE

N

[204]

and on the left 3 British Division (Sword sector): both of which were under 1 Corps.

50 Division assault was made on a two brigade front. The intention for D-day was to penetrate the beach defences between Le Hamel and La Rivière and to secure a covering position which would include the town of Bayeux and the high ground in the area of St Leger, astride the main road from Bayeux to Caen. The division had under command 8 Armoured Brigade, of which two regiments were amphibious, assault teams of 79 Armoured Division, and a Royal Marine Commando: which was to land immediately behind the leading right-hand brigade and move west along the coast to seize Port-en-Bessin.

As on Omaha beach, the weather was extremely unfavourable; the sky was overcast and visibility only moderate, while a Force 5 wind raised a considerable sea in the anchorage and it was considered too rough to launch the amphibious tanks. The landing craft carrying the tanks were therefore ordered to beach behind the assault craft of the leading infantry, which touched down within a few minutes of H-hour—which was 0725 hours. On the right, the main opposition came from Le Hamel, which had escaped reduction by the initial air and sea bombardment. Here the infantry were pinned to the beach for some time by machine gun and mortar fire, but the opposition was gradually by-passed and the troops started to push inland. On the left, the task of the assaulting infantry was somewhat easier, for the bombardment of La Rivière had been more effective and the enemy resistance was conducted with less spirit. The leading brigade moved quickly inland to its objective on the Bayeux–Caen road. Eventually the situation at Le Hamel was cleared up; meanwhile reserve brigades were landed successfully and by last light the forward positions of 50 Division were roughly on the line Manvieux–St Sulpice–Vaux–Breçy–Creully. At Creully contact was made with patrols of 3 Canadian Division, but touch had not been gained with V United States Corps on the right; the Royal Marine Commando had experienced difficulty during its landing and got delayed, so that by nightfall it was about one and a half miles south of the objective Port-en-Bessin.

Although not all the D-day objectives had been secured, the situation in the 50 Division sector was satisfactory and an advance inland had been made of some five miles.

In 1 Corps sector, 3 Canadian Division assaulted with two brigades, and 3 British Division on a frontage of one brigade. The initial task of these formations was to secure a covering position on the general line Putot-en-Bessin–Caen–River Orne to the sea, joining up with 6 Airborne Division on the left. With 3 Canadian Division there was 2 Canadian Armoured Brigade (including one amphibious regiment), while 27 Armoured Brigade (with two amphibious regiments) was under command 3 British Division; both formations were supported by appropriate detachments from 79 Armoured Division.

The two leading Canadian brigades assaulted astride Courseulles-sur-Mer about 0800 hours. The rough sea caused casualties to the amphibious tanks and delay to some of the assault craft, and the fact that the landing was behind schedule (H-hour was 0735–0745 hours) proved a great handicap to the engineers who had less time than planned to deal with the under-water obstacles before the incoming tide covered them. The enemy resistance was stiff, as a number of strong points had survived the preliminary bombardment and it was some time therefore before the beach exits could be cleared. Once clear of the beaches steady progress was made; because the advance was more rapid on the left of the sector, the reserve brigade was brought in on that flank, and throughout the day the Canadians pushed forward steadily; by nightfall they were on the general line Lantheuil–Le Fresne–Camilly–Villons-les-Buissons. Tanks of 2 Canadian Armoured Brigade had given great assistance to the advance, and two troops had, in fact, succeeded in reaching one of the final objectives for the day— Bretteville L'Orgueilleuse, on the Bayeux–Caen road; there they inflicted considerable casualties on the enemy before withdrawing for the night to the main divisional line.

The task of 3 British Division was to assault the beaches just east of Lion-sur-Mer and advance on Caen to secure a bridgehead there over the River Orne. The leading brigade was to secure a firm base on the Periers-sur-le-Dan feature, through which the following brigades were to advance on Caen. The division was to link up with 6 Airborne Division on the bridges over the canal and river at Benouville. The plan provided for troops of 4 Commando Brigade clearing up the area between 3 Canadian and 3 British Divisions. 1 Commando Brigade was made responsible for capturing enemy posts on the left flank of the Corps sector and the port of Ouistreham; this brigade was subsequently to join 6 Airborne Division east of the Orne, and continue clearing up enemy posts on the coast up to and including Cabourg.

H-hour for 3 British Division was fixed for 0725 hours and the assault waves reached the beaches well on time. A fairly heavy sea was running but two squadrons of amphibious tanks were launched about 4,500 yards from the shore and about half of them were able to reach the beaches abreast of the leading infantry. In general, the assault in this sector went according to plan and the leading brigade was soon a mile inland attacking Hermanville, Colleville, and battery positions on the southern outskirts of Ouistreham. The follow-up brigade came ashore shortly after 1000 hours, by which time heavy fire was coming down on the beaches and their exits: but the brigade reached its assembly positions near Hermanville quickly and pushed on southwards, meeting considerable opposition from infantry and strong points protected by concrete and minefields. The reserve brigade of 3 British Division landed soon after midday; it was moved to the left of the divisional area owing to the heavy opposition which had been encountered at Douvres-la-Delivrande.

By late afternoon Bieville had been secured, and an enemy counter attack by infantry and some twenty tanks of 21 Panzer Division was broken up with the assistance of our own armour. By nightfall, the division was well established with forward elements on the line Bieville–Benouville, where contact was made with 6 Airborne Division. Ouistreham had almost been cleared, but the Commandos had not succeeded in capturing the heavily fortified strong point at Douvres.

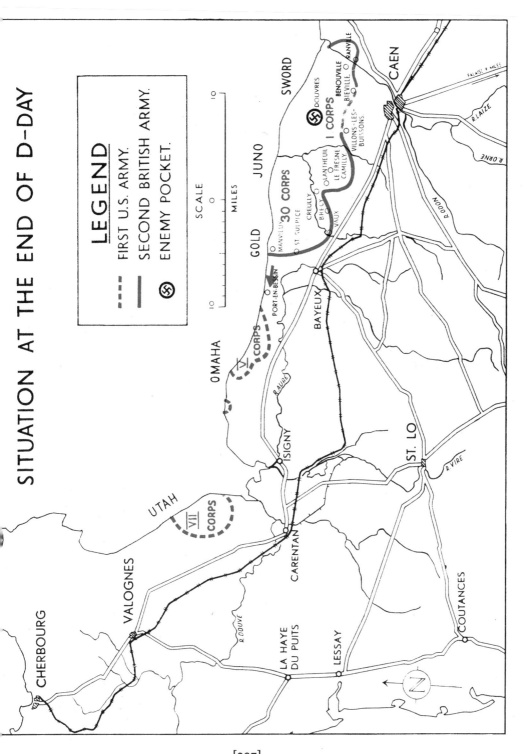

SITUATION AT THE END OF D-DAY

LEGEND

FIRST U.S. ARMY.

SECOND BRITISH ARMY.

⊗ ENEMY POCKET.

SCALE

10        0        10
MILES

CHERBOURG

VALOGNES

UTAH

VII CORPS

LA HAYE DU PUITS

LESSAY

CARENTAN

R. DOUVE

ISIGNY

OMAHA

V CORPS

PORT-EN-BESSIN

R. AURE

BAYEUX

GOLD

JUNO

30 CORPS

MANVIEU

ST. SULPICE

CREULY

BRECY

VAUX

OLANTHEUIL

LE FRESNE CAMILLY

DOUVRES

SWORD

BENOUVILLE

BIEVILLE

RANVILLE

CAEN

VILLONS-LES-BUISSONS

I CORPS

R. ODON

R. ORNE

R. LAIZE

FALAISE 9 MILES

ST. LO

R. VIRE

COUTANCES

N

East of the River Orne, 6 Airborne Division withstood a number of counter attacks during the day; in spite of heavy casualties the airborne troops succeeded in frustrating repeated attempts by enemy infantry and tanks to capture Ranville and to wipe out the Benouville bridgehead. The division was joined during the afternoon by Commandos of 1 Brigade, but attempts to expand the bridgehead northwards towards the coast were held on the line Breville–Sallenelles. At 2100 hours the gliders of 6 Air Landing Brigade arrived and served to strengthen our positions on the left flank.

### REVIEW OF THE SITUATION AT THE END OF D-DAY

As a result of our D-day operations we had gained a foothold on the Continent of Europe.

We had achieved surprise, the troops had fought magnificently, and our losses had been much lower than had ever seemed possible. We had breached the Atlantic Wall along the whole 'Neptune' frontage, and all assaulting divisions were ashore. In spite of the bad weather the sea passage across the Channel had been successfully accomplished and following this the Allied Naval Forces had given valuable support by fire from warships and craft; the Allied Air Forces had laid the foundations of success by winning the air battle before the invasion was launched, and by applying their whole collective striking power, with magnificent results, to assist the landings.

In spite of the enemy's intentions to defeat us on the beaches, we found no surprises awaiting us in Normandy. Our measures designed to overcome the defences proved successful. But not all the D-day objectives had been achieved and, in particular, the situation on Omaha beach was far from secure; in fact we had only hung on there as a result of the dogged fighting of the American infantry and its associated naval forces. Gaps remained between Second British Army and V United States Corps and also between V and VII United States Corps; in all the beachhead areas pockets of enemy resistance remained and a very considerable amount of mopping up remained to be done. In particular, a strong and dangerous enemy salient remained with its apex at Douvres.

It was early to appreciate the exact shape of the German reaction to our landings. The only armoured intervention on D-day was by 21 Panzer Division astride the Orne, north of Caen. Air reconnaissance, however, showed that columns of 12 SS Division, quartered in the area Lisieux–Laigle–Bernay, were moving west.

To sum up, the results of D-day were extremely encouraging, although the weather remained a great anxiety. I ordered the Armies to proceed with the plan; First United States Army was to complete the capture of its D-day objectives, secure Carentan and Isigny so as to link up its beachheads, and then to thrust across the base of the peninsula to isolate Cherbourg as a prelude to its reduction. Second British Army was to continue the battle for Caen, develop the bridgehead southwards across the Bayeux–Caen road and link up with V United States Corps at Port-en-Bessin.

# CHAPTER EIGHT

# The Battle of Normandy:
## 2. The Establishment of the Initial Bridgehead and the Capture of Cherbourg

### THE INITIAL PROBLEMS

I T was clear to me that we should now have to deal with three immediate problems, the solution of which was vital in order to start the campaign on a proper footing.

First it was necessary to join the individual beachheads into one continuous bridgehead. This was a task of considerable magnitude since the two Armies had assaulted on a front of about fifty miles, and in particular the American assaults were separated by the deep Carentan estuary and the system of water lines and floods associated with it. The second essential was to retain the initiative during the early stage when we were concentrating on forming a secure bridgehead; we had started with the initiative and we had to retain it in order that the battle should be swung our way. The third problem was to guard against any setback or reverse. During the initial days the Allied forces were relatively thin on the ground and time was necessary to get the whole organization sorted out and working smoothly; while this was happening there was a danger of the enemy catching us off balance. A reverse would have had very serious repercussions, not only in Normandy but also throughout the world, and it was therefore important to avoid any setback.

It was apparent on 7 June that the solution of these immediate problems was going to be complicated by the situation in the Omaha beachhead and also by the tenacity of the German defenders in a number of strong points which had been by-passed during the first day's operations. These difficulties were, however, overcome; V United States Corps fought with outstanding gallantry and retrieved the situation, while the mopping up of enemy centres of resistance inside the beachheads was eventually accomplished: although the process took some time, during which the rear areas abounded in snipers and small enemy parties which considerably hindered circulation.

### FIRST PHASE: LINKING UP THE BEACHHEADS

#### 7–12 June

On the American sectors the situation demanded the firm establishment of the Omaha beachhead, and the rapid development of operations to capture Isigny and Carentan in order to provide a proper link between V and VII United States Corps;

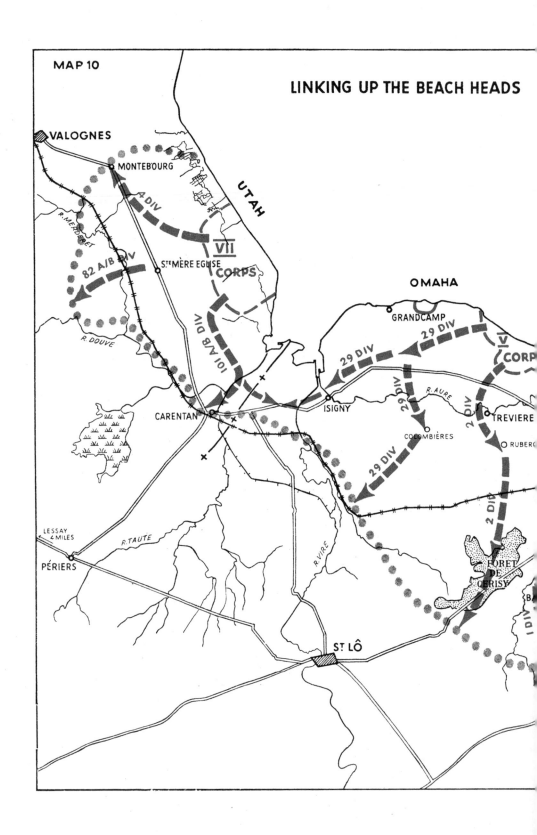

MAP 10

LINKING UP THE BEACH HEADS

VALOGNES

MONTEBOURG

UTAH

4 DIV

R. MERDERET

VII

82 A/B DIV

STᴱMÈRE EGLISE

CORPS

OMAHA

GRANDCAMP

29 DIV

V

101 A/B DIV

29 DIV

CORPS

R. DOUVE

R. AURE

TREVIERE

CARENTAN

ISIGNY

COLOMBIÈRES

RUBERC

29 DIV

2 DIV

LESSAY
4 MILES

R. TAUTE

R. VIRE

FORET
DE
OBRISY

PÉRIERS

BA

1 DIV

ST LÔ

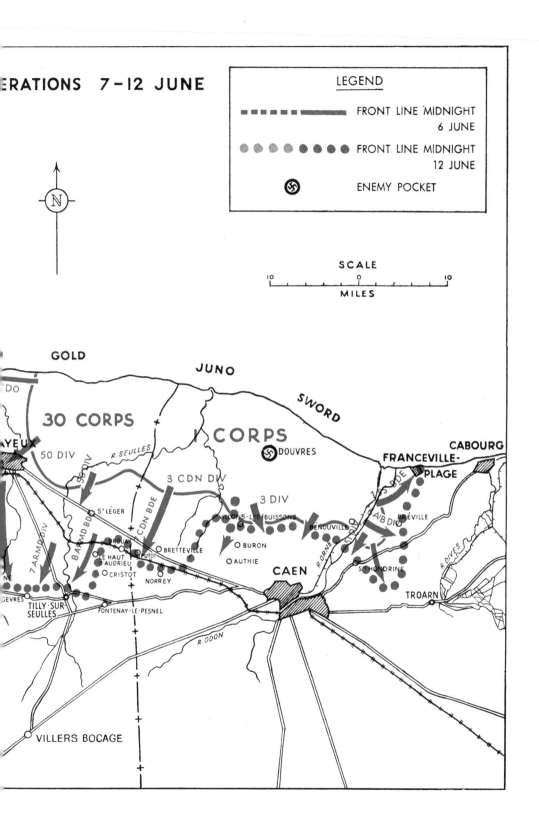

ERATIONS 7-12 JUNE

LEGEND

- - - - - - - FRONT LINE MIDNIGHT 6 JUNE
●●●●●●●● FRONT LINE MIDNIGHT 12 JUNE
✪ ENEMY POCKET

N

SCALE

10 — 0 — 10
MILES

GOLD

JUNO

SWORD

30 CORPS

I CORPS

CABOURG

50 DIV

R. SEULLES

DOUVRES

FRANCEVILLE-PLAGE

3 CDN DIV

3 DIV

BRÉVILLE

ST LÉGER

CDN BDE

VILLONS-LES-BUISSONS

BÉNOUVILLE

A/B DIV

BROUAY

BURON

PUTOT

BRETTEVILLE

LE HAUT D'AUDRIEU

AUTHIE

Sr HONORINE

CRISTOT

NORREY

CAEN

R. ORNE

R. DIVES

TROARN

TILLY-SUR-SEULLES

FONTENAY-LE-PESNEL

R. ODON

VILLERS BOCAGE

meanwhile VII Corps required to reorganize its front with the airborne divisions and set about the task of securing Cherbourg. The gap had to be closed between Omaha and Gold areas, as Port-en-Bessin was still in enemy hands; at the same time Second British Army had to develop its operations with all possible speed for the capture of Caen. On the 30 Corps front the object was to develop a thrust southwards on Tilly-sur-Seulles and Villers Bocage, in order to establish armour on commanding ground well inland, thus facilitating the development of the bridgehead.

At first light on 7 June the Omaha beaches were still under close fire from enemy weapons of all calibres, but the American troops fought sturdily and gradually extended their initial holding. Any attempt to move westwards from the bridgehead met severe enemy reaction, but progress was slowly made to the south. Patrols eastwards along the coast made contact with British troops, who captured Port-en-Bessin. On the following day advances were more substantial and the opposition on the west flank was overcome, so that by 9 June, having by-passed Grandcamp, American troops captured Isigny with a bridge over the River Vire about one mile to the south-west. Further east, crossings were effected over the River Aure and Colombières was reached. 2 United States Division came into action in the centre of the Corps bridgehead and by-passed Trévières, reaching Rubercy on 9 June. Meanwhile, on the left of the beachhead 1 United States Division made good progress and linked up with 50 British Division just west of Bayeux on 8 June.

By 10 June V United States Corps, pushing on rapidly on a three-divisional front, secured the Forêt de Cerisy with practically no opposition, and pushed patrols into Balleroy. The enemy continued to make determined efforts to prevent the junction between V and VII United States Corps and the road between Isigny and Carentan was under heavy fire; by 10 June, however, patrols of 29 United States Division were in contact with 101 Airborne Division and two days later, when Carentan was finally captured, the beachheads had been securely linked. The enemy put up a fierce fight for Carentan and 101 Airborne Division was much hampered in the operation by the difficult nature of the flooded country. With the joining of V and VII United States Corps, our bridgehead was made continuous throughout the invasion frontage.

Operations from Utah beach developed well on 7 and 8 June. 101 Airborne Division was relieved in order to concentrate on the capture of Carentan, and junction was effected with 82 Airborne Division in the Ste Mère Eglise area. Thereafter, while 82 Airborne Division pushed westwards beyond the River Merderet, 4 United States Division was advancing north towards Montebourg, where heavy fighting took place on 10 June.

The operations for the capture of Caen were continued from the north by 3 British Division and from the north-west and west by 3 Canadian Division; but it quickly became apparent that the enemy was concerned for the security of this nodal point, and was quick to bring forward reserve formations to hold us off from the town and to prevent the expansion of our bridgehead south of the Caen–Bayeux road. On 7 June, 3 Canadian Division pressed forward and reached its objectives on the Bayeux–Caen road at Putot-en-Bessin and Bretteville L'Orgueilleuse, with forward troops south of the road at Norrey-en-Bessin, while further east Authie was reached. The enemy resistance became increasingly severe and culminated in a major counter attack against Authie; after a heavy engagement the Canadians withdrew to Villons-les-Buissons to reorganize. At 2200 hours a further counter attack developed from Buron, but this was successfully beaten off. In these engagements the Canadians were faced by tanks of 21 Panzer Division and infantry from 12 SS Panzer Division, both of which suffered severe casualties. Over the next three days further enemy counter attacks developed, but the Canadians stood firm and on 11 June launched a further attack in the same area which became heavily engaged with enemy tanks and anti-tank guns.

Meanwhile 3 British Division was pressing attacks towards Caen from the north against strong opposition which included tanks. The enemy was well concealed and in strength, and his positions were covered by minefields and anti-tank ditches; although fighting was continuous our troops were not able to make any great headway in this sector.

While 1 Corps operations were developing round Caen, 30 Corps was engaged in heavy fighting in the Tilly-sur-Seulles sector. The intention was to thrust south through Tilly-sur-Seulles towards Villers Bocage, employing initially 8 Armoured Brigade, which was to be followed by 7 Armoured Division (then coming ashore). On the morning of 9 June, Le Haut d'Audrieu was seized and the advance continued towards the road triangle east of Tilly. In addition to 12 SS Panzer Division, tanks of Panzer Lehr Division were identified in this sector and although 7 Armoured Division came into action near Tilly on 10 June, progress was slow. On the following day elements of 7 Armoured Division fought their way into Tilly, but were subsequently driven out by a very heavy counter attack.

On the morning of 12 June the 30 Corps advance had reached the general line La Belle Epine–Lingevres–Tilly–Fontenay-le-Pesnel–Cristot–Bronay. In these villages the enemy had established strong points with a co-ordinated system of anti-tank defences backed up by detachments of infantry and armour. It was therefore decided by Second Army to regroup and to launch 7 Armoured Division on a new thrust line, which would sweep down from the right flank of 50 Division and come in on Villers Bocage from the west; this drive would continue eastwards towards Evreçy and the high ground between the Rivers Odon and Orne. The attack, if successful, would threaten the enemy forces covering Caen on the north and north-west.

East of the River Orne our troops were concerned in maintaining the bridgehead in face of continuous counter attacks, and in developing operations towards the coastal sector and Cabourg.

1 Commando Brigade secured Franceville Plage, but efforts to capture Cabourg were held up by strong enemy defences. On 8, 9 and 10 June, 6 Airborne Division withstood persistent enemy attacks and took heavy toll of the enemy. Meanwhile 51 Division was arriving and concentrating in the Orne bridgehead in preparation

for attacks which were to be developed towards the eastern outskirts of Caen. This move was to be complementary to 30 Corps thrust from the west.

### THE ENEMY SITUATION IN THE OPENING PHASE

### 6–12 June (*Map 3*)

The enemy's detailed dispositions in the assault area were quickly clarified by our identifications: by 9 June the estimated number of prisoners taken was 6,000. It was soon evident that the West Normandy area had been, as we suspected, considerably reinforced during May. The sectors of the two original coastal divisions covering the immediate assault frontage had been shortened by the introduction of 352 Division in Omaha area and by the move of 243 Division to the north-west. The Cotentin peninsula had been strengthened by the arrival of 91 Division with a parachute regiment.

Although these identifications were no surprise, the location of 352 and 91 Divisions within the coastal 'crust' obviously made our initial task more formidable: and betrayed Rommel's influence in the siting of reserves.

When the battle began the principal enemy armoured and motorized divisions in reserve in the west were disposed at intervals covering the coast from Antwerp to Avignon. Immediately available for action in Normandy were the following divisions: 21 Panzer (area Caen), 12 SS Panzer (area Evreux), Panzer Lehr (area Chartres). 17 SS Panzer Grenadier Division was south of the Loire, while the other formations were 116 Panzer (north of the Seine), 2 Panzer (area Amiens), 11 Panzer (area Bordeaux), 1 SS Panzer (Belgium), 2 SS Panzer (area Toulouse), and 9 Panzer (area Avignon). Our immediate attention was therefore directed to these ten divisions; but the enemy had also a number of field infantry divisions at ready call. These included 3 and 6 Parachute and 77 Divisions in Brittany, with 84 and 85 Divisions north of the Seine.

21 Panzer Division was in action on D-day north of Caen, and main bodies of 12 SS, Panzer Lehr and 17 SS Panzer Grenadier Divisions were identified on 7, 9 and 12 June respectively, the first west of Caen and the others south of Bayeux and astride the Aure. By 9 June, 1 SS Panzer was moving south and 2 SS Panzer, 2 Panzer and 11 Panzer Divisions were all making preparations for a move or were actually en route. By 12 June, 3 Parachute and 77 Divisions had been identified on our front, bringing the total number of enemy divisions involved to twelve. It will be remembered that we had reckoned that we might have to face twenty enemy divisions by this date, including eight Panzer. The 'missing' infantry was still, however, north-east of the Seine awaiting a landing in the Pas de Calais, while the 'missing' armour had been forced by air attacks to move on side roads and mainly by night. In the case of 2 Panzer Division, coming from Amiens, the approach march was so delayed that the division did not arrive till 13 June. These delays were a convincing revelation of the power of our Air Forces and of the selling power of our Cover Plan.

# MAP II

## ENEMY ORDER OF BATTLE IN WEST NORMANDY AS AT 6 JUNE, 1944.

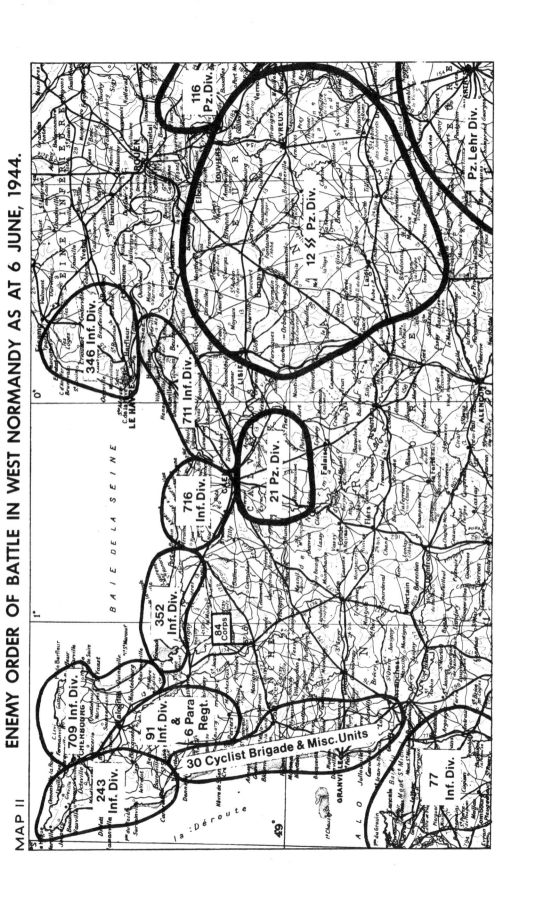

What was the reaction of the German High Command to the assault and the rapid penetration of the coastal defences?

We now know that the extent of the surprise we attained was more than could have been imagined possible. The disruption of enemy communications caused by our bombing, and the breakdown of his radar caused by our counter measures, left the enemy for a considerable time in doubt about the actual extent and strength of our assault. It was some considerable time before adequate information got back to Hitler, and even more before coherent orders were issued from higher headquarters to the fighting formations.

That 21 Panzer Division counter attacked, and 12 SS moved, on 6 June was due to their commanders' own initiative. Not only did the enemy appreciate that our landings in the Cotentin peninsula were intended merely as a diversionary effort, which they could deal with easily, but the notion persisted that the whole operation was in itself a diversionary operation which was only the prelude to the main Allied invasion to be delivered in the Pas de Calais. As a result, the enemy completely misappreciated the scope of our landings and of our subsequent build-up, and this in turn was vitally to affect his decisions regarding calling divisions from northern France into Normandy.

The reaction of the German Supreme Command on receiving news of our landings is shown in a telephone conversation at 1655 hours on D-day between von Rundstedt's Chief of Staff and the Chief of Staff Seventh German Army. Hitler desired that the bridgehead should be annihilated by the evening of 6 June. This order, fantastic in retrospect, shows how little was known in Paris or Berlin of the magnitude of the Allied operation. Owing to bad communications, it is doubtful whether these orders were ever in fact passed on to the divisions concerned. The Chief of the German General Staff had apparently already said he thought the task impossible to carry out, but Rommel ordered that 21 Panzer Division should attack immediately.

Post-war interrogation of the German generals who were in Normandy shows the considerable confusion which existed in the enemy formations on D-day. A good example is 21 Panzer Division, the commander of which heard news of our approach just after midnight but received no order of any kind from his superior headquarters until 0700 hours that morning. Although he had been ordered to make no move until the arrival of instructions from Army Group 'B', on his own initiative he decided to attack the British 6 Airborne Division, and gave orders to this effect at 0630 hours. At 0700 hours he did not get any definite order as to the role his division was to play in resisting the invasion, and it was not until 1000 hours that an Operation Order arrived which cancelled his move against 6 Airborne Division and ordered him west to assist the forces covering Caen.

To add to the confusion caused by the breakdown of communications, it was apparent that the enemy plans for meeting our attack were vague and that, because of the differences between von Rundstedt and Rommel, no co-ordinated plan as to how to deal with a major onslaught in Normandy had been made. This fact, together with the manner in which the enemy reserve divisions were disposed and the delays caused by our bombing designed to impede the German concentration, led to the commitment piecemeal of the enemy formations as they arrived in the battle area. Our offensive policy, and our thrusts designed to 'peg out claims' inland, forced Rommel to adopt a policy of plugging the holes.

As we had planned, the enemy also misappreciated our local intentions. Uncertain initially of our flanks owing to the size and success of our airborne landings, he became immediately apprehensive of a rapid exploitation towards the ports of Cherbourg and Rouen and of the possible design of striking towards the Pas de Calais to link with the main assault he was anticipating. His first reactions were attempts to block Caen and destroy our bridgehead on the right bank of the Orne; to oppose VII US Corps in strength at Montebourg (in order to protect Cherbourg); and to split the beachhead strip by contesting Carentan.

These three efforts were essentially defensive. His offensive efforts consisted of strong local attacks by the three Panzer divisions—21, 12 SS and Lehr—all along the front between the Orne and the Seulles. These attacks should have been co-ordinated, but owing to Allied air attacks, shortage of petrol, bad communications, and the inability of the infantry to hold its ground, they degenerated into a series of bitter local engagements. Very soon it was realized that it was beyond their strength alone to regain the beaches, and they settled down to the uncomfortable task of containing our beachhead while more Panzer and infantry divisions were brought up.

## The Situation, 12 June

The beachheads had now been firmly linked into a continuous bridgehead on a front of over fifty miles, varying in depth eight to twelve miles. With the arrival of 51 Division, the Orne bridgehead was more secure and additional bridging over the river and canal was put in hand.

We had firmly retained the initiative. The enemy was engaging his formations piecemeal in response to our thrusts. I appreciated that the vigour of his attacks to the west of Caen would be further strengthened as fresh reserves became available and felt that the plan for engaging his reserves on my eastern flank was beginning to take shape. Meanwhile it was likely that he would react further to the threat to Cherbourg; to do this he would endeavour to hold open a corridor on the west of the Cotentin and try to hold our thrust towards St Lô.

At this stage, in spite of the signs of movement already mentioned, no enemy formation had made the difficult journey from north of the Seine; a long detour was imposed by the wrecked bridges over the river and the bulk of the Fifteenth German Army waited grimly for an assault in the Pas de Calais.

The weather remained a great anxiety. Our build-up was already getting behind schedule; it reflects great credit on the Navy and the beach organizations that so much was accomplished in spite of the continually unfavourable weather conditions.

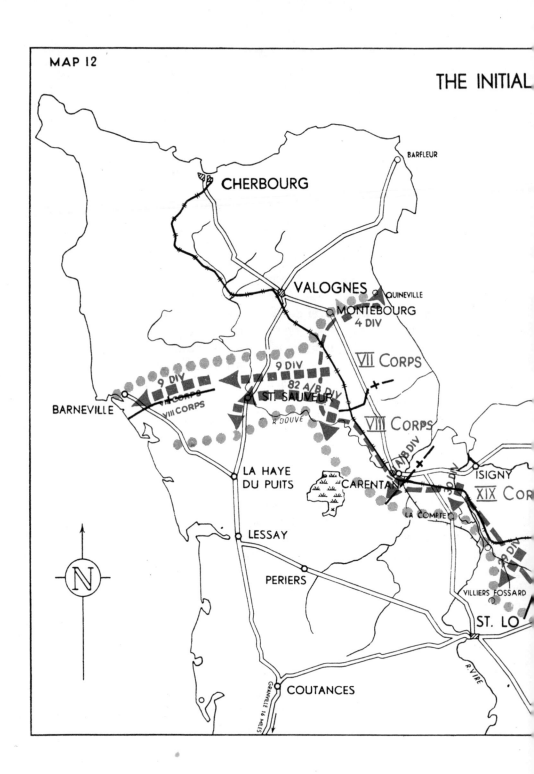

MAP 12

THE INITIAL

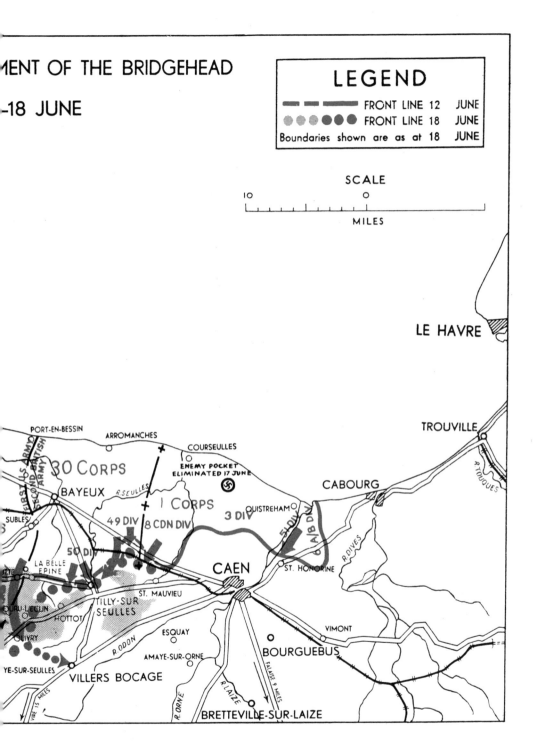

MENT OF THE BRIDGEHEAD

-18 JUNE

LEGEND

FRONT LINE 12 JUNE
FRONT LINE 18 JUNE
Boundaries shown are as at 18 JUNE

SCALE

10                    0

MILES

LE HAVRE

TROUVILLE

PORT-EN-BESSIN

ARROMANCHES

COURSEULLES

30 CORPS

ENEMY POCKET
ELIMINATED 17 JUNE

BAYEUX   R.SEULLES

CABOURG

1 CORPS

SUBLES

49 DIV  8 CDN DIV

3 DIV

QUISTREHAM

51 DIV

6 A/B DIV

50 DIV

LA BELLE
EPINE

CAEN

ST. HONORINE

R. DIVES

R.TOUQUES

TILLY-SUR
SEULLES

ST. MAUVIEU

URU-LECLIN

HOTTOT

ESQUAY

VIMONT

IVRY

R. ODON

AMAYE-SUR-ORNE

BOURGUEBUS

YE-SUR-SEULLES

VILLERS BOCAGE

R. ORNE

R. LAIZE

BRETTEVILLE-SUR-LAIZE

VIRE 15 MILES

FALAISE 9 MILES

FIRST US. ARMY   SECOND BRITISH ARMY

[219]

During the first six days 326,000 men, 54,000 vehicles and 104,000 tons of stores had been landed.

### THE SLOW-DOWN IN OUR OPERATIONS

It was inevitable that after the successful outcome of the assault, the pace of operations slowed down. The assault formations needed time for a 'breather', while they reorganized and re-absorbed the echelons which had been left behind for the first days, but without which no unit could function for long. The beach organization had to be established and built up to its full efficiency. The whole administrative machine had to commence functioning on shore and initial shortages made up.

As mentioned, the build-up was falling behind schedule and this added to our difficulties.

In spite of these circumstances it was vital to retain the initiative, which could only be ensured by continuing the offensive. I therefore ordered a policy of limited offensive operations in furtherance of the plan, which were carried out although they often involved great risks. But the policy was successful mainly owing to the fine quality of the assaulting formations and the excellent support they were afforded by the Allied Air Forces. My immediate objects remained to capture Cherbourg and Caen, and to develop the central sector of the bridgehead to Caumont and Villers Bocage. Examination was made of the possibility of using airborne forces to hasten the capture of Caen, but conditions were found to be unsuitable for their employment.

### SECOND PHASE:
### THE INITIAL DEVELOPMENT OF THE BRIDGEHEAD

#### 13–18 June

On the western flank, operations against Cherbourg continued with the cutting off of the Cotentin peninsula and the concentration of forces for the drive on Cherbourg, while further east enemy attempts to regain Carentan were successfully resisted. In Second British Army the operations in the Tilly-sur-Seulles sector were maintained, still with the object of developing a southern pincer movement towards Caen by 30 Corps, while 1 Corps maintained steady pressure on the mounting enemy forces grouped round the town.

The enemy made urgent attempts to break the junction between Utah and Omaha sectors by counter attacking in the Carentan area, and committed 17 SS Panzer Grenadier Division for this purpose. On 13 June, 101 Airborne Division, assisted by tanks from 2 United States Armoured Division, not only withstood the enemy onslaught but made some progress in the general direction of Periers, though the marshlands in the area greatly restricted manœuvre. Further enemy counter attacks developed in this sector on 15 June. Meanwhile the fighting round Montebourg continued; the enemy was resisting strongly in this area, but the Americans gradually closed in on the town and also captured Quineville on 14 June. Enemy attempts to recapture Carentan and to block the main road to Cherbourg in the Montebourg area had left him weak in the centre, and the American forces were now well placed to cut off the peninsula. On 14 June 9 Infantry Division, assisted by 82 Airborne Division drove west through St Sauveur-le-Vicomte directed to the sea coast about Barneville. St Sauveur fell on 16 June to the airborne troops, who then wheeled south to protect the left flank, while 9 Division continued the advance to the coast which was reached on 18 June.

A regrouping of the American divisions in the peninsula had meanwhile been taking place. On 15 June, VIII United States Corps became operational and took under command both airborne divisions and 90 Infantry Division. The Corps task was to face south and protect the rear of the forthcoming operations for the capture of Cherbourg. XIX Corps took the field on 14 June, with 2 Armoured and 30 Infantry Divisions together with 29 Infantry Division from V Corps. This Corps was to develop the bridgehead in the Carentan–Isigny area and to advance on St Lô round the east of the marshland area. On 15 June, La Compte was occupied and the advance continued towards the Canal de Vire. Attempts to make further ground west of the Vire were ineffective; all bridges over the canal had been blown and the enemy covering the waterway was located in strong defensive positions strengthened by mines. On the right bank of the Vire, however, 29 Infantry Division made progress, so that by 18 June First United States Army was disposed with VII United States Corps facing north with three divisions, while facing south, from Barneville on the west coast of the Cotentin to Caumont, were VIII, XIX and V United States Corps. The line ran north of both La Haye du Puits and St Lô, between which places the floods and marshes greatly handicapped our deployment.

30 Corps of Second British Army launched 7 Armoured Division in its new thrust towards Villers Bocage in the late afternoon of 12 June on the axis Subles–La Butte–La Paumerie–Amaye-sur-Seulles, roughly along the inter-army boundary. V United States Corps assisted by granting running rights over certain routes. 7 Armoured Division was to seize the high ground north-east of Villers Bocage by by-passing the town from the south, and was to be followed up by 50 Division. The advance in the afternoon made good progress, and leading tanks reached Livry about three miles north-east of Caumont at 1745 hours, by which time main bodies were some three miles in rear. By dark the leading troops had completed the southwards thrust and were beginning to wheel to the east. The following morning the area of Villers Bocage was reached and the town entered, while patrols were pushed to the east and south. During this manœuvre little opposition was encountered from Panzer Lehr Division, but on 13 June 2 Panzer Division, which was fresh from Amiens and had been ordered to the Caumont sector to stabilize the line in front of the Americans, arrived unexpectedly at Villers Bocage. Each side was surprised to find the other in the town; enemy counter attacks came in from the south-west and south-east and there was some heavy fighting at close quarters. At 1800 hours it was decided to

withdraw from Villers Bocage to the high ground about two miles west of the town and this was successfully accomplished, after which further enemy counter attacks were broken up. Meanwhile 50 Division had started its advance south, but it met heavy opposition and little progress was made beyond the Balleroy–Tilly road.

On 14 June, 7 Armoured Division was holding a line from just west of Villers Bocage to the inter-army boundary near Caumont and was in touch with 1 United States Infantry Division. During the afternoon, a series of heavy enemy attacks developed, and as 50 Division was held up on the line La Belle Epine–Tilly-sur-Seulles, the exposed position of 7 Armoured Division became untenable. Orders were issued for a withdrawal of about five miles to the area of Parfouru–l'Eclin, on the River Aure. In the evening two columns of enemy made further attacks and heavy fighting ensued in which great execution was caused by our artillery fire, including the support of guns of V United States Corps. The disengagement began at 2300 hours and was successfully completed during the night. Claims for the day's fighting were forty tanks knocked out, while very heavy losses were inflicted on the enemy infantry.

7 Armoured Division was now ordered to hold firm, while 49 Division (which landed on 13 June) and 50 Division were to press south and south-west to capture Hottot and Tilly. By 18 June this fighting had been going on for three days and was particularly violent round the town of Tilly, which was eventually captured on 19 June.

The north-eastern pincer movement on Caen did not make very much progress. 51 Division attacked St Honôrine on 13 June, but, having taken the village, was unable to hold it in the face of subsequent enemy counter attacks. Thereafter any attempt to enlarge the Orne bridgehead met very determined enemy reaction.

In the centre of the British sector, 1 Corps was concerned in maintaining its positions in face of the steady and continuous pressure exerted by the German armour of 12 SS Panzer and 21 Panzer Divisions. As a result little progress was possible.

On 15 June, 8 Corps began to arrive on the Continent but, owing to delays in the build-up, the leading formation (11 Armoured Division) was two days behind schedule. This retarding of the build-up was to have unfortunate repercussions on the subsequent development of my plans.

By 18 June the enemy had deployed four armoured divisions between the Caumont area and Caen, while 17 SS Panzer Grenadier Division was committed in the Carentan sector. 2 Panzer Division, the latest armoured arrival, was committed astride our inter-army boundary. The three fresh infantry formations identified were all located on the west; 3 Parachute Division in the St Lô sector, and 77 with 353 Division in the Cotentin. It has been seen that the enemy continued to employ his reserves in Caen, and in the recapture of Carentin and the saving of Cherbourg. When we cut the Carentin peninsula the enemy was left with remnants of four different infantry divisions defending the fortress.

### The Situation, 18 June

Although the enemy had managed to delay our progress towards Cherbourg, and to prevent us getting into Caen, he had been unable to release his Panzer divisions in order to regroup them for a properly mounted major counter attack. We had retained the initiative and were steadily pursuing our plan. We had so far achieved our object in drawing the bulk of the enemy armour on to the eastern flank, which was the first basic point upon which the design of operations was formed. The second factor was the development of our own build-up, and in this disappointments had to be faced: not only from the delay in taking the port of Cherbourg, but also owing to the adverse effect the weather was having on our beach working. To offset this, success in the third basic matter, that of delaying the enemy build-up, was achieved to a remarkable degree. The strategic bombing policy of the pre-D-day period was now yielding good dividends, and the growing paralysis over enemy communications was beginning to give us a tremendous advantage. The remorseless air offensive against enemy headquarters, communications and detraining stations had caused disorganization which was aggravated by the activities of our SAS troops and the French Resistance. These facts are well illustrated by the following quotation from a report by von Rundstedt:

> 'Marching during day time in good weather is definitely excluded. It is therefore necessary to make the most of the short summer nights . . . but the troops must be prepared for low level attacks at any time. Rail transports can hardly be brought up nearer to the front than 150 to 200 kilometres; even this must be done without any definite schedule. The routes must be changed hourly . . .'

My immediate aim remained to capture Cherbourg and Caen, and to get both Armies into position facing south in order to prepare for the break-out on the western flank. I wrote in my directive on 18 June that once the enemy's 'roping off' policy could be snapped, he would obviously find it very difficult to gather resources to stabilize the situation. With all the Allied forces facing south the enemy would be confronted with a very difficult problem, and it was to be expected that he would then make the threat in Normandy take precedence over other potential threats, including his fear of a thrust in the Pas de Calais. 'It was then that we might have a mighty chance to make the German Army come to our threat, and to defeat it between the Seine and the Loire.'

My orders on 18 June, which were finalized the following day, instructed First United States Army to capture Cherbourg and clear the peninsula of enemy. Moreover, operations were to be developed against La Haye du Puits and Coutances at the earliest possible moment without waiting for the fall of Cherbourg. XV United States Corps (of three infantry divisions) was to be brought through the Omaha beaches beginning 24 June, and as soon as additional American troops were available First United States Army was to break away to the south directed on Granville, Avranches and Vire. The left wing of the army was to maintain the closest touch with Second Army in order to protect the British right flank. Second Army was to capture Caen and provide a strong eastern flank for the Army Group: continuing the policy of

[223]

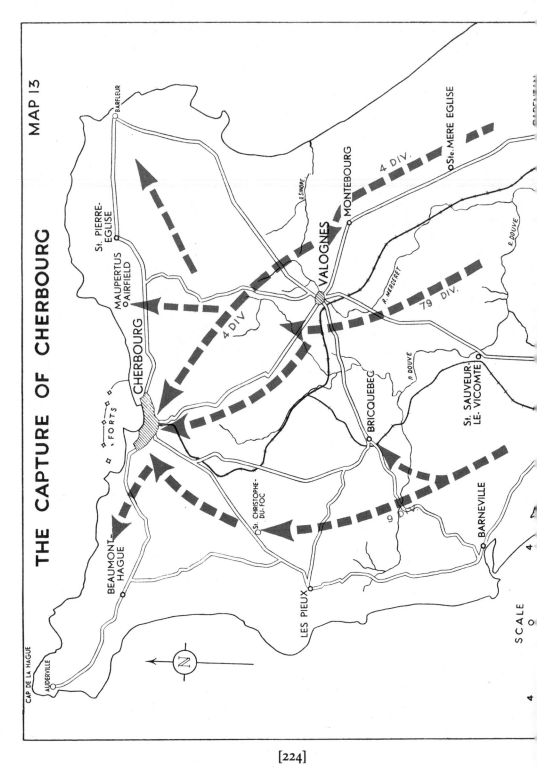

THE CAPTURE OF CHERBOURG

MAP 13

[224]

absorbing the enemy reserve divisions in its sector. The operations against Caen were to continue on the basis of two enveloping movements; the western arm of the pincer was to be launched across the Rivers Odon and Orne on the axis St Mauvieu–Esquay–Amaye-sur-Orne, while the eastern arm was to operate from the Orne bridgehead north of Caen. I had originally intended that 8 Corps would carry out the eastern pincer movement, but detailed examination of the problem revealed that it would be very difficult to form up a whole corps in the bridgehead east of the river; the area was exposed and subject to continual enemy fire, and there were insufficient routes and space generally at this stage for a major deployment. I therefore had to scale down the eastern thrust, which was made the responsibility of 1 Corps. Meanwhile 8 Corps was to provide the main movement from the west with the object of establishing itself, strong in armour, to the south-east of Caen in the area Bourguebus–Vimont–Bretteville-sur-Laize. It will be noticed that the intention to get a strong force into this area remained from now onwards the fundamental object of my strategy on the eastern flank: it was the key to ensuring the retention of the bulk of the enemy armour on the Second Army front. I had hoped to launch the offensive on 18 June, but at that time certain essential units and types of artillery ammunition were still waiting in the anchorage to be unloaded. I was forced to postpone the date of the operation to 22 June owing to the delays caused by unfavourable weather. My calculations were to be further upset by a gale of unprecedented violence which lasted from 19 to 22 June.

### THIRD PHASE: THE CAPTURE OF CHERBOURG AND THE ESTABLISHMENT OF THE ODON BRIDGEHEAD

#### 19–30 June

Following the isolation of Cherbourg, VII United States Corps continued operations northwards on a front of three divisions. On the right flank, 4 United States Infantry Division delivered a surprise attack on 19 June without artillery preparation and advanced to seize the high ground north-west of Montebourg. Prepared defences were encountered and the town held out until the evening; by nightfall the division was very close to Valognes. In the centre, 79 United States Division thrust towards the high ground north-west of Valognes and by night was astride the approaches to the town from the west, while 9 United States Division made a rapid advance, capturing Bricquebec by midday and reaching St Cristophe-du-Foc by the end of the day. On 20 and 21 June the Corps closed in on the defences of Cherbourg itself and began preparations for the final assault, which commenced in the afternoon of 22 June. The attack was preceded by heavy air action on the enemy positions, but although much damage was done to the defences, there were many points of resistance and the main progress was made on the flanks. On 23 June, the airfield about five miles east of Cherbourg was secured together with commanding

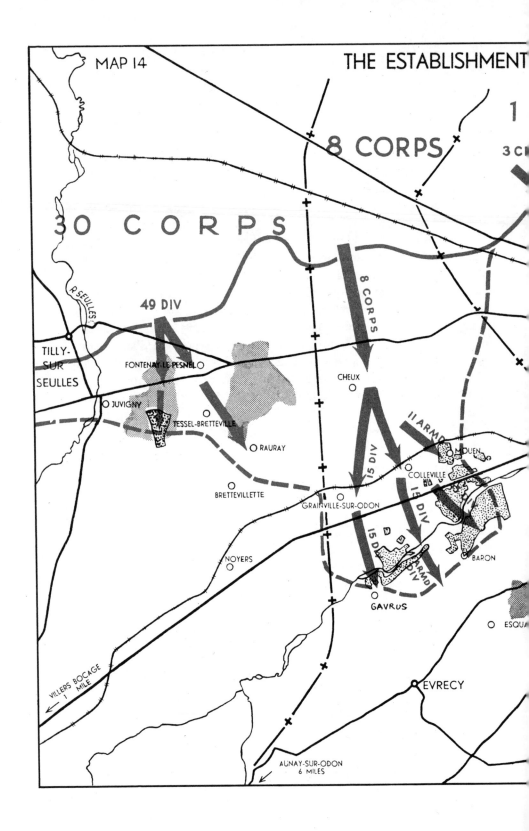

MAP 14                    THE ESTABLISHMENT

1

8 CORPS ✕

3 C[

30 CORPS

8 CORPS

R SEULLES

49 DIV

TILLY-
SUR-
SEULLES

FONTENAY-LE-PESNEL○

CHEUX
○

○ JUVIGNY

TESSEL-BRETTEVILLE

II ARMD

○UEN

COLLEVILLE

○ RAURAY

15 DIV

○
BRETTEVILLETTE

15 DIV

○
GRAINVILLE-SUR-ODON

15 DIV

ARMD
DIV

○ BARON

○
NOYERS

○ ESQUA

○
GAVRUS

○ESQUA

VILLERS BOCAGE
1   MILE
←

○EVRECY

AUNAY-SUR-ODON
6 MILES
←

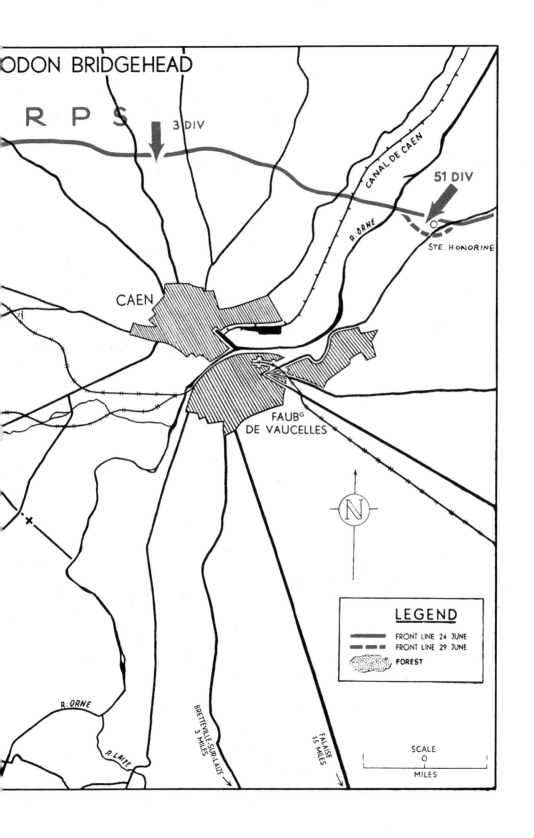

ODON BRIDGEHEAD

R P S

3 DIV

CANAL DE CAEN

51 DIV

R. ORNE

STE. HONORINE

CAEN

FAUB<sup>G</sup>
DE VAUCELLES

N

R. ORNE

BRETTEVILLE-SUR-LAIZE
3 MILES

FALAISE
15 MILES

R. LAIZE

LEGEND

FRONT LINE 24 JUNE
FRONT LINE 29 JUNE
FOREST

SCALE
0
MILES

ground on that flank and on the following day all three divisions reached the outskirts of the town. On 25 June, supported by naval gunfire, artillery and the air forces, troops broke into Cherbourg; two of the main forts were captured and the area of the arsenal was reached. The following day the dominating fortification, St Sauveur, was secured and the German garrison commander surrendered with the local Admiral. They were, however, unable to communicate with all the isolated groups of enemy still offering resistance and sharp fighting continued at various points. On 27 June the garrison of the arsenal was persuaded to surrender with the aid of a sound truck operated by a Psychological Warfare unit, and during the next two days resistance ceased from the outlying forts in the harbour. Forces in the north-west corner of the peninsula had not been included in any of the surrenders and it was necessary for 9 Division to clear them out, a task which was finally accomplished on 1 July.

As a result of these operations the enemy lost some 39,000 prisoners, and VII United States Corps was now free to concentrate to the south in preparation for the next phase of operations. The port installations at Cherbourg had been very considerably wrecked by the enemy, and the anchorages and basins mined. The task of opening the port was energetically tackled by the Allied navies, but it was to be late August before Cherbourg was in a fit state to receive heavy lifts alongside berths.

To implement my instructions for the development of the pincer movement on Caen, Second Army regrouped in order to launch 30, 8 and 1 Corps into the operation. I was determined to develop this plan with the utmost intensity with the whole available weight of the British forces. I wanted Caen, but realized that in either event our thrusts would probably provoke increasing enemy resistance: which would fit in well with my plan of campaign.

Second Army plan provided for the start of the main thrust to be in the 30 Corps sector; the intention was to hold firm on the right and central sectors of the Corps front, and on the left to advance and secure the area of Noyers. This movement would protect the right flank of 8 Corps and was to be exploited towards Aunay-sur-Odon. 8 Corps was to be launched through the front of 3 Canadian Division, with a view to forcing crossings over the Rivers Odon and Orne and gaining a position on the high ground north-east of Bretteville-sur-Laize, dominating the exits from Caen to the south. The operation was planned in two phases, the first culminating with the seizure of the Orne crossings. 8 Corps had two infantry divisions and two armoured divisions, with two additional armoured brigades available for the task. In the 1 Corps sector, the intention was to ensure the security of the bridgehead, and prepare to eliminate the enemy salient north of Caen and clear the city, as the 8 Corps thrust took shape.

I have already mentioned that my orders provided for the main effort of Second Army to be launched on 22 June, but the continued bad weather made it impossible to adhere to this date. I have also referred to the gale which raged between 19 and 22 June; by 20 June we were already five days behind in our planned build-up, and I had to inform the Supreme Commander that owing to the late arrival of 8 Corps formations the earliest date on which I could deliver its attack was 25 June: and then only provided the weather improved. Eventually 30 Corps attack was fixed for 25 June, with the 8 Corps thrust commencing twenty-four hours later.

On 23 June, 1 Corps carried out a preliminary operation in the Orne bridgehead as a result of which 51 Division captured St Honôrine. This provoked a fierce counter attack by 21 Panzer Division which was driven off.

30 Corps started its thrust on 25 June with the object of occupying a commanding feature in the Rauray area. The attack by 49 Division with 8 Armoured Brigade under command began in darkness and thick mist at 0415 hours. During the morning steady progress was made on the right, and by the afternoon the high ground at Tessel Bretteville was reached and patrols pushed through the wood to the south. Meanwhile on the left considerable opposition was encountered in Fontenay and progress was halted. At 2100 hours a fresh attack with tank support was successful and Fontenay was in our hands by midnight in spite of the opposition. During the day we had been opposed mainly by 12 SS Panzer and Panzer Lehr Divisions. On the morning of 26 June the attack on Rauray was resumed from the high ground at Tessel Bretteville, but progress was soon brought to a halt by fierce resistance and the fact that the country was unsuitable for tanks; the armour, therefore, disengaged and was switched to resume the attack from the left flank. During the night 8 Armoured Brigade reached the outskirts of Rauray with infantry in close support. Heavy fighting continued throughout the following day, and the enemy mounted several tank attacks from the south and south-west; but our positions held, and on 28 June Brettevillette was captured, but subsequently lost again in the face of a counter attack by 2 SS Panzer Division.

Meanwhile the 8 Corps attack was launched at 0730 hours on 26 June with 15 Division leading. The enemy was well concealed in difficult country, and extensive minefields covered his positions. The weather was bad with heavy rain and low cloud, but progress was made during the day in spite of heavy fighting, particularly around Cheux. By the end of the day leading troops were well south of the village with patrols in Grainville-sur-Odon and with a battalion established in Colleville; elements of 11 Armoured Division were in Mouen.

During 27 June operations continued in order to square up to the River Odon, pass 11 Armoured Division through to the high ground in the Evreçy–Esquay area, and subsequently to secure a bridgehead across the Orne. During the morning there was confused fighting, the main core of enemy resistance being in the Grainville area. This was gradually by-passed and by late afternoon infantry were across the Odon. A little later a bridge was secured intact about one mile west of Baron and tanks were able to join the infantry on the east bank of the river.

The intention now was to widen the corridor down to the river by eliminating the enemy in the Grainville area, and to widen the Odon bridgehead by establishing additional crossings further south on the Evreçy road.

Early on the morning of 28 June the bulk of 11 Armoured Division was across the river moving towards Esquay and the dominating feature called Point 112, both of which the enemy was holding with Panzer detachments and anti-tank guns. By mid-afternoon our tanks were in the area of Point 112 and were working round to the north-east of Evreçy, but the enemy fought stubbornly and at the end of the day our armour was withdrawn into the bridgehead from its isolated positions on the high ground. Meanwhile a series of separate attacks was launched to mop up resistance on the flanks of the Corps axis, in addition to which a second bridgehead was secured across the Odon in the area of Gavrus.

On 29 June operations continued to enlarge the Odon bridgehead and finally to stabilize the corridor as a prelude to launching 11 Armoured Division to the River Orne. In the corridor, progress was made by 15 Division across the railway near Grainville and, further south, towards the main Noyers–Caen road. On its left, 43 Division was dealing with determined opposition in the woods and orchards about the Odon and by evening had one brigade east of the river. At this stage in the operation the enemy made a determined effort to restore the situation. He put in a strong counter attack from the south-west, with one thrust astride the River Odon and the other astride the Noyers–Caen road; enemy detachments also infiltrated towards Cheux. Heavy fighting went on along the whole right flank of the Corps salient and the southern bridge at Gavrus was lost. By evening the situation had gradually improved and the enemy was driven off after having sustained heavy casualties.

During the day both 1 and 2 SS Panzer Divisions were encountered, and 9 SS Panzer Division with reconnaissance elements of 10 SS Panzer Division, both from the Eastern Front, also made their appearance. There were now elements of no fewer than eight Panzer divisions on the twenty mile stretch of the Second Army front between Caumont and Caen. In view of this it was decided that 8 Corps should concentrate for the time being on holding the ground won, and regrouping started with the object of withdrawing our armour into reserve ready for renewed thrusts.

In 1 Corps sector the divisions continued offensive activity and some local gains were made, but there was no major progress, since the 8 Corps operation had not progressed sufficiently far to threaten the enemy defenders north of Caen, who continued to fight stubbornly.

*The Situation, 30 June*

The enemy had committed 21 Panzer, 12 SS and Panzer Lehr Divisions to a series of desperate but unco-ordinated attacks to regain the beaches, and these had failed.

The next step was obviously to try and seal off the beachhead until a really strong armoured force could be concentrated for a decisive attack. Owing, however, to the delays imposed by air attack and sabotage, this concentration of the armour in Normandy took over a fortnight to achieve. In the period 13–30 June five more Panzer divisions—2 Panzer, 1 SS, 2 SS, 9 SS and 10 SS—joined those already involved.

Late as they were, their combined effort would have been very formidable had

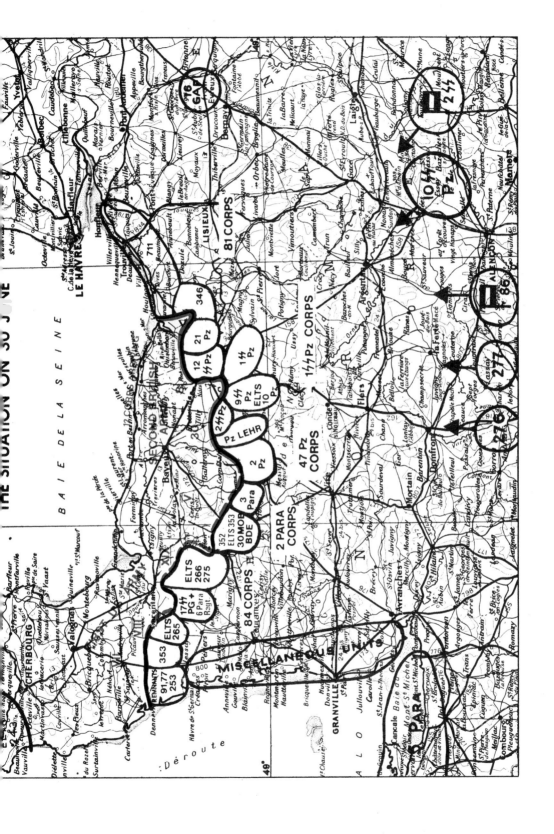

THE SITUATION ON 30 JUNE

they been launched in a properly organized attack. As it was, their concentration was never achieved because it was forestalled by our own series of heavy attacks in the Odon sector from 25 June onwards. The enemy had no option but to resist with everything available, and one by one the Panzer divisions were flung in.

The presence of seven Panzer divisions (with elements of an eighth)—two-thirds of the enemy armour in France—along a 20-mile front gives some idea of the heavy fighting which took place there in the last week of June, and of the importance which the enemy attached to preventing the isolation of Caen.

'Crust' and 'cushion' had failed already, and the pledging of the Panzer divisions in a defensive role signified the failure of the 'hammer'; and with it all hopes of ever driving the Allies out of France.

The equipment and supply arrangements of the enemy Panzer divisions are of interest. Most of them joined battle with very nearly their full establishment of armoured fighting vehicles (about 160 Mark IV and Mark V tanks and self-propelled guns), but the enemy was never able at any given moment to employ more than a small proportion of them in a mobile role. The dense bocage alone was not responsible for this. It was due mainly to the serious shortage of petrol, and also to a reduced rate of tank serviceability resulting from Allied artillery and fighter-bomber harassing missions over the forward areas. This interfered with tank maintenance, and generally necessitated the siting of workshops very far back from their Panzer regiments.

Another of the enemy's serious deficiencies, particularly from the defensive aspect, was his shortage of artillery ammunition. He had large numbers of guns, but through maldistributed dumps and irregular supply they fired remarkably little.

The situation in the German Fifteenth Army area remained obscure; but apparently no infantry from the Pas de Calais area had yet been moved south, and it thus appeared that the enemy was still anticipating landings in the Pas de Calais. Meanwhile, of the twelve Panzer divisions in western Europe, eight were now in Normandy (and the remainder were apparently not yet battle-worthy), yet the enemy had failed to deliver a single major co-ordinated counter stroke against us.

As the story of the moves of the latest arrivals in Normandy was pieced together, the effectiveness of Allied air action in reducing the enemy's mobility became increasingly apparent. 9 and 10 SS Panzer Divisions took as long to travel from eastern France to Normandy as from Poland (where they had been refitting) to the French frontier. The wrecking of all the Seine bridges below Paris, together with the principal crossings of the Loire, had virtually isolated Normandy except for the routes which led into it through the Paris–Orleans gap. There the roads and railways inevitably became congested and afforded rich opportunities for sabotage and bombing. The enemy's difficulties were immeasurably increased by his shortage of fuel. We know that during the first six months of 1944 German oil production was reduced by at least forty per cent as a result of the bombing of plants by the strategic air forces; moreover, his supply columns were subjected to constant attack in their movements towards the front, and the outcome began early to be apparent in Normandy. Units were even moved on seized bicycles, with much of their impedimenta on horse transport, while heavy equipment had to follow as best it could by rail, invariably arriving some time after the men.

We had continued to retain the initiative, forcing the enemy to react to our thrusts; this had been accomplished by sustained offensive action; it had cost us considerable casualties and the Allied divisions had been kept going without respite and were inevitably tired. It was fortunate indeed that, in spite of the delays caused to our build-up by the weather, and above all by the gale of 19–22 June, it had been possible to mount the Second Army offensive by 25 June. Any further delays that had been forced upon us would have given Rommel some opportunity to form up properly his four SS Panzer divisions, and our problems might thereby have been greatly increased.

It is interesting to speculate upon the effect on our operations that really fine weather might have had in these early weeks. In fairer conditions the build-up of formations and stores might have been kept to schedule; with greater weight and increased resources the American operations could have proceeded more rapidly, and 8 Corps operations might have succeeded in taking Caen before the flower of the SS Panzer formations had become available in its defence. In the first five days on the American sectors only thirty-eight per cent of the planned tonnage of stores was actually discharged, and after a fortnight the figure was still only seventy per cent. At the time of the storm, no further bad weather reserves of ammunition were available to the United States forces, who faced an extremely critical situation and had to cut expenditure to an emergency minimum. In the British sector, during the period of the storm, the effects on our intake were equally severe.

In the overall sense, however, we had been very successful in developing the plan. Cherbourg had fallen and First United States Army was now ready to proceed with its reorganization and regrouping, while the bulk of the enemy armour was concentrated in a formidable array on our eastern flank, where it was receiving a heavy punishment. Dietrich, Commander of 1 SS Panzer Corps in Normandy, has recorded that by 20 June the average company fighting strength of Lehr, 12 SS and 21 Panzer Divisions was down to about 25–35. At the end of the month we know that Panzer Lehr averaged 9–10 fighting men per company, in spite of having received 1,800 reinforcements since D-day. These figures give some indication of the heavy fighting which went on in June.

Our tactics remained unchanged, and were based on retention of the initiative, the avoidance of setbacks and the relentless pursuit of the plan to break out from the west.

On 30 June my orders to First United States Army emphasized the need for speed in starting the drive to the south, to take advantage of the existing enemy dispositions to stage the break-out quickly; I hoped at that time to commence operations on 3 July, and that it would be possible to strike straight through, without pause, to the line Caumont–Vire–Mortain–Fougères. Subsequently operations would continue with minimum delays, to successive objectives in the areas Laval–Mayenne and Le

Mans–Alençon. A subsidiary thrust was to be launched into the Brittany peninsula directed initially on Rennes and St Malo.

My plan at this stage for developing the break-out operation remained to pin and fight the maximum enemy strength between Villers Bocage and Caen, while the main American thrust swung south and then east to the Le Mans–Alençon area and beyond. In this way I intended to cut the line of withdrawal from Normandy through the Paris–Orleans gap, and so force the Germans back against the Seine below Paris; this would have placed the enemy in a difficult situation as there were no bridges left intact over the river between Paris and the sea.

It was essential to the success of the plan that, once the American break-out operation began, it should be carried through without pause; the momentum had to be maintained, and all our resources had to be directed to ensuring this.

Second Army meanwhile was ordered to continue operations for the capture of Caen, and to maintain maximum pressure in order to hold the enemy forces. At the same time it was to ensure that our east flank positions remained firm. The enemy had now very great strength in the Caen sector and might well be contemplating a co-ordinated counter attack in strength; it was vital to the overall plan that Second Army should not suffer any reverse which might unbalance us.

# CHAPTER NINE

# The Battle of Normandy:
## 3. The Break-out. The Battle of the Mortain-Falaise Pocket, and the Advance to the River Seine

THE battlefield in Normandy was now assuming the layout desired for launching the break-out from the western flank. I had hopes of starting the operation on 3 July, but events proved this to be optimistic, and in fact it was not launched until 25 July.

The overriding factor was speed, in order to take advantage of the general enemy situation in Normandy and to achieve our designs before greater enemy strength was brought against us from other areas. This fact was patently obvious, yet there was no way of avoiding a series of delays which were imposed upon us. The basic difficulty was that before General Bradley could launch his break-out operation in strength, he had to undertake difficult and laborious preliminary operations to secure a suitable starting position. The extent of the flooded marshy country associated with the Carentan estuary made it necessary to go as far south as the general line of the Periers–St Lô road before an area could be found adequate for the deployment of major assault forces. The degree of enemy resistance in such ideally defensive terrain greatly hampered progress; to the difficulties of bocage and marshland was added the handicap of persistently inclement weather, which restricted air support.

Delays on the western flank had, of course, direct repercussions on operations in Second Army. The pressure had to be maintained at full intensity in order to retain the enemy in the east, and with this object attacks were staged south-west, south and south-east of Caen.

FIRST PHASE: THE PRELIMINARY OPERATIONS; SECURING THE AMERICAN START LINE AND EXTENDING THE BRITISH BRIDGEHEAD BEYOND CAEN

*American Operations 1–9 July*

While VII United States Corps was completing the capture of Cherbourg during the last week of June, the rest of the American Army was building up and regrouping. This process was delayed by the retarded schedule of the build-up, and in particular by the effects of the storm in the second half of June. The attack southwards started on 3 July with a thrust by VIII United States Corps employing 82 Airborne, 79 and 90 Divisions. The object was to converge on La Haye du Puits, and on the first day 82 Airborne Division secured Hill 131 about two miles north of the town. Further

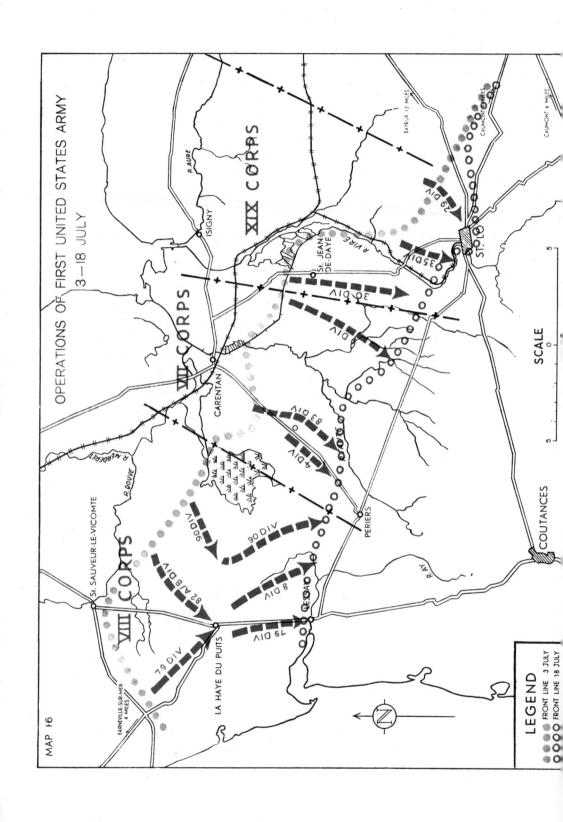

MAP 16

OPERATIONS OF FIRST UNITED STATES ARMY
3–18 JULY

XIX CORPS

VII CORPS

VIII CORPS

R. AURE

ISIGNY

St. JEAN DE-DAYE

R. VIRE

29 DIV

35 DIV

ST. LO

BAYEUX 13 MILES

CAUMONT 3 MILES

CAUMONT 6 MILES

30 DIV

DIV

CARENTAN

83 DIV

4 DIV

PERIERS

9 DIV

R. MERDERET

R. DOUVE

St. SAUVEUR-LE-VICOMTE

90 DIV

82 A/B DIV

8 DIV

LESSAY

79 DIV

LA HAYE DU PUITS

79 DIV

BARNEVILLE-SUR-MER
4 MILES

R. AY

COUTANCES

SCALE

N

LEGEND

FRONT LINE   3 JULY
FRONT LINE 18 JULY

progress was made on the following day, but the enemy exerted stubborn resistance and launched a series of counter attacks which considerably delayed the advance, and it was not until the late afternoon of 8 July that 79 Division secured the objective. The enemy had rushed 353 Infantry Division to stem the advance on La Haye du Puits and the bocage country in the area greatly assisted the enemy's defensive tactics.

Meanwhile, on 4 July, VII United States Corps attacked south-west of Carentan with 83 Division. Again progress was very difficult owing to the numerous water obstacles and bocage, but by 5 July the edge of the flooded area north of St Eny was reached. In this area the enemy was located in very strong positions from which he counter attacked. Attempts to outflank the opposition on the night 6/7 July by 4 Division were unsuccessful, but in the morning further progress was achieved north-east of St Eny. The following day 83 Division was heavily attacked by 2 SS Panzer Division which had been switched from the Odon sector.

Further east XIX United States Corps captured St Jean-de-Daye on 7 July, and continued its advance to within four miles of St Lô.

Clearly the enemy was now becoming increasingly anxious about his western flank, and I determined to redouble our efforts on the Second Army front to prevent the switching of additional armoured forces against the Americans. It was moreover apparent that the American operations, designed to secure the general line of the Periers–St Lô road, as a preliminary to the main assault to the south, were going to take time. The terrain gave the German defenders every advantage; there were very few good roads across the extensive marshlands and floods; the bocage country was extremely thick; the weather was atrocious and not only restricted mobility and caused great discomfort to the troops, but seriously limited any attempts to give them support from the air; and, owing to maintenance difficulties, ammunition remained in short supply.

*The Capture of Caen, 7–9 July*

On 1 July the SS formations made their last and strongest attempt against the Second Army salient. 1, 2, 9, 10 and 12 SS Divisions formed up with their infantry and tanks and made repeated, though not simultaneous, attacks against our positions. All of these attacks were engaged by our massed artillery with devastating effect, and all but one were dispersed before reaching our forward infantry positions.

At the time, the strength of these attacks was perhaps under-estimated owing to the efficacy of our defensive fire. Later, identifications and captured strength returns showed how many units were involved and how heavy their casualties had been. At one place alone, on the Rauray spur, the enemy got to grips with our defences. An infantry battalion of 2 SS Division and a tank battalion of 9 SS Division closed with a battalion of 49 Division and a regiment of 8 Armoured Brigade. Heavy fighting continued at intervals throughout the day, and at the end of it our positions were intact, while thirty-two enemy tanks had been knocked out.

Although no further attacks on this scale were made by the enemy, local counter

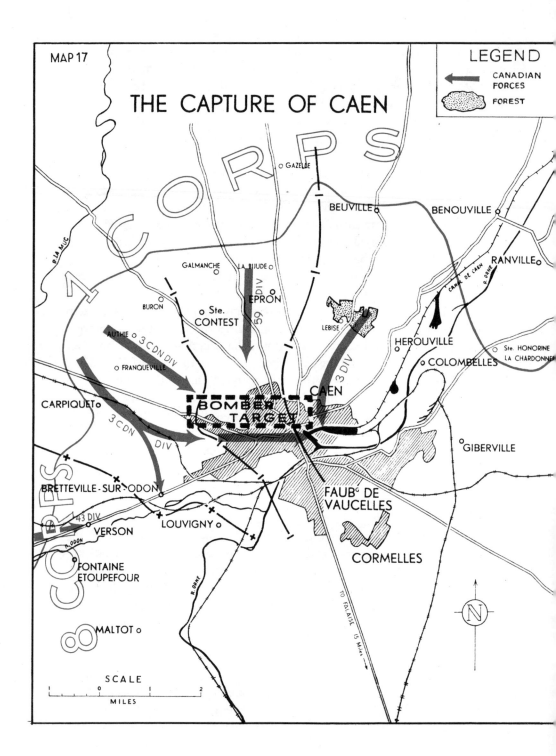

MAP 17

THE CAPTURE OF CAEN

LEGEND

CANADIAN FORCES

FOREST

O GAZELDE

BEUVILLE O

BENOUVILLE O

RANVILLE O

GALMANCHE

LA BIJUDE O

EPRON

BURON

Ste. CONTEST

LEBISE

HEROUVILLE O

Ste. HONORINE LA CHARDONNEN

AUTHIE O 3 CDN DIV

O FRANQUEVILLE

COLOMBELLES O

CARPIQUET O

3 CDN DIV

CAEN

BOMBER TARGET

GIBERVILLE O

BRETTEVILLE - SUR - ODON

43 DIV

LOUVIGNY O

VERSON

FAUB^G DE VAUCELLES

FONTAINE ETOUPEFOUR

R. ORNE

CORMELLES

MALTOT O

N

SCALE

0        1        2

MILES

TO FALAISE 15 Miles

R.ODON

R. LA MUE

CANAL DE CAEN

R. ORNE

59 DIV

3 DIV

[238]

attacks continued. The enemy went over to the defensive again, and showed himself particularly sensitive to further efforts to outflank Caen from the south-west.

It was about this time that von Rundstedt was relieved of his command, to be replaced by von Kluge. From then on Hitler's personal, and, as it proved, fatal interference in the strategy and even the tactics of the battle for France was unchecked.

Meanwhile it became apparent that the enemy was bringing in fresh infantry on our eastern flank, presumably with the intention of relieving his armour; 16 GAF Division was identified east of the Orne and 276 Division near Tilly-sur-Seulles on 3 and 4 July respectively.

Second Army's intention now was to continue the battle for Caen by a direct assault from the north. As a preliminary, 3 Canadian Division attacked Carpiquet on 4 July with the object of securing the airfield and of freeing the western exits from Caen. The village of Carpiquet was entered quickly, but round the airfield to the south fierce fighting took place and continued for several days. 12 SS Panzer Division put up a stout fight and delivered a series of counter attacks, with the result that the airfield area was not finally cleared until 9 July. In conjunction with the operation at Carpiquet, 43 Division attacked north-eastwards astride the Odon from the 8 Corps salient, in order to loosen the opposition on the Canadian front. This move was also strongly contested.

For the direct assault on Caen, 1 Corps employed three divisions with two armoured brigades in immediate support, and a third readily available. The plan involved an assault against well organized and mutually supporting positions based on a number of small villages which lay in an arc north and north-west of the city, and, in view of the strength of these defences, I decided to seek the assistance of Bomber Command RAF in a close support role on the battlefield.

For some time previously the problem of applying the tremendous weight of heavy bombers in immediate support of a major assault had been under consideration. There were many factors involved both from the Air Force and the Army points of view before assistance of this nature could be sought. There was the higher policy question whether it was justifiable to divert heavy bomber effort from its main strategic role; and there were technical problems concerning the practicability of bringing the bombline close enough to the starting position of the assault troops to ensure that the attack would strike the vital enemy defensive area. An added complication arose from the problem of cratering, and a compromise had to be made between delay-fused bombs, which entailed cratering, and the instantaneous-fused bombs which, while causing less obstruction to subsequent mobility, had less destructive effect on pre-pared defences. To some extent this problem had to be decided by experience.

The Supreme Commander supported my request for the assistance of Bomber Command, and the task was readily accepted by Air Chief Marshal Sir Arthur Harris.

Since this was the first time that we had attempted a battle of this nature, it was jointly decided with Bomber Command that the bombline would not be brought nearer than six thousand yards from our leading troops; on theoretical calculation this left an adequate safety margin. The plan was for the three attacking divisions to converge on Caen, clear the main part of the town on the west bank of the Orne and seize the river crossings. The air bombardment was designed to destroy enemy defensive positions and artillery, and to cut off the enemy's forward troops from their lines of supply in rear. The target area was a rectangle on the northern outskirts of Caen approximately four thousand yards wide and fifteen hundred yards deep, in which there were known to be an enemy headquarters and defensive positions. In addition to the material damage, much was hoped for from the effects of the percussion on the enemy defenders generally, and from the tremendous moral effect on our own troops. The defences between the bomber target area and the front line were to be dealt with by concentrated artillery fire. It was obviously desirable that the bombing attack should immediately precede the ground assault, but owing to the weather forecast it was decided to carry out the bombing on the evening before the attack and aircraft were therefore timed over the target between 2150 and 2230 hours 7 July, while the ground attack was to commence at 0420 hours on the following morning. 460 aircraft, each carrying approximately five tons of mixed 500 lb and 1,000 lb bombs, carried out a remarkably accurate operation.

The ground attack started as planned and good progress was made during 8 July. The brunt of the attack fell on 16 GAF Division newly arrived from north of the Seine; 21 and 12 SS Panzer Divisions were hurriedly committed to assist in stemming our progress. By nightfall, 3 Canadian Division had secured Franqueville, while tanks and armoured cars closed in on the western outskirts of Caen. In the centre 59 Division cleared St Contest and La Bijude, while 3 Division got into the north-east corner of Caen and directed 33 Armoured Brigade to the bridges. During the night armoured patrols came up against anti-tank guns and large numbers of mines and were impeded by the cratering and obstruction caused by the bombing. On the morning of 9 July, 3 Division reached the dock area and met troops from 3 Canadian Division who had entered the town from the west; at the end of the day Canadian troops were firmly established in the Carpiquet airfield area with elements at Bretteville-sur-Odon. Mopping up in the town continued on 10 July. The bridges over the river in the city were either destroyed or completely blocked by rubble, and the enemy remained in occupation of the suburb of Faubourg-de-Vaucelles on the east bank.

Investigation showed the tremendous effect of the heavy bombing on the enemy; some German defenders were found still stunned many hours after the attack had been carried out. The troops in the defences north of the town were cut off and received no food, petrol or ammunition as a result, while one regiment of 16 GAF Division was wiped out. The Bomber Command attack played a vital part in the success of the operation. Difficulties, however, arose from the cratering and the obstruction from masonry and debris caused by the bombing, and it will be seen that in our next operation of this nature it was decided to employ small bombs with instantaneous fuses.

The capture of Caen greatly simplified our problems on the eastern flank, as we had now eliminated the enemy salient west of the river and were well placed to continue operations for extending our bridgehead to the east of it.

## *The Situation, 9 July*

My aim remained to launch the break-out operation on the western flank as soon as possible, and meanwhile to hold the main enemy forces on my eastern flank.

There were two very disquieting developments in the enemy situation during the first week in July. The identification of 2 SS Panzer Division in the American sector round St Eny showed the enemy's determination to strengthen his resistance in the west in spite of Second Army's endeavours to prevent it. Moreover we had identified fresh infantry divisions on the eastern sectors, which were relieving Panzer formations in the line; during the week 1 SS, 2 SS, Lehr and 21 Panzer Divisions were known to have been withdrawn wholly or partially into reserve.

It was vital for us to counter these measures urgently.

Therefore the impetus of Second Army operations had to be maintained at maximum pressure, and in a manner which would have the most direct and immediate effect on the enemy and force him to react.

Before discussing the courses of action open to us to achieve this object, it is important that I should explain in detail my conception of how operations should develop on the eastern flank.

It has been made abundantly clear that the role of Second Army was to contain the main enemy strength and to wear it down by sustained offensive action. Thereby I was creating the opportunity to launch the break-out by First United States Army under the best possible conditions. Second Army was succeeding in its role because the enemy was determined to ensure that we were prevented from exploiting our armoured resources and superior mobility in the better country south-east of Caen. Once we became established in strength on the high ground south of Bourguebus, with lateral routes south of Caen, and with our eastern flank up to the sea secure, we would be able to launch attacks in strength to the south and south-east. By this means we could immediately threaten the important communication centres of Falaise and Argentan, which were vital to the enemy in Normandy in view of the main east–west lateral routes which passed through them. We could moreover threaten to drive into the Seine basin either towards Paris, or the Seine ports of Rouen and Le Havre; such moves would immensely increase the existing difficulties on the enemy's lines of communication, and drive a wedge between the German Seventh and Fifteenth Armies.

It followed, as I have already remarked, that the key to retaining strong enemy forces on the eastern flank was the establishment of strong forces in the area south-east of Caen, and the violence of the enemy's reaction to our operations in the Caen sector had amply shown the measure of his determination to prevent our progress in that direction. We were thus achieving our immediate object.

Meanwhile I had in mind also the longer term aspect of our eastern flank operation.

[241]

It has been shown that my intention was to swing the main break-out thrust from the west flank eastwards to the area Le Mans–Alençon. It would then be necessary for Second Army to wheel south and east to come into line with the American forces, so that the whole front would face east and north-east. While the American right flank closed the routes from Normandy to the gap between the Loire and Seine, the rest of the Allied strength would drive the enemy back against the Seine below Paris, while the air forces kept the bridges out and harassed the ferries.

Second Army had therefore to position itself for delivering a major thrust east of the Orne when the right time came: that would be when the American break-out operation had gathered momentum and was striking east.

There were other urgent reasons for wanting to develop our bridgehead east of the Orne. The eastern sectors of the bridgehead were becoming very cramped; we required more space for airfield construction and for administrative development.

What were the main tactical requirements to be attained in order to establish major forces south-east of Caen and to exert with maximum intensity the direct threat to Falaise?

*First*: we had to extend the bridgehead in order to gain space to manœuvre; this could be achieved best by attacking from the existing bridgehead to the south, south-east and east. *Secondly*: we required a firm left flank, so that we could launch major attacks to the south without fear of becoming unbalanced by enemy action on our left rear; if we could extend our bridgehead to the River Dives this requirement would be satisfied. *Thirdly*: we required lateral east-west routes, which passed south of the Caen bottleneck. We should not achieve our object if we created a salient south-east of Caen and had to rely on maintenance routes which involved a long detour to the north through Caen or across the bridges north of the town; it follows that we had to thrust south between the Odon and the Orne in order to open lateral routes to the west.

To sum up, there were two major projects to be undertaken on the Second Army front; an attack east of the Orne to extend the existing bridgehead and establish armour in strength east of the river, and a thrust between the Odon and the Orne to open lateral routes.

The immediate problem was to prevent the transfer of enemy reserves to the American sector. Speed was the paramount factor and it was therefore decided to begin with operations between the Odon and the Orne, because they could be started more quickly than a major attack east of the Orne. An added advantage was that a thrust directed on Thury Harcourt–Mont Pinçon would closely threaten the rear of enemy forces operating in the area west of St Lô, and would strike towards the dominating Mont Pinçon feature.

I therefore ordered Second Army to operate immediately in strength towards the south, with its left flank on the River Orne. The objective was the general line Thury Harcourt–Mont Pinçon–Le Beny Bocage.

At the same time rapid preparations were to be made to launch a major armoured thrust east of the Orne. This task was to be undertaken by 8 Corps with a force of three armoured divisions; Headquarters 8 Corps was to be relieved in the line by Headquarters 12 Corps, which was coming ashore at this time.

I also ordered Second Army to prepare to take over the left divisional sector of First United States Army, in order to free additional resources for the American break-out.

There were no changes in my orders for First United States Army. I emphasized again the need for speed. We required to get going before the enemy found the means to increase his forces on the western flank, and to take advantage of the situation I was creating on the eastern flank in the renewed Second Army offensives. An additional important factor was the urgency of securing the Brittany ports; we were reaching the limit of the beach capacities and experience at Cherbourg showed that the enemy's demolition policy was very thorough and that considerable time would be required to develop facilities in the ports we captured. Moreover we could not count on continuing beach working after the early autumn, by which time it was vital to have deep water port facilities at our disposal. I planned to swing the right-hand American corps into the Brittany peninsulas as soon as the base of the Cotentin peninsula was reached; at this time Headquarters Third United States Army would become operational and take charge of the operations in Brittany. Planning was in hand for securing St Malo quickly; the desirability of employing airborne troops to seize the port was studied, though I preferred to retain them for use in the Vannes area, from which they could operate to capture Lorient or Quiberon Bay. It was at this time thought preferable to concentrate on ports at the base of the Brittany peninsula, since the railway and road routes through the peninsula itself were very vulnerable to demolition and would therefore probably involve difficult and lengthy repairs. Again the immensity of the task of reopening demolished ports resulted in plans being prepared for creating a deep sea port in Quiberon Bay.

*Second Army Operations, 10–18 July*

During the period 10–18 July, Second Army delivered a series of thrusts, with the primary object to make progress southwards towards Thury Harcourt: all operations were related to this task and to the maintenance of pressure on as broad a front as possible.

At 0500 hours 10 July, 43 Division with a tank brigade attacked towards the high ground at Point 112 and the villages of Feuguerolles and Maltot, in the Orne valley. The high ground about Point 112 and Eterville was secured, but a strong counter attack drove our troops out of Maltot. Because Maltot was overlooked from the east bank of the Orne it was untenable until we had secured the high ground on that side of the river. On the following day Point 112 was held in spite of further counter attacks, mainly by 10 SS Panzer Division, assisted by 9 SS Panzer Division, which had recently been withdrawn from the line for a rest.

On 11 July, 50 Division attacked the Hottot area in 30 Corps sector, and captured

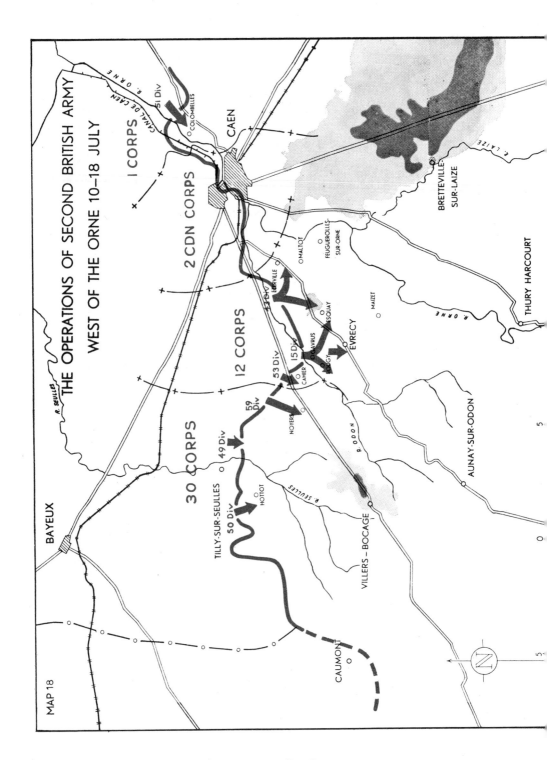

THE OPERATIONS OF SECOND BRITISH ARMY
WEST OF THE ORNE 10–18 JULY

MAP 18

[244]

the high ground north-west of the village, while further east 49 Division made some limited advances. On the same day, on 1 Corps front, 51 Division attacked Colombelles and its factory area on the east bank of the Orne. After some initial success the Highlanders were forced back in the face of strong counter attacks.

During 12 and 13 July considerable regrouping was taking place within Second Army. 12 Corps took over the 8 Corps sector of the line, while 2 Canadian Corps became operational with 2 and 3 Canadian Infantry Divisions under command; this Corps took station between 12 Corps and 1 Corps.

30 and 12 Corps continued major attacks on 15 July. The object of the 30 Corps operation was to secure the Noyers area and to exploit towards the high ground north-east of Villers Bocage. 59 Division led the attack, and by the evening of 16 July had enveloped Noyers on three sides; further west, 50 Division made limited progress. These operations advanced our line west of Tilly-sur-Seulles about three miles; in all sectors the enemy had reacted sharply, and was still succeeding in plugging the holes.

The attack by 12 Corps began on the night of 15 July. 'Movement light', or the employment of searchlights directed to reflect from the clouds and give a degree of visibility at night over the area of operations, was used for the first time in battle, and proved a great success. The object of the attack was to secure the line Bougy–Evrecy–Maizet, and by the morning of 16 July Gavrus, Bougy and Esquay had been occupied; a number of counter attacks round Bougy were repulsed and mopping-up was in progress. On the left, supporting operations were mounted in the area of Point 112; meanwhile 53 Division attacked north of the Odon and, after some hard fighting, secured Cahier which had changed hands several times. At night a strong attack was put in to secure Evrecy and continued for some twenty-four hours; the fighting was confused; the enemy made repeated counter attacks and succeeded in holding on to the village.

The 12 and 30 Corps attacks had thus not made much ground by 18 July, but the fighting had been severe, and above all we were attaining our object by pulling the enemy armour back into the line. 1 SS Panzer Division was identified in counter attacks round Esquay, where 10 SS Panzer Division was also heavily engaged; 9 SS Panzer Division was committed at Evrecy and Maltot; the 1 Corps operations at Colombelles had prevented 21 Panzer Division from continuing with its projected refit. To sum up, the enemy had now only 12 SS Panzer Division out of the line in the woods north of Falaise, where it was refitting, in spite of having brought 16 GAF, 276 and 277 Divisions into the line.

*First United States Army Operations, 10–18 July*

First United States Army continued its advance southwards; by steady pressure and hard fighting it gradually overcame the difficulties of terrain and the increased enemy opposition.

On the right, VIII Corps made good progress in the sector between the marshlands and the western coast, and by 14 July had reached the general line of the north bank of the River Ay, with patrols west of Lessay. Here they were checked while operations developed further east. In the centre sector VII Corps made ground west of the River Taute, and XIX Corps pushed on between the Taute and the Vire. An enemy counter attack on 11 July aimed at St Jean de Daye was beaten off by VII Corps after some heavy fighting. Just as 2 SS Panzer Division had been rushed from the western flank to stem the American progress towards Periers, Panzer Lehr Division was switched to the east to bolster the defence of St Lô; its efforts were however abortive, and cost the enemy heavily in personnel and material. On 16 July, XIX Corps mounted a strong attack with two divisions against St Lô. The formations were to converge on the town from the north and east, and heavy fighting continued for three days; on 17 July some accurate close support bombing from the air proved decisive in driving back a strong enemy attack by infantry and armour, and on the following day assaulting forces closed in on St Lô; by evening, 29 Division had forced its way into the town and completed its capture. On the extreme left V Corps improved its positions in conjunction with the XIX Corps operation towards St Lô.

Thus by 18 July First United States Army was in possession of St Lô, and of the ground west of the River Vire which was required for mounting the major break-out assault operation to the south.

*The Situation, 18 July*

We were now on the threshold of great events. We were ready to break out of the bridgehead.

We still firmly retained the initiative. We had prevented the enemy from switching further reinforcements to the western flank and had forced him to commit again the armoured forces he had sought to withdraw into reserve. We had continued to punish the enemy severely, and force him into what I call 'wet hen' tactics—rushing to and fro to stem our thrusts and plug the holes in his line.

The sooner we got going on the western flank the better, while the setting for the break-out remained favourable. Apart from the local conditions in Normandy, it seemed impossible that the enemy should continue much longer to anticipate an invasion in the Pas de Calais; however great his anxiety for the safety of the flying bomb sites, he must surely soon give overriding priority to the Normandy battlefield, and when he took that decision substantial reinforcements would become available from Fifteenth Army.

I have said how important it was to my plans that, once started, the break-out operation should maintain its momentum. It was therefore essential to ensure that the assault would make a clean break through the enemy defences facing the Americans, and that a corridor would be speedily opened through which armoured forces could be passed into the open country. To make sure of this, it was decided to seek heavy bomber assistance; but because of the weather, the operation had to be progressively postponed until 25 July in order to obtain favourable flying conditions.

Meanwhile on the eastern flank offensive operations were sustained; by 17 July 8 Corps was ready to begin the offensive east of the Orne.

The operations of 8 Corps between 18 and 21 July gave rise to a number of misunderstandings at the time. It was a battle for position, which was designed first to bring into play the full effect on the enemy of a direct and powerful threat to Falaise and the open country to the east of the town, and secondly to secure ground on which major forces could be poised ready to strike out to the south and south-east, when the American breakout forces thrust eastwards to meet them. I now believe that the misconception concerning this operation arose primarily because the forthcoming battle for position was in fact the prelude to operations of wider scope, which, when the time came, were to form part of the Allied drive to the Seine. Added to this, the break-out operation by First United States Army was, for obvious reasons, being kept a close secret, and, since it was clearly time we broke the enemy cordon surrounding us, it was understandable that a major operation of this kind should suggest wider implications than in fact it had.

### The British Offensive east of the Orne, 18–21 July

While 12 and 30 Corps operations were in progress west of the River Orne, preparations for a major thrust east of the river were completed with all possible speed. Additional bridges were constructed north of Caen and ultimately there were five Class 40 crossings available between Ouistreham and Blainville. Three corps were employed in the operation, the major role being played by 8 Corps, which was to pass over the Orne bridges through 1 Corps bridgehead and establish an armoured division in each of three areas: Hubert Folie–Verrières, Vimont, and Garçelles Secqueville. The armoured divisions were to dominate the area described and fight the enemy armour which would come to oppose them, and opportunities were to be exploited of pushing armoured cars south towards Falaise in order to cause maximum dislocation to the enemy.

2 Canadian Corps was to cross the Orne and clear the Colombelles factory, the suburb of Faubourg de Vaucelles and the village of Giberville. These operations were designed to open up the south-eastern exits from Caen and to mop up the enemy in that area. 1 Corps was made responsible for ensuring that the existing bridgehead was firmly held, and was to protect the left flank of 8 Corps by securing the villages and woods west of Troarn.

The air programme was arranged for first light 18 July in direct support of the attack. About 1,100 heavy bombers of Bomber Command and 600 of Eighth United States Air Force, together with 400 medium bombers of Ninth United States Air Force were to be employed. It was planned for the heavy bombers to strike, with delayed fuse bombs, on the flanks of the frontage of attack and on strong points and concentration areas in rear. The medium bomber aircraft, using fragmentation bombs with instantaneous fuses, in order to avoid cratering, were to strike in the area directly facing the frontage of the 8 Corps assault. On 18 July, heavy bombers attacked between

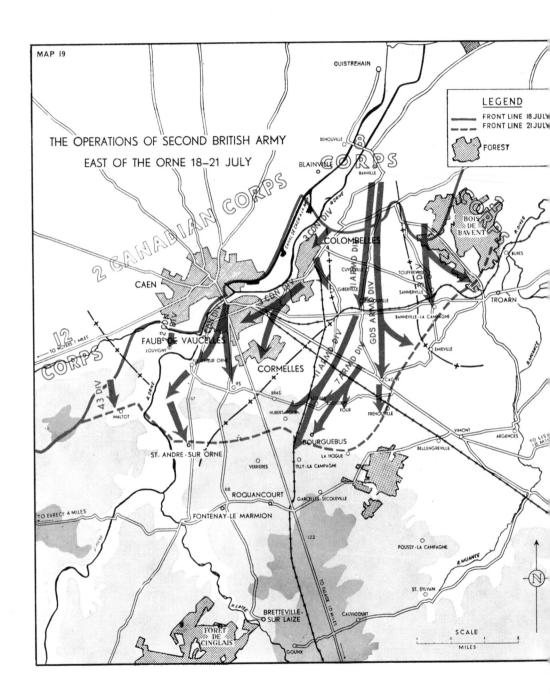

MAP 19

THE OPERATIONS OF SECOND BRITISH ARMY
EAST OF THE ORNE 18–21 JULY

[248]

0545 and 0630 hours, followed by the medium bombers which operated from 0700 to 0745 hours. The leading troops began the assault at 0745 hours, and both 1 and 8 Corps started off well. 11 Armoured Division, leading the 8 Corps attack, was directed on the area Hubert Folie–Verrieres. By 0900 hours an advance of three or four miles had been made, leading tanks reaching the line of the railway near Demouville while infantry was clearing the village of Cuverville in rear. At the same time 3 Division was attacking the villages west of Troarn and had got into the outskirts of Touffreville. On the right 3 Canadian Division, leading 2 Canadian Corps, made slower progress owing to bomb craters and to the very determined enemy resistance at Colombelles.

Throughout the morning the attack continued to make progress; Guards Armoured Division operated on the east flank of 11 Armoured Division and was directed on Vimont. By midday, 11 Armoured Division was in the area Tilly la Campagne–La Hogue. Guards Armoured Division had reached Cagny–Emiéville and 7 Armoured Division, whose task was to deploy between the other two formations, was moving forward to the front. Progress was being made in spite of considerable anti-tank gun-fire, as there were a number of German 88 millimetre dual purpose guns in the area which had originally belonged to the flak defences of Caen.

In the afternoon the enemy opposition stiffened considerably and counter attacks were developed, the largest being delivered by some fifty to sixty German tanks which advanced against 11 Armoured Division from the Bourguebus area. Resistance was stubborn in the villages about the railway and road from Caen to Lisieux, and in particular a strong anti-tank gun screen south-east of the line Emiéville–Frenouville prevented further progress in that direction. On the flanks progress was maintained. 3 Canadian Division cleared Colombelles and occupied Giberville, while, west of the Orne, 2 Canadian Division was fighting hard near Louvigny. On the left flank 3 Division was firmly established in Touffreville, Sannerville and Banneville, but an attack to secure Troarn had met with little success.

The plan for 19 July was for the armoured divisions of 8 Corps to push on to their objectives, while 2 Canadian Corps opened the routes from Caen through the east bank suburbs and 1 Corps continued its operation against Troarn. Our tank casualties on 18 July had been considerable; over 150 tanks were reported out of action in the three armoured divisions.

Progress during the day was slow, as increased enemy reserves were concentrated against us. 3 Canadian Division cleared Faubourg de Vaucelles and Cormelles, and 2 Canadian Division captured Louvigny on the left bank of the Orne and Fleury and Ifs on the right bank. In the 8 Corps sector, Guards Armoured Division occupied Cagny. 1 Corps operations continued round Troarn. The enemy made strenuous efforts to stem our advance and to deny us the high ground in the Bourguebus area. Apart from 21 Panzer Division and 16 GAF Division operating on our east flank, elements of 1 SS, 9 SS and 10 SS Panzer Divisions were all brought into this battle, having been rushed from west of the Orne, and even a battle group of 2 Panzer

Division, switched from the Caumont sector, was identified; this latter arrival was clear evidence of the enemy's anxiety and provided an excellent indication of the success of our strategy in working for the establishment of what I shall now call 'the threat to Falaise'.

On 20 July our attacks continued although heavy rain after midday began to slow down operations. 2 Canadian Corps captured St André sur Orne but later attempts to secure the high ground about Verrieres were unsuccessful. The enemy counter attacked 2 Canadian Division in this sector repeatedly, employing battle groups of infantry and tanks. The armoured divisions of 8 Corps made some further progress, as a result of which both Bourguebus and Frenouville were captured.

But the rain continued and began to turn the battlefield, which previously had been inches deep in dust, into a sea of mud. We had, however, largely attained our purpose; in the centre 8 Corps had advanced ten thousand yards, fought and destroyed many enemy tanks, caused considerable casualties to the enemy infantry, and taken two thousand prisoners. The eastern suburbs of Caen had been cleared and the Orne bridgehead had been more than doubled in size. On the evening of 20 July our new line ran from the Orne near St André to Bourguebus, Cagny and the outskirts of Troarn. We had mounted 'the threat to Falaise' and the enemy had thrown in his available resources, being forced once again to react strongly to our thrust.

Orders were now issued for infantry to take over from the armour, which was to be withdrawn into reserve.

### The Situation, 21 July

The situation on the eastern flank was now greatly improved, and we had drawn the German armour east of the Orne again and caused heavy losses to the enemy. We had not yet pushed the extreme left flank up to the Dives, and we still needed more ground in the area between the Odon and the Orne. In order to be properly poised for subsequent operations to the south, I wanted to establish our line along the River Dives from the sea to Bures, thence along the Muance to St Sylvain, and on through Cauvicourt, Gouvix and Evreçy to Noyers and Caumont.

My orders on 21 July were for First Canadian Army and Second British Army to develop operations in order to secure this line.

Headquarters First Canadian Army (General Crerar) was to take the field on 23 July, when it would assume responsibility for the extreme left flank sector, taking 1 Corps under command. 2 Canadian Corps was to remain under Second Army for the moment. On 24 July, Second Army was to take over the left divisional sector of First United States Army, thus releasing American troops for operations elsewhere.

I further ordered Second Army to hold in reserve a corps containing at least two armoured divisions ready to strike south from our Orne bridgehead when the opportunity came to implement the manœuvre which I have already described.

There was no change in the roles for First and Third United States Armies; it should be noted, however, that as soon as Third United States Army became operational, Headquarters Twelfth United States Army Group were also to become operational, under the command of General Omar Bradley, in order to control the two American Armies. This Army Group was to remain under my operational control.

At this stage I appreciated that I should have to be ready to launch a major attack by Second Army on Falaise early in August, on the assumption that the American drive would make rapid progress once it turned eastwards. While the break-out was gathering speed I planned to continue operations on the Second Army front which, in addition to drawing the enemy's attention, would improve our bridgehead east of the Orne and our positions between the Orne and the Odon, with a view to facilitating the ultimate operations against Falaise. The first attack was planned east of the Orne in order to secure Garçelles Secqueville and Point 122 on the Falaise road; 2 Canadian Corps was to undertake this task.

*Operations, 21–24 July*

During the period 21–24 July the United States forces were still waiting for favourable weather which would enable the Air Forces to give them the required send-off for the break-out operation.

Meanwhile in order to give the enemy no respite and to adjust the Second Army front between the Orne and the Odon, 43 Division of 12 Corps carried out limited operations during the period 22–24 July. At long last Maltot was captured and a fresh attack was made on Point 112 north of Esquay. This provoked a strong counter attack as a result of which the enemy regained possession of the high ground.

*The Situation, 24 July*

The enemy was continuing his policy of trying to contain us. Every time we punched a hole in the infantry, he made desperate efforts to plug it with his Panzer reserves. As soon as he got a respite, as many of them as possible would be withdrawn to await the next crisis.

There was no long term plan behind this dogged defence in the bocage. In Berlin, it is true, they were nursing hopes of one day being able to concentrate for a final blow to drive the Allies back to the sea. Such dreams were not shared by the local commanders, many of whom were already pressing for a planned withdrawal to the Seine before the armies were completely destroyed where they stood. Meanwhile, they tried to sustain the morale of their troops by promises of new and secret weapons. If only they could hold on for a little while longer, they were told, it would give sufficient time for terrible weapons to be brought into action and victory would be assured.

About this time, Rommel was severely injured in a road strafing attack and took no further part in the campaign.

The enemy was forced to thin out from the Pas de Calais in view of his growing weakness in Normandy, and infantry divisions from Fifteenth Army north of the Seine were called down as fast as the limited transport facilities permitted.

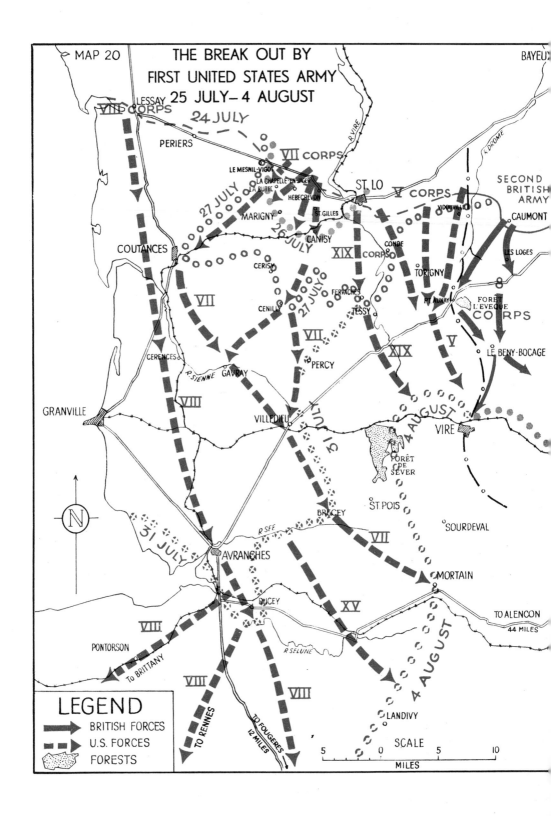

MAP 20

# THE BREAK OUT BY
# FIRST UNITED STATES ARMY
## 25 JULY – 4 AUGUST

BAYEUX

LESSAY
VIII CORPS
24 JULY
PERIERS
VII CORPS
R. VIRE
R. DROME
LE MESNIL-VIGOT
LA CHAPELLE-EN-JUGER
LA BUTTE
HEBECREVON
ST LO
V CORPS
SECOND BRITISH ARMY
27 JULY
MARIGNY
ST. GILLES
VIDOUVILLE
CAUMONT
26 JULY
CANISY
CONDE
LES LOGES
COUTANCES
CERISY
XIX CORPS
TORIGNY
CERISY
FERVACHES
PT AUNAY
FORÊT L'EVEQUE
VII
27 JULY
CENILLY
TESSY
CORPS
CERENCES
VII
PERCY
XIX
V
LE BENY-BOCAGE
R. SIENNE  GAVRAY
VIII
GRANVILLE
VILLEDIEU
31 JULY
4 AUGUST
VIRE
FORÊT DE SEVER
ST POIS
SOURDEVAL
BRECEY
VII
R. SEE
31 JULY
AVRANCHES
MORTAIN
DUCEY
XV
TO ALENCON
44 MILES
VIII
R. SELUNE
PONTORSON
To Brittany
VIII
TO RENNES
TO FOUGERES
12 MILES
VIII
4 AUGUST
LANDIVY

N

# LEGEND
➤ BRITISH FORCES
➤ U.S. FORCES
FORESTS

SCALE
5   0   5   10
MILES

The decision was made too late: the divisions arrived so slowly and so piecemeal that they were to find themselves reinforcing failure.

### SECOND PHASE: THE BREAK-OUT

*The Launching of the Break-out, 25–27 July*

The break-out operation made a false start on 24 July. Two thousand aircraft took off for the air bombardment and arrived over the target area, but heavy cloud and thick mist greatly restricted visibility, and the majority of the aircraft had to return to their bases without dropping their bombs, and the ground attack was postponed. This unavoidable setback would, I feared, betray to the enemy our intentions and the frontage of our proposed attack, and caused me considerable anxiety. I feared lest the enemy would take some immediate steps to strengthen his forces on the First United States Army front. There was nothing I could do about it at this stage except to ensure that the Second Army projected operations were carried through at once and with the utmost intensity. I hoped that thereby the enemy might be persuaded that the bombing on the American front was a form of feint. I have mentioned that I had already ordered Second Army to start the next stage in its operations by securing Garçelles Seçqueville and Point 122 on the Falaise road; I gave orders that this attack was to start at all costs on 25 July. 2 Canadian Corps, which was responsible for the operation, was ready and in fact started at 0330 hours on 25 July.

On 25 July weather conditions improved and the break-out operation began.

First United States Army plan was to deliver a break-in assault against the enemy defensive positions with VII United States Corps employing three infantry divisions. The attack was to cross the Periers–St Lô road roughly between Le Mesnil Vigot and Hebecrevon directed on a frontage from Marigny to St Gilles. The attacking divisions were then to face outwards in order to establish the flanks of the break-in area. Meanwhile a force of two armoured and one infantry divisions was to thrust through the corridor thus formed. The right hand division was to wheel right towards Coutances, by which means it was hoped to cut off all the enemy in the area of Lessay and Periers; the left hand armoured division was to pass through Canisy followed by the infantry division, directed on the general line Notre Dame le Cenilly–Fervaches in readiness for further exploitation as decided. Twenty-four hours after the VII Corps assault, VIII Corps in the coastal sector was to advance south; this formation had four infantry divisions and one armoured division. XIX United States Corps was also to launch attacks in the St Lô sector, beginning simultaneously with VIII United States Corps.

These operations were the prelude to the American advance to cut off the Brittany peninsula, reach the Loire and swing east to the line Le Mans–Alençon.

The air plan for the assault phase included bombardment of an area 6,000 yards wide by 2,500 yards deep on the frontage of VII United States Corps by 1,500 heavy bombers of the Eighth United States Air Force, together with an attack by some 400 medium bombers on an adjacent target area. In order to strike the foremost enemy defenders, the American troops were withdrawn 1,200 yards to the north of the heavy bomber target area. Zero hour for the assaulting infantry was 1100, and it was hoped that the assaulting troops would regain their start line before the enemy had time to recover from the air attack.

At 1100 hours the infantry of VII United States Corps moved forward, and it quickly became apparent that the results of the air bombardment had been devastating. Enemy troops who were not casualties were stunned and dazed, and weapons not destroyed had to be dug out and cleaned before they could be used; communications were almost completely severed. By the end of the day the American troops had advanced some two miles to the general line La Butte–La Chapelle-en-Juger–Hebe-crevon. On 26 July, although there was heavy resistance in the west of the penetration area, opposition on the front was light and considerable advances were made; the armoured divisions were set in motion, Marigny and St Gilles were captured and the advance soon reached Canisy and the line of the Canisy–St Lô railway.

Meanwhile, on the right, VIII Corps attacked at 0530 hours. Attempts to pinch out Periers were unsuccessful, but by dark the main Periers–St Lô road had been cut. In V Corps sector, advances of 2,000–3,000 yards were made east of St Lô.

On 27 July the decisive actions of the operation took place. The enemy began to withdraw along the entire front, and Lessay and Periers were occupied. In the central sector, mobile columns were sent within two miles of Coutances where the enemy was trying desperately to keep open an escape corridor for his troops withdrawing along the coast. On XIX Corps front the enemy was cleared out of the loop in the River Vire immediately south of St Lô.

*Operations on the Eastern Flank, 25–27 July*

I have already shown that an attack by 2 Canadian Corps southwards along the Falaise road started at 0330 hours on 25 July. Steady progress was made and by midday St Martin de Fontenay and the high ground about Verrieres were reached, and Tilly la Campagne had been captured. As the advance continued, however, enemy opposition hardened and a considerable number of enemy tanks came into action north of the line May-sur-Orne–Roquancourt. During the afternoon a strong tank counter thrust pushed our line back, and our troops were evicted from Tilly. The German forces in the sector included 1 SS, 9 SS, 12 SS and 21 Panzer Divisions, and it was clear that any further thrust in this sector would not only be contested by a great weight of armour, but also that there were strong contingents of 88 milli-metre guns, well sited, in support. It was therefore necessary to discontinue our thrust during the night 25/26 July.

*The Situation, 27 July*

The break-out thrust had been delivered, and the operation was making excellent progress. It was now essential to ensure that all our efforts went to further the speed and progress of the American drive, and on 27 July I was carefully considering the proposed plan of action for the British and Canadian forces in the sectors east of the River Odon, and wondering whether these projects were in fact the most profitable we could devise from the point of view of helping the Americans forward.

The enemy had very powerful forces in the Orne sector; there were six Panzer and SS Panzer divisions on the Second Army front, all of which were east of Noyers. West of that place there was no German armour facing the British, and therefore the situation was favourable for delivering a very heavy blow on the right wing of Second Army in the Caumont sector. If we could regroup speedily and launch a thrust in strength southwards from the Caumont area directed on Le Forêt l'Eveque and Le Beny Bocage, and ultimately to Vire, the effect would be to get behind the German forces which had been swung back to face west by the American break-through; any attempt by the enemy to pivot on the River Vire or in the area between Torigny and Caumont would thus be frustrated, as we should knock away the hinge. I therefore ordered Second British Army to regroup in order to deliver a strong offensive on these lines; not less than six divisions were to be employed, and the operation was to proceed with all possible speed. In the meantime First Canadian Army and the remainder of Second Army were to maintain the maximum offensive activity on the rest of the front in order to pin the enemy opposition and wear it down.

*United States Operations, 28 July–4 August*

While Second British Army was switching its main weight to the Caumont sector, the progress of the break-out operation proceeded apace. On 28 July, 4 and 6 Armoured Divisions passed through the infantry on the western sector and thrust south towards Coutances. The town was captured in the afternoon and firm contact was established there between VIII and VII Corps. To the south-east, troops of VII and XIX Corps had got to within five miles of the main Avranches–Caen road. All reports indicated that west of the River Vire to the coast the enemy was completely disorganized.

First United States Army ordered VIII Corps to continue the drive to the foot of the Cotentin peninsula with VII Corps on the left; XIX and V Corps were to continue their eastern thrusts in conformity. On 29 July, with its armoured divisions leading, VIII Corps forced the crossing of the River Sienne west of Coutances and captured Cerences; on its left VII Corps made good progress towards Gavray and Percy. Progress was slower in XIX and V Corps sectors, where some substance of enemy organization existed, helped by the arrival of 2 Panzer Division from the east, and it became evident that the enemy was trying to wheel back the line, pivoting on the general area Tessy-sur-Vire–Torigny-sur-Vire–Caumont.

During the last two days of the month the advance in the coastal sector maintained its momentum. On 31 July both Granville and Avranches were captured. A bridgehead was seized over the River See and forward troops pushed on to Ducey where a crossing was made over the River Selune. The See was also crossed in the Brecey area.

On V and XIX Corps sectors the enemy opposition continued to be desperate, but V Corps succeeded in capturing Torigny on 31 July, by which time it will be seen that Second Army was thrusting south in the Caumont area in order to break the enemy hinge on which he was attempting to pivot and re-form the front. On 1 August, Headquarters Third United States Army became operational, taking command of VIII United States Corps. This Corps moved south and west into Brittany with the task of cleaning up the peninsula and capturing its ports. While VII United States Corps continued its advance southwards, XIX Corps closed up to the general line Percy-Tessy, and on the left flank V Corps continued its progress towards the River Vire. On the left, V Corps troops pushed on behind Forêt l'Eveque in conjunction with Second Army which was approaching Le Beny Bocage. On the following day VII Corps reached St Pois and Mortain, while XIX Corps crossed the Villedieu–Caen main road; west of Le Beny Bocage, V corps secured bridgeheads over the River Vire.

The enemy established some strong centres of resistance on 3 August which delayed VII Corps progress, but by the following day spearheads of the American advance had reached the general line Fougères–Mortain–Forêt de St Sever—exclusive Vire. On the right of this frontage XV Corps was brought into the line, and placed under Third United States Army; VII Corps was in the centre, and on the left XIX Corps was gradually pinching out V Corps which was closing towards Vire. On the left sector of the American line the enemy was now exerting considerable pressure as 116 Panzer, as well as 2 Panzer, had joined 2 SS Panzer Division in covering Vire.

*British and Canadian Operations, 28 July–4 August*

Second Army regrouped with creditable speed, and it was found possible to commence the thrust southwards from the Caumont area on 30 July.

The Army right flank followed the River Drôme about Vidouville, some four miles west of Caumont; on the west bank of the river, V Corps, of First United States Army, was at this time advancing on Torigny-sur-Vire. From Vidouville the British front skirted Caumont to the south and then swung north-north-east to Livry, and on to the River Seulles near Hottot. The enemy opposing Second Army between Caumont and Esquay about 29 July was believed to be 326, 276 and 277 Infantry Divisions.

The main weight of the attack was to be developed by 8 and 30 Corps on a narrow front. 30 Corps was to wheel south-west, initially to the line Villers Bocage–Aunay-sur-Odon, while 8 Corps, in a wider sweep on its right, swung down to Le Beny Bocage and on to the Vire–Tinchebray–Condé triangle. Operations were then to be developed eastwards to the Orne, hinging on 12 Corps which was to conform. The initial objective was the general area St Martin des Bésaces–Le Beny Bocage–Forêt l'Eveque. While the country in the line of the proposed thrust was typical Norman bocage, it was more hilly and wooded than the areas further north; the principal feature was formed by a series of hills running south-east between Le Beny Bocage and Aunay-sur-Odon. Some of these hills were over 1,000 feet high and they included the Mont Pinçon massif.

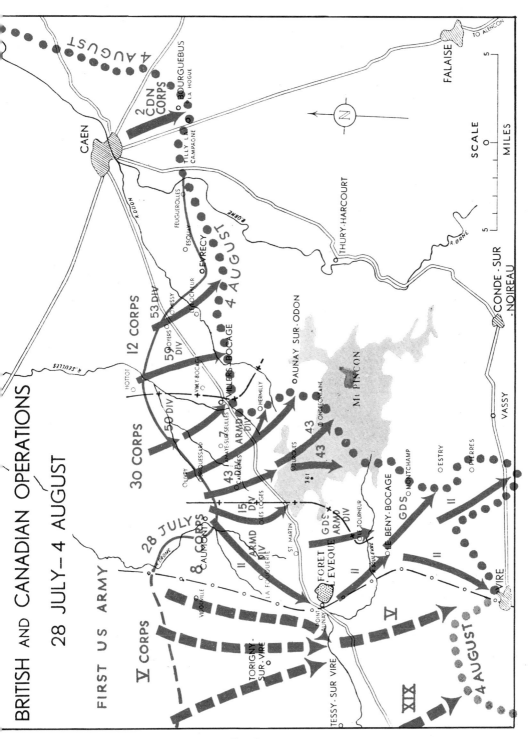

BRITISH AND CANADIAN OPERATIONS
28 JULY – 4 AUGUST

FIRST US ARMY

CAEN

2 CDN CORPS
BOURGUEBUS
LA HOGUE
TILLY LA CAMPAGNE

FEUGUEROLLES
ESQUAY
EVRECY
4 AUGUST
LE LOCHEUR
VASSY

12 CORPS
53 DIV
59 DIV
VILLERS BOCAGE
4 AUGUST
VINEY BOCAGE

30 CORPS
50 DIV
HOTTOT
7 ARMD DIV
AMAYE-SUR-SEULLES
HERMILLY
AUNAY-SUR-ODON
ONDEFONTAINE
Mt PINCON
43

43
361
43
BRIOUELLE
OLENDY
CAHAGNES

28 JULY
8 CORPS
15 DIV
LES LOGES
ST MARTIN
GDS ARMD DIV
LE TOURNEUR
BENY-BOCAGE
MONTCHAMP
GDS
ESTRY
PERRES
II

CAUMONT
II
11 ARMD DIV
FORET L'EVEQUE
LA FERQUERIE
PONT AUNAY
R SOULEUVRE
II
VIRE

V CORPS
VIDOUVILLE
TORIGNI-SUR-VIRE
TESSY-SUR-VIRE
XIX
V
4 AUGUST

R SEULLES
R ODON
R ORNE
R ORNE

THURY-HARCOURT

CONDE-SUR-NOIREAU

FALAISE
TO ALENCON

N

SCALE
MILES

[257]

The attack started on 30 Corps front at 0600 hours 30 July. 43 Division was to secure the hill feature about Point 361 to the west of Jurques, while 50 Division on its left was to secure the high ground west and north-west of Villers Bocage. The attack by 8 Corps was timed to start one hour later with 11 Armoured and 15 Divisions, which were to establish themselves in the area of St Martin des Bésaces, protect the right flank of 30 Corps and exploit round the Forêt l'Eveque to Point Aunay. Orders provided that, if the situation permitted, 11 Armoured Division was to push on to the south and west irrespective of the progress of 15 Division.

The initial attack was supported by heavy and medium bombers which carried out their attacks in spite of low cloud and bad weather.

Progress on the 8 Corps flank proved easier than on 30 Corps front. The former advanced astride the Caumont–Le Beny Bocage road; La Fouquerie and Les Loges were soon reached. Meanwhile 30 Corps was experiencing difficulty in crossing a stream which ran through Bricquessard (two miles east of Caumont). This stream had steep banks which were heavily mined and the approaches were covered by well sited anti-tank guns and machine guns. Some progress was made, however, on the right, though 50 Division on the left was held up till nightfall.

On 31 July the attacks continued at first light. 8 Corps secured crossings over the River Soulevre and reached the high ground just west of Le Beny Bocage, while Guards Armoured Division reached Le Tourneur; 15 Division was engaged in mopping up in rear. 30 Corps cleared Cahagnes and approached Jurques, and 50 Division forced the Bricquessard stream and was pushing forward. The opposition in the Le Beny Bocage area began to stiffen; 21 Panzer Division was now identified with 326 Infantry Division, having been switched from the extreme eastern flank. On 1 August 8 Corps cleared Le Beny Bocage, and the Guards made for Estry; 15 Division, holding a firm base for the armour, repulsed counter-attacks delivered by the enemy from the south and south-east. 30 Corps brought 7 Armoured Division in on the left flank and directed it on Aunay-sur-Odon, while 50 Division made further progress towards Villers Bocage. 43 Division continued its advance during the night with the object of securing Ondefontaine, and was to be followed up by 7 Armoured Division at first light in the morning. On 2 August, 43 Division, having made good progress during the night, moved forward towards Aunay while 50 Division secured Amaye and continued the advance up the Seulles valley. Opposition to 8 Corps was now becoming more stubborn; elements of 11 Armoured Division reached the northern outskirts of Vire and patrols crossed the Vire–Vassy road, but the enemy had not evacuated Vire and there were signs of his being reinforced in the area south of Mont Pinçon. The Air Force found good targets among tanks and vehicles moving west in the Condé area. In its advance on Estry, Guards Armoured Division met heavy opposition and was eventually held up. By this time it was known that already 9 SS, 10 SS as well as 21 Panzer Divisions had been swung across from the east to oppose our thrust. In order therefore to add weight to the drive, 3 Division was placed under command of 8 Corps.

13.  (*top left*) This is the first time this corporal in the 50th Division has been able to take his boots off since landing. 13 June 1944.

14.  (*top right*) Major Lord Ashley with 'Tilly', a puppy found when Tilly sur Seulles was captured, which became the Army H.Q. mascot. 19 June 1944.

15.  (*bottom*) Allied reinforcements arriving in Normandy.

16. Hitler's West Wall—German tank obstacles which stretched for miles behind the West Wall along the coast. 4 July 1944.

17. Bath time for the 21st Argyll and Sutherland Highlanders. 6 July 1944.

18.   General Montgomery with his two puppies, 'Hitler' and 'Rommel', and in the background his cage of canaries, at the 21st Army Group H.Q. at Blay. 6 July 1944.

19.   (*left to right*) General Patton, General Bradley and General Montgomery at the 21st Army Group H.Q. 7 July 1944.

20.  View of the ruins of Caen. 9 July 1944.

21.  A Diesel railway engine arriving ashore from landing craft on the beach at Courseulles, Normandy. 26 July 1944.

Heavy fighting continued on 3 August; south of the Vire–Vassy road 11 Armoured Division was engaged with strong enemy forces, while the Guards continued to be heavily engaged round Estry. 7 Armoured Division was prevented from making further progress by a series of counter attacks. Meanwhile 12 Corps, operating with 53 and 59 Division, was closing up to the Villers Bocage–Noyers road and captured Noyers itself together with Missy.

On the following day 12 Corps troops crossed the Villers Bocage–Noyers road, and 53 Division reached the general line from the Odon near Le Locheur through Evrecy to the Orne near Feuguerolles. The reconnaissance regiments of the attacking divisions began closing up to the Orne from Thury Harcourt northwards.

Progress was slow in both 8 and 30 Corps owing to enemy counter attacks and the great difficulty of the country. 11 Armoured Division, however, made some progress round the south side of Mont Pinçon while 7 Armoured Division secured Hermilly, about two miles north-west of Aunay-sur-Orne. Further north, 50 Division entered Villers Bocage. During the first days of August 2 Canadian Corps mounted three attacks east of the Orne as part of the general programme of maintaining pressure in that area. Its operations took place in the area of Tilly la Campagne and La Hogue. They produced violent infantry and tank counter attacks.

### The Situation, 4 August

The enemy had been unable to reform his left flank. As the American armour approached Avranches he attempted to hold a hinge between Percy and Tessy with 2 and 116 Panzer Divisions, but this was frustrated by First United States Army pressure and by the Second Army attack towards Vire. On 31 July, 363 Infantry Division, also from Fifteenth Army, appeared at Villedieu on the Avranches–Caen main road. Meanwhile, as a result of the Second Army advance to Le Beny Bocage, the enemy brought in 21, 9 SS and 10 SS Panzer Divisions and the front began to firm up between Aunay-sur-Odon and Vire. Desperate resistance continued between these two places, because it was vital for the enemy to hold firm in this sector while his forces to the south-west swung back. At this stage it was assumed he would try to bring his whole line back behind the Orne because, from a strictly military point of view, he was now placed in a situation in which the only logical answer was a staged withdrawal to the Seine. However it was very difficult to forecast the enemy's plans because of the erratic dictation from Berlin. There was still a chance that Hitler would decide to fight the Battle of France south of the Seine which would give us an opportunity of sealing the fate of the Seventh German Army. Meanwhile in Brittany, there appeared to be four divisions in danger of being cut off: and another division in the Channel Islands.

The general situation was now very good. We had broken out of the bridgehead and had destroyed the first hinge on which the enemy had tried to pivot. We were now pressing hard against the next 'key rivet' of his line on the slopes of the Pinçon massif. Meanwhile the American drive was beginning to swing towards the east according to

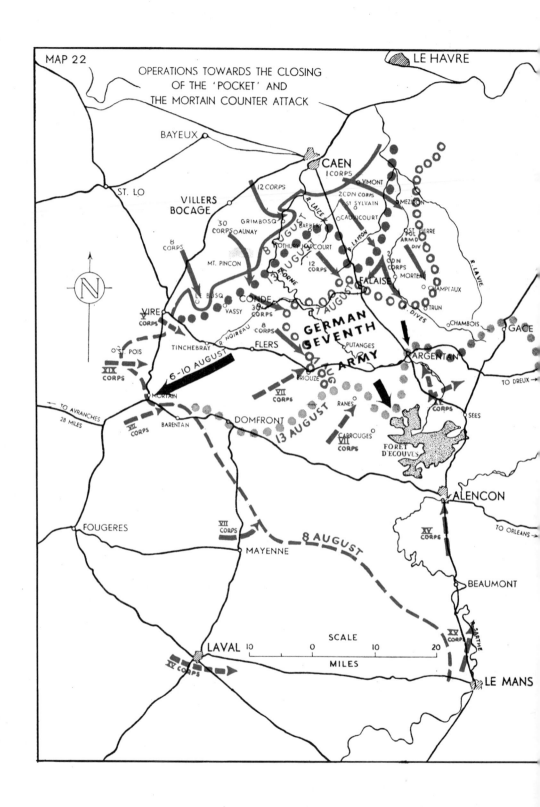

MAP 22

OPERATIONS TOWARDS THE CLOSING
OF THE 'POCKET' AND
THE MORTAIN COUNTER ATTACK

LE HAVRE

BAYEUX

ST. LO

CAEN
I CORPS

VIMONT

12 CORPS

2 CDN CORPS
ST SYLVAIN

MEZIDON

VILLERS
BOCAGE

CAUVICOURT

30
CORPS AUNAY

GRIMBOSQ

BARBERY

ST. PIERRE
ARMD
DIV

8
CORPS

MT. PINCON

THURY HARCOURT

12
CORPS

R. LAISON

CDN
CORPS

CHAMPEAUX

MORTEEN

R. LA VIE

R. ORNE

FALAISE

LE BUSQ

CONDE

VIRE
CORPS

VASSY

39
CORPS

DIVES

TRUN

CHAMBOIS

GACE

R. NOIREAU

8
CORPS

FLERS

PUTANGES

ST. POIS

TINCHEBRAY

BRIOUZE

ARGENTAN

TO DREUX

XIX
CORPS

6-10 AUGUST

MORTAIN

VII
CORPS

RANES

X
CORPS

SEES

TO AVRANCHES
28 MILES

VII
CORPS

BARENTAN

DOMFRONT

13 AUGUST

CARROUGES

VII
CORPS

FORET
D'ECOUVES

GERMAN
SEVENTH
ARMY

ALENCON

FOUGERES

VII
CORPS

8 AUGUST

MAYENNE

XV
CORPS

TO ORLEANS

BEAUMONT

SCALE

LAVAL

10

0

10

20

MILES

XV
CORPS

LE MANS

XV
CORPS

plan, and at the same time Third United States Army had turned VIII United States Corps westwards into Brittany.

The time had now come to deliver the major attack towards Falaise, which had so long been the fundamental aim of our policy on the eastern flank. I planned that the Canadians should drive south-east from Caen to gain as much ground as possible in the direction of Falaise, in order to get behind the enemy forces facing Second Army, and to continue the process of wearing down the enemy formations in the sector. I envisaged this operation as a prelude to subsequent exploitation of success.

My orders on 4 August provided for the First Canadian Army attack to be launched as quickly as possible. Meanwhile Second British Army was to continue pivoting on 12 Corps, swinging down towards Thury Harcourt, Condé and Flers; subsequent operations were to be developed towards Argentan. I provided that the northern flank of Twelfth United States Army Group should operate on the axis Domfront–Alençon.

I was continuing with my broad strategy of swinging the right flank round towards Paris, so as to force the enemy back against the Seine. Plans were under preparation for the use of airborne forces in advance of the American columns in order to hasten the closure of the Orleans gap.

*Twelfth United States Army Group begins to swing East, 5–6 August*

On 5 August, Third United States Army held the line Fougères–Mortain with XV Corps; to the north the First United States Army front ran from Mortain through the Forêt de St Sever to a point of junction with Second Army immediately north of Vire. From right to left the corps in First Army were VII, XIX and V.

XV Corps developed operations to capture Laval and Mayenne and to secure a crossing over the River Mayenne between those places. Progress was rapid and the objectives were secured, but VII Corps ran into heavy opposition, provided by 84 Infantry Division which had recently arrived from Fifteenth Army. XIX Corps was now passing across the front of V Corps as it made further ground to the west of Vire.

VIII United States Corps had turned into the Brittany peninsula and Rennes was liberated on 3 August. Armoured columns pushed on rapidly south of Chateaubriant and by 5 August reached the coast near Quiberon Bay, while in the centre of the peninsula advanced elements were only fifty miles short of Brest.

On 6 August troops of VIII United States Corps reached the River Loire about fifteen miles east of Nantes. On VII Corps front resistance continued to prove stubborn on the left flank; but on the right, forward troops reached Mayenne, where contact was made with XV Corps, and armoured elements were pushed into Domfront. Vire was occupied by XIX Corps in spite of considerable resistance.

Progress in the Brittany peninsula continued, and it was clear that there was no properly organized enemy resistance except in the neighbourhood of the ports. Much useful work had been done before the arrival of the troops by the Resistance Movement, and by the Allied parachute detachments.

*Second Army Operations, 5–6 August*

As American troops advanced on Vire from the south-west, tanks of 11 Armoured Division were fighting north of the town. In the 8 Corps sector most of 5 August was spent mopping up the enemy pockets which were hindering the supply routes, but in the centre of Second Army front 43 Division continued to converge on Mont Pinçon. 7 Armoured Division entered Aunay-sur-Odon during the afternoon and forward troops pushed on about four miles in the direction of Thury Harcourt. 12 Corps troops closed up to the River Orne on a frontage of seven miles from Grimbosq northwards, but mobility was impeded by the rubble and craters which blocked the roads and villages between the Odon and the Orne.

Throughout 6 August the enemy was attacking between Vire and Mont Pinçon. 10 SS Panzer Division made a determined attack against 11 Armoured Division and achieved some initial success, but the ground lost was quickly retaken. Guards Armoured Division was also fighting heavily in the area Le Busq. On 30 Corps front, 43 Division gained a footing on Mont Pinçon after severe fighting. Further east, 59 Division on 12 Corps front attacked across the Orne near Grimbosq and by midnight had forded the river and was holding a shallow bridgehead some two miles in width.

During 5 and 6 August First Canadian Army was making final preparations for its attack southwards in the direction of Falaise.

*The Situation, 6 August*

On 6 August I issued orders for the advance to the Seine.

I was still not clear what the enemy intended to do. There was no evidence to show on what line he was intending to reform his front; it was evident from the British and Canadian troops in close contact with the Germans east, south-east and south of Caen that he was definitely holding his ground in this sector: he was evidently trying to pivot on the Caen area. Beyond this I was mystified as to how he was endeavouring to conduct his withdrawal; but, as far as the Allies were concerned, I ordered that we should continue relentlessly with our plans to drive him against the Seine, denying him escape routes through the Orleans gap. I emphasized the need for continued and sustained pressure; the enemy was off his balance and we had to keep him in this plight. Having frustrated his attempts to establish a hinge in the Caumont–Vire sector, Second Army by its operations in the Thury Harcourt area on 4 August prevented the establishment of a hinge on the River Orne. The next essential was to smash the hinge south of Caen: and this was to prove a very difficult task.

I instructed First Canadian Army to make every effort to reach Falaise itself in the forthcoming attack; in the subsequent advance to the Seine the main Canadian axis was to be the road Lisieux–Rouen. On its right I intended Second British Army to advance with its right directed on Argentan and Laigle, whence it was to reach the Seine below Mantes. Twelfth United States Army Group was to approach the Seine on a wide front with its main weight on the right flank, which was to swing up towards Paris. Plans for using airborne and air-portee forces to secure the Chartres area ahead of the main advance were to be held ready. As the eastward move progressed flank protection along the line of the River Loire was to be provided, particularly at the main crossing places of Saumur, Tours, Blois and Orleans.

### THIRD PHASE: THE GERMAN COUNTER STROKE, AND THE BATTLE OF THE MORTAIN–FALAISE POCKET

The arrival of 116 Panzer Division, 84, 89 and 363 Infantry Divisions and elements of 6 Parachute Division from north of the Seine, together with the reports of other formations on their way from that direction and from the south of France, indicated that the Normandy front was now taking priority over all others in the west of Europe; the enemy was reducing his Biscay and Mediterranean coast garrisons to a mere façade, while Fifteenth Army in the Pas de Calais was no longer to be organized in strength to meet a cross-Channel thrust. Divisions were being thrown straight into the Normandy battle rather than being positioned as a firm base upon which hard pressed formations of Seventh Army could regroup.

I have already stated that from the military point of view the enemy had reached the stage where withdrawal to the Seine offered the only hope of saving his armies; and personally I was surprised and delighted that he had not tried to do so already. Indeed he was even sending more troops into Normandy. Why?

The answer was now to be provided. The German High Command had by this time fully realized that the critical moment had arrived in Normandy, and that the outcome of the battle now raging would decide the issue of the struggle in western Europe and possibly even of the war itself. Refusing no doubt to believe the situation as it was presented to him, and disregarding the advice of his generals, Hitler himself ordered that the Panzer divisions should be disengaged, formed up outside Mortain facing west, and launched into an attack which was to drive down the rivers See and Selune and reach the sea at Avranches, thereby restoring the old 'roping-off' line and severing the communications of Third United States Army whose advanced columns were even now beginning to cut across his own.

The following order signed by the Commander of Seventh Army, plainly reveals these facts:

'The Fuehrer has ordered the execution of a breakthrough to the coast to create the basis for the decisive operation against the Allied invasion front. For this purpose, further forces are being brought up to the Army.

'On the successful execution of the operation the Fuehrer has ordered depends the decision of the War in the West, and with it perhaps the decision of the war itself. Commanders of all ranks must be absolutely clear about the enormous significance of this fact. I expect all corps and divisional commanders to take good care that all officers are aware of the unique significance of the whole situation. Only one thing counts, unceasing effort and determined will to victory.

For Fuehrer, Volk and Reich,
HAUSSER.'

Even after the costly battles along the Odon a month before, Hitler could not, or would not, understand that armoured operations on such a scale must be secure from air attack. The Germans were playing into our hands by hurling against us the concentrated strength of their surviving armour in the west, most of which had already received a heavy battering and was tired and dispirited. Instead of reforming on a prepared line of defence, the enemy was exhausting his resources in a way which would give us the opportunity of defeating his Army west of the Seine and administering one of the greatest defeats of the war.

The German field commanders were under no illusion about the appalling risk of the Mortain counter stroke. We know, for example, that Dietrich, who took over Fifth Panzer Army during this operation, protested to von Kluge for over an hour about the impracticability of the Mortain attack. He pointed out that there was insufficient petrol; that if three armoured divisions were sent westwards it would be impossible to hold Falaise; that it was impossible to concentrate such a mass of tanks without inviting disaster from the air; that there was manifestly not enough space to deploy such large armoured forces; and that the Americans were already very strong to the south of Falaise so that such an attack would only serve to wedge the German forces tighter into the trap rather than to destroy the trap itself. To each argument von Kluge had only one reply, 'It is a Fuehrerbefehl (Hitler's Order)'.

Five Panzer divisions—2 Panzer, 1 SS, 2 SS, 116 Panzer, and finally 10 SS as well—took part in the attack, together with 84 and 363 Infantry Divisions, which were both fresh.

It began on 7 August and the brunt of it fell on 30 United States Infantry Division which held the onslaught sufficiently long to enable two American divisions who were moving south between Avranches and Mortain to be switched to the danger area. Fortunately the weather was ideal for air operations and the tremendous power of the Allied Air Forces was brought to bear against the enemy columns. All day they kept up their attacks and apart from the material damage caused, the intensity and continuity of the attacks undermined the morale of the enemy tank crews. Although they failed to do more than recapture Mortain, the Germans maintained their desperate efforts and continued to despatch reinforcements to the Mortain–Domfront area. On 8 August elements of 9 Panzer Division from the Mediterranean coast were identified and heavy pressure continued against VII Corps; but with the assistance of the Tactical Air Forces these attacks were also repulsed. On the ground, the American counter measures were swift and efficient, and the result of the battle was never for a moment in doubt.


*Canadian Operations, 7–8 August*

First Canadian Army was ready to launch its thrust southwards in the direction of Falaise on the night of 7 August. The object was to break the enemy defences astride the Caen–Falaise road, and to exploit as far as Falaise itself. The German

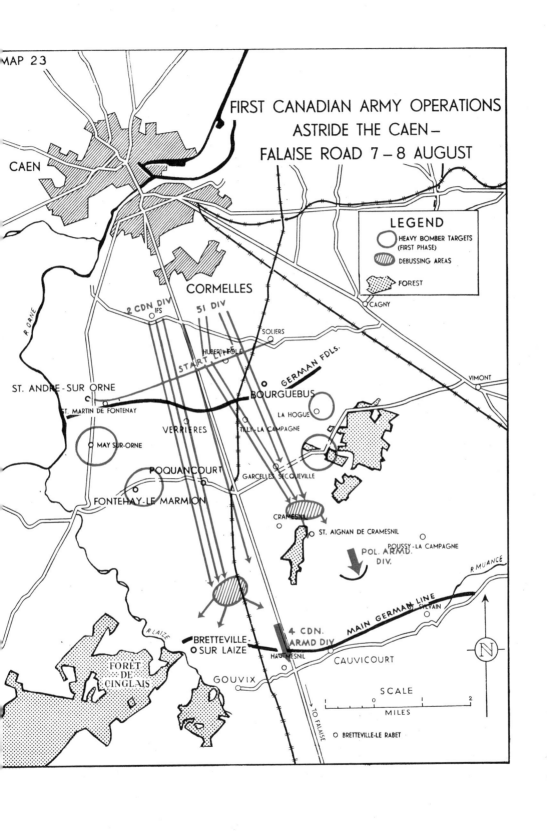

MAP 23

FIRST CANADIAN ARMY OPERATIONS
ASTRIDE THE CAEN –
FALAISE ROAD 7 – 8 AUGUST

CAEN

CORMELLES

LEGEND

HEAVY BOMBER TARGETS
(FIRST PHASE)

DEBUSSING AREAS

FOREST

CAGNY

2 CDN DIV
IFS

51 DIV

SOLIERS

HUBERT-FOLIE

START LINE

GERMAN FDLS.

VIMONT

ST. ANDRE-SUR ORNE

ST. MARTIN DE FONTENAY

BOURGUEBUS

LA HOGUE

VERRIERES

TILLY-LA CAMPAGNE

MAY-SUR-ORNE

POQUANCOURT

GARCELLES SECQUEVILLE

FONTENAY-LE-MARMION

CRAMESNIL

ST. AIGNAN DE CRAMESNIL

POUSSY-LA-CAMPAGNE

POL. ARMD.
DIV.

R. MUANCE

MAIN GERMAN LINE

R. LAIZE

CLEVAIN

BRETTEVILLE-
SUR LAIZE

4 CDN.
ARMD DIV

HAUTMESNIL

CAUVICOURT

N

FORET
DE
CINGLAIS

GOUVIX

SCALE

0        1        2

MILES

TO FALAISE

BRETTEVILLE-LE-RABET

R. ORNE

defences were formidable; it was known that, during its period out of the line, 12 SS Panzer Division had been hurriedly preparing successive defence lines covering the approaches to Falaise. About sixty dug-in tanks and self-propelled guns were supplemented by some ninety 88 millimetre flak guns sited in an anti-tank role. The defence positions proper were manned by elements of 12 SS Panzer Division with 89 Infantry Division (newly arrived from north of the Seine) and 272 Infantry Division. Unlocated in rear was 85 Infantry Division, another Fifteenth Army formation.

The plan was to attack under cover of darkness after a preliminary action by heavy bombers; the infantry was to be transported through the enemy's zone of defensive fire and forward defended localities in heavy armoured carriers. These vehicles, which became known as 'Kangaroos', were self-propelled gun carriages specially converted for transporting infantry. To ensure accurate navigation by night the positions and bearings of thrust lines were fixed by survey from the leading tanks; directional wireless, Bofors guns firing tracer and 'artificial moonlight' were also employed to facilitate mobility in the darkness. Once the infantry had penetrated the forward enemy defended area, it was to debus and fan out in order to mop up the defenders.

The night attack was to break through the Fontenay-le-Marmion–La Hogue position and exploit to Bretteville-sur-Laize. The following morning armour was to tackle the defences along the line Hautmesnil–St Sylvain and to exploit towards Falaise.

At 2300 hours 7 August the heavy bomber operation began, and half-an-hour later 2 Canadian and 51 Divisions with their armoured brigades moved forward. The assault was organized in eight columns of armour, each with vehicles four abreast, which advanced preceded by gapping teams of assault engineers and flail tanks. The enemy was greatly confused by these armoured columns driving through his defences. At first light the infantry debussed in their correct areas after a four miles' drive within the enemy lines, and proceeded to deal with their immediate objectives. In rear of the advance other troops began mopping-up operations, which in fact proved to be a most difficult task.

By midday 2 Canadian Division had secured May-sur-Orne, Fontenay and Roquancourt, while 51 Division secured Garçelles Secqueville; soon afterwards Tilly la Campagne was taken.

The first phase of the operation had been successful, and following an attack by strong formations of Flying Fortresses, the armoured formations began to move south at 1355 hours. 4 Canadian Armoured Division on the right was held up eventually by an anti-tank gun screen, and on the left Polish Armoured Division was also unable to make much headway.

It was clear that the attack had come up against a very strong lay-back position astride the high ground from about Bray-en-Cinglais through Bretteville-le-Rabet to Poussy-la-Campagne.

*Other Operations, 7–8 August*

While VII United States Corps and 8 British Corps were held up in their respective sectors, the right wing of Twelfth United States Army Group proceeded with its planned operations. On 7 August XV Corps, in spite of opposition from 708 Infantry Division recently arrived from the Biscay front, continued to make progress and on the following day entered Le Mans.

In Brittany, Third United States Army units were engaged in heavy fighting at the approaches to St Malo, Brest and Lorient.

In the British sector, 43 Division finally secured Mount Pinçon and some villages on the southern slopes, but heavy fighting continued and the enemy launched repeated counter attacks in which considerable casualties were inflicted by both sides. Meanwhile 30 Corps made progress towards Condé, while in the Orne bridgehead 59 Division was attempting to swing down on Thury Harcourt from the north-east; a series of strong enemy counter attacks by 12 SS Panzer Division on 8 August frustrated this plan.

*The Situation, 8 August*

I have shown that up to this period my plan was to make a wide enveloping movement from the southern American flank up to the Seine about Paris, and at the same time to drive the centre and northern sectors of the Allied line straight for the river. In view of the Mortain counter stroke, I decided to attempt *concurrently* a shorter envelopment with the object of bottling up the bulk of the German forces deployed between Falaise and Mortain. It was obvious that if we could bring off both these movements we would virtually annihilate the enemy in Normandy.

XV Corps of Third United States Army was sweeping all before it and was admirably placed at Le Mans to swing north towards the Canadian forces coming southwards to Falaise and Argentan; if the Germans continued to attack at Mortain for a few days while the British and Canadians progressed through Falaise and on to Argentan, and the Americans came north to Alençon, it seemed to me that the enemy would be unable to get away.

On 8 August, therefore, I ordered Twelfth United States Army Group to swing its right flank due north on Alençon at full strength and with all speed. At the same time I urged all possible speed on First Canadian and Second British Armies in the movements which were converging on Falaise.

*American Operations, 9–12 August*

The plan of Twelfth United States Army Group was for First United States Army to continue to reduce the enemy salient, and pivoting on Mortain, to advance to the line Domfront-Barenton, prepared for further action against the German flank and rear in the direction of Flers. The task of Third United States Army was to advance on the axis Alençon–Sees up to the line Sees–Carrouges, prepared for further action against the enemy flank and rear in the direction of Argentan. At the same time a bridgehead was to be seized over the River Sarthe in the vicinity of Le Mans, while Nantes and Angers were to be occupied to cover the southern flank. The responsibility for completing the reduction of the Brittany peninsula remained with Third United States Army. XII and XX Corps were now becoming operational in Third United States Army.

On 9 August XV Corps regrouped with the following divisions under command: 5 United States and 2 French Armoured Divisions, 79, 80 and 90 Infantry Divisions. Approaches east and south of Le Mans were blocked and crossings were built over the River Sarthe preparatory to the advance on Alençon. On 10 August XV Corps attacked north towards Alençon with 5 Armoured Division and 79 Division on the right, 2 French Armoured Division and 90 Division on the left. The enemy exerted desperate resistance to the initial advance but on 11 August progress was rapid, and while main bodies were some six miles south of the town, reconnaissance elements were in Alençon and beyond it. By the following day XV Corps was firmly established on the line Sees–Carrouges, and forward elements were converging on Argentan.

On First Army front operations were directed to driving in the enemy salient between Domfront, Mortain, St Pois and Vire; and on the Second Army sector conforming attacks were in progress towards Condé, Tinchebray and Flers. The enemy's attacks made no progress against VII Corps; on 10 August a major enemy attack north-west of Barentan was driven off and VII Corps continued to push forward. Further north XIX Corps made some progress south-west of Vire where the enemy had thrown in 331 Infantry Division, recently arrived from the Pas de Calais on bicycles.

### British and Canadian Operations, 9–12 August

The two main movements on the north of the enemy pocket comprised the converging movements of 8 and 30 Corps towards the Tinchebray–Condé area and the attacks of 12 Corps and First Canadian Army towards Thury Harcourt–Falaise. The enemy infantry opposing 8 and 30 Corps fought in the excellent defensive country with great stubbornness, and progress was therefore slow; 3 Division of 8 Corps crossed the Vire–Condé road about two miles east of Vire, while 30 Corps troops made some progress south from Mont Pinçon towards Condé. By 12 August heavy fighting was continuing on the high ground three miles south-east of Vire, and at the same time leading troops were only a few miles short of Condé.

In 12 Corps sector, 53 and 59 Divisions advanced on Thury Harcourt astride the Orne; leading elements reached the outskirts of the town on 11 August and found it held. East of the river the bridgehead was extended to the south-east, and also to the north-east to link up with elements of 2 Canadian Division who had crossed the River Laize.

On 9 August Canadian Army made appreciable advances. 4 Canadian Armoured Division secured Bretteville-le-Rabet after bitter fighting, and the Poles captured Cauvicourt and St Sylvain. Repeated attempts, however, to make a clean break through the enemy's anti-tank gun screen met with little success and our armour sustained heavy casualties; in particular, it was obvious that the line of the River Laison had been developed into a strong defensive position.

While the armoured divisions were fighting astride the Falaise road, the two infantry divisions completed the task of securing the corps flanks. On 11 August, 2 Canadian Division was ordered across the River Laize and by the afternoon of the following day had taken Barbery, and linked up with 12 Corps. On the left flank, 51 Division cleared the woods and villages south of the Caen–Mezidon railway, and reverted to command of 1 Corps which took over responsibility for that area. In conjunction with 51 Division, 49 Division made progress and reached Vimont on 10 August; in this area elements of 344 Infantry Division from Fifteenth Army were identified.

## *The Situation, 12 August*

After four days' fighting around Mortain, the enemy had suffered enough and began to pull back his Panzer divisions to meet the threat to his flanks: particularly on the south, where hitherto protection had been afforded by inadequate battle groups. The enemy plan was evidently to extricate as many troops as possible, both Panzer and infantry, from the salient and reform a north–south line much further to the east. By 12 August reconnaissance reports clearly showed a general trend of enemy movement to the east from the Mortain area through the 'neck' between Falaise and Argentan and on towards the Seine ferries. But the enemy was still fighting back hard and apparently trying to stand his ground within the salient; it was reasonable therefore to assume that this movement comprised the rearward elements of the German forces, and that if we could close the jaws of our 'short' enveloping movements across the Falaise–Argentan neck, we should have in our grasp the bulk of the fighting formations of von Kluge's forces. The Allied Air Forces were pounding the enemy in the pocket but the problem of completing the encirclement was no easy one; the Germans realized that their existence depended on holding open the corridor, and bitter fighting ensued as a result of our attempts to frustrate them. On the north side of the corridor it must be recalled that the enemy had long been in possession of the vital ground north of Falaise, and had thus had ample opportunity for the development of strong, well sited defences; the large number of 88 millimetre guns which had previously defended the Caen area in the anti-aircraft role, were now taking heavy toll of our armour north of Falaise. On the south side of the corridor the enemy piled his resources not only to oppose XV United States Corps, but ultimately to launch an endeavour to break our cordon in that area.

There was no change in my orders or intentions. I was watching carefully the mounting of the 'wide' envelopment around to the Seine, and kept plans ready for dropping airborne forces in the Paris–Orleans gap. It was essential from my point of view to continue with the wide envelopment movement, concurrently with closing the Falaise–Argentan corridor, as we wanted to round up those enemy formations which were outside the actual Mortain pocket; we wanted to make certain of writing off all the Germans in the Normandy battle. General Bradley therefore carried out further regrouping in Third United States Army, so that General Patton could continue his drive to the Seine while the battle of the 'neck' continued. The major difficulty was administration, since the maintenance of the southern American wing from the original beach areas had to be effected along a long and badly damaged line of communication, which passed through the congested Avranches area and made a wide sweep southwards and eastwards. Very great credit is due to the American administrative machine, greatly assisted by rapidly developed air supply arrangements, for the outstanding administrative improvisation and ingenuity which enabled us to continue offensive operations on our southern flank.

*Operations, 13–20 August*

The battle of the Mortain–Falaise pocket continued with undiminished ferocity. While strenuous efforts continued to close the corridor between Falaise and Argentan, British and American forces pressed in from all sides of the pocket to annihilate the enemy which it contained. XV United States Corps was well established in the Argentan area on 13 August and had elements some ten miles to the east towards Gace, feeling for the enemy flank and closing on the routes to the east; on 14 August this Corps was ordered to extend yet further to the east towards Dreux in order to get round the enemy holding the southern shoulder of the corridor and to prevent leakage of the enemy forces towards the Orleans gap.

VII United States Corps advanced north from Mayenne to positions on the western flank of XV United States Corps; as this movement was in progress the enemy made a determined but unsuccessful effort to break out of our cordon in the area of the Forêt d'Ecouves.

Meanwhile V and XIX United States Corps pressed in on the extreme western and north-western sectors of the pocket; by 14 August XIX Corps had fought its way into Domfront and troops of V Corps were within two miles of Tinchebray. 8 Corps, of Second British Army, was closing in on Tinchebray from the north, and 30 Corps pushed the enemy back on Vassy, Condé and the River Noireau. East of the Orne, leading troops of 12 Corps were now about six miles to the west and north-west of Falaise. The main Canadian thrust on Falaise from the north was resumed on 14 August, when it was planned to by-pass the resistance astride the main road and come down on the town from the north-east, after breaking through the enemy positions on the River Laison. By the end of the day an advance of some five miles had been made and the Canadians were only four miles short of Falaise itself.

By 15 August it was quite clear that the enemy intended to evacuate his armour from the pocket and to withdraw, regardless of the infantry, east of the Falaise-Argentan area. Although the opposition in the west of the salient lessened considerably, fighting on the flanks of the corridor was fierce, as the Germans exerted every possible effort to hold open a line of escape for their forces. The enemy was becoming

MAP 24

THE FALAISE POCKET AS AT 18 AUGUST

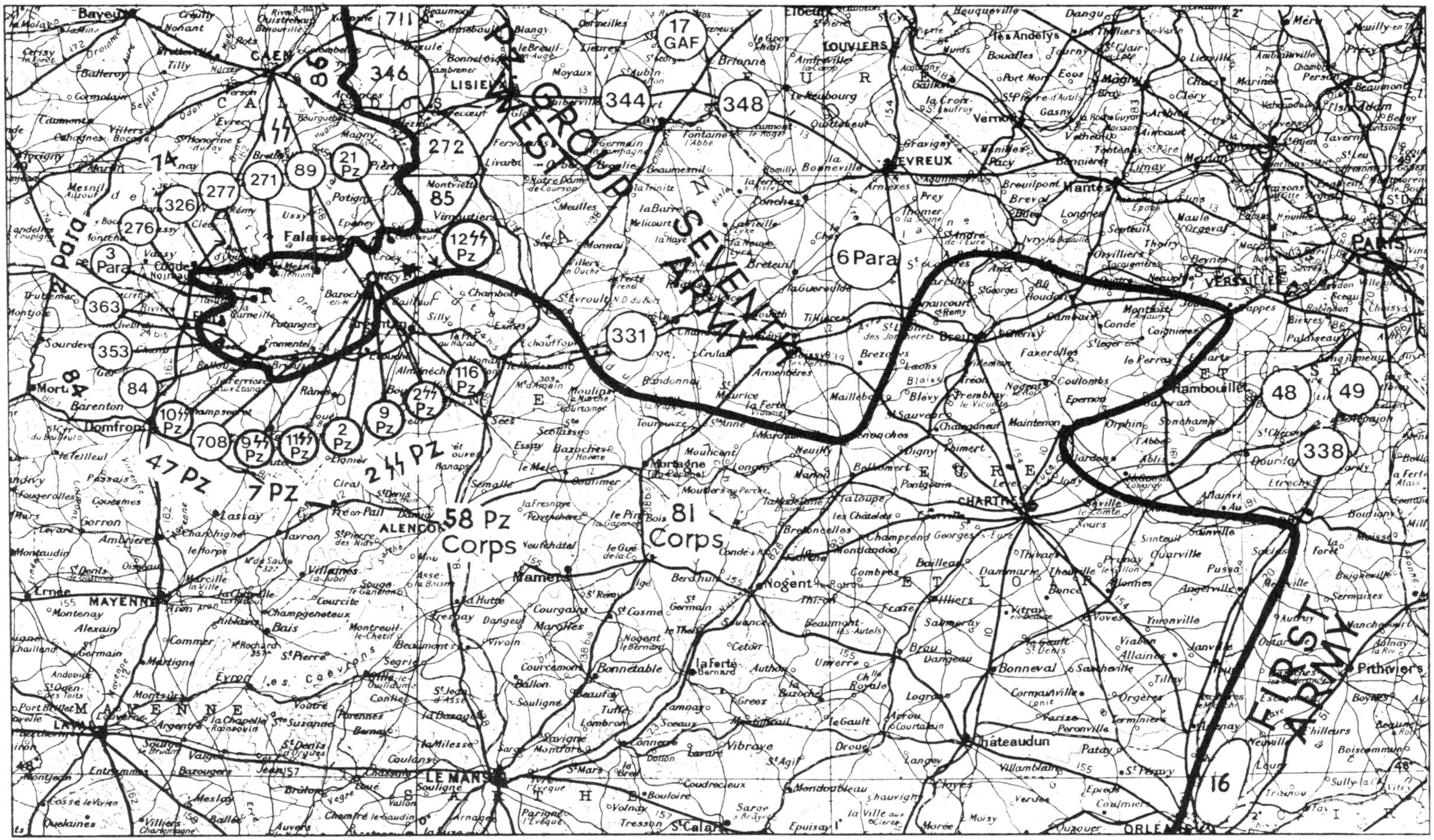

very disorganized; elements from no less than eleven different divisions had been identified near Argentan on 14 August. The same day saw very heavy fighting on VII United States Corps front in the area of Rânes, and XIX Corps on its left was having difficulty with stubborn rearguards to the north-east of Domfront. V United States Corps captured Tinchebray from the west as Second Army troops came in from the north; 30 Corps made progress astride Condé, and 12 Corps drove in closer to Falaise. 4 Canadian Armoured Division made progress east of the Caen–Falaise road and the Polish Armoured Division secured bridgeheads over the River Dives some six to ten miles north-east of Falaise. Further north, 1 Corps was thrusting towards St Pierre-sur-Dives.

Meanwhile Twelfth United States Army Group continued to develop the wide encircling movement to the Seine. The plan was to line up Third United States Army facing east, and to develop its operations on three main axes directed on Dreux, Chartres and Orleans. At the same time First United States Army was to face north along the southern flank of the pocket and to complete its reduction in conjunction with the British and Canadian forces. Headquarters V United States Corps, when pinched out in the Tinchebray sector, was to take over from Headquarters XV Corps in the Argentan area. The Third Army drives were to be conducted by XV Corps to Dreux, by XX Corps from Le Mans to Chartres and by XII Corps to Orleans along the north bank of the Loire. General Bradley also ordered XIX United States Corps, when pinched out of the Mortain area, to be swung round to join the drive to the Seine. The limiting factor remained administration, yet on 15 August General Patton's troops were only some five miles short of Dreux, and ten miles short of Chartres. On 16 August elements of XII Corps liberated Orleans, and on the same day XX Corps entered Chartres. Twenty-four hours later Dreux was captured by XV Corps. The speed of these three thrusts was such that there was no call for the employment of airborne forces ahead of the Third Army troops. Between 17 and 20 August, XII United States Corps became established to the north-east of Orleans, while XX Corps reorganized in the Chartres area pending additional maintenance resources for the continuance of their advance.

The movement continued with the swing of General Patton's northern flank up to the Seine from the Dreux area. Orders were issued on 17 August directing XV Corps to the Seine about Mantes Gassicourt. The supply situation made it impossible to maintain major forces east of Dreux, but by 19 August (D + 75) 79 United States Division had secured a small bridgehead over the Seine a few miles below Mantes. Elsewhere patrols had pushed to within a few miles of the suburbs of Paris, and reported the general area full of small and disorganized bodies of Germans moving towards the capital. On 19 August, maintenance conditions permitted Twelfth United States Army Group to order an advance along the southern bank of the Seine by both XV and XIX Corps on a frontage running from Mantes to Dreux and Verneuil.

Meanwhile the battle of the pocket continued; but by 16 August it had diminished considerably. 30 Corps secured Condé and continued its thrust towards the Orne. 12 Corps made further progress and finished the day just short of the Falaise–Condé railway, while troops of First Canadian Army virtually surrounded Falaise. On the south side of the enemy's corridor fierce fighting continued in the Argentan–Briouze sector.

On 17 August, Second Army troops advanced seven miles east of Flers, and on their right were in contact with VII United States Corps in the Briouze sector. Advancing south-east from Condé we were across the River Noireau on a broad front, and 12 Corps troops also made progress in the sector to the west of Falaise. Meanwhile 2 Canadian Division cleared Falaise, to the east of which 4 Canadian Armoured Division advanced on Trun, crossing the River Dives near Morteaux. On its left, Polish Armoured Division advanced its right flank to within a mile of Trun, but was experiencing fierce fighting about Champeaux, four miles to the north.

On the north side of the corridor the most desperate action on 18 August was in the Chambois area. Here the enemy was making an attempt to retrieve the situation by attacking towards Chambois with fresh troops newly arrived in Normandy. Meanwhile V United States Corps struck north towards Chambois from the Argentan sector, in a bid to link up with the Polish and Canadian thrusts. On the western sector of the pocket the resistance was crumbling; 30 Corps troops reached Poutanges and Ecouche, while further advances were made by 12 Corps.

On 19 August the neck of the pocket was finally closed when American troops from the south linked up at Chambois with the Polish Armoured Division. On this day, 4 Canadian Armoured Division captured St Lambert-sur-Dives and held it in face of desperate enemy attacks; the Polish Armoured Division experienced equally hard fighting. In the difficult tank country south of Les Champeaux, both armour and infantry detachments fought a confused battle with Panzer elements attacking from the east, south and west in a desperate attempt to keep open a narrow passage for escape. By midday, Ecorches had been captured and Polish tanks were in the area Coudehard–Mont Ormel. The Poles captured Chambois at 1900 hours, about which time contact was established with V United States Corps.

On the night of 19 August the general situation showed that we had in Trun, and to the north of it, 3 Canadian Infantry and 4 Canadian Armoured Divisions, with a small force of tanks and infantry gallantly holding St Lambert-sur-Dives on the road to Chambois. Polish Armoured Division was in Chambois and the area of Coudehard and Ecorches. From Chambois to Argentan V United States Corps had two infantry divisions and one (French) armoured division. In Argentan and extending to Bailleu on the Argentan–Trun road, was 11 Armoured Division of 30 Corps with 50 Division clearing the area further west. To the north, 53 Division of 12 Corps was closing on the Bailleu and Trun area from the west.

At the beginning, the German forces inside the pocket had retained a semblance of cohesion and plan: the Panzer divisions concentrated near the neck, where Allied

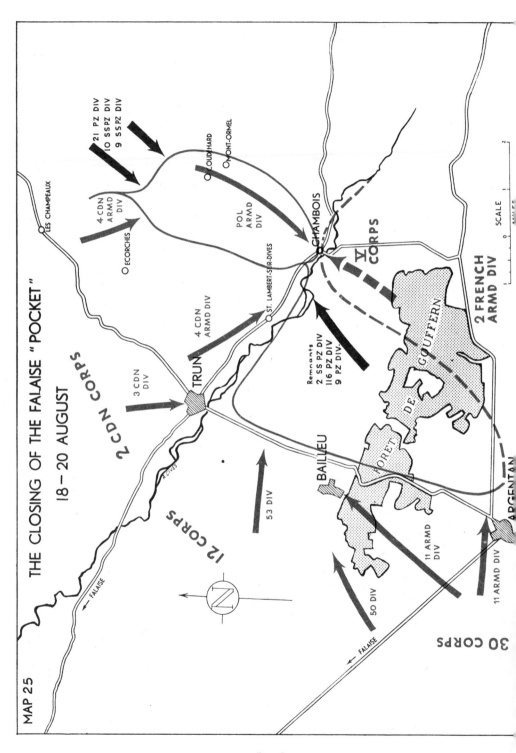

THE CLOSING OF THE FALAISE "POCKET"

18–20 AUGUST

MAP 25

2 CDN CORPS

12 CORPS

30 CORPS

V CORPS

LES CHAMPEAUX

ECORCHES

CLOUDEHARD

MONT-ORMEL

CHAMBOIS

ST. LAMBERT-SUR-DIVES

TRUN

BAILLEU

ARGENTAN

FORET DE GOUFFERN

21 PZ DIV
10 SSPZ DIV
9 SSPZ DIV

4 CDN ARMD DIV

POL ARMD DIV

4 CDN ARMD DIV

Remnants
2 SS PZ DIV
116 PZ DIV
9 PZ DIV.

3 CDN DIV

53 DIV

50 DIV

11 ARMD DIV

11 ARMD DIV

2 FRENCH ARMD DIV

R. DIVES

FALAISE

FALAISE

N

SCALE

pressure was strongest, in order to try and keep it open while the infantry divisions, notably the parachutists, conducted a rearguard action as best they could. By 16 August, however, almost all cohesion had been lost: divisions were hopelessly jumbled up and commanders were able to control no more than their own battle groups. Batch after batch of prisoners contained members of a dozen different divisions. The wreckage of German transport and equipment as a result of our air attacks littered the countryside. The Allied Air Forces were presented with targets probably unparalleled in this war: aircraft formations were engaging endless columns of enemy transport packed bumper to bumper and rendered immobile by the appalling congestion. While there were some attempts by the enemy to break out in formed detachments, there were in all sectors small parties of Germans trying to infiltrate across the fields to safety, and the problem of rounding them up was very considerable.

On 20 August the enemy made his last co-ordinated attempt at forcing our cordon. Fifth Panzer Army was ordered to make a gap; elements from 9 SS, 10 SS and 21 Panzer Divisions, which were outside the pocket, attacked from the north towards Trun and Chambois, while from inside, detachments of 2 SS, 116 and 9 Panzer Divisions tried to break out towards the east. The attack was contested by the Canadians and Poles, who inflicted tremendous casualties on the enemy, and it seems unlikely that the enemy succeeded in getting any great number of tanks out of the pocket. After this attack, the battle of the Mortain–Falaise pocket was virtually at an end, though the process of mopping up took some time.

At the same time I was endeavouring to develop operations eastward from the 1 Corps sector on our extreme northern sector. On 16 August I had directed First Canadian Army to mount a thrust towards Lisieux. General Crerar gave this task to 1 Corps, to which 7 Armoured Division was transferred from the Condé area. 51 Division captured St Pierre-sur-Dives and had advanced two miles beyond the town on 16 August, while 49 Division crossed the Dives at Mezidon. Nearer the coast, 6 Airborne Division found the enemy holding firm along the river, which constituted a difficult obstacle. By the night of 20 August we had crossed the River Vie on a broad front; 7 Armoured Division secured Livarot, and on the Lisieux road 51 Division reached St Julien-le-Faucon with 49 Division on its left. 6 Airborne Division was still engaged in the marshlands of the Dives valley, and in Cabourg was having difficulty in reducing the enemy defences.

*The Situation, 20 August*

The enemy situation in France was now desperate.

Our first enveloping movement completed, I was concentrating on ensuring that the wider encirclement along the Seine should be achieved with the maximum possible speed, so as to cut off the survivors from the Falaise–Mortain pocket.

There was little enough that the enemy could do: he had realized the inevitable fate of Seventh Army too late, so that the formations of Fifteenth Army, and those arriving from the south of France, had become involved in the battle piecemeal and had merely served to increase the numbers of our victims. By 20 August, the garrison of the Pas de Calais, once so strong, had been reduced to three divisions, while there was only one division in Flanders and one in the Somme–Seine sector.

Meanwhile, on the Mediterranean coast Allied forces had started landing on 15 August by sea and air between Toulon and Cannes. The German Nineteenth Army, which controlled the nine divisions remaining on the Riviera, began to withdraw in the face of these landings, but, owing to its own immobility, it attempted to delay as much as possible the advance of the United States Seventh Army up the Rhône Valley.

Speed, then, was now the vital necessity, in order to take advantage of the favourable circumstances presented to us: first, we had got to block the withdrawal of enemy survivors across the Seine, and second, we were to drive quickly across the Pas de Calais to capture ports to facilitate our maintenance requirements, and the flying bomb sites in order to diminish the effects that the 'V' weapons were having on the United Kingdom.

In my orders of 20 August I gave as my intention the completion of the destruction of enemy forces in north-west France, and the preparation for an advance northwards in order to destroy the enemy forces in north-east France.

First priority was to be given to clearing up the Mortain–Falaise pocket. It was essential to maintain the cordon until all the enemy forces had been destroyed or rounded up. As soon as this had been completed 21 Army Group was to form up facing east in order to drive with all possible speed to the Seine. This requirement was a complicated manœuvre, as it involved swinging back First Canadian Army to the north, leaving the axis Falaise–Bernay–Louviers available for Second Army. It was also my intention to give Second Army another axis, running from Argentan through Evreux to Vernon, which was to involve withdrawal across its front of the Americans who were sweeping down the left bank of the Seine.

While waiting for the redistribution of British and Canadian forces, and their drive to the river, the advance from the Mantes Gassicourt–Dreux–Verneuil area along the south bank of the Seine was to continue, with the object of establishing with maximum speed forces to block the escape routes to the river ferries. As soon as the British and Canadian troops got forward to their sectors on the Seine, the American forces on their front would withdraw within the Twelfth Army Group boundary. Twelfth Army Group was to assemble its right flank to the west and south-west of Paris; it was the Supreme Commander's intention that Paris should be captured when General Patton considered that a suitable moment had arrived, and not before; it was important not to attempt to secure the capital until it was a sound military proposition.

On 20 August it was the intention that the subsequent advance of Twelfth United States Army Group would be to the general area Orleans–Troyes–Chalons–Reims–Laon–Amiens: on its left, Second British Army was to advance to the Somme between Amiens and the sea, while Canadian Army would cross the Seine about Rouen and tackle the Havre peninsula. I wanted to secure the port of Le Havre as quickly as possible, and also Dieppe; it was appropriate that 51 Division was on the northern flank and available for the capture of St Valery, and I had no doubt that General Crerar would arrange for 2 Canadian Division to deal suitably with the enemy in Dieppe.

### THE FINAL PHASE: THE ADVANCE TO THE RIVER SEINE AND THE LIBERATION OF PARIS

The formations of Twelfth United States Army Group advanced to the Seine as maintenance conditions permitted. On 21 August, XII United States Corps liberated Pithiviers and crossed the River Loing on the following day. Montargis was occupied and forward troops reached Sens on the River Yonne. On the southern flank Auxerre was reached, while elements pushed forward to Troyes on the Seine.

On 22 August, XX United States Corps resumed its advance from the Chartres area towards Etampes and Rambouillet. The following day this Corps crossed the Seine in the area of Fontainebleau and Melun and was then directed to the Marne about Reims.

XV United State Corps wheeled to the north-west along the left bank of the Seine, while 79 Division extended its bridgehead at Mantes Gassicourt. By 24 August, Heudebouville was reached, only some five miles short of Louviers. At the same time, XIX Corps, on the left of XV Corps attacked north from the Dreux–Verneuil area on 20 August. The towns of Nonancourt and Verneuil were liberated on 22 August, and Evreux was reached on the following day. The advance continued rapidly across the front of Second British Army, and on 25 August Elbeuf was reached; in this area considerable fighting was experienced, since enemy forces were trying desperately to keep open routes from the Forêt de la Londe to the ferries at Rouen. Meanwhile troops of First Canadian Army reached the area and began to relieve the Americans. The enemy was in great confusion in the Forêt de la Londe. The American drive along the south bank of the Seine had deflected enemy survivors making for the river ferries further and further to the north, so that there became a great concentration of enemy vehicles and personnel in the sector between Rouen and the sea.

It was General Bradley's intention to take Paris by crossing the Seine astride the city and encircling it; it was hoped in this way to avoid fighting within the city itself. The rising of the Resistance Movement in the capital brought matters to a crisis, however, and the Supreme Commander ordered troops to enter the city before the encircling movements were completed. V United States Corps, having been relieved at Argentan by 30 Corps, was directed to Paris from the west; the advance was led by 2 French Armoured Division. Considerable resistance was met in the Versailles area and at the western exits from Paris itself, but on 25 August French troops entered the city and the German commander surrendered to General Leclerc. The French Armoured Division was followed by an American formation, for there was a considerable amount of clearing up required.

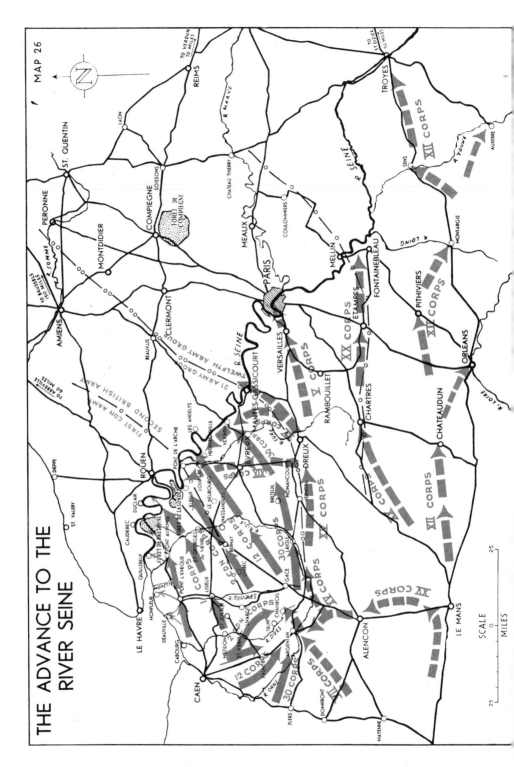

THE ADVANCE TO THE
RIVER SEINE

MAP 26

Second Army advanced to the Seine with 30 Corps on the right and 12 Corps on the left. The former was directed to the sector Mantes–Vernon, and the latter on Les Andelys–Louviers. On 20 August, 30 Corps began to pass through the American troops north-east of Argentan, and on the following day 11 Armoured Division by-passed resistance in Gace and reached Laigle twenty-four hours later. Meanwhile 50 Division came up on the left of 11 Armoured Division and on 23 August reached the area Verneuil–Breteuil. Here the advance was halted as XIX United States Corps was moving across the front in its drive towards Elbeuf.

12 Corps started from the Chambois area and met no opposition to its advance except from extensive demolitions and mines. By last light 23 August, armoured car patrols were in Bernay, and 15 Division, which was to force the Seine at Louviers, had concentrated south-west of Le Neubourg by 25 August. On the following day this division passed across the axes of XIX United States Corps and reached Louviers preparatory to crossing the river on the following day.

Since the time that it had been pinched out in the Flers sector, 8 Corps remained grounded while its transport was taken to assist in the advance to the Seine.

First Canadian Army moved east with 2 Canadian Corps on the right, directed on Rouen, and 1 Corps on the left directed on the lower reaches of the river.

The Polish Armoured and 3 Canadian Divisions were left to complete operations in the pocket, while the remainder of 2 Canadian Corps reached the River Touques on 22 August; there was considerable fighting round Orbec but by 24 August Bernay had been reached and a bridge over the River Risle seized at Nassandres. Contact was made with XIX United States Corps in the general area Elbeuf and Canadian troops took over the battle that was ranging round the Forêt de la Londe.

The advance of 1 Corps was delayed by considerable opposition round Lisieux, but 7 Armoured Division passed through the southern outskirts of the town on 22 August. On their left, 49 Division crossed the Touques south of Pont L'Evêque, at which place 6 Airborne Division was involved with German rearguards. On the coastal sector the Belgian Brigade (under command 6 Airborne Division) reached Deauville. 1 Corps advance continued slowly, since the enemy forces on their front had not been involved in the Falaise debacle, and were conducting a planned and orderly withdrawal, leaving considerable demolitions, obstacles and mines in their path. By 24 August, however, the pace of the advance quickened. On the right, St Georges du Vievre was captured and patrols were approaching Pont Audemer on the River Risle. After clearing Pont L'Evêque, 6 Airborne Division advanced ten miles to the River Morette together with the Royal Netherlands Brigade. On 27 August the Corps was nearing the river between the Forêt de la Londe and Quillebeuf, and the task of clearing the Forêt de Bretonne and the bends in the river was under-taken.

The Allied Air Forces throughout the drive to the river had carried out relentless attacks against the ferries which provided the only means of escape to the enemy. During the last days of August considerable bodies of enemy were still sandwiched

[279]

against the river in the bends and forests between Elbeuf and the sea. They made desperate attempts to hold perimeter lines, while the ferries endeavoured to continue operation in spite of day and night attacks from the air. The most successful air action was carried out at Rouen where an enormous conglomeration of enemy fighting vehicles and transport was jammed round the ferry quay. Subsequent survey of the area revealed destruction second only to that in the Falaise–Mortain pocket.

In spite of everything, the Germans in fact managed to get a very considerable proportion of their surviving manpower away to the north of the river. Some sixty main ferries were employed across the Seine, in addition to boats and rafts of all kinds. But because the Allied Air Forces had destroyed every bridge between Paris and the sea, and had successfully kept them out of operation, the amount of equipment that the enemy lost was staggering.

### OPERATIONS IN BRITTANY

Meanwhile VIII United States Corps continued its operations in the Brittany peninsula. In early August efforts were concentrated on reducing St Malo and Dinard, but some delay was experienced owing to the shortage of ammunition. On 11 August, infantry units entered the old part of the town of St Malo but the enemy held out in the citadel until 14 August and in the harbour forts for several subsequent days; by 18 August, with the exception of Cezembre Island the defences of St Malo and Dinard were finally reduced. By 20 August, Brest and Lorient had been completely surrounded; attacks to reduce the Brest fortress were launched on 26 August and the Plougastel peninsula was soon cleared, but the city continued to hold out. The enemy defenders of the ports had received very precise instructions from the High Command as a result of which they continued to resist with stubborn and bitter intensity our efforts to capture them. At the same time the demolition of port facilities was carried out in a most thorough manner, so that it was evident that when at last the harbours fell into our hands we were going to be confronted with major clearance problems before use could be made of them.

# CHAPTER TEN

## *Review of the Battle of Normandy*

WITH the gradual clearance of the Mortain–Falaise pocket and the lining up of the Allied armies on the Seine, the extent of the crushing defeat suffered by the Germans in Normandy became apparent.

The enemy losses in manpower were not far short of half a million men; 210,000 were prisoners in our hands and the figures for killed and wounded were estimated at about 240,000. Material losses were equally severe; some 3,500 guns and 1,500 tanks were captured or destroyed, together with a vast amount of mechanical transport, horse transport and equipment of all kinds.

A total of forty-three enemy divisions had either been eliminated or severely mauled, apart from the formations isolated in the Brittany ports and the Channel Islands. Of the Army, Corps and Divisional Commanders, twenty had been killed or captured and two others wounded; the Supreme German Commander had been changed twice.

The outstanding point about the Battle of Normandy is that it was fought exactly as planned before the invasion. This plan had been relentlessly followed in spite of the inevitable delays and minor setbacks which the changing course of the battle had imposed upon us, and had brought us finally to overwhelming victory. The measure of our success was, in the event, far greater than could ever have been foreseen, because of the faulty strategy of the enemy. Hitler's personal intervention in the direction of the battle provided us with opportunities we were not slow to exploit; he refused to face the only sound military course open to the Germans at the end of July, which would have involved staging a withdrawal to the Seine barrier and with it the sacrifice of north-western France. Instead he decided to fight it out between the Seine and the Loire, and thus committed the first vital error the Germans made in the campaign. As a result the Allies had caused the enemy staggering losses in men and material, and won a victory which ended the German domination of France; the repercussions throughout Europe (and indeed the world) were of first importance to the Allied cause, as the peoples of the occupied countries saw at long last real grounds for hope of speedy liberation, and the world became inspired with confidence in the power of Allied arms to overcome and defeat the Wehrmacht.

I have made it clear that in planning to break out from the bridgehead on the western flank, a prerequisite was the retention of the main enemy strength on the eastern flank. The extent to which this was achieved is well illustrated in the following table, which shows the estimated enemy strength opposing us in the eastern and western areas of our front during June and July:

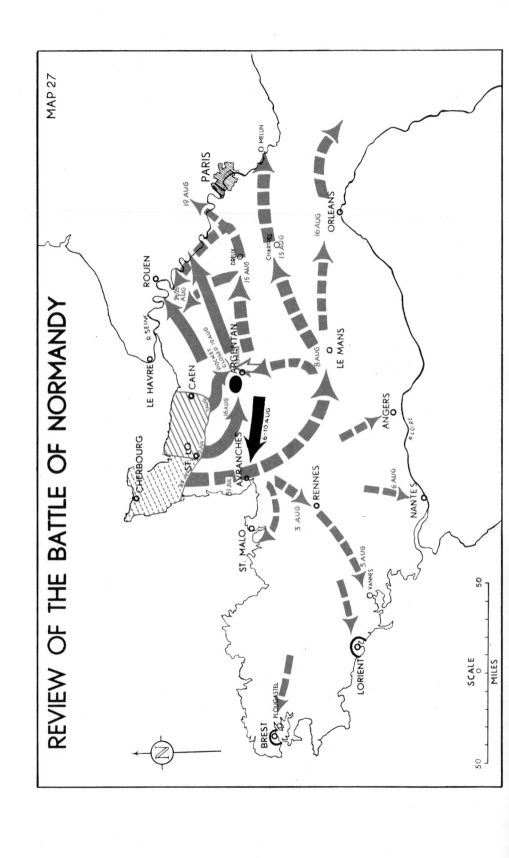

REVIEW OF THE BATTLE OF NORMANDY

MAP 27

| | Estimated enemy strength opposite Caumont–Cotentin sectors | | | Estimated enemy strength opposite Caumont–Caen sectors | | |
|---|---|---|---|---|---|---|
| | Panzer Divisions | Tanks | Infantry Battalions | Panzer Divisions | Tanks | Infantry Battalions |
| 15 June | — | 70 | 63 | 4 | 520 | 43 |
| 25 June | 1 | 190 | 87 | 5 | 530 | 49 |
| 30 June | ½ | 140 | 63 | 7½ | 725 | 64 |
| 5 July | ½ | 215 | 63 | 7½ | 690 | 64 |
| 10 July | 2 | 190 | 72 | 6 | 610 | 65 |
| 15 July | 2 | 190 | 78 | 6 | 630 | 68 |
| 20 July | 3 | 190 | 82 | 5 | 560 | 71 |
| 25 July | 2 | 190 | 85 | 6 | 645 | 92 |

This result was achieved by the retention of the initiative and by very hard fighting, which enabled us to expand our territorial gains in the west and to engage and wear down the enemy strength along the whole of the Allied front. We never had to conform to enemy thrusts, and were able to remain firm and balanced until we were at last ready to stage the break-out operation. During this period the enemy was forced to commit his reserves in piecemeal fashion in order to splice the cordon with which he tried to rope us off in the bocage country. The maintenance of the threat to the Pas de Calais immobilized meanwhile very considerable enemy forces, and reserves which were despatched to Normandy had to run the gauntlet of the splendid action of the Allied Air Forces, making use of circuitous and uncertain routes owing to this interdiction of roads and railways throughout western Europe, and particularly over the Rivers Seine and Loire.

The mounting of the break-out operation suffered considerable delays. One of the main reasons was the weather, which not only upset the schedule of our beach working, causing delay in the arrival of troops and stores, but also hampered the action of the air forces. A good example of the latter effect was the week's delay between 19–25 July until conditions were suitable for heavy bombers in the Periers–St Lô sector. The high quality of the enemy reserve divisions, coupled with the ideally defensive nature of the bocage country, was another delaying factor, and it must be remembered that the original assault and follow-up divisions were getting very tired by the beginning of July: though there was no opportunity of relieving them.

We also found the development of the bridgehead to the south-east of Caen a slow and difficult matter. I have shown, in discussing the plan, that the Air Forces were anxious to expand our territory rapidly into the good airfield country, and that I had undertaken to do this as soon as conditions permitted. In the event it became impossible to meet this requirement without altering the whole strategy of the battle: and this I was not prepared to do. The Allied Air Forces had achieved a remarkable degree of air superiority over the bridgehead, and the provision of air support was of the highest order; on the other hand the success of the plan involved pulling the enemy's reserves against our eastern flank, and this was achieved to such a degree that in spite of all our efforts it was impossible to make rapid headway in the sector which the enemy obviously regarded as the most vital.

There was a period, after we had secured our bridgehead, when criticism began to appear in the Press on both sides of the Atlantic, as a result of what was termed 'the danger of a stalemate in Normandy'; there were those who found our progress slow and who foresaw the failure of our operations to force a break-out from the bridgehead. There was indeed a stage when the progress of operations was not as fast as had been hoped, but it has been seen that I had given D + 90 as the target date for being lined up on the Seine, and that in fact the first crossing of the river was made on D + 75. That there were critics who became despondent and lacking in confidence at a time when well laid plans for victory were maturing satisfactorily is understandable, because they could not be given, for obvious reasons, the basic design within which those plans were being executed.

When at last the break-out operation was delivered, it carried all before it. Initially my intention was to push the enemy back against the Seine, closing meanwhile, with all possible speed, the escape routes through the Paris–Orleans gap. I had not reckoned on Hitler's fling at generalship, and when it was realized that the Germans were concentrating against Avranches, I ordered an inner envelopment through Falaise and Argentan. At this stage the important thing was to conduct enveloping movements concurrently, so that the enemy who escaped from the one, would be rounded up in the other.

It took time to close the Falaise–Argentan corridor, and some enemy escaped us there; but the degree of resistance was desperate in the extreme for the Germans realized full well that holding open the neck of the pocket was vital to their withdrawal. The Allied problem was made more difficult by the relative paucity of routes, because movement was made across the main road axes, and also by the great congestion, which was aggravated, as the enemy retreated, by the mass of German transport and equipment which littered the countryside.

The major difficulty in the wider envelopment to the Seine was administration. The American forces were being maintained from Cherbourg and the beaches, and transport echelons had to pass through the congested Avranches bottleneck, close behind formations which were resisting the German counter stroke. The actual rate of progress was therefore an outstanding achievement, which was greatly facilitated by delivery of stores by air.

Once the Mortain–Falaise pocket was sealed, it became essential to get the British and Canadian armies up to the Seine as rapidly as possible, but this was a much more difficult matter than is at first sight apparent. It was necessary to readjust the axes of formations which had been converging on the Falaise area, to the routes running east and north-east to the Seine: a process which involved inevitable congestion and delays on roads damaged, mined and littered with derelict enemy vehicles. Moreover,

:he advance eastwards was opposed by organized enemy formations which had not experienced the fighting in the pocket, and which were therefore able initially to stage an organized withdrawal.

It has not been possible in this account of the Battle of Normandy to make more than passing reference to the tremendous achievements of the Allied Air Forces. They maintained complete air supremacy over the battle area, so that finally the enemy became virtually immobilized during the hours of daylight. The interdiction programme, particularly on the line of the Seine and Loire, isolated the Normandy battlefield, and greatly hampered the enemy's reinforcement and supply arrangements. The results of the strategic bombing offensive were apparent in the battle, for the enemy's lack of oil reduced the mobility of his formations and thus added further difficulties to the problems confronting the High Command. It has been seen that in addition to the part played by the Tactical Air Forces in direct support of land operations, heavy bombers were employed on the immediate battlefield with devastating results.

The outstanding administrative problems in Normandy arose from the unfavourable weather conditions, which resulted in the tonnage of stores landed over the beaches being 25 per cent less than had been planned throughout the early stages; from the difficulty of expanding the major maintenance installations rapidly from the beaches into the confined area of the bridgehead; from the great traffic congestion within the bridgehead; and from the sudden change from intensive short-range operations to the fast moving battles up to the Seine and beyond.

Initially the armies were supplied from hastily stacked dumps on the beaches; within fifty days the vast and complicated organization of the Rear Maintenance Area had been brought into being. The degree of the expansion is reflected in the fact that in the British sector alone on D-day 8,900 vehicles and 1,900 tons of stores were landed, while by D + 50 631,000 personnel, 153,000 vehicles and 689,000 tons of stores had been handled in the bridgehead as well as 68,000 tons of bulk petrol, oil and lubricants.

Difficulties occurred in beach working owing to shortage of ferry craft, and to the fact that anchorages, except for shallow draft shipping, were some distance offshore. Shortage of ferry facilities arose from the rough sea conditions in which the specially constructed 'Rhino' ferries proved of little value, and from the losses due to bad weather. It therefore became necessary to beach for discharge landing craft, and even tank landing ships, in order to speed up unloading.

Amphibious lorries (Dukws) proved of outstanding value in discharging cargoes.

The storm of 19–22 June caused very grave dislocation of our beach working arrangements. Some eight hundred craft of all types were damaged or driven ashore, and the Mulberries were also seriously damaged. Except to a very limited extent inside the Gooseberries, unloading came to a standstill, and it has been estimated that the overall unloading loss caused by the gale was in the neighbourhood of 20,000 vehicles and 140,000 tons of stores. The Mulberry in the Omaha area was so badly

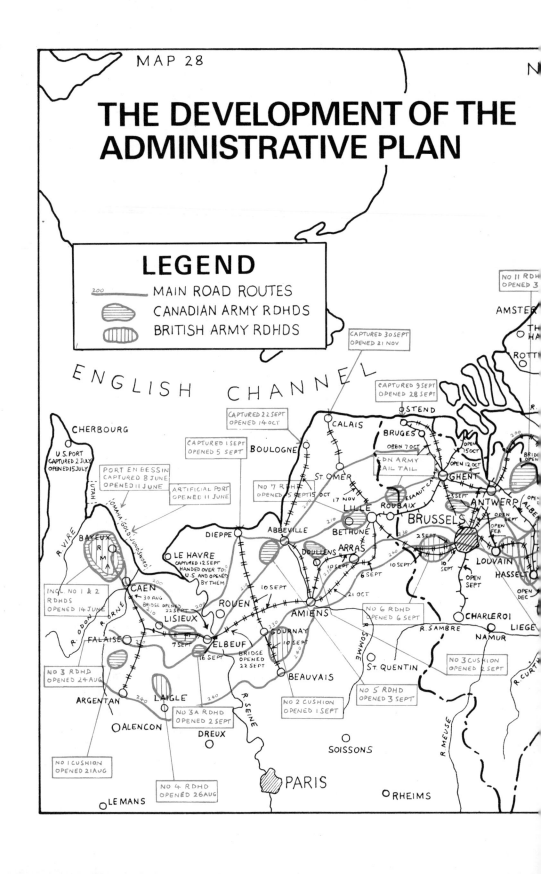

MAP 28

# THE DEVELOPMENT OF THE ADMINISTRATIVE PLAN

## LEGEND

─────── MAIN ROAD ROUTES

CANADIAN ARMY RDHDS

BRITISH ARMY RDHDS

ENGLISH CHANNEL

CHERBOURG

U.S. PORT
CAPTURED 2 JULY
OPENED 15 JULY

PORT EN BESSIN
CAPTURED 8 JUNE
OPENED 11 JUNE

ARTIFICIAL PORT
OPENED 11 JUNE

BAYEUX

INCL. NO 1 & 2
RDHDS
OPENED 14 JUNE

CAEN
30 AUG
BRIDGE OPENED
22 SEPT

LISIEUX

FALAISE

NO 3 RDHD
OPENED 24 AUG

ARGENTAN

LAIGLE

NO 3A RDHD
OPENED 2 SEPT

ALENCON

DREUX

NO 1 CUSHION
OPENED 21 AUG

NO 4 RDHD
OPENED 26 AUG

LE MANS

CAPTURED 1 SEPT
OPENED 5 SEPT

BOULOGNE

CAPTURED 22 SEPT
OPENED 14 OCT

CALAIS

St OMER

NO 7 RDHD
OPENED 5 SEPT

ABBEVILLE

LILLE

DIEPPE

LE HAVRE
CAPTURED 12 SEPT
HANDED OVER TO
U.S. AND OPENED
BY THEM

ROUEN

ELBEUF
16 SEPT

BRIDGE
OPENED
22 SEPT

GOURNAY
10 SEPT

BEAUVAIS

NO 2 CUSHION
OPENED 1 SEPT

PARIS

SOISSONS

RHEIMS

CAPTURED 30 SEPT
OPENED 21 NOV

CAPTURED 9 SEPT
OPENED 28 SEPT

OSTEND

BRUGES
OPEN 7 OCT

CDN ARMY
TAIL TAIL

GHENT

ANTWERP

BRUSSELS

ROUBAIX

BETHUNE

DOULLENS

ARRAS

AMIENS

NO 6 RDHD
OPENED 6 SEPT

NO 5 RDHD
OPENED 3 SEPT

St QUENTIN

NO 3 CUSHION
OPENED 2 SEPT

LOUVAIN

HASSELT

CHARLEROI

NAMUR

LIEGE

R. SAMBRE

R. MEUSE

AMSTER

THE
HA

ROTT

NO 11 RDH
OPENED 3

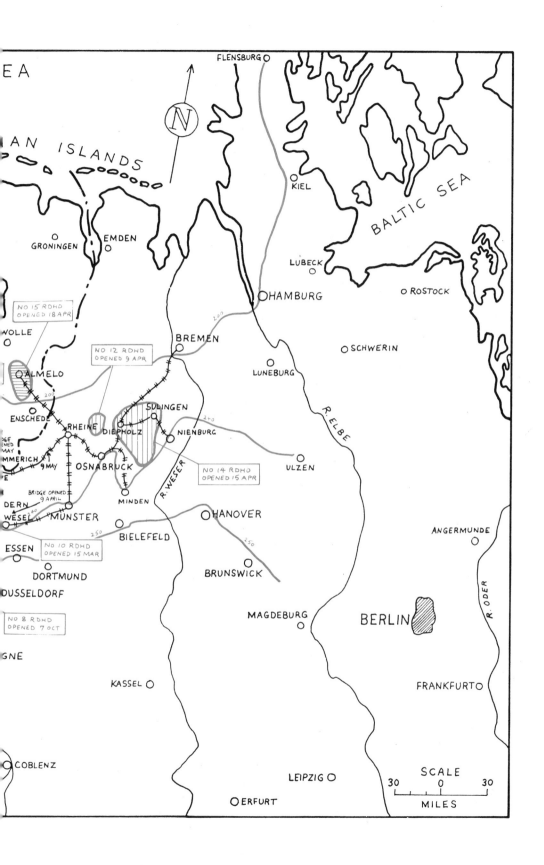

damaged that further construction was abandoned, and resources were diverted to the Arromanches Mulberry: which was speedily completed.

The congestion of transport in the bridgehead was immense. At one check post 18,836 vehicles passed in one day, giving an hourly average of 785 vehicles, or one every four seconds throughout the twenty-four hours. Road repair, traffic control, and the construction of diversions became a major commitment.

Mention has been made of the shortage of ammunition which occurred owing to unloading delays. This problem was solved by ordering selective discharge of ships; in particular, ships carrying field ammunition were given top priority for unloading. At the same time, petrol and oil shipments were reduced in order to provide more space for ammunition; it is invariably found that the expenditure of petrol, oil and lubricants rises and falls in inverse ratio to ammunition requirements; we had built up large reserves of the former and could now concentrate on the latter.

The British assault troops landed with two twenty-four hour ration packs, while the Americans carried K rations. Thereafter fourteen-man 'Compo packs' were used, until, towards the end of July, the normal Field Service Ration was introduced. This was wholly a preserved ration except for bread, which became available in limited quantities from the beginning of July.

Ordnance stores were landed in special packs, initially designed to contain sufficient reserves for a brigade group or its equivalent for thirty days. Subsequently, larger packs scaled for thirty days' requirements of a division were used; they weighed 500 tons each.

The Medical Service evacuated casualties and seriously sick cases to England during the initial stages. Air evacuation began as early as 13 June and worked with pronounced efficiency throughout.

The local administration of the dumps in the bridgehead was taken over on D + 5 from Second Army by the Headquarters of a Lines of Communication Area, and in mid-July Headquarters Lines of Communication itself assumed responsibility for co-ordination and administration of the rear areas. Shortly after Headquarters 21 Army Group assumed full administrative control. In the event, it might have been preferable to have brought in Rear Headquarters of the Army Group earlier, in order to avoid the difficulties of so many changes of responsibility.

As operations in the beachhead continued into July, the problem of lack of port facilities became more pressing. Experience at Cherbourg showed that clearing captured ports was going to constitute a lengthy and major undertaking; the breaks in beach working under autumn conditions were likely to become more frequent, and the urgency of securing the Brittany ports in time to get them working before weather conditions further deteriorated was apparent. Although circumstances subsequently caused an alteration in our dependence on the Brittany ports, in early July they were of first importance in our administrative planning. Meanwhile the stocks in the Rear Maintenance Area were being increased at full pressure in order to provide a cushion for emergencies in the future.

At the end of July, the rapid change over to mobile conditions resulted in speedy administrative arrangements to meet the changing requirements of the Armies.

Additional transport units, which had been held back in the United Kingdom, were now called forward, and the import of stores and reserves was reduced in order to free more transport for clearing loads from the administrative centres to the forward troops. As the advance gained momentum the transport in rear areas was progressively cut, and some lines of communication units were grounded in order to increase resources for sustaining operations.

By the time the Armies began to close to the River Seine, it was evident that the administrative machine was to be faced with a prolonged and rapid pursuit, and it will be seen that major maintenance risks had to be taken in order to maintain the momentum of the advance.

# CHAPTER ELEVEN

## *The Development of Allied Strategy North of the Seine*

THE Supreme Commander decided that he would take over direct control of the land battle from 1 September. Twelfth United States Army Group would then no longer be subject to my operational control.

As the Allied Armies drove to the Seine the problem of the future conduct of operations against Germany was being resolved. During the period 23 August–12 September I discussed at length with General Eisenhower the future plan of campaign.

At the end of August the current appreciation of the enemy's capabilities suggested that German resistance in western Europe was on the verge of collapse. It was thought that north-west of the Ardennes the enemy disposed two weak Panzer and nine infantry divisions, which were in full retreat and therefore unlikely to offer strong resistance provided they were given no respite. South of the Ardennes enemy forces were estimated at two Panzer Grenadier and four weak infantry divisions. Heterogeneous German forces were withdrawing from south-west France but had only minor fighting value, while, in the Rhône valley, Allied forces were driving northwards the equivalent of half a Panzer division and two infantry divisions. In such circumstances it was obvious that the enemy would have to produce fresh divisions from other fronts, and from Germany, if he were to succeed in preventing our advance into the Reich; the dependence of his war potential on the industrial areas of the Ruhr and Saar suggested that he would concentrate his available resources in defending them. His preoccupation with 'V' weapon sites in Flanders added to the possibility that he would allocate the preponderance of his available resources to the north. It was reckoned (on 22 August) that he would allot about sixteen divisions to the northern sectors of the front, leaving the remainder to delay the American advances towards Metz.

How best could we exploit this situation to finish the German war as quickly as possible?

My own view, which I presented to the Supreme Commander, was that one powerful full-blooded thrust across the Rhine and into the heart of Germany, backed by the whole of the resources of the Allied Armies, would be likely to achieve decisive results. Success in such a plan would have been, to my mind, dependent upon our ability to concentrate sufficient strength, supported by adequate administrative resources, to ensure the maintenance of the momentum from the time we crossed the Seine. The project therefore involved calling upon combined Allied resources in the widest sense, and would have entailed reverting sectors of the Allied front to a purely static role.

There appeared to be two feasible axes along which such a thrust into Germany

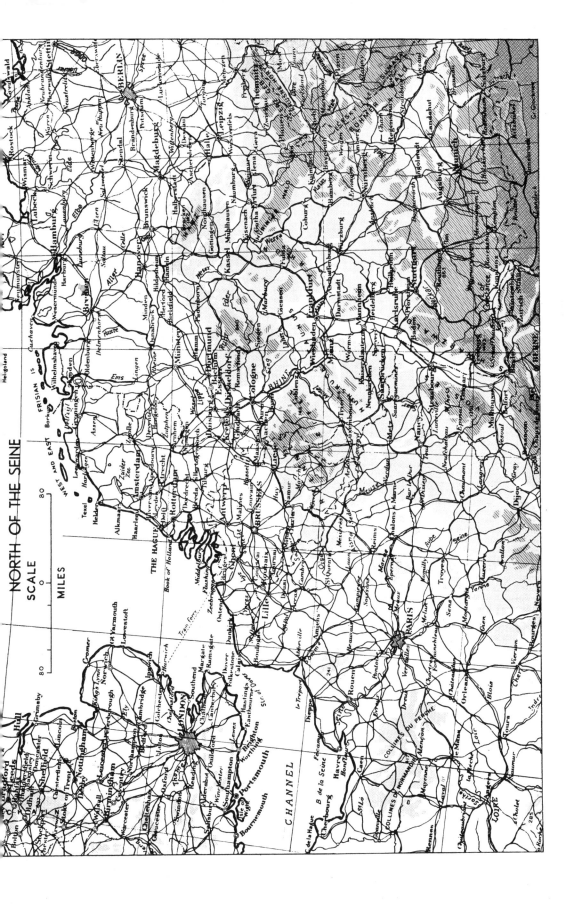

NORTH OF THE SEINE

SCALE

MILES

80    0    80    160

could be mounted. The first was the northern axis through Belgium to the Rhine, crossing the river north of the Ruhr industrial region; once over the Rhine, this route led into the open plains of northern Germany. The alternative axis was through Metz and the Saar area, leading into central Germany.

I favoured the northern route since it would enable us to exploit our greatly superior mobility and strength of armoured forces in the plains of northern Germany, with greater effect than would be possible in the more difficult southern country. The development of this plan would logically fall into certain stages, and it is very important, in order to understand the subsequent development of the campaign from the 21 Army Group point of view, to be quite clear what these stages were.

In my view, once we had crossed the Seine the major problem confronting the Allies was getting over the Rhine. This great waterway formed an obstacle of tremendous military value, and I considered that the necessity for establishing bridgeheads on its eastern bank was a factor of overriding importance in our plans for finishing the war. If we could maintain the strength and impetus of our operations beyond the Seine sufficiently to keep the enemy on the run straight through to the Rhine, and 'bounce' our way across that river before the enemy succeeded in reforming a front to oppose us, then we should achieve a prodigious advantage. If, on the other hand, we were to give the enemy sufficient respite to enable him to organize a cohesive front to oppose our advance and to check our progress, we might well become involved in a heavy 'dog-fight' west of the Rhine obstacle, the effects of which, combined with the advent of winter weather, might well hold us up until the spring of 1945. Moreover, should the enemy once establish a proper defensive system based on the Meuse and the Rhine, we should be involved in an opposed river crossing operation of the first magnitude: which would inevitably take time and prove costly in lives and material.

Assuming we should succeed, by the concentration of our resources, in gaining rapidly and cheaply a bridgehead east of the Rhine, we should then have a springboard from which to develop operations into the heart of Germany; if this projected thrust were delivered over the river north of the Ruhr, logically our immediate objective would become the Ruhr industrial region itself, because it was estimated that without it, the German capacity for waging war would peter out within six months. Having isolated the Ruhr, we should be free to develop operations in the open plains of northern Germany. Since the Ruhr was the enemy's premier industrial region, it was obvious that he would concentrate his available military resources in the north to defend it; in tackling this objective, therefore, we should bring the German Army in the north to battle and could finish it off in country suitable for the development of our superior mobility. Providing, therefore, the essential prerequisites of speed *and concentration of maintenance resources* could be effected, I favoured a drive into Belgium with the clearance of the Channel coast as far as Antwerp, the establishment of our air forces in Belgium, and a speedy and all-out drive along the northern axis into Germany.

The alternative course open to the Allies on crossing the Seine was to drive to the Rhine on a broad front. I shall refer to this as the 'broad front' policy: to distinguish it from the single concentrated thrust project I have discussed above.

The broad front policy implied lining up the Allied Armies along the length of the River Rhine, and then developing operations for the capture of both the Ruhr and the Frankfurt areas. Subsequently, operations into Germany could be staged either on the northern axis, or through the Saar and Frankfurt, or along both routes: according to the situation at the time. The main point of difference in the two plans was that the broad front policy avoided the risks of developing long range operations on a relatively narrow front; it was the opposite of 'sticking our neck out' in a single deep thrust into enemy territory. On the other hand it clearly involved a slower and more deliberate campaign, because the Allied Armies would have to develop offensive operations on a very wide frontage; our available administrative resources would be spread accordingly, and in my opinion would not stand up to the strain.

Apart from the administrative difficulties, my objection to the broad front policy was that nowhere should we be strong enough to get decisive results quickly; the Germans would thus have time to recover and we should become involved in a long winter campaign.

The crux of the problem appeared to be whether the Allies could concentrate sufficient strength in the broadest sense to ensure the success of a single deep thrust; if such concentration could not be effected, then the broad front plan was the available alternative.

The Supreme Commander eventually decided on the broad front policy. He came to the conclusion that it would not be feasible immediately to concentrate adequate administrative resources to carry us in sufficient strength across the Rhine and deep into Germany. The lines of communication still stretched rearwards to the Normandy beaches and Cherbourg peninsula, and the autumn weather was close upon us; he decided that the early opening of deep water ports and improvement of our maintenance facilities were essential prerequisites to the undertaking of the final all-out assault on Germany.

General Eisenhower's orders were that the Allied Armies should line up along the River Rhine, establishing bridgeheads wherever feasible, and that operations would not be developed further east until the port of Antwerp was opened and functioning. Meanwhile a firm link-up was to be made with Sixth United States Army Group advancing from the Mediterranean, in order to complete our front from Switzerland to the North Sea. Within the compass of this plan, the mission allotted to 21 Army Group, together with that portion of Twelfth United States Army Group operating north of the Ardennes, was to secure the port of Antwerp, to reach the sector of the Siegfried Line covering the Ruhr, and then seize the Ruhr. The boundary between 21 and Twelfth Army Corps was on the general line Amiens–Brussels–Krefeld, all inclusive to us. Concurrently Twelfth United States Army Group was ordered to occupy the Siegfried Line covering the Saar and to seize

Frankfurt. First Allied Airborne Army was allocated in support of 21 Army Group operations up to and including crossing the Rhine.

In considering the tasks allotted to me, my chief preoccupation was the degree to which I could maintain the momentum of our pursuit with the forces and administrative resources at my disposal: in order to take advantage of the disorganized state of the enemy. 21 Army Group at this time disposed fourteen divisions and seven armoured brigades; but with my own maintenance resources *alone* it was very doubtful whether all of these formations could be maintained from Normandy to Belgium and beyond.

It was very soon made clear that 21 Army Group was not strong enough to carry out unaided the task of capturing the Ruhr; but the time was ripe for securing other important results cheaply. Experience in large scale retreats has always shown the tremendous difficulty of organizing troops who have carried out a long and painful march after being overwhelmed in battle; if we could give the Germans no respite, it was possible that, with their lack of immediate reserves behind, they would not be able to recover sufficiently to oppose serious resistance to our progress.

Was it going to be possible with my own resources alone to keep the enemy on the run right back to the Rhine? This was the overriding problem that faced me.

I have mentioned the great importance I placed on establishing quickly bridgeheads over the Meuse and Rhine; I was deeply impressed with the magnitude of the military problem of fighting an opposed crossing over these great water barriers, and wanted to avoid it at all costs. Although the broad front policy restricted our present aims to reaching the Rhine, I continued to plan the concentration of such resources as I had into a drive that would hustle the enemy straight through to that river: in order to jump it quickly before the Germans could seriously oppose us. The degree of difficulty which this project involved was directly dependent on the vital factor of speed; for this reason I considered it worth while to employ all our resources for its accomplishment, at the expense of any other undertaking.

The Supreme Commander agreed with this conception of the development of my operations, and I therefore gave first priority to the seizure of a bridgehead over the Rhine. North of the Seine, the operations of 21 Army Group were managed with this object in view, and the chief problem became the accumulation of adequate strength to ensure success.

# CHAPTER TWELVE

## The Drive Across the Pas de Calais to Belgium, the Clearance of the Channel Ports and the Battle of Arnhem

### THE PLAN OF ADVANCE INTO BELGIUM

On 26 August, I issued detailed orders for the conduct of the advance north of the Seine.

Twelfth Army Group was to operate on our right flank, and directed First United States Army along the general axis Paris–Brussels, with the object of getting established in the general area Brussels–Maastricht–Liège–Namur–Charleroi.

I agreed with General Bradley on a forward boundary on the line Mantes–Beauvais–Tournai–Alost–Antwerp (all inclusive to Second Army).

The immediate tasks confronting 21 Army Group were the destruction of the enemy in north-east France, the clearance of the Pas de Calais with its 'V' bomb sites, the capture of airfields in Belgium, and the opening of the port of Antwerp. I made it clear that our ultimate aim was the isolation of the Ruhr.

I ordered Second Army to cross the Seine with all possible speed and to advance to the area Arras–Amiens–St Pol, irrespective of the progress of the armies on its flanks. From that area, the Army was to be prepared to drive forward through the industrial area of north-east France and into Belgium. Alternatively, General Dempsey was to be ready to operate forces to the north-west in support of an airborne operation which might be developed in the Pas de Calais area. I instructed Second Army to move its armoured strength deployed well ahead; the spearheads were to by-pass resistance and push on with all possible speed in order to cut the east-west communications of enemy forces in the coastal belt; Amiens was to be secured as quickly as possible.

The task of First Canadian Army was to operate along the coastal belt initially as far north as Bruges. As first priority, Dieppe was to be seized and a corps swung into the Havre peninsula to destroy the enemy forces in that area and secure the port. I specified that First Canadian Army was to operate with its main weight on the right flank, dealing with enemy centres of resistance by 'right hooks'.

### CROSSING THE RIVER SEINE

Second Army's intention was to cross the River Seine in the vicinity of Vernon with 30 Corps, and between Les Andelys and Louviers with 12 Corps. The concentration of these corps within striking distance of the river took time, because they had

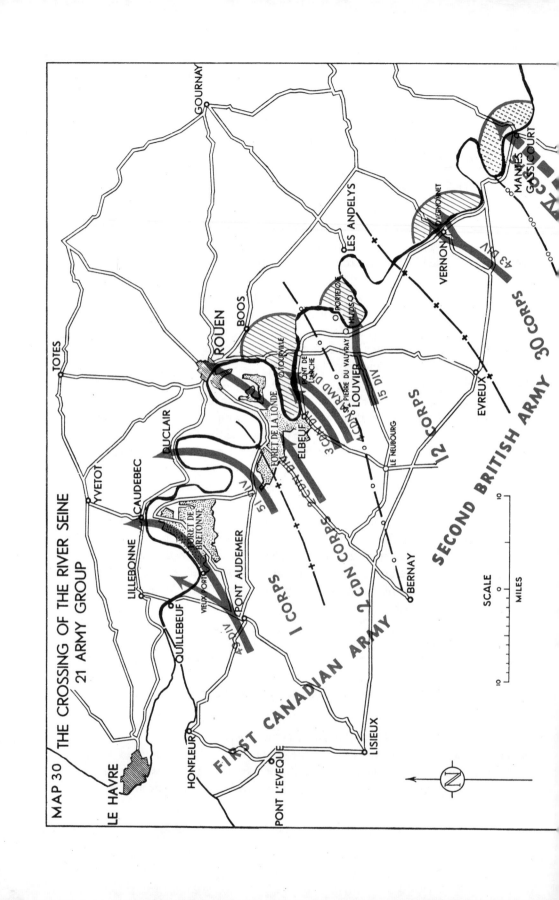

MAP 30    THE CROSSING OF THE RIVER SEINE
21 ARMY GROUP

to pass across the axes of the two American corps which had driven north-west from the Dreux area to Elbeuf.

At 1900 hours on 25 August the leading brigade of 43 Division (30 Corps) started to cross the river in stormboats under cover of artillery concentrations. The enemy had no prepared defensive positions on the north bank and opposition to the crossing was generally light. The German troops in the area belonged to 49 Division, which was fresh but had been weakened by draft-finding; the enemy was posted in the village of Veronnet and in the hills on the south bank, and from these positions made some attempt to interfere with ferrying and bridging operations. By the afternoon of 26 August this opposition had been cleared, and a second brigade was across the Seine before nightfall. The whole division, together with 8 Armoured Brigade, was on the north bank by 28 August and, in the evening, captured the high ground over-looking the crossing area and established a bridgehead some four miles wide and three miles deep. Behind 43 Division 11 Armoured Division began to cross, while Guards Armoured Division was already moving forward from Condé on transporters.

In 12 Corps sector, 15 Division assaulted on 27 August in the bend of the Seine some three miles due east of Louviers. The northern crossing, near St Pierre du Vauvray, was virtually unopposed; but the second crossing, about a mile upstream, sustained severe losses and operations in the area were eventually discontinued. The leading brigade completed its crossing at the St Pierre ferry and gradually extended the bridgehead up to the line Muids–Portejoie; the bridge sites were shelled, but by 29 August 15 Division was across the river complete, and the whole loop west of Les Andelys was in our hands. 4 Armoured Brigade and 53 Division began to move into the bridgehead on 30 August, followed by 7 Armoured Division.

On First Canadian Army front, 2 Canadian Corps planned to secure crossings about Pont de l'Arche and Elbeuf, astride a sharp bend in the river about eight miles south of Rouen. On the right, 4 Canadian Armoured Division got patrols across during the evening of 26 August, and the following morning infantry of the division crossed the river on rafts and stormboats and began to expand the bridgehead east-wards. At first light on 27 August, 3 Canadian Division began crossing, and during the day the bend of the river was gradually cleared of the enemy and Tourville was captured. The two divisions now advanced on Boos and Rouen, in order to cut off the escape routes of the enemy who were still south of the Seine engaged in opposing 2 Canadian Infantry Division in the Forêt de la Londe. Boos was secured on 29 August, and leading troops of 3 Canadian Division entered Rouen the following day without opposition. 2 Canadian Division had three days' hard fighting in order to clear the Forêt de la Londe; enemy rearguards and remnants put up a stiff fight in the thick woods, and considerable casualties were sustained by both sides. By 30 August, however, 2 Canadian Division was able to cross into the Seine bridge-head.

The two infantry divisions of 1 Corps were the last to force the Seine; they were opposed by relatively strong opposition in the area of the Forêt de Bretonne and the

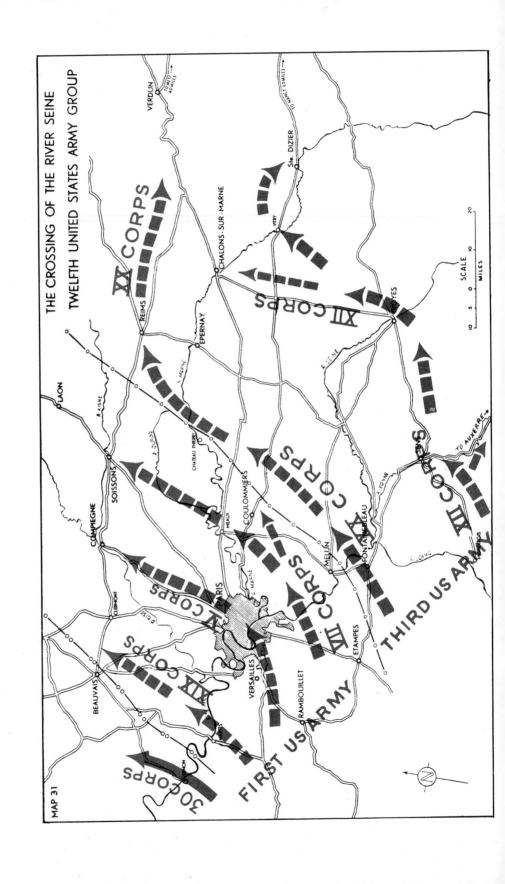

MAP 31

THE CROSSING OF THE RIVER SEINE

TWELFTH UNITED STATES ARMY GROUP

mouth of the river. On 29 August, 51 Division reached the loop near Duclair and pushed patrols across the river on the following day, while 49 Division with Royal Netherlands Brigade also got elements over the river on that day between Caudebec and Vieux Port, using assault boats, ferries and any other craft they found on the river bank. By 1 September both divisions were on the northern bank and began pushing forward.

In the Twelfth United States Army Group sector, Third United States Army swept forward to Troyes, Chalons-sur-Marne and Reims; Troyes was reached on 27 August by XII Corps which subsequently liberated Chalons on 30 August and crossed the Marne. XII Corps then swung south-east towards St Dizier. Meanwhile on 28 August, XX Corps approached the Marne near Château Thierry and two days later entered Reims, after which it was directed due east towards Verdun. XV Corps, which had taken part in the drive along the south bank of the Seine, reverted to Third United States Army on 29 August and was withdrawn to the east of Paris.

First United States Army crossed the Seine between Melun and Mantes Gassicourt and advanced to seize the line Laon–Peronne, whence the advance was to be pushed rapidly to the north-east. On 26 August, VII Corps began to cross the Seine immediately south of Paris and two days later was approaching Coulommiers. Bridgeheads were quickly established over the Marne and by 31 August the Corps crossed the Aisne and had liberated Soissons and Laon. V Corps meanwhile was occupied in restoring order in Paris; on 30 August it advanced north from the city and by the following day had elements just south of Compiègne. XIX Corps took over the Mantes Gassicourt bridgehead and speedily expanded it. On 30 August it moved forward directed on Clermont and Beauvais.

## THE ADVANCE OF SECOND ARMY TO ANTWERP
### AND BRUSSELS

On 29 August, 11 Armoured Division, with 8 Armoured Brigade under command, led the advance from 30 Corps bridgehead. There were two main axes, on each of which an armoured brigade advanced preceded by an armoured car regiment. On the first day the pace of the advance was restricted by bad weather, extensive demolitions, and small pockets of infantry backed by anti-tank and self-propelled guns. By nightfall the division had reached the Mainneville area, some twenty miles from the Seine. About midday on 30 August, Guards Armoured Division took over the right-hand axis from 8 Armoured Brigade, and in the afternoon the Corps Commander ordered 11 Armoured Division to drive on to Amiens through the night in order to seize bridges over the Somme in and to the west of the town. Amiens was reached early on 31 August, and a bridge over the Somme was secured intact with the assistance of the local Resistance Movement.

Just outside Amiens, General Eberbach, who succeeded Hausser as Commander

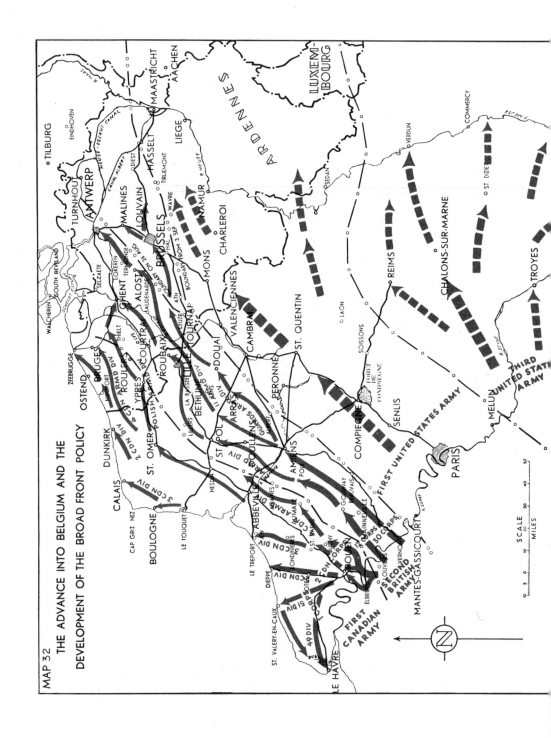

MAP 32

THE ADVANCE INTO BELGIUM AND THE
DEVELOPMENT OF THE BROAD FRONT POLICY

of the Seventh Army, was surprised and captured with his Tactical Headquarters. He had just signed an operation order which revealed the plan of the High Command to withdraw to and fortify the line of the Somme: as the right-hand sector of a new defence line that was to extend to Switzerland.

East of Amiens, Guards Armoured Division crossed the river, and by evening had elements astride the Albert–Amiens road. A brigade group of 50 Division, which was closely following the armoured spearheads, also reached Amiens.

When the advance north from the Seine started, I had plans ready for an airborne drop in the Tournai area, to the east of the bend in the River Escaut; my idea was for the airborne forces to operate offensively from the Tournai area in order to destroy enemy elements attempting to escape eastwards from the coastal belt. In conformity with this plan, forward boundaries between the Armies were adjusted generally with the object of swinging the axes more to the east. From Tournai, Second Army's right boundary was altered to run through Ath, on to Brussels, Louvain and Diest; First Canadian Army's right boundary beyond Ypres included Roulers, Thielt and Selzaete, whence it followed the Dutch frontier to the Scheldt.

On 30 August the advance began from 12 Corps bridgehead with 4 Armoured Brigade leading, closely followed by 53 Division. The armour moved twenty-five miles during the day and reached Gournay, with 53 Division about ten miles to the left rear. On the following day 7 Armoured Division passed through the leading troops, picking up 4 Armoured Brigade on its way, and by nightfall was on the line Poix–Aumale, some fifteen to twenty miles short of the Somme. There was some opposition on the 12 Corps axes and mines, craters and blown bridges were met with frequently. On 1 September, 7 Armoured Division drove on, by-passing enemy opposition at Airaines, and by mid-morning a bridge was secured at Hangest, about midway between Amiens and Abbeville.

Rapid advances were made by troops of 30 Corps during 1 September. Guards Armoured Division outflanked Arras, 11 Armoured Division got astride the Arras–St Pol road, and 8 Armoured Brigade reached Doullens. Patrols reported Lens clear of the enemy. The following day the Guards captured Douai and Tournai and 11 Armoured Division reached the outskirts of Lille, which was by-passed. On the left, 7 Armoured Division reached St Pol and elements crossed the Béthune–Lillers road.

The speed of advance was such that the necessity for an airborne drop in the Tournai area no longer existed, and the plan was cancelled; the revised boundaries, however, remained unaltered.

Orders were now issued for the next stage of the advance. Guards Armoured Division was directed on Brussels, 11 Armoured Division on Antwerp and 7 Armoured Division on Ghent.

The drive north continued with speed. In the early hours of 3 September armoured cars of Guards Division crossed the Belgian frontier; during the afternoon Hal, some twelve miles short of Brussels, was reached in spite of sporadic resistance.

Before nightfall the whole Guards Armoured Division was in the capital and reconnaissance elements were fanning out round the city to control the main approaches. On the left, 11 Armoured Division was temporarily delayed by enemy holding out between Tournai and Lille; the resistance was brushed aside and the division pressed on and concentrated for the night a few miles east of Alost; in rear, 50 Division closed up quickly in order to enter the town in the morning.

On 12 Corps front there was considerably more resistance. In order to provide some protection for the Channel ports, the enemy had moved two fresh divisions, 59 and 712, into the La Bassée–Béthune area; further west in the area north of St Pol, 64 Infantry Division was encountered, having lately arrived from Germany. While 53 Division and 4 Armoured Brigade were engaged against these enemy formations, 7 Armoured Division swung east before Lille in order to by-pass resistance and get on to its objective at Ghent.

11 Armoured Division entered Antwerp on 4 September and quickly disposed of the enemy elements in the residential quarters of the city. In the dock areas to the north, however, hostile elements hung on for some days, and caused considerable trouble before they were eventually cleaned out. The docks were secured virtually intact—a major dividend of the great victory in Normandy, and of the subsequent rapid advance. During the following two days, 30 Corps reorganized in the general area Antwerp–Malines–Louvain–Brussels–Alost–Termonde, and made hasty preparations for the resumption of the advance towards the Albert and Meuse–Escaut canals. At the same time 12 Corps was clearing up the area St Pol–Béthune–Lille, while 7 Armoured Division drove on the axis Roubaix–Audenarde to Ghent, which was captured on the evening of 5 September. With Ghent and the area south of it securely in our hands, 12 Corps relieved 30 Corps in Alost and Antwerp on 7 September and assumed responsibility for the northern flank of Second Army, thus freeing 30 Corps for a swing to the north-east.

Second Army had advanced 250 miles in six days. Spearheads had been provided from three armoured divisions behind which infantry formations, supported by armoured brigades, took over the ground won and conducted the very considerable mopping-up operations which the method of advance involved.

On the right flank of Second Army security was afforded by an equally forceful advance by First United States Army, which had reached the general line Namur–Tirlemont. During the advance this Army had collected no less than 25,000 prisoners in a pocket centring on the Forêt de Compiègne. On the western flank the enemy had still a heterogeneous collection of troops estimated on 4 September to be some 150,000 in number, west of the general line Antwerp–Lille–Béthune–Hesdin. Some of these gradually collected into the fortress defences made round the Channel ports; for the remainder the only line of escape now lay across the Scheldt estuary and into the islands to the north of it. In the first days of September First Canadian Army was closing in on Le Havre with troops of 1 Corps, while 2 Canadian Corps reached the line of the Somme on 3 September.

Elsewhere on the Allied front, Third United States Army had reached Commercy and Verdun on the Meuse, while the Allied Mediterranean invasion force continued to make progress along the Rhône valley.

## *The Situation, 3 September*

On 3 September I issued fresh instructions to 21 Army Group for the further development of operations.

I have already explained in the previous chapter that the main object constantly before me was to 'bounce' a crossing over the Rhine with the utmost speed before the enemy could reorganize sufficiently to stop us. Speed, and still greater speed, was the essential factor, and I now ordered Second Army to drive forward to the Rhine as quickly as possible. The boundary between Second Army and First United States Army was laid down on the line (all inclusive to First United States Army) Wavre–Tirlemont–Hasselt–Sittard–Leverkusen; the latter place is on the Rhine some six miles north of Cologne. Beyond the Rhine the boundary inclusive to 21 Army Group ran along the southern face of the Ruhr to Warburg and Brunswick. This boundary involved 21 Army Group in a very long frontage along the Rhine, and I directed Second Army to move its main weight up the river between Wesel and Arnhem. It was my intention at this period to threaten the western face of the Ruhr frontally, to jump the river north of the Ruhr and, subsequently, to by-pass that region round its northern face; at the same time preparations were to be made to swing forces from the Rhine bridgehead round into southern Holland, directed on the ports of Rotterdam and Amsterdam.

The Supreme Commander had instructed First United States Army to move forward in conjunction with us, directing its left flank to the Rhine between Bonn and Cologne. There was no change in the tasks of First Canadian Army, which were to clear the coastal belt up to Bruges and subsequently develop operations for the clearance of the Scheldt estuary, in order to give access to Antwerp from the North Sea.

The rapidity of our advance from Normandy had placed severe strains on our administration. With our arrival in Brussels and Antwerp, the lines of communication became some 300 miles long, but we now had the opportunity of establishing our advanced base in Central Belgium, which, as soon as the Scheldt was cleared, could be served by a first class port in good condition.

At the time, however, the advance produced administrative problems of great complexity; it had been expected that there would be some pause in operations between Normandy and Belgium which would have afforded an opportunity for the building up forward of essential stores. There was no pause; our dumps remained in the Rear Maintenance Area in Normandy, and the problem of supplying two corps advancing up to forty miles a day had to be solved. 8 Corps was grounded and all its second line transport, together with half its first line transport, was switched to the maintenance of 12 and 30 Corps. In First Canadian Army also, it soon became necessary to ground some units in order to maintain the momentum of others.

On 30 August a decision was made to rely on the early capture of a Channel port such as Dieppe or Boulogne, and to reduce meanwhile the quantities of stores and vehicles being brought in through Normandy. In view of the satisfactory level of supplies of all natures it was decided to cut down our imports from an average of some 16,000 tons per day to 7,000 tons per day. It thus became possible to release a considerable amount of transport from beach and port clearance for the task of supplying the forward troops.

The consumption of petrol during the pursuit was enormous and the greater part of the available transport was used in bringing it forward. The principle remained that the expenditure of ammunition is in inverse ratio to that of petrol; demands for the transport of ammunition did not therefore often conflict with those for petrol.

Road control became a factor of the utmost importance, particularly in view of the temporary bridges over the Seine and numerous other rivers. Tank transporters, which had formerly been severely restricted on the roads, now had to travel in large numbers over great distances, and special convoys frequently had to be shepherded along prearranged routes by Military Police detachments. To achieve the necessary flexibility, all third line transport was pooled and placed directly under Army control, and the tasks of all supply columns had to be extended. First line transport collected from the Field Maintenance Centres, second line transport from the Army Roadheads, while third line and GHQ transport brought supplies from the rear Maintenance Area to the Army Roadhead. The RASC columns concerned sometimes covered two hundred miles a day during this period.

One of the greatest difficulties in our rapidly lengthening lines of communication was the lack of signal communications, as the telephone lines had been destroyed and distances soon became too great for field wireless apparatus. This meant that despatch riders had frequently to be used, with attendant delays. The slowness of communications affected flexibility of supply as it was difficult to give sudden switches of priority when they were required.

It might have been expected that in such a lengthy advance the Armies could have found some relief to supply problems from captured enemy dumps. In the event, a very minor dividend was obtained from this source, probably due to the accuracy of our bombing of the enemy dumps themselves and of the communications leading to them. The maintenance of the pursuit was largely achieved by the cutting of our imports and by the grounding of fighting formations.

### THE ADVANCE OF SECOND ARMY TO THE
### MEUSE–ESCAUT CANAL

Second Army continued its advance from the Brussels–Antwerp area with minimum delay.

Stretched along a general line between Hasselt and Antwerp, facing Second Army front, the enemy disposed 176, 719 and elements of 347 Divisions. These troops were bolstered up with battle groups from parachute formations and remnants from 1 SS Panzer Division.

Second Army's intention was to advance with 30 Corps leading, while 12 Corps deployed to guard its left flank; on the right flank was First United States Army. As a first stage in the advance to the Rhine, 30 Corps plan was to position Guards Armoured Division in the Eindhoven area and 11 Armoured Division in the area Turnhout–Tilburg. These manœuvres entailed the passage of a number of water obstacles, in particular the Albert Canal and the Meuse–Escaut Canal. On the morning of 7 September Guards Armoured Division advanced on Diest, while armoured cars fanned out to reconnoitre the line of the Albert Canal from Beeringen to Herenthals. All bridges were reported blown, and the division planned to force a crossing near Beeringen. Meanwhile, 11 Armoured Division was attempting to cross the canals north of Antwerp, but encountered considerable resistance and began to search for weaker spots to the east; orders were subsequently issued for 50 Division to secure a bridgehead on the left of Guards Armoured Division, in some suitable area between Beeringen and Gheel.

On 8 September, Guards Armoured Division crossed the Albert Canal at Beeringen and established a bridgehead despite considerable opposition. The advance was now directed north-east with the immediate object of seizing the De Groot bridge over the Escaut Canal near Neerpelt. By nightfall on the same day, 50 Division had secured a small bridgehead over the canal south-west of Gheel; in this area, also, stiff resistance was encountered and the enemy delivered a number of well staged counter attacks.

The bridgeheads were gradually extended and on 10 September the Guards broke through to Overpelt, and made contact with the perimeter defences of the De Groot bridge. Confused fighting ensued, not only in the vicinity of the canal but also further south round Hechtel and the wooded areas to the south-west; by last light, however, the bridge was secured and infantry and tanks began crossing. The position was strengthened on 11 September. In view of the opposition and the exposed nature of the eastern flank, 11 Armoured Division was switched to the general area Peer–Bree–Helchteren, and 50 Division was subsequently relieved in the Gheel bridgehead by 15 Division of 12 Corps. 15 Division gradually pushed the enemy back to the Escaut Canal and on the night 13 September secured a bridgehead over it near the Gheel–Rethy crossing. The remainder of 12 Corps was now being relieved by Canadian Army in the Ghent area, and was moving across into the area Gheel–Diest–Malines–Antwerp.

The enemy was developing more spirit in his attacks against our bridgeheads over the Escaut Canal, and had clearly received reinforcements of better calibre; a number of sharp counter attacks were delivered, particularly in the area of the De Groot bridge.

It was now necessary for Second Army to make another short pause. Administrative difficulties had to be overcome and some stocks built up forward. Although

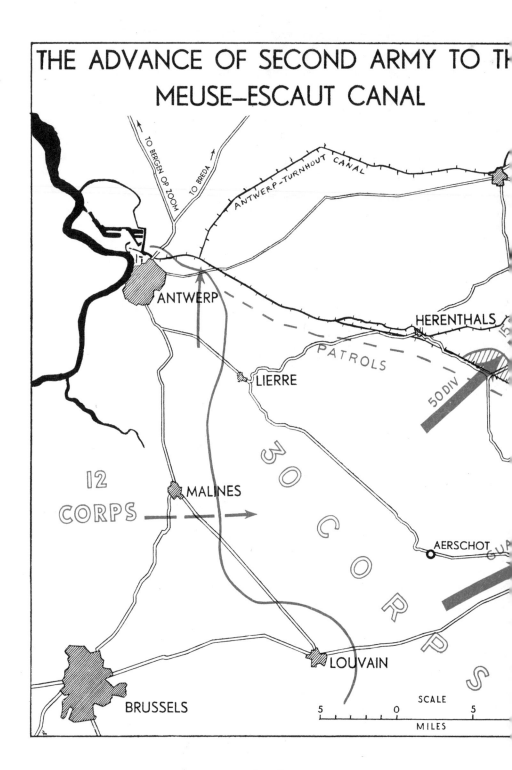

# THE ADVANCE OF SECOND ARMY TO TH
## MEUSE–ESCAUT CANAL

TO BERGEN OP ZOOM

TO BREDA

ANTWERP–TURNHOUT CANAL

ANTWERP

HERENTHALS

PATROLS

LIERRE

50 DIV

12

CORPS

30 CORPS

MALINES

AERSCHOT

LOUVAIN

BRUSSELS

SCALE

5    0    5

MILES

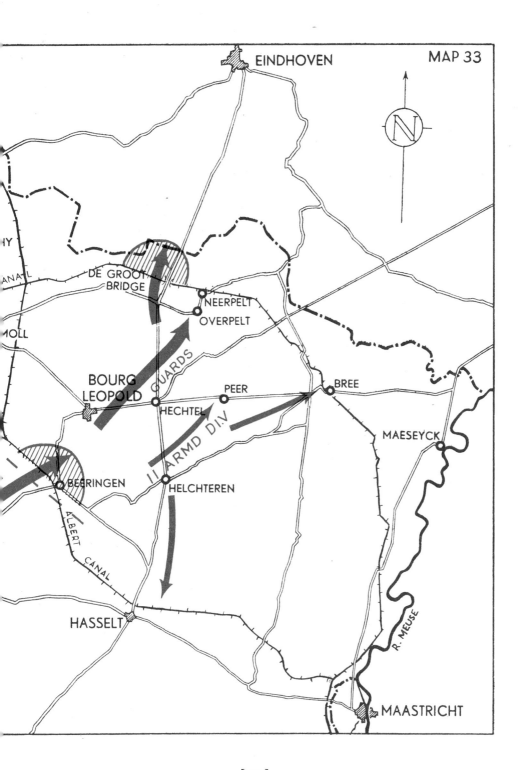

MAP 33

EINDHOVEN

N

DE GROOTE
BRIDGE

NEERPELT

OVERPELT

BOURG
LEOPOLD

GUARDS

PEER

BREE

HECHTEL

MAESEYCK

II ARMD DIV

BEERINGEN

HELCHTEREN

ALBERT

CANAL

HASSELT

R. MEUSE

MAASTRICHT

NY

CANAL

MOLL

it was apparent that the clearance of Havre was going to be a lengthy undertaking, Dieppe was opened on 8 September and the first coaster arrived there two days later. The capacity of this port increased rapidly and by the end of the month it was handling between 6,000 and 7,000 tons a day.

The control of transport over the long lines of communication had become a major problem which was solved by the establishment in Amiens of an organization called 'Tranco', under which transport working in rear of Army Roadheads was centralized.

In spite of our efforts and improvisations, however, I was not happy that the administrative build-up was proceeding fast enough for our purpose, and on 7 and 9 September I reported to the Supreme Commander that even with a port working in the Pas de Calais I should be unable to get over the Rhine without additional administrative assistance. On current reckoning I feared that Second Army would have to wait until 23 September, if not later, before sufficient resources had been built up forward to permit resumption of the advance; this delay would give the enemy his chance of strengthening and co-ordinating resistance before the German frontier. On 12 September, General Bedell Smith visited me on behalf of the Supreme Commander and, after discussing the situation, undertook to provide us with an increased daily air lift together with some American truck companies, in order to speed up our preparations. At the same time, First United States Army was to receive priority of maintenance requirements in Twelfth Army Group so that its operations on our right flank could be intensified. In subsequent weeks air freight deliveries averaged 400 to 500 tons per day, and by road special American fast convoys brought 500 tons per day to our Army Roadhead near Brussels. The main commodities delivered consisted of petrol and the special requirements for American airborne divisions.

With this assistance I was able to advance the date of Second Army's thrust to the Rhine to Sunday, 17 September.

The approach of autumn weather was now giving cause for anxiety but, providing weather conditions permitted the full development of our air power and unhindered use of airborne forces, I was confident that we now had sufficient resources to secure our Rhine bridgehead. But we were working on a minimum margin, particularly from an administrative point of view.

FIRST CANADIAN ARMY OPERATIONS ON THE
CHANNEL COAST

1–12 September

2 Canadian Corps moved out of the Rouen bridgehead on 31 August, and 4 Canadian Armoured Division on the right flank advanced twenty miles during the day to Forges and Buchy. In the centre, 3 Canadian Division advanced on the axis

St Saens–Londiniers, and captured Eu and Le Treport on 1 September. On the left, 2 Canadian Division drove straight through Totes on to Dieppe, meeting virtually no resistance; the division entered the port towards the evening of 1 September.

Advancing from Buchy through Aumale, 4 Canadian Armoured Division reached the Somme on 2 September, and by the next morning had a bridgehead across the river in the area of Pont Remy. It then concentrated astride the Somme while 1 Polish Armoured Division crossed the river on its left north of Abbeville; the advance was subsequently continued towards St Omer and the area Ghent–Bruges.

49 and 51 Divisions of 1 Corps advanced north of the Seine on 1 September, and while the former swung left into the Havre peninsula, the Highlanders went straight for St Valery and liberated the town on 2 September. The same day reconnaissance elements of 49 Division made contact with enemy outposts about three miles short of the River Lezarde. On the following day, the enemy covering troops were driven back to the perimeter defences of Le Havre, which ran across the peninsula from the mouth of the Seine to the Channel coast about six to eight miles from the centre of the town. Probing on 3 September showed that the elaborate defences of Havre were fully manned, and that a full scale set piece attack would be necessary to reduce the city. 51 Division was ordered to take over the northern sector of the perimeter and preparations for the assault were put in hand.

2 Canadian Corps continued to advance rapidly north of the Somme; the Polish Armoured Division crossed the canal at St Omer on 6 September, while on its left 3 Canadian Division closed in on the defences of Boulogne and Calais on 5 September; reconnaissance revealed that the enemy was intending to fight in defence of both these ports. 2 Canadian Division followed the leading troops north and passed through 3 Division in order to close on Dunkirk, into which a strong enemy garrison had retired; detachments were pushed on to Nieuport and Ostend, both of which were occupied on 9 September.

At this stage 4 Canadian Armoured Division began to come up on the left of the Poles and was directed on the Ghent–Bruges canal, which was held in some strength by the enemy. On 9 September a crossing was secured south-east of Bruges and mopping up of the town and surrounding area was undertaken. The Polish Armoured Division was now moved into the Ghent area to relieve 12 Corps and began local operations to clear the area to the north-east, while on the coast light forces progressed speedily as far as Zeebrugge.

As a result of these operations we were now investing enemy garrisons in Boulogne, Calais and Dunkirk; elsewhere the Pas de Calais was clear.

The attack on Le Havre by 1 Corps began at 1745 hours on 10 September, after the defences had been softened by the heavy guns of the Royal Navy and by a series of attacks by Bomber Command. The air preparations culminated in a ninety-minutes attack before H-hour in which nearly five thousand tons of bombs were dropped. 49 Division broke into the enemy positions at the north-east corner of the perimeter, and by midnight 51 Division had also penetrated the enemy defences.

By dark on 11 September both divisions were working their way into the town itself and had reached the high ground overlooking the harbour; operations continued with vigour during the night and the following morning, until at 1145 hours the garrison commander surrendered. 12,000 prisoners were collected. Le Havre constituted one of the strongest fortresses of the Atlantic Wall and had been provided with most elaborate concrete defences, extensive minefields and other obstacles, but it had been reduced after forty-eight hours' fighting.

The Canadian advance along the coast had been conducted with creditable speed. Great difficulty was experienced owing to the bad routes astride the Seine below Rouen; the Somme bridges below Amiens had been blown; and organized resistance continued in the coastal sector from the time of our advance across the Dives. As Second Army forged ahead cutting the east-west communications of the enemy on the coast, however, the opposition to Canadian Army loosened, with the result that the pace of advance quickened. The 'V' bomb sites were overrun, and very considerable numbers of prisoners were rounded up.

### THE ADVANCE TO THE MEUSE AND RHINE:
### THE BATTLE OF ARNHEM

*The Enemy Situation*

It was at this time that Field-Marshal Model, who, a fortnight previously, had succeeded temporarily to the Western Command (following von Kluge's suicide), managed to rally his demoralized forces and, by remarkable improvisation, to reestablish a front. Regimental and divisional commanders were empowered to form battle groups with such troops as they could muster locally from stragglers, reinforcements, lines of communication units, etc. These battle groups had, of course, no more than light infantry weapons, but they were able to base their anti-tank defence on a large number of 88 millimetre flak guns turned to a ground role with good effect. Such battle groups could not stop us, but, making full use of the numerous water obstacles, they could reduce our impetus. As our lines of communication grew longer, this improvised screen hardened.

Later in the month von Rundstedt was reinstated as Commander-in-Chief, but Model remained the Commander of Army Group 'B'.

*The Administrative Situation*

Maintenance difficulties remained our major problem. Although it had been possible to get Dieppe working very quickly, the damage and dislocation caused to the French railway system by the Allied air offensive made the restoration of rail traffic extremely difficult. In particular, shortage of locomotives and railway stock, combined with the destruction of signal facilities and bridges, demanded the expenditure of very considerable resources in manpower and materials in order to restore even a limited degree of train working.

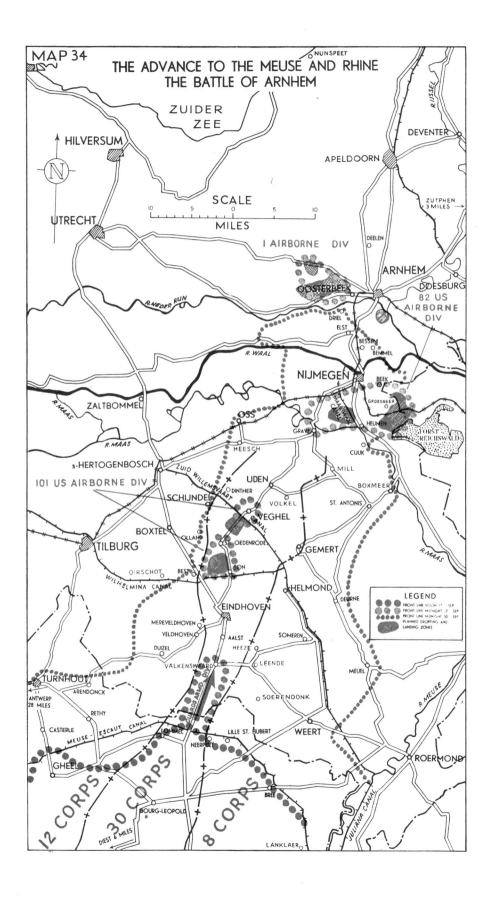

MAP 34

# THE ADVANCE TO THE MEUSE AND RHINE
## THE BATTLE OF ARNHEM

NUNSPEET

ZUIDER ZEE

HILVERSUM

N

DEVENTER

APELDOORN

ZUTPHEN
3 MILES →

SCALE

10      5      0      5      10

MILES

DEELEN

UTRECHT

I AIRBORNE DIV

R. NEDER RUN

OOSTERBEEK

DRIEL

ELST

ARNHEM

DOESBURG

82 US
AIRBORNE
DIV

R. WAAL

BESSEN

BEMMEL

NIJMEGEN

BEEK

GROESBEEK

R. MAAS

ZALTBOMMEL

OSS

R. MAAS

HEESCH

GRAVE

HEUMEN

FORST
REICHSWALD

CUIJK

s-HERTOGENBOSCH

ZUID WILLEMSVAART

MILL

101 US AIRBORNE DIV

DINTHER

UDEN

BOXMEER

SCHIJNDEL

VOLKEL

ST. ANTONIS

VEGHEL

CANAL

BOXTEL

OLLAND

ST. OEDENRODE

GEMERT

TILBURG

OIRSCHOT

BEST

SON

R. MAAS

WILHELMINA CANAL

HELMOND

DEURNE

LEGEND

FRONT LINE NOON 17  SEP
FRONT LINE MIDNIGHT 17  SEP
FRONT LINE MIDNIGHT 18  SEP
PLANNED DROPPING AND
LANDING ZONES

EINDHOVEN

MEREVELDHOVEN

VELDHOVEN

AALST

SOMEREN

DUIZEL

HEEZE

VALKENSWAARD

LEENDE

MEIJEL

TURNHOUT

SOERENDONK

R. MEUSE

ANTWERP
28 MILES

ARENDONCK

RETHY

CASTERLE

MEUSE - ESCAUT CANAL

LOMMEL

LILLE ST. HUBERT

WEERT

NEERPELT

GHEEL

ROERMOND

12 CORPS

30 CORPS

BREE

8 CORPS

JULIANA CANAL

BOURG-LEOPOLD

DIEST 8 MILES

LANKLAER

## Operations by United States Forces

During the first half of September, First United States Army, in face of considerable opposition, thrust to the German frontier and was in contact with the defences of the Siegfried Line; it was planned that the Army should continue its operations to Bonn and Cologne, while the left hand Corps was responsible for the northern American flank operating along the inter-Army Group boundary. Further to the south General Patton's Third United States Army had established bridgeheads over the Moselle.

## Orders to 21 Army Group, 14 September

My intention now was to establish bridgeheads over the Meuse and Rhine in readiness for the time when we could advance eastwards to occupy the Ruhr. I ordered Second Army to secure crossings over the river obstacles in the general area Grave–Nijmegen–Arnhem. I had decided upon this thrust line after detailed study of the possible routes in the 21 Army Group sector. Although this axis involved the additional obstacle of the Lower Rhine (Neder Rijn) as compared with more easterly approaches, and would carry us to an area relatively remote from the Ruhr, it satisfied three major overriding considerations: we should outflank the Siegfried defences; we should strike on the least likely line from the enemy's point of view; and our airborne forces would be operating in the most favourable conditions of range from home bases.

The Airborne Corps (General Browning) of three divisions was placed under Second Army's command.

Having secured the crossings, operations were to be developed to establish strong forces on the line Arnhem–Deventer–Zwolle, facing east, with bridgeheads on the east bank of the Ijssel River. Preparations were then to be made to advance east on the general axis Rheine–Osnabruck–Munster–Hamm, with the main weight on the right flank directed to Hamm: whence a thrust would be made along the eastern face of the Ruhr. My instructions were that the drive northwards to secure the river crossings would be made with the utmost rapidity and violence, and without regard to events on the flanks. The corridor of supply was to be widened and consolidated while the main advance continued.

Meanwhile the whole energies of First Canadian Army were to be directed towards opening up the port of Antwerp, which involved clearance of both banks of the Scheldt estuary. It was also necessary to capture Boulogne and Calais, as they would be useful subsidiary ports, and we required to release our containing forces for operations elsewhere. I decided it would be necessary to continue the investment of Dunkirk, as its reduction would have demanded the diversion of relatively major resources which at this time we could not afford. In order to provide transport for the Army it was necessary to ground 51 Division in the Havre area, but Headquarters 1 Corps and 49 Division were to be brought up to Antwerp as quickly as possible. Canadian Army was to take over the Antwerp sector from Second Army beginning on 17 September, and subsequently the inter-Army boundary, all inclusive to Canadian Army, would become Herenthals–Turnhout–Tilburg–'s Hertogenbosch–Zaltbommel–Utrecht–Hilversum. Initially the main drive to the north by Canadian Army would be directed on the port of Rotterdam, but at a later stage it was my intention that it should be brought up on the northern flank of Second Army directed on Bremen and Hamburg.

### THE SECOND ARMY PLAN FOR THE BATTLE OF ARNHEM

The Second Army task involved establishing crossings over five major obstacles; the Neder Rijn at Arnhem, the Waal at Nijmegen, the Maas at Grave, and two main transverse canals between our Escaut Canal bridgeheads and Grave. The canals concerned were the Wilhelmina, north of Eindhoven, and the Zuid Willemsvaart which runs parallel to the River Maas and links the towns of Helmond and 's Hertogenbosch. There was a third canal running partially across the line of advance, which connected the Mass and the Waal just west of Nijmegen. There were both road and railway bridges at Nijmegen and Arnhem and a road bridge at Grave—all of which were intact.

The essential feature of the plan was the laying of a carpet of airborne troops across these waterways on the general axis of the main road through Eindhoven to Uden, Grave, Nijmegen and Arnhem, culminating in a bridgehead force north of Arnhem. The airborne carpet and bridgehead force were to be provided by the Allied Airborne Corps consisting of two American and one British airborne divisions and the Polish Parachute Brigade. Along the corridor established by the airborne carpet, 30 Corps was to advance to the Arnhem bridgehead whence it would develop operations to establish a northern flank on the Zuider Zee and an eastern flank on the River Ijssel with bridgeheads beyond it. As 30 Corps advanced north, 8 Corps was to relieve it of responsibility for the right flank of the corridor, and was to widen it to the east; on the left flank, 12 Corps had a similar task with responsibility for widening the corridor to the west.

1 Airborne Corps detailed 1 Airborne Division, with Polish Parachute Brigade under command, to capture the Arnhem bridges. 82 United States Airborne Division was to seize the bridges at Nijmegen and Grave in connection with which the capture of the high ground between Groesbeek and Nijmegen was vital. 101 United States Airborne Division was to capture the bridges and defiles on 30 Corps axis between Grave and Eindhoven. The plan provided that 52 Division (air portable) was to be flown in north of Arnhem as soon as airstrips could be made available, in order to strengthen the bridgehead. Our resources in transport aircraft made it impossible to fly in the whole of the Airborne Corps in one lift, and in fact four days were required to convey the Corps to the battle area, together with the provision of re-supply by air. The air lift programme therefore provided that on D-day of the operation the American divisions were each to land three parachute Regimental Combat Teams,

while the remainder were scheduled to arrive on D+1 and D+2. 1 British Airborne Division was to land initially one parachute brigade and two-thirds of the air landing brigade; the rest of the division was to land on D+1. The Polish Parachute Brigade was phased in on D+2.

In general terms, when airborne troops are to deliver a coup de main against an objective such as a bridge, it is desirable to land them on both sides of the water obstacle, so that they can close in from all directions. Unfortunately, available reports concerning the terrain between the Waal and the Neder Rijn, including the opinion of Dutchmen living there, was that the area was basically unsuitable for airborne dropping or landing zones. Moreover, the flak defences at Arnhem and in the region of the Deelen airfield made it necessary to land some eight miles from Arnhem itself. These were difficulties which had to be accepted, but in the event they placed us at a great disadvantage.

30 Corps intention was to thrust north with all possible speed from the Meuse–Escaut Canal bridgehead along the airborne carpet to secure the general area Arnhem –Nunspeet, both inclusive. The Guards Armoured Division was to be the spearhead of the advance and had the ultimate task of dominating the area between Apeldoorn and the Zuider Zee; 43 and 50 Divisions were to follow up. Should any of the bridges at Grave, Nijmegen or Arnhem have been destroyed, the plan was for the armour to fan out along the river bank and, in conjunction with airborne troops, facilitate bridging operations, which were to be carried out by 43 Division. The ultimate task of 43 Division was to secure the area from Apeldoorn south to points of contact with 1 Airborne Division, and to secure crossings over the River Ijssel at Deventer and Zutphen. 50 Division was designated Corps reserve, and was ultimately to reorganize on the high ground north of Arnhem, pushing forces to the east in order to secure a crossing over the Ijssel at Doesburg. The task of opening initially the main road axis to the north fell to the United States airborne divisions; 8 Armoured Brigade was to join 101 United States Airborne Division to assist in holding the corridor through Eindhoven, Veghel and Grave.

Plans were made for a very heavy scale of air escort and air support; the task of neutralizing the enemy flak in the majority of the area covered by the airborne carpet fell to the air forces, but arrangements were made to bring normal artillery into action as quickly as possible in support of the airborne troops.

The operation involved the most detailed traffic control. Until the corridor was widened, all traffic of 30 Corps and the seaborne transport echelons of the airborne divisions had to move tactically along one route, supplemented by a subsidiary axis, which joined the main road at various bottlenecks.

The plan involved provision for bridging on a vast scale; preparation had to be made for the construction and maintenance of crossings over the major obstacles, apart from subsequent requirements in the advance over and beyond the River Ijssel. 8 and 12 Corps on the flanks of the main thrust also required considerable quantities of bridging to provide for their respective advances across the canals of southern Holland. The bridging resources were assembled in the Bourg Leopold area, and organized in columns of pre-arranged composition which were held in readiness to be called forward if and when required.

Most intensive measures were taken to build up stocks forward for Second Army to carry through this long advance. Meanwhile a rapid regrouping was carried out. 8 Corps assumed responsibility for the right flank of Second Army, taking over 11 Armoured Division, which continued to probe east and south-east to the line of the Meuse–Escaut Canal in the Lanklaer–Bree area. 1 Belgian Brigade also passed to command of 8 Corps, while 3 Division, which was being called forward from south of the Seine, was due to arrive in the Bree–Neerpelt sector by 17 September. 12 Corps, with 7 Armoured, 15 and 53 Divisions, adjusted its dispositions to the east from Antwerp and took over the bridgehead north of Gheel, where 15 Division was in the line. Within 30 Corps, 50 Division relieved the Guards in the De Groot bridgehead, so that the latter might concentrate for the drive north; 43 Division assembled to the north-east of Diest.

During the process of our regrouping the enemy made a number of counter attacks against the bridgeheads over the Meuse–Escaut Canal, and it was becoming increasingly evident that he was succeeding in the organization of a co-ordinated defensive system. For our part, the very utmost drive and energy was centred on speeding up preparations; in deciding on the target date of 17 September for the attack, time had been cut to the absolute minimum, bearing in mind the available resources at our disposal and the time taken to plan an operation of this scope involving the employment of major airborne forces.

THE BATTLE OF ARNHEM

*Operations, 17 September*

On the morning of 17 September the weather was fine and generally favourable for an airborne operation. During the morning the vast fleets of aircraft and gliders converged on their landing and dropping zones, the initial drops having been planned for 1300 hours. In general terms surprise was achieved and initially light opposition was encountered.

Paratroops of 101 United States Airborne Division were quickly established at Son, between Eindhoven and St Oedenrode; they secured the bridge at Veghel intact, though at Son the crossing over the Wilhelmina Canal was blown by the enemy when paratroops were within a few hundred yards of it. 82 United States Airborne Division landed according to plan and seized the bridge over the Maas at Grave intact, and later secured two bridges over the Maas–Waal Canal between Grave and Nijmegen. Efforts by this formation to rush the Nijmegen bridge were unsuccessful, but they reported the bridge intact. News from 1 British Airborne Division was scarce, but it appeared that the north end of the Arnhem bridge was in our hands and air reconnaissance showed gliders in its vicinity.

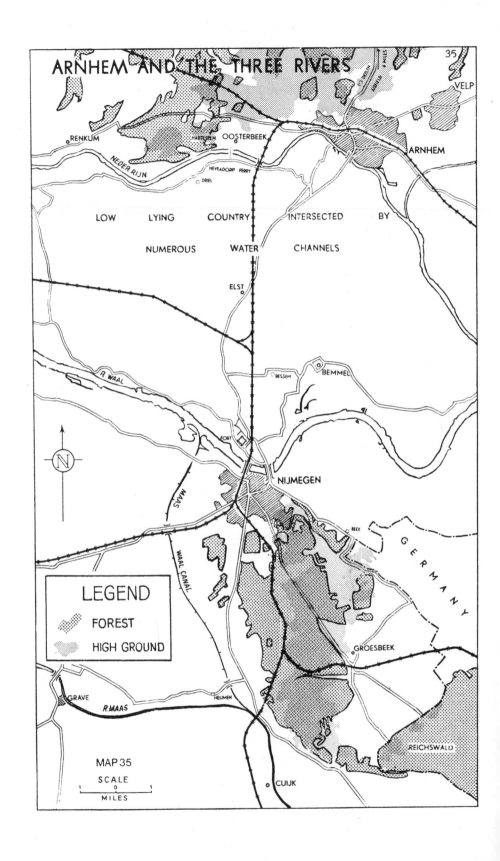

ARNHEM AND THE THREE RIVERS

VELP

RENKUM

HARTESTEIN OOSTERBEEK

ARNHEM

NEDER RIJN

HEVEADORP FERRY

DRIEL

LOW LYING COUNTRY INTERSECTED BY

NUMEROUS WATER CHANNELS

ELST

R WAAL

BESSEM BEMMEL

FORT

N

NIJMEGEN

BEEK

MAAS

G E R M A N Y

WAAL CANAL

LEGEND

FOREST

HIGH GROUND

GROESBEEK

GRAVE

R. MAAS

HEUMEN

REICHSWALD

MAP 35

SCALE
0
MILES

CUIJK

30 Corps gave the order to Guards Armoured Division to commence the advance at 1425 hours, as the airborne echelons came into view. The advance was preceded by a rolling barrage astride the Eindhoven road, in conjunction with rocket firing Typhoons which worked on the 'cab rank' system controlled from the forward area. Strong opposition was encountered from parachute infantry dug in along the road axis and supported by some self-propelled guns, but after hard fighting an advance of six miles was made and the village of Valkenswaard was occupied. On the flanks of 30 Corps the enemy was active, while 8 and 12 Corps completed their arrangements for making further crossings of the Meuse–Escaut Canal.

*Operations, 18 September*

The fighting along the canal had shown the need for more infantry, and a brigade of 50 Division was therefore brought forward. The advance from Valkenswaard was resumed at 0600 hours on 18 September by the Guards, while 50 Division mopped up behind the armoured spearhead. Enemy defending Aalst were brushed aside and attempts made to enter Eindhoven; it was, however, soon determined that the town was strongly held. Efforts were then directed to by-passing the opposition, initially to the east, but strong enemy positions were found four miles from the main road. The bridges on the western approaches to the town would not take tanks, but armoured cars managed to get through and to make contact with elements of 101 United States Airborne Division to the north-west of Eindhoven. The American troops reported the Son bridge blown and engineer material was ordered forward. The battle for Eindhoven continued; the Americans were first into the town, in the northern sector, while at 1700 hours an attack by the Guards finally broke the enemy resistance. The advance was pressed on to Son where bridging was put in hand. 50 Division continued mopping up to the south, and ensured the security of the De Groot bridge-head, which the enemy again counter attacked from the north-east; in order to relieve 30 Corps of the responsibility for this bridgehead, 50 Division was transferred to command of 8 Corps.

North of Eindhoven, 101 United States Airborne Division organized its hold on the nodal points astride the axis up to the Grave bridge, while 82 Airborne Division continued attempts to get through to the Nijmegen bridge, but an increase in the enemy defenders prevented its capture. Meanwhile the first of a series of counter attacks was made from the direction of the Reichswald Forest; this achieved some temporary success and reached one of our landing zones before the enemy was eventually repulsed. During the counter attack a glider lift of reinforcements arrived, some four hours behind schedule, owing to bad weather at the bases in England.

Reports from the Arnhem area were still scanty. While the main body of airborne troops was established west of the town, it appeared that elements of the parachute brigade were holding out at the road bridge, which remained intact. The Germans, however, were holding the town in strength with a garrison which included tanks and self-propelled guns. The reinforcements for 1 Airborne Division arrived four

[317]

hours late, and formed up with the object of pushing into Arnhem, but were held at the western exits and became virtually surrounded. At the end of the day, therefore, it appeared that the division was in three parts, and although losses to the fly-in on this day had been almost negligible, re-supply had failed owing to poor visibility and heavy flak.

On the right flank, 8 Corps planned to force a crossing of the Escaut Canal with 3 Division after midnight on 18 September in the vicinity of Lille St Hubert. The bridgehead was to be pushed to the line Weert–Soerendonk, while 11 Armoured Division pressed forward to the Helmond–Deurne area east of Eindhoven. 12 Corps, by the morning of 18 September, had secured a new bridgehead near Lommel and during the day was building up on the north bank of the canal in face of considerable opposition, while further to the west 15 Division was strengthening the Gheel bridgehead. 12 Corps planned to push 53 Division west of Eindhoven astride the Eindhoven–Turnhout road, while 15 Division secured the area Rethy–Casterle–Arendonck, whence operations were to be developed further to the north.

*Operations, 19 September*

The Guards Armoured Division started to cross the Son bridge at 0615 hours, and by 0900 hours leading elements had advanced twenty-five miles and linked up with 82 United States Airborne Division at the Grave bridge. Further north, the bridge over the Maas–Waal Canal was found unfit for tanks, and a detour became necessary to the canal crossing just north of Heumen. By early afternoon armoured cars had reached the banks of the Waal, and the armoured brigade was concentrated about three miles south of Nijmegen. Meanwhile the American paratroops were having very stiff fighting, particularly on the eastern flank, which was being counter attacked from the Beek area. Enemy action delayed the plans for launching an attack on the Nijmegen bridge for several hours, but at 1845 hours armour broke in to part of the town; it proved impossible, however, to get to the bridge, the approaches to which were covered by a number of self-propelled guns and concrete pill-boxes. It was therefore decided to renew the assault the following day with a frontal attack by the Guards Division, together with an assault crossing west of the bridge by American paratroops, who were subsequently to swing in against the northern end of the objective.

At Arnhem the situation was still obscure. 1 Airborne Division was endeavouring to concentrate all its forces some four miles west of the bridge, while troops of the parachute brigade maintained their hold on a small area in the immediate vicinity of the bridge itself. Other parties were still holding out in houses on the west side of the town but the enemy had brought up tanks and artillery which were gradually reducing the buildings to rubble. Food and ammunition were getting short owing to the failure of re-supply on 18 September.

101 United States Airborne Division had considerable fighting during the day; the enemy was in fair strength in the area of Schijndel, and also held the Helmond

area. Meanwhile the first of what was to be a long series of counter attacks against the Eindhoven–Nijmegen axis was developing, for quite unexpectedly a small but well-equipped 'pocket' Panzer division, 107 Panzer Brigade, arrived from the Rhineland via Venlo. A strong attack with tanks against the bridge at Son was successfully driven off, but some anxiety was felt about the stability of the situation in the Uden area, and operations were developed to 'firm up' the corridor here.

The weather on 19 September was generally bad, and the resultant dislocation of the air lift programme was to have serious repercussions on the course of the operations. Apart from its effect on airborne reinforcement and re-supply, the weather began seriously to restrict the action of the Allied Air Forces. Not only was close support of the ground troops limited, but we were unable to interdict the enemy's reinforcement routes. The concentration of enemy forces, in particular against the Arnhem bridgehead, continued rapidly whereas close support of the Arnhem bridgehead forces, which were extremely weak in artillery, was virtually precluded.

Although transport aircraft braved the weather, most of the re-supply for 1 Airborne Division again fell into enemy hands, as the dropping zones were occupied by Germans, and it had not been possible to alter them owing to faulty communications. In the case of 82 United States Airborne Division, only about twenty-five per cent of the re-supply tonnage reached the troops and the glider lift for 101 United States Airborne Division was only two-thirds effective. The balance of the glider lift for 82 Airborne Division was not flown, nor was it possible for the Polish Parachute Brigade to take off from its bases in England. The latter setback was particularly grave, as this brigade was intended to land south of Arnhem in order to reinforce the operations of 1 Airborne Division, and at the same time it was hoped that it would establish contact with the forces investing Nijmegen.

The enemy anti-aircraft artillery was increasing rapidly and the columns of aircraft encountered heavy fire in approaching their landing and dropping zones.

Meanwhile efforts were intensified to speed up the operations of 8 and 12 Corps in order to widen the corridor. The extreme congestion on the main Eindhoven road axis was making it difficult to increase our forces in the foremost area in order to hasten operations for the relief of 1 Airborne Division. The deterioration of the weather made it essential to reinforce the Arnhem forces by ground troops and particularly by artillery; but the enemy opposition was increasing, and our own troops were fighting without their accustomed scale of artillery support owing to shortage of ammunition.

In the 8 Corps sector, 3 Division secured its bridgehead at Lille St Hubert early on 19 September, and 11 Armoured Division began to push north. By midday our armour was in contact with enemy at Leende; patrols subsequently reached Heeze, two miles further north. On the 12 Corps sector a project to secure a bridgehead at De Maat was abandoned in view of the opposition, and it was decided to concentrate on exploiting north from the bridgehead at Lommel. Troops of 53 Division attacked from this area, reaching the line of the Eindhoven–Turnhout road near Duizel, where there was considerable fighting. Meanwhile one brigade struck north-east and captured Veldhoven, and made contact with 50 Division at Mereveldhoven.

The progress of the two flank corps was thus depressingly slow; apart from the enemy resistance, the difficult nature of the country, which was flat and intersected by a great number of minor water lines, greatly impeded progress; we were not strong enough to accelerate further these operations, and as a result the flanks of the long 30 Corps salient were thinly held and lay open to attacks by the enemy battle groups assembling against us.

### Operations, 20 September

There were now three major considerations in the conduct of the battle. First, it was imperative to secure the Nijmegen bridge; second, it was necessary to strengthen 82 United States Airborne Division, as the enemy was building up considerable forces in the Reichswald Forest; third, relief had to be brought to 1 Airborne Division at Arnhem.

Guards Armoured Division planned to capture the Nijmegen bridge in a joint operation with 504 Regimental Combat Team. During the morning of 20 September the Anglo-American forces gradually cleared the town of Nijmegen up to the southern approaches to the bridge. It was apparent that the enemy had been reinforced during the previous night with elements of SS troops, and bitter fighting took place in the town. Meanwhile American troops received some rapid instruction in the use of British assault boats preparatory to forcing a crossing of the river west of the bridge, and while these preparations were in hand there was heavy fighting on the east flank where the enemy launched a series of counter attacks. At 1500 hours the assault across the Waal started, about one mile west of the town. The operation was in full view of the enemy and there were only sufficient boats to carry one battalion at a time; on the north bank the assault had to be carried across several hundred yards of flat open country in order to capture an old fort surrounded by a moat. Subsequently the attack was to be swung in on the northern exits of the main road and railway bridges. Fire support was limited, and in the event smoke cover proved ineffective on account of the weather. In spite of these difficulties the American troops carried out a magnificent operation; although they suffered considerable casualties, they pressed on desperately and by 1845 hours had secured the northern end of the railway bridge and soon afterwards the exit from the road bridge. On the south side of the river the Guards were having a hard fight near the southern ends of the bridges; the sight of the United States flag on the northern end of the railway bridge was the signal for the Guards' tanks to launch a head-on attack which carried the defences and enabled leading elements to cross the river and join up with the Americans. Considerable mopping up was necessary in the bridge areas, while the demolition charges were removed and the last defenders eliminated. Plans were now made to push on north to Arnhem on the following day, while 43 Division closed up rapidly from the south.

At Arnhem the situation was becoming acute. Although supplies were successfully dropped on 20 September, it was still impossible to bring in the Polish Parachute Brigade; therefore the vital airborne link between Arnhem and Nijmegen was still lacking while the enemy concentrated increasing forces of high calibre against 1 Airborne Division. The British troops had by now withdrawn into a small perimeter covering the Heveadorp ferry and the wooded area round Oosterbeek. The perimeter was subjected to concentrated artillery and mortar fire and pressed on all sides; the town of Arnhem was by now completely in enemy hands and nothing was known of the survivors of 1 Parachute Brigade.

In the southern sector, 101 Airborne Division held its positions firmly in face of a series of attacks launched against the corridor. Renewed attacks on Son were driven off, though enemy detachments from the Helmond area, backed by tanks and self-propelled guns, infiltrated on to the main road during the morning. A counter attack by American paratroops and units of the Royal Tank Regiment and Yeomanry restored the situation by midday, and the flow of traffic north was resumed.

11 Armoured Division on the right flank made strong efforts to increase the pace of advance to the north. Some progress was made and Someren was captured. In 12 Corps area slow progress was made against stiff opposition towards Best and Oirschot.

*Operations, 21–30 September*

Every possible effort was now concentrated on relieving the Arnhem bridgehead forces. With the exception of 23 September, adverse weather conditions continued severely to restrict air operations; on 22 September it was impossible to carry out any troop carrier operations at all. As a result we continued to suffer from lack of support from the air in its widest sense.

On 21 September the Guards resumed attempts to progress northwards, while 43 Division came into the Nijmegen bridgehead. The advance was eventually halted by a strong anti-tank gun screen south of Bessem. It was almost impossible to manœuvre armoured forces off the roads, which generally ran about six feet above the surrounding country and had deep ditches on both sides. On this day, however, it was found possible to drop about two-thirds of the Polish Parachute Brigade in the area north-west of Elst. Unfortunately the drop was nearer the village itself than had been intended and the brigade sustained considerable casualties from the enemy holding it. The paratroops suffered delays in concentrating for their task, which was to cross the Neder Rijn and reinforce 1 Airborne Division. The latter meanwhile was cut off from the river, as the enemy garrison from Arnhem had now captured the Heveadorp ferry terminal.

On 22 September, 43 Division resumed the attack north from the Nijmegen bridgehead while armoured car patrols pushed west towards 's Hertogenbosch. The attack was held up outside Elst, but a mixed column of tanks and infantry succeeded in making a detour to the west and in joining up with the Poles near Driel, and in reaching the Neder Rijn. The river was under close and concentrated enemy fire, and it was found that the banks were too steep for the amphibious lorries which were carrying relief supplies; as a result only very small quantities of stores were got across that night.

Meanwhile to the south, the 30 Corps axis was cut during the middle of the day between Uden and Veghel by enemy infantry and tanks attacking from the north-west. The infantry brigade of Guards Armoured Division from Nijmegen was despatched to assist in re-opening the axis; this was successfully achieved and the road was re-opened by the afternoon of 23 September.

43 Division continued its operations from the Nijmegen bridgehead on 23 September, but was unable to break through Elst. In the afternoon the Glider Regiment of 82 Airborne Division and the balance of the Polish Brigade were flown in, and at night about 250 Poles were ferried across the Neder Rijn to reinforce 1 Airborne Division. The following night infantry detachments crossed the river, but intense fire from the high ground on the north bank put a stop to these operations at first light. These troops did not make contact with 1 Airborne Division, and it was now decided that it would not be possible to fly in 52 (air portable) Division as had been hoped. Fighting continued violently in the area of Elst and Bemmel and it was not until the afternoon of 25 September that this area was cleared. The main axis was again cut south of Veghel during the afternoon of 24 September and in spite of strenuous efforts by 101 Airborne Division the enemy built up considerable forces astride the road. Fighting to re-open the axis continued throughout 25 September and traffic was not able to resume until the following day.

Meanwhile 8 and 12 Corps made some further progress on the flanks of the salient. Weert was captured on 22 September and Deurne two days later. By the evening of 25 September, Helmond and Gemert were in our hands and 8 Corps was in contact with elements of 30 Corps at St Antonis. 12 Corps made progress in the triangle between the Eindhoven–Turnhout road and the Eindhoven–'s Hertogenbosch axis, but the enemy still held out in Best and Boxtel.

On the morning of 25 September I decided to withdraw the gallant Arnhem bridgehead that night. Owing to the casualties they had suffered and the shortage of ammunition and supplies, their positions were no longer tenable in face of the mounting enemy opposition. The Germans now dominated in strength all possible crossing places of the Neder Rijn, so that reinforcements and supplies could only be ferried over the river in minor quantities with great risk by night. During the night 25/26 September the withdrawal was carried out with assault boats. The greatest gallantry and skill was shown in this operation, both by the detachments evacuating from north of the river and by a battalion of 43 Division which assisted them; by 0600 hours on 26 September, when intense enemy fire made further crossings impossible, about 2,400 men of 1 Airborne Division, Polish Parachute Brigade, and 4 Battalion The Dorsetshire Regiment had been safely evacuated. Other detachments of the Dorsets were left on the north bank of the river still fighting in a most gallant manner to cover the operation.

Following the withdrawal from Arnhem, it became my immediate object to ensure

22. A Sherman tank crossing the Seine. 28 August 1944.

23. American tank crossing the Seine west of Paris on a treadway bridge constructed by U.S. Army engineers. 26 August 1944.

24. A new section of the 'Mulberry' roadway under tow across the Channel. 11 October 1944.

25. American units cross the Rhine on a bridge built in the record time of $6\frac{1}{2}$ hours. 26 March 1945.

YOU ARE NOW
CROSSING THE
RHINE RIVER
THROUGH COURTESY
OF E CO. 17 ARMD
ENGR. BN. AND
'C' CO. 202
ENGR. C. BN

26.   A U.S. Army train crosses the newly completed bridge over the Rhine at Wesel which was built by the Ninth U.S. Army engineers in the remarkable time of 11 days. March 1945.

27.   U.S. Third Army troops ride through a gap blasted in the 'Dragons Teeth' of the Siegfried Line.

28.  The Germans ask for surrender terms at 21st Army Group H.Q. on
3 May 1945.

29.  Field-Marshal Montgomery signing the Instrument of Surrender
document. 4 May 1945.

the security of the Nijmegen bridgehead and to firm up the salient leading to it. By this time enemy reactions to our operation were fully aroused, and attacks against both salient and bridgehead were developing from every quarter.

The German troops were told that the Nijmegen road bridge was the 'gateway to the Fatherland' and that its destruction was essential to avert defeat. All available land and air forces were committed to the task. Between 19 September, when the Guards Division reached Nijmegen, and 4 October there were no less than twelve attacks of divisional or greater strength against the Eindhoven–Arnhem salient. Of these the strongest were delivered north-east from the Reichswald Forest on 28 September and south from Arnhem on 1 October. Both were directed on to the road bridge and both were repulsed, but only after some heavy fighting.

In these operations the enemy employed the remnants of 9, 116, 9 SS and 10 SS Panzer Divisions together with a very large force of infantry from the formations of Fifteenth Army and from locally organized battle groups.

In addition the enemy made a number of determined air attacks to put the Nijmegen bridges out of action, notably on 27 September, when nearly six hundred aircraft appeared over the area. These attacks fortunately failed, but he soon resorted to other methods. On the night 28/29 September, specially trained swimmers equipped with demolition charges seriously damaged the railway bridge and also caused the road bridge to be closed for twenty-four hours. A pontoon Bailey bridge was at once put under construction, and measures taken to frustrate further attempts by swimmers or floating mines.

Between the Waal and the Maas operations continued; north-east of Nijmegen, 30 Corps made ground east of Bemmel and Elst, while 82 Airborne Division improved its positions east and south of Nijmegen itself and between 29 and 30 September repulsed four enemy attacks from the direction of the Reichswald Forest. 8 Armoured Brigade was fighting on the west sector of the bridgehead and disposed of an enemy force which had crossed the Neder Rijn. South of the Waal, Oss was occupied by our troops.

At the time that 8 Corps made contact with 30 Corps at St Antonis, patrols reached the Maas south of Boxmeer, and, to the west, entered Mill and Volkel. By the end of September the Corps was on the general line Weert–Meijel–Deurne–Boxmeer and thence along the Maas to the area of Cuijk, which was the point of contact with 82 Airborne Division.

West of the salient, 12 Corps continued operations in the Schijndel area. North of the town progress was made to the area Heesch–Dinther, and on 29 September the line of the Oss–'s Hertogenbosch railway was reached. Meanwhile the enemy held out stubbornly in Schijndel and Olland and counter attacked our troops at Best. The accompanying map shows the position in the Second Army salient on 30 September. At its narrowest part south of Grave, the corridor was only twenty miles wide, but we were now sufficiently well placed to ensure holding it firmly in spite of the increased enemy forces containing it.

[323]

### REFLECTIONS ON THE BATTLE OF ARNHEM

The battle of Arnhem had been designed to gain us quickly and at relatively cheap cost a bridgehead beyond the Rhine (or Waal) and lower Rhine (or Neder Rijn). It had had to be undertaken with resources which left very little margin for the insurance of success in view of the remarkably rapid recovery of the enemy, and at a time of year when it was necessary to accept considerable risks with the weather.

The plan involved initially driving a deep salient of over sixty miles into country occupied by a stubborn enemy, in which manœuvre was very limited and observation restricted. It was necessary to rely on the weather permitting large scale airborne operations over a period of four days, in order to reinforce and link up the airborne detachments; we had also relied on a heavy scale of intimate air support, since the depth of the airborne operation carried it far beyond artillery support from the ground forces. It had moreover been assumed that the airborne divisions would be strong enough to dominate the enemy in their respective areas for a relatively lengthy period of time, because we were not strong enough, particularly in supporting weapons, to guarantee forcing rapid progress by major ground forces on a wide front from the Meuse–Escaut Canal bridgehead.

We had undertaken a difficult operation, attended by considerable risks. It was justified because, had good weather obtained, there was no doubt that we should have attained full success.

Had 1 Airborne Division received the planned measure of airborne reinforcement and re-supply, together with the full scale of support from the air, I am confident that the result would have been very different. In particular, I believe that the link-up with 1 Airborne Division would have been effected had it been possible accurately to drop the Polish Parachute Brigade on D+2 together with the Glider Regiment of 82 Airborne Division. At the same time the normal scale of action by the Allied Air Forces would not only have impeded the enemy pressing in on our Arnhem bridgehead, but would have greatly retarded the speed with which he was able to react and bring forward his reinforcements.

A great tribute is due to 1 Airborne Division for the magnificent stand at Arnhem; its action against overwhelming odds held off enemy reinforcements from Nijmegen and vitally contributed to the capture of the bridge there. Such reinforcements as did reach Nijmegen were forced to use a long detour to the east and a ferry crossing, and there is no doubt that the delays thus imposed were instrumental in enabling us to secure the Nijmegen bridges intact.

The battle of Arnhem was ninety per cent successful. We were left in possession of crossings over four major water obstacles including the Maas and the Waal, and it will later be seen that the Waal bridgehead proved a vital factor in the subsequent development of operations, culminating in crossing the Rhine and advancing to the Baltic. Full success at Arnhem was denied us for two reasons; first, the weather prevented the build-up of our airborne forces in the battle area; second, the enemy managed to effect a surprisingly rapid concentration of forces to oppose us. In face of this resistance the British Group of Armies in the north was not strong enough to retrieve the situation created by the weather by intensifying the speed of operations on the ground. We could not widen the corridor sufficiently quickly to reinforce Arnhem by road.

# CHAPTER THIRTEEN

## The Clearance of the Scheldt Estuary and Opening of the Port of Antwerp

### REVIEW OF THE SITUATION AFTER THE BATTLE OF ARNHEM

WE had failed in our object of gaining quickly a bridgehead over the Lower Rhine at Arnhem, but the Nijmegen bridgehead over the Rhine itself gave us excellent strategic and tactical advantages.

It seemed likely that the enemy would now aim at stabilizing the northern front on the Waal, contesting our advance north of Antwerp and denying us the Scheldt estuary with all the means at his disposal, and at the same time concentrate on organizing a firm defensive system on our eastern flank to keep us remote from the Ruhr.

For 21 Army Group the prize remained the Ruhr. I continued to work on the problem of how best to thrust towards that area. During the winter months we were to suffer many delays and setbacks to the project, but it remained always the ultimate aim of 21 Army Group to cross the barrier of the Rhine and to develop operations for the isolation of the Ruhr. We had now the ability to strike south-east and south from the Nijmegen bridgehead, between the Rhine and the Meuse, towards the western extremity of the Ruhr; such a thrust combined with American operations directed on Cologne and Düsseldorf would clearly place the enemy in great difficulties. It was my idea that as we progressed along the west bank of the Rhine we should take any opportunity afforded us of jumping the river; if enemy opposition made this impossible the Allies would be in a position to undertake an opposed crossing operation once we had cleared the sector between Düsseldorf and Nijmegen.

At the same time we could maintain a constant threat of resuming operations into southern Holland, which could be used to pin down enemy forces in the Arnhem sector.

The project of clearing the area between the Rhine and the Meuse, as a preliminary to striking at the Ruhr, I called the 'Battle of the Rhineland', and it now became my preoccupation to prepare and launch this operation as quickly as possible. The extent of the German recovery was increasingly apparent and to achieve our objects we were clearly destined to have another 'dog-fight' battle west of the Rhine. Additional strength was necessary to overwhelm the enemy in the northern sectors of the Allied front and to ensure opening up again mobile operations on a decisive scale. The longer we delayed the greater would become the magnitude of the task before us, and in the last days of September I was hoping to be able to undertake the Rhineland thrust about 10 October.

While the battle of Arnhem was still in progress I was trying to accumulate

[326]

additional forces for the offensive operations in the north, and asked the Supreme Commander for the inter-Army Group boundary to be changed in order to relieve 8 Corps from the long defensive flank on the east of the 30 Corps salient. On 22 September orders were given for moving the boundary northwards to the line Weert–Deurne–Maashees.

### DEVELOPMENT OF THE PLAN OF OPERATIONS IN THE NORTHERN SECTOR UP TO THE END OF 1944

By the end of the first week in October, I realized that I should not be able to carry out my plans as speedily as I had hoped.

Apart from the major consideration of getting up to the Rhine and crossing it, there were three commitments facing 21 Army Group. We had to provide for the early opening of the Scheldt. I had hoped that the Arnhem operation would draw the enemy away from the front of First Canadian Army, but with the stabilization of the front in the northern sector, it was increasingly evident that the enemy would be able to provide considerable forces to cover the Scheldt estuary, and that we were going to have difficulty in clearing him out of the very difficult country astride that waterway. Meanwhile the American armies in particular were greatly hampered in their operations by lack of resources, and the solution of their difficulties lay in opening the port of Antwerp.

The second commitment was the need for additional strength in the Nijmegen bridgehead. The enemy continued to engage our forces there, and it was vital to ensure that we retained firmly our territory north of the Waal, because it was the springboard from which the Rhineland battle was to be developed and therefore the key to our future strategy in the north. I considered that two infantry divisions would be required in the bridgehead.

Thirdly, the enemy west of the Meuse on our eastern flank was in greater strength than had originally been anticipated, and he evidently intended to fight for his bridgehead; the country greatly favoured defensive tactics so that we should have to deploy some strength to push him east of the river. One American armoured division was sent to deal with the enemy in the sector west of Venlo, but experience quickly showed that it was insufficient for the task.

These three commitments had a direct bearing on future plans for the battle of the Rhineland. In view of the degree of the enemy's recovery, it was clearly unsound to advance between the Rhine and the Meuse with two hostile flanks and risk being hemmed in between those obstacles. We had to clear the west bank of the Meuse and ensure the opening of lateral routes across the river as the operation progressed to the south. Again, we had to be firmly balanced in the Nijmegen salient so that enemy action against the bottlenecks in rear of the Rhineland front could not divert us from our purpose. Lastly, we could not strike on an axis so remote from the Scheldt until we were certain that the operations there would proceed quickly and relentlessly and that there would be no sudden difficulties demanding reinforcements for the Canadian Army.

It is thus clear that we had not sufficient strength in the northern sectors to compete with our commitments concurrently. It was necessary to ensure balanced dispositions, and to devote first priority to opening Antwerp.

The battle of the Rhineland would have to wait. Apart from the considerations enumerated above, American action against Bonn and Cologne was, to my mind, an essential part of the Rhineland plan; but the First United States Army was not yet in a position to strike at the Rhine. The Americans were very heavily engaged in fierce fighting in the Siegfried Line round Aachen, and it was going to take time to break through the enemy defences in that area.

By 9 October, therefore, my immediate object had been reduced to completing the clearance of the Scheldt estuary and the undertaking of operations against the enemy bridgehead west of the Meuse. It was very soon necessary further to reduce the scope of our plans. The Allied need for Antwerp had become imperative; in 21 Army Group the administrative machine was working on a narrow enough margin, while in the American armies the maintenance situation had become extremely grave. To add to our difficulties, there was a gale in early October which had considerable repercussions cn beach-working in Normandy. It became increasingly apparent that the enemy was determined to prevent our opening the Scheldt for as long as possible, and that if Antwerp was to be opened quickly we should have to deploy additional forces in our west flank operations.

It had thus become necessary to devote the whole of our resources into getting Antwerp working at once, and I had to shut down all other offensive operations in 21 Army Group until this object was achieved.

By the end of October completion of the clearance of the Scheldt estuary and of the operations directed to the mouth of the River Maas was in sight, and I was then able to return to my plans for clearing the enemy salient west of the Meuse. When these operations had in turn been completed towards the end of November, I was able once more to concern myself with getting ready for the battle of the Rhineland. Preparations were in fact in hand when events again caused delay in execution of the operation: the German counter stroke in the Ardennes caused us to react strongly, and it was not until that situation had been cleared up that we were able to undertake operations towards the Ruhr from the Nijmegen bridgehead.

### CANADIAN ARMY OPERATIONS

#### 13–30 September

In mid-September First Canadian Army was commanding 1 Corps, which was relieving 12 Corps in the Antwerp area, and 2 Canadian Corps, which was operating in the coastal belt. The intention was for 1 Corps to advance north across the Antwerp–

Turnhout canal, while 2 Canadian Corps cleared the country west of Antwerp up to the southern shores of the Scheldt estuary and at the same time invested Dunkirk and reduced the garrisons of Boulogne and Calais.

The enemy forces opposing the Canadian Army had by now split into two groups. Some 30,000 troops were left behind to hold the fortresses of Boulogne, Calais and Dunkirk, while further north Fifteenth Army, with eight nominal divisions (worth about four) was withdrawing slowly across the estuary of the Scheldt.

A slow withdrawal was greatly facilitated by the canal barriers which lay across our path. The Canal de Ghent joins with Bruges and continues to the sea at Zeebrugge, the later stretch being called the Bruges Ship Canal. Further north, the Leopold Canal runs from near Terneuzen to the North Sea north of Zeebrugge, while between these main arteries is the Canal de Derivation de Lys which runs from the sea parallel to the Leopold Canal for about twelve miles and then swings south-east to cross the Ghent Canal about ten miles west of Ghent. The Ghent–Terneuzen Canal runs north from Ghent to the West Scheldt, and parallel to the Scheldt itself there is the Canal de Hulst. These waterways were major obstacles, and between them existed a network of minor water lines and considerable areas of flooding.

4 Canadian Armoured Division had crossed the Ghent Canal and had cleared the Bruges area by about 12 September; the division then continued its advance towards the Canal de Derivation and the Leopold Canal and secured a small bridgehead over them on the night 13/14 September. There was considerable enemy opposition and it was decided to reconnoitre the hostile defences along the canal lines in other areas in the hope of finding 'soft spots'. On 15 September a bridgehead over the Canal de Derivation was established near Balgerhoek, and in the following days the area west of the Ghent–Terneuzen Canal and north to the town of Sas Van Ghent was cleared. By 22 September the whole area south of the Leopold Canal, across which all the bridges were blown, was clear of the enemy, and in addition the pocket between the Terneuzen Canal and the Savojaards Plaat was also in our hands. Reconnaissance showed that the enemy was concentrating on holding the line of the Leopold Canal, and it became clear that additional resources would be necessary in order to continue the advance to the north.

The Polish Armoured Division relieved 7 Armoured Division in Ghent on 12 September and then moved to Lokeren and St Nicolas and northwards across the Dutch frontier. On 19 September a bridgehead was forced across the Canal de Hulst and on the following day Hulst and Axel were occupied. By 22 September Terneuzen had been taken, and the enemy was now confined to the Breskens 'island', which was formed by the area between the Savojaards Plaat, the Leopold Canal and the sea. The line of the canal was held by 4 Canadian Armoured Division, while the Poles moved east to join 1 Corps.

On 17 September 2 Canadian Division investing Dunkirk was relieved by 4 SS Brigade and moved to the Antwerp area, in connection with the relief of 12 Corps. I then undertook the clearance of the dock areas immediately north of Antwerp, and

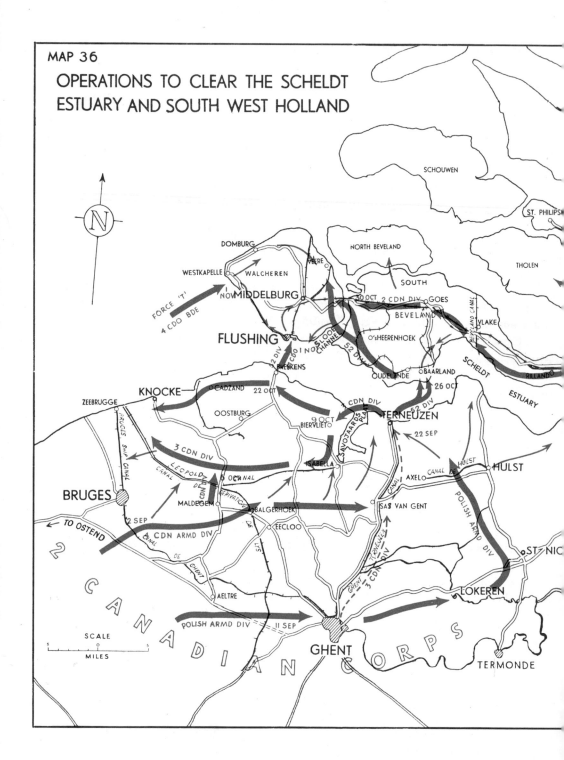

MAP 36

OPERATIONS TO CLEAR THE SCHELDT
ESTUARY AND SOUTH WEST HOLLAND

SCHOUWEN

ST. PHILIPS

DOMBURG

WESTKAPELLE
WALCHEREN
NOV

MIDDELBURG

NORTH BEVELAND

THOLEN

VEERE

SOUTH

30 OCT
2 CDN DIV
GOES

BEVELAND

FORCE 'T'
4 CDO BDE

FLUSHING

CDO I NOV

SLOOE
CHANNEL

2 DIV

BRESKENS

O'SHEERENHOEK

VLAKE

52 DIV

OUDELANDE

BAARLAND

SCHELDT

RILLAND

KNOCKE

CADZAND
22 OCT

ZEEBRUGGE

OOSTBURG

BRUGES SHIP CANAL

3 CDN DIV

CANAL

LEOPOLD

BIERVLIET

ISABELLA

9 OCT

CDN DIV

26 OCT

ESTUARY

TERNEUZEN

52 DIV

22 SEP

AXELO CANAL DE

HULST

HULST

SAVOJAARDS PLAT

BRUGES

LEOPOLD
CDN
DERIVATION

OCT CANAL

ST. NIC

BALGERHOEK

MALDEGEM

TO OSTEND

2 SEP

3 CDN ARMD DIV

EECLOO

SAS VAN GENT

POLISH ARMD DIV

CANAL DE GHENT

TERNEUZEN

3 CDN DIV

LOKEREN

2 CANADIAN CORPS

AELTRE

SCALE

POLISH ARMD DIV     II SEP

GHENT

MILES

TERMONDE

[330]

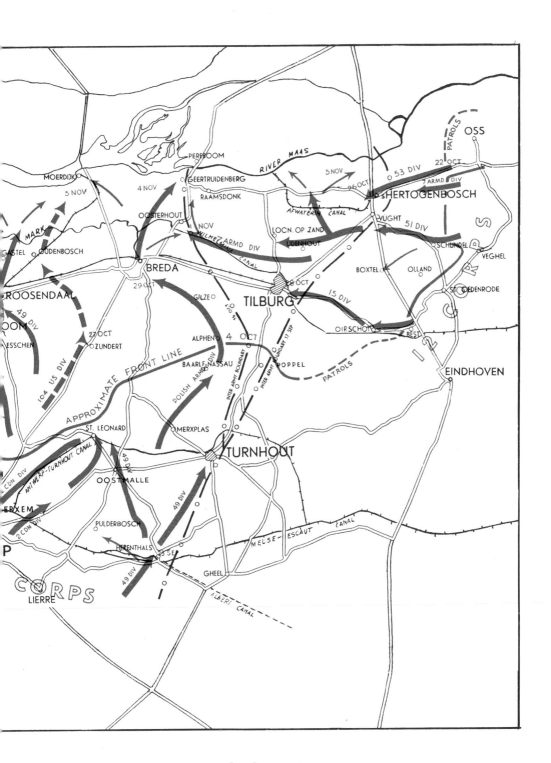

subsequently began to push north. On 22 and 23 September patrols from 1 Corps had reached Herenthals and Pulderbosch, and on the next day Turnhout was occupied and a small bridgehead gained over the Antwerp–Turnhout canal south of St Leonard. In the following days this bridgehead was extended in face of strong opposition, and leading troops of 2 Canadian Division were brought round through the bridgehead with the object of swinging west and advancing towards the River Scheldt and the South Beveland isthmus. On 29 September Polish Armoured Division was brought up on the right of 49 Division and directed on Tilburg; Merxplas was captured on 30 September.

While the operations for clearing the banks of the Scheldt were developing, Boulogne and Calais were stormed.

The garrison at Boulogne was estimated at about 9,000 men. The defences ran along an irregular semi-circle of high ground, and a number of the main features had been turned into strong points with concrete emplacements, minefields and other defensive works. The attack on the fortress was delayed by bad weather, and by the necessity to await the arrival of some of the special resources and medium artillery which were engaged in the Havre battle. During this waiting period some 8,000 civilians were evacuated from the town. The assault was launched on 17 September by two brigades of 3 Canadian Division supported by a great weight of artillery and air support. The battle for Boulogne lasted six days, chiefly because the hostile batteries and concrete strong points in many cases withstood our artillery and air action, and had to be reduced in turn by the ground troops. On 22 September the garrison commander surrendered and the total prisoners amounted to 9,535. It is interesting to record that during the Boulogne fighting guns on the South Foreland near Dover engaged enemy batteries near Calais, and on 17 September a direct hit was scored on an enemy battery at a range of 42,000 yards.

The attack on Calais began on 25 September. The defences were of the same pattern as those at Havre and Boulogne and the defenders were assisted by batteries at Cap Gris Nez and Sangatte. It was necessary to deliver the assault on the west side of the town, owing to extensive flooding in other sectors. Some delays were caused by mines and inundations but the citadel fell and the town was entered on 28 September, when an armistice was granted for the evacuation of civilians. The attack was resumed at midday on 30 September and by the evening all organized opposition had ceased. The total prisoners amounted to some 10,000.

Canadian Army was now free to concentrate all its energies on the clearance of the Scheldt. In my instructions of 27 September I ordered General Crerar to proceed with all possible speed.

The right flank of the Army was to be brought up on the axis Tilburg–'s Hertogenbosch in order to relieve Second Army of the defence of its long western flank. It was moreover important to push the enemy north of the Maas in order to establish a firm northern flank along the river as economically as possible.

Dunkirk continued to be invested and as Canadian Army pushed north the esponsibility for this commitment was reverted to Army Group. The Czech Armoured Brigade took charge of the investing forces.

### INITIAL STAGES OF CLEARING THE SCHELDT ESTUARY

The task of clearing the Scheldt estuary involved the capture of three distinct areas: he Breskens 'island', the peninsula of South Beveland, and the Island of Walcheren.

In the Breskens 'island' there were heavy enemy coastal batteries at Breskens and Cadzand covering the approaches to the estuary, while on Walcheren there were some twenty-five heavy batteries which could engage shipping in the Scheldt. The main strength of the enemy south of the estuary was provided by 64 Division, which included a high proportion of troops who had fought on the Russian front. The Walcheren garrison was from 70 Division, while in South Beveland there were elements of a divisional battle group, and between the isthmus and Turnhout we had identified 346, 711 and 719 Divisions.

The plan to clear the estuary was made in three main phases. First: the sealing off of South Beveland isthmus by a thrust from the Antwerp area together with the clearance of the Breskens 'island'. Second: the clearance of South Beveland by an advance along the isthmus in conjunction with a waterborne assault across the estuary from the south. Third: the capture of Walcheren by concentric assaults from the east, south and west, which entailed a second crossing of the estuary to seize Flushing and a sea-borne expedition from one of our Channel ports.

On 1 October 2 Canadian Division crossed the Antwerp–Turnhout Canal and thrust west towards the northern suburbs of Antwerp. Enemy resistance was spasmodic; by the evening of 4 October the Merxem–Eekeren area had been cleared and leading troops were within two miles of Putte, half-way to the isthmus. Steady progress continued, but as the Canadians closed on their objective the opposition stiffened considerably and initial attempts to secure Korteven were unsuccessful. The enemy launched some counter attacks, but on 16 October the village of Woensdrecht was captured.

Meanwhile, on the right wing of First Canadian Army, 1 Corps continued its advance from the general line of the Antwerp–Turnhout Canal. Polish Armoured Division crossed the Dutch frontier north of Merxplas on 1 October and 49 Division was at this time fighting north of St Leonard. By 5 October leading troops were about four miles south of Tilburg and on the left were in Alphen. These advances were followed in the next few days by a number of enemy counter attacks along the length of the Corps front, all of which were successfully held. In the third week of October 4 Canadian Armoured Division was switched from the Leopold Canal sector to join 1 Corps, and 104 United States Infantry Division also moved up into the sector. From 20 October steady progress was made to the north and, by the evening of 23 October, 4 Canadian Armoured Division had crossed the Dutch frontier near Esschen and was swinging in towards Bergen-op-Zoom. This manœuvre, combined with the gradual reduction of the enemy positions round Woensdrecht, sealed off the South Beveland isthmus and opened the way for our troops to advance into the peninsula.

In the Leopold Canal sector 3 Canadian Division planned to assault due north from Maldegem over the canal, while a brigade was to carry out an amphibious operation, landing in the north-east corner of the Breskens 'island'. The enemy positions on the north bank of the Leopold Canal were dug in on the reverse slope of the canal dyke and were therefore extremely difficult to neutralize with high explosive and small arms fire, and it was decided, after a series of experiments, to use flame throwers as a prelude to the attack. Early on the morning of 6 October the flame firing began and immediately it ceased attacking companies clambered over the dyke and launched their assault boats; on the right of the assault the canal was negotiated without undue difficulty, but severe losses were incurred on the left flank from machine gun fire. Nevertheless a footing was made on the far bank, and our troops held on during the day in spite of repeated counter attacks and heavy mortaring. On 7 October further reinforcements were with difficulty transferred to the north bank but still the bridgehead consisted only of a series of isolated detachments and it was clear that until the enemy pressure was reduced it would be impossible to construct Bailey bridges. It was in fact four days before bridging could be completed, and meanwhile the troops across the canal were maintained by assault boats, foot bridges and ferries. The enemy was now fighting desperately, and we subsequently learned that he sustained very heavy losses among his best fighting troops in trying to eliminate our Leopold Canal bridgeheads.

Meanwhile the amphibious operation got under way shortly after midnight on 8 October, and landed successfully some two hours later. Opposition was negligible and complete surprise was attained, but after daylight the Flushing battery and guns in the Biervliet area opened fire on the beaches and sea approaches and delayed vehicles already ashore from joining their units. By 0500 hours most of the Buffaloes used by the assault waves had turned round to collect the follow-up troops, who started to arrive on the beaches about 0900 hours. During the day enemy reaction stiffened, but the advance westwards continued along the coast while other detachments were pushed inland to the south-west. By nightfall the bridgehead was two to three miles deep. In view of the stiff nature of the fighting on the Leopold Canal, it was decided to reinforce the bridgehead with the primary task of swinging down along the western bank of the Savojaards Plaat and opening a land route into the island. This was effected by the evening of 14 October when an axis was opened through the village of Isabella.

52 Division was now arriving in the theatre and came under command of Canadian Army. It took over the Leopold Canal bridgehead. The increased weight of our attacks, together with extremely effective support from the air, now began to quicken the pace of operations, and on 22 October Breskens was captured and more than half the island was in our possession; clearance of the remaining area was left to 3 Canadian Division, while 52 Division began to prepare for the crossing of the Scheldt estuary.

SECOND ARMY OPERATIONS, 1–17 OCTOBER, AND THE DECISION
TO DIVERT ALL RESOURCES TO OPENING ANTWERP

While Second Army operations were continuing in the last days of September to widen and strengthen the salient to Nijmegen, I issued orders for preparations to commence for the battle of the Rhineland. I was examining the possibility of launching the operation about 10 October. I was hopeful that the plans to open Antwerp would proceed quickly and that continuance of Second Army's operations would loosen the enemy facing the Canadian Army. On the right flank, First United States Army took over up to the new boundary on the line Hasselt–Weert–Deurne–Maashees, and despatched 7 United States Armoured Division to tackle the enemy west of the Meuse.

In accordance with my instructions Second Army commenced regrouping in the first days of October.

On the western flank the Germans made some withdrawal as a result of our progress north of Turnhout, but the area 's Hertogenbosch–Schijndel–Olland–Boxtel–Tilburg remained firmly in enemy hands.

Meanwhile 7 United States Armoured Division started south from Overloon towards Venraij, but was unable to make much progress against the strong opposition.

*The Situation, 7 October*

At the end of the first week in October I had to inform the Supreme Commander that it was necessary to postpone the projected Rhineland attack, because my resources were not sufficient to enable me to continue with this plan in view of other more immediate commitments. The strength of enemy action against our Nijmegen bridgehead showed the necessity for a considerable reinforcement there to ensure its firm retention. Secondly, on the front of First Canadian Army there had been a very noticeable stiffening of enemy opposition, and our initial operations on the Leopold Canal indicated the enemy's determination to prevent us clearing the banks of the Scheldt. Thirdly, the efforts of 7 United States Armoured Division against the enemy bridgehead west of the Meuse gave indications of considerable strengthening in this sector. In spite of our withdrawal from the Arnhem bridgehead, the enemy feared a further thrust north-east across the Neder Rijn, directed either at invading Germany itself or at reaching the Zuider Zee and cutting off Fifteenth Army. Apart from his desire to deny us Antwerp for as long as possible, these considerations obliged him to reinforce his front opposite 21 Army Group as much as his strained resources permitted. By 7 October there were about twenty weak divisions, or battle groups of comparable size, including four Panzer divisions, around our front from Roermond to Breskens. Their lack of armour and mobility was offset by the nature of the country, and we had to fight for every water crossing.

Behind this line the remnants of the Panzer, SS and parachute divisions were hastily reforming, but they were kept ready for action in case of a sudden Allied break-through or further airborne landings.

Towards the middle of October, the Panzer divisions left 21 Army Group front to meet a more pressing threat from First United States Army, but infantry resistance remained as dogged as before.

I therefore ordered that the offensive between the Rhine and the Meuse would be postponed and that our immediate objects would be to open Antwerp, using First Canadian Army, and to undertake the clearance of the enemy bridgehead west of the Meuse by Second Army.

### Operations west of the Meuse, 12–17 October

The progress of the Canadian Army in the battle for the Scheldt has already been described. Meanwhile, in Second Army, 8 Corps was given the responsibility for launching a thrust from the Boxmeer area directed on Venraij; 7 United States Armoured Division was to co-operate in attacks eastwards from Deurne. After taking Venraij, the intention was to pass 11 Armoured Division through towards Venlo, while another thrust from the Weert area would be directed to the Maas in order to assault Roermond. The target date for this operation was 12 October.

8 Corps operation started as planned from the area north of Overloon; armour supporting the attack was held up by minefields, but the infantry succeeded in capturing Overloon by the evening. In the following days our troops slowly closed in on Venraij; the enemy fought doggedly in the thickly wooded country, and was greatly assisted by flooding and extensive use of mines and other obstacles. On 15 October it was decided to swing the main thrust to the right flank south-east of Rips, while 7 United States Armoured Division advanced along the general axis of the Deurne–Venraij road. Venraij was eventually occupied on 17 October.

### The Situation, mid-October

The Allied drive to the Rhine had now virtually come to a halt. We had won a great victory in Normandy and had advanced north of the Seine on a broad front. Great successes had been achieved, but we had nowhere been strong enough to secure decisive results quickly.

The opposition along the whole front was hardening. In the central sectors, First and Third United States Armies continued to fight hard along the Siegfried Line from the Aachen area through the Ardennes to the region of Trier and southwards in the sector of the upper Moselle. Further south, Sixth United States Army Group was deployed on the right of Twelfth United States Army Group and carried the area of operations down to the Swiss frontier.

The administrative situation was such that until Antwerp was opened the Allies would be unable to sustain further full-scale offensive operations, and, in view of the obvious difficulties we were going to have in dislodging the enemy from the Scheldt, we had clearly reached the stage when it was necessary to divert the entire resources of 21 Army Group to the task. On 16 October I issued orders shutting down all offensive operations in 21 Army Group except those concerned with the opening of the Scheldt

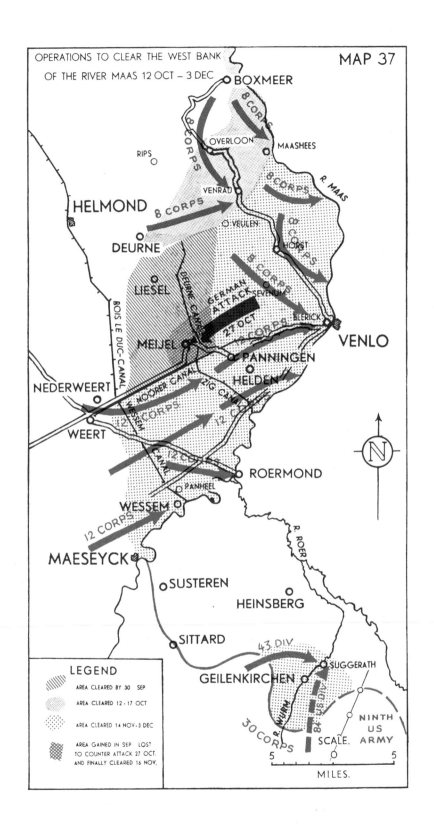

OPERATIONS TO CLEAR THE WEST BANK
OF THE RIVER MAAS 12 OCT – 3 DEC

MAP 37

BOXMEER

8 CORPS

RIPS

OVERLOON

MAASHEES

8 CORPS

VENRAD

R. MAAS

HELMOND

8 CORPS

VEULEN

DEURNE

8 CORPS

HORST

8 CORPS

LIESEL

GERMAN ATTACK 27 OCT

SEVENUM

BLERICK

DEURNE C. NZL

MEIJEL

VENLO

PANNINGEN

HELDEN

NEDERWEERT

NOORER CANAL

ZIG CANAL

12 CORPS

WESSEM CANAL

12 CORPS

WEERT

12 CORPS

ROERMOND

12 CORPS

PANHEEL

BOIS LE DUC CANAL

WESSEM

12 CORPS

N

MAESEYCK

SUSTEREN

HEINSBERG

R. ROER

SITTARD

43 DIV

SUGGERATH

GEILENKIRCHEN

R. WURM

43 DIV 18

NINTH
US
ARMY

30 CORPS

SCALE.

LEGEND

AREA CLEARED BY 30 SEP

AREA CLEARED 12 – 17 OCT

AREA CLEARED 14 NOV – 3 DEC

AREA GAINED IN SEP LOST
TO COUNTER ATTACK 27 OCT.
AND FINALLY CLEARED 16 NOV.

5            0            5

MILES.

estuary, and instructed Second Army to carry out immediate regrouping so as to bring its weight to bear on the west and to operate in conjunction with First Canadian Army.

My intention was for Second Army to thrust westwards initially towards 's Hertogenbosch and Tilburg, while Canadian Army transferred its weight further to the left. The inter-Army boundary was changed to give the road Turnhout–Tilburg to Second Army. The two incoming divisions (52 and 104 United States) had been allotted to Canadian Army to increase its resources.

Second Army planned to develop its maximum offensive power in a strong thrust on the general axis 's Hertogenbosch–Breda, with the right flank on the Maas. Its objective was the general line Moerdijk–Breda–Poppel. Meanwhile Canadian Army was to make every effort to accelerate its operations in South Beveland and against Walcheren, and with its right flank was to thrust northwards from the Antwerp–Turnhout Canal towards Breda–Roosendaal–Bergen-op-Zoom. I intended not only to clear up the Antwerp situation with all possible speed, but also to push the enemy back across the Maas in order to establish a firm and economical northern flank along the river. I hoped that, as Second Army operations developed, the enemy opposite Canadian Army would weaken in face of the threat to the main escape routes to the north.

As the weight of Second Army was switched into the 12 Corps sector on the west, 8 Corps operations in the Venraij area were brought to a halt.

COMPLETION OF THE CLEARANCE OF THE SCHELDT

For the sake of clarity I will now describe the operations of 2 Canadian Corps which were directly concerned with clearing the banks of the Scheldt, before dealing with other operations which were concurrently pushing the enemy north of the Maas.

It has already been seen that troops of 2 Canadian Corps captured Woernsdrecht at the approaches to the neck of the Beveland isthmus on 16 October; by 23 October the action of 4 Canadian Armoured Division, coming up on the right of 2 Canadian Corps, made it possible to swing troops into the isthmus with a secure flank to the north and north-east.

Early on 24 October 2 Canadian Division began its advance along the isthmus, but progress was inevitably very slow owing to the extremely difficult nature of the country. There were large areas of flooding, particularly at the approaches to the Beveland Canal, and existing roads were cratered and mined. The Canadians forced their way westwards, often waist deep in water, and by 25 October had reached a line running north and south through Rilland. On the following day they were only six miles short of the Beveland Canal. Meanwhile on the night 25/26 October a brigade of 52 Division sailed from Terneuzen, in Buffaloes and LCAs, to make an assault landing near Baarland. On the westernmost beach the troops got ashore without opposition, but on the east there was some shelling which caused casualties to craft; a squadron of DD tanks safely negotiated the Scheldt, but the mud flats and dykes prevented them from accompanying the infantry inland. In spite of counter attacks the bridgehead was extended to Oudelande and beyond.

On 27 and 28 October while operations from the bridgehead continued, leading troops of 2 Canadian Division reached the Beveland Canal and found the bridges blown, but during the night 27/28 October a crossing was forced, and by noon the following day a Class 9 Bridge was opened near Vlake. By this time 4 Canadian Armoured Division had captured Bergen-op-Zoom, thus strengthening the base of the 2 Canadian Division operation.

The clearance of South Beveland continued rapidly in spite of all difficulties and on 30 October the east end of the causeway carrying the road and railway across to Walcheren Island was reached. South Beveland was now clear of the enemy, and, in order to avoid any possibility of the enemy holding out in North Beveland, a column was despatched to clear that island.

Meanwhile operations in the Breskens 'island' had continued successfully and, by the evening of 1 November, Cadzand and Knocke were in our hands and it remained only to clear the area between the Leopold Canal and Zeebrugge. Early on 3 November the last enemy pockets were eliminated and the whole of the southern bank of the Scheldt Estuary was in our hands. In four weeks' fighting, which was as fierce as any we had yet experienced in north-west Europe, First Canadian Army had taken 12,500 prisoners and accounted for many enemy dead and wounded.

It now remained to clear the island of Walcheren.

The defences of this island were primarily sited to cover the entrance to the West Scheldt and to prevent a seaborne landing on the west side of the island. There was a number of heavy coastal batteries, many of them housed in concrete emplacements, while on the west and south the defences included under-water obstacles and extensive wiring and mining of the beaches and beach exits. Flushing had a perimeter defence system with a double line of anti-tank ditches.

The strength of the island garrison was estimated at between 6,000 and 7,000 men and it was clear that its reduction presented an extremely difficult problem. The nature of the terrain, which was closely intersected by dykes and steep banks, did not offer scope for an airborne landing and it was eventually decided that the most effective way to capture the place quickly would be to 'sink' it: by breaching the sea dykes which ran round its circumference. If the dykes could be broken, it was believed that many of the enemy artillery positions would be rendered untenable and the movement of enemy troops would be restricted; moreover, if the breach were large enough, assaulting forces could be launched into the island in their own amphibious craft and would thus be able to take the defences in rear.

Early in October Bomber Command carried out an operation of truly magnificent accuracy, as a result of which the sea dykes were breached at four points on the island. The gaps were improved by further attacks during the month and the island was gradually flooded so that at the end of October it resembled a saucer filled with water. The most important gap was 380 yards wide in the dyke near Westkapelle. The precision and weight of the Royal Air Force operation may be gauged from the fact that at Westkapelle the dyke was 330 feet wide at its base and about 30 feet high above the low water mark.

It was planned to make two seaborne landings on Walcheren by troops conveyed and supported by Force 'T' of the Royal Navy; one force was to move from Breskens to secure Flushing, while the second, mounted from Ostend, was to assault the West-kapelle area, passing into the island through the breach in the dyke. The latter force was subsequently to operate along the dunes in order to link up with the Flushing attack, and was also to send detachments northwards along the coast. In conjunction with the seaborne assaults an attack was to be made across the South Beveland causeway.

Operations began on 1 November. Early in the morning Commando troops landed near Flushing and reached the water front without heavy casualties. They were followed by troops of 52 Division, and the attack was developed into the town. Mean-while the Westkapelle force approached the coast supported by naval units; it had been planned to provide heavy air attacks as a preliminary to the assault, but weather over the home airfields limited the air effort to Continental-based units, which pressed home a determined attack just as the assault troops were about to land, and had a profound effect on the operation at a time when the support craft were suffering heavy casualties.

The Naval support programme included action by a bombardment squadron, consisting of HM Ships Warspite, Roberts and Erebus, and by various types of support craft. The latter closed in to the coast and engaged enemy batteries at point blank range and were mainly responsible for the assault troops reaching the beaches with comparatively few losses; the support craft themselves, however, suffered severely in the process.

On the east of the breach a Commando quickly secured the major strong points and by evening had advanced two miles in the direction of Flushing, while on the left another Commando negotiated the gap in the dyke, dismounted, and captured West-kapelle. Later in the day the advance was continued towards Domburg.

Meanwhile on the causeway, the Canadians made some minor initial progress but were subsequently forced back.

On 2 November Flushing was captured after hard fighting, and on the following day a link up was made with the Westkapelle force, which had reduced the enemy batteries along the dunes, and had already reached Domburg in the north. On the causeway, 52 Division took over from 2 Canadian Division, and hard fighting con-tinued. Eventually an assault crossing was made over the Slooe Channel, about two miles south of the causeway, and a bridgehead secured which was eventually linked with the causeway itself.

From 3 November the reduction of Walcheren became a problem of mopping up many enemy parties marooned in the island, a process which was completed by 8 November. The total number of prisoners taken was about 8,000.

Meanwhile one of the most intricate minesweeping operations of the war had been put in hand. On 4 November the first minesweeper ships reached Antwerp and in the next three weeks one hundred craft were employed clearing the seventy-mile channel, which had to be swept sixteen times. On 28 November the first convoy was safely berthed at Antwerp and the port was opened for the maintenance of both American and British Armies.

It was now possible to commence full stocking of the Advance Base in Belgium. Up to this time the depots were fed with commodities brought in by road and rail from the Channel ports and from the Rear Maintenance Area in Normandy.

There were between 300,000 and 400,000 tons of stocks in the Rear Maintenance Area alone, and 100,000 personnel were employed there. It was decided that once Antwerp was opened, the Rear Maintenance Area should begin closing down, leaving the commodities no longer required by us to be handed over to the War Office for disposal.

The opening of Antwerp also enabled us to close some of the Channel ports and thus release key personnel and transportation resources for the establishment of the Advance Base in Belgium. It was planned that Antwerp could accept 40,000 tons per day exclusive of petrol, oil and lubricants; of this total 22,500 tons were allotted to the American forces. There was ample capacity for bulk petrol and the installations were shared by the Americans and ourselves.

The only anxiety at Antwerp was due to the 'V' bomb and rocket attacks which were soon developed by the enemy. Great credit is due to the excellence of the American and British anti-aircraft units which accounted for an exceptionally high percentage of the V1 projectiles, and to the military personnel and Belgian civilians who worked under the strain of the continual attacks.

### CLEARING SOUTH-WEST HOLLAND
### TO THE LINE OF THE RIVER MAAS

As already explained, while Canadian Army was clearing the banks of the Scheldt, 1 Corps on its right wing, together with 12 Corps of Second Army, were engaged in clearing south-west Holland up to the River Maas; at the same time 1 Corps was protecting the right flank of 2 Canadian Corps operating in Beveland and Walcheren.

1 Corps advanced on 20 October with Polish Armoured Division on the right, 49 Division in the centre and 4 Canadian Armoured Division on the left. The right and centre were directed to the general line exclusive Tilburg–Breda–Roosendaal, while 4 Canadian Armoured Division advanced on Bergen-op-Zoom.

On 22 October 12 Corps launched its attack west of the general line Oss–Veghel–St Oedenrode–Best, directed initially on 's Hertogenbosch and Tilburg. The three enemy divisions on the front were reinforced by 256 Division the day before our attack started. 12 Corps plan was to advance to 's Hertogenbosch with 7 Armoured and 53 Divisions, which were to be followed up by 51 Division; on the left, 15 Division was to clear the area to the south and capture Tilburg.

Operations were impeded by widespread minefields, but there was very little enemy artillery fire; 51 Division reached the vicinity of Schijndel on the morning of 23 October and the following day 53 Division was in the outskirts of 's Hertogenbosch. The main road to Eindhoven was cut and Boxtel was captured, but the enemy held out in some strength covering Vught. Meanwhile, 15 Division made good progress through Oirschot.

On 1 Corps sector, 104 United States Infantry Division came into the line in the centre, between the Poles and 49 Division. The advance continued steadily and by 27 October the Poles had occupied Gilze and cut the Tilburg–Breda road. On their left the Americans repulsed a sharp counter attack from Zundert on 26 October and captured the town the following day. At the same time 49 Division was two miles south of Roosendaal, and 4 Canadian Armoured Division occupied Bergen-op-Zoom. In the last days of October 12 Corps was through 's Hertogenbosch and across the canal west of it, had captured Vught and moved on towards Loon-op-Zand, and Udenhout had been occupied. 15 Division completed clearing Tilburg on 28 October.

It is now necessary to turn to the enemy salient west of the River Meuse.

With the object of unbalancing us and relieving the pressure in the western sectors, the enemy launched a spoiling attack on 27 October against 8 Corps. The Germans employed 15 Panzer Grenadier and 9 Panzer Divisions to help the parachute formation already in the sector, and thrust across the Noorer Canal at Nederweert and over the Deurne Canal between Meijel and Liesel. The main weight of the attack fell on 7 United States Armoured Division; the enemy made some progress and captured Meijel and subsequently reached an area two or three miles further west along the road towards Helmond. To seal off this penetration, 15 Division, which had now completed its Tilburg operation, was transferred to the sector together with a tank brigade. 51 Division followed, as it also became pinched out on the 12 Corps front. By 30 October the position had been stabilized.

The final stages of the 1 and 12 Corps operations were soon completed. 7 Armoured Division struck west towards Oosterhout and made contact with the Poles thrusting from the south on 30 October. Patrols pushed north to Geertruidenberg. The following day hard fighting took place in Raamsdonk, where the enemy was making a stand in order to cover the Pereboom bridge as long as possible. By 1 November, 12 Corps task was completed except for the clearance of the area between Afwaterings Canal and the Maas; 51 Division carried out this task by 5 November.

Meanwhile 1 Corps advanced quickly across the Tilburg–Bergen-op-Zoom road. On 29 October Breda fell, and the Americans reached Oudenbosch on the following day. 49 Division cleared Roosendaal and 4 Canadian Armoured Division, after overcoming some stubborn resistance north of Bergen-op-Zoom, was about one mile south of Steenbergen. The enemy's attempt to form a last line south of the Maas was along the River Mark, across which 1 Corps established crossings on a wide front, despite enemy counter attacks designed to cover his troops withdrawing across the Moerdijk bridges. Geertruidenberg was taken on 4 November by the Poles, and within four days the enemy had been cleared from the last pocket south of the Maas. Tholen and the St Philipsland peninsula were reported clear and patrols visited Schouwen.

The enemy's withdrawal from south-west Holland had been very greatly facilitated by the adverse flying weather. Under cover of mist and low clouds he had escaped the inevitably heavy punishment which, in more favourable conditions, our Air Forces would have given him. The total prisoners taken in this phase of the operation were about 8,000.

# CHAPTER FOURTEEN

# Preparations for the Battle of the Rhineland. The Clearance of the West Bank of the River Meuse

## DISCUSSIONS ON THE DEVELOPMENT OF ALLIED PLANS

*The Brussels Conference, 18 October*

WHILE the battles of the Scheldt and south-west Holland were progressing, discussions continued concerning the development of Allied plans. On 18 October the Supreme Commander held a conference in Brussels with General Bradley and myself. We discussed the situation on the Allied front and plans for the future. My opinion was that the situation bore a close resemblance to that existing in Normandy before we broke out of the bridgehead. It seemed to me that the decisive battle for Germany might well be fought west of the Rhine, just as the battle for France was fought south of the Seine; since, however, the Germans obviously were determined to hold us back from the Ruhr with all the means at their disposal, the battle of the Rhineland would not be won easily. We would require to deploy great strength in order to ensure its success.

As I saw our problems, the Ruhr remained the objective of highest value. Having defeated the enemy in the northern sector and having seized this vital industrial region, it remained in the spring to develop mobile warfare into the heart of Germany across the North German plains.

The main conclusions reached at the conference were that 21 Army Group should continue its operations to open the port of Antwerp as quickly as possible, and should subsequently launch an attack south-eastwards from the Nijmegen bridgehead towards Krefeld. Meanwhile First United States Army was to advance to the Rhine about Cologne and gain a bridgehead over the river, starting early in November. Ninth United States Army, which was now operational, was to operate on the left flank of First United States Army during the advance to the Rhine, and subsequently attack northwards between the Rhine and the Meuse, in order to meet the Second Army offensive driving southwards; during the latter stage Ninth United States Army was to pass to command of 21 Army Group. It was further decided that Twelfth United States Army Group would be responsible for commanding the operations to capture the Ruhr, and that 21 Army Group would examine the possibility of thrusting northwards over the Neder Rijn towards the Zuider Zee.

It was thus agreed that the battle of the Rhineland should consist of two converging offensives: one from the Nijmegen bridgehead southwards, the other from the left flank of Twelfth United States Army Group northwards. The basic essential now was to deliver these thrusts in overwhelming strength in order to write off the German forces in the northern sector of the Rhineland and to burst across the Rhine north of the Ruhr.

## *The Situation, 31 October*

In the last days of October it became apparent that the Allies were not in a position to implement the plan of 18 October as speedily as had been hoped.

The situation in the 21 Army Group sector showed that the opening of the Scheldt was now in sight, and that in a short time we should have our northern flank established along the line of the lower Maas. On the other hand, with the object of diverting us from the western sector, it has been seen that the enemy launched an attack in some strength on our eastern flank. It was evident that the Germans were quite determined to hold on to their bridgehead west of the Meuse so that it would constitute an embarrassment to our Nijmegen salient. As long as this threat remained in strength it was clearly unsound to launch Second Army into the battle of the Rhineland.

If the American thrust to Cologne developed quickly and in great strength, I had hopes that it would draw off the enemy from his Meuse bridgehead. On 31 October General Bradley and I discussed the situation; he told me that owing to his 250-mile front, and requirements for offensive operations against the Saar, the number of divisions available for the First United States Army thrust to Cologne was not as great as might have been hoped. From this I deduced that the operation might not result in the desired thinning out of the enemy west of the Meuse, and that therefore operations on a considerable scale might have to be undertaken in order to push the enemy east of that river.

The prerequisites for launching the battle of the Rhineland were now the elimination of the enemy bridgehead west of the Meuse and the release of Ninth United States Army for the offensive from the south. The latter was dependent upon the completion of the Twelfth United States Army Group attack on Cologne, and it was therefore logical that 21 Army Group should do all in its power to assist this American offensive and at the same time undertake the clearance of the west bank of the Meuse.

Revised plans were agreed by the Supreme Commander on 1 November. Having completed operations on the western flank, 21 Army Group was to regroup and line up along the River Meuse, and was to extend its flank to the south in order to take over additional territory from the Americans; at the same time the American divisions serving in the British sectors were to be returned to Twelfth Army Group. As far as resources permitted we were to develop offensive operations on the immediate flank of Twelfth Army Group in order to assist directly its operations towards the Rhine.

I issued orders on 2 November to give effect to these decisions. As soon as the Scheldt and south-west Holland operations were completed, First Canadian Army was to take over our northern sector as far east as Middelaar, which included assuming responsibility for the Nijmegen bridgehead. Second Army was to line up facing east for the drive to the line of the Meuse, and the target date for the commencement of these operations was 12 November. By 15 November I intended to extend our flank to the south as far as Geilenkirchen exclusive. Second Army would then undertake offensive operations in conformity with Ninth United States Army. 82 and 101 United States Airborne Divisions, together with the American 7 Armoured and 104 Infantry Divisions, were to be returned to Twelfth Army Group as soon as possible.

General Dempsey planned to face the Meuse with 8 Corps in the north, 12 Corps in the centre and 30 Corps in the south. On 9 November 2 Canadian Corps relieved 30 Corps in the Nijmegen bridgehead; the latter moved south and as it came into position took over the left sector of Ninth American Army as far as the River Wurm, south of Geilenkirchen. At the opposite end of the Army Group front, 1 Corps was made responsible for the line of the Maas from about Oss to the sea and as far west as Walcheren.

I provided in my instructions that when the time came, First Canadian Army would be responsible for launching the northern offensive of the battle of the Rhineland, and intended that subsequently Second Army would undertake the forcing of the Rhine.

### PREPARATIONS FOR THE BATTLE OF THE RHINELAND

I refer to Second Army operations for the elimination of the enemy bridgehead west of the Meuse as the 'Preparations for the Battle of the Rhineland'.

Our front ran roughly along the Wessem Canal from about ten miles north of Maeseyck, across the front of Weert, and then followed the Noorer Canal to the enemy salient round Meijel. The line then joined the Deurne Canal north of Meijel and later swung north-east to Veulen, Venraij and Maashees. The enemy territory was completely flat and largely waterlogged, and the only three roads of any consequence converged on Venlo. We had to expend very considerable engineer resources in order to establish communications capable of carrying military traffic in the area.

The Second Army plan provided for operations by 8 Corps in the north, including the occupation of Meijel, while 12 Corps advanced from the line of the Wessem Canal on Venlo, with its right flank on the River Maas and its left on the Noorer Canal.

12 Corps started on 14 November, when troops of 53 and 51 Divisions secured bridgeheads across both the Wessem and Noorer Canals, while 7 Armoured Division secured the locks at Panheel, giving us control of the canal waters. The enemy was not particularly strong on the ground, but had sown very extensive minefields in order to delay the advance, and the extremely difficult muddy country, coupled with unusually bad weather, precluded rapid progress. On 16 November patrols reached the next major water obstacle, the Zig Canal, with main bodies a few miles behind; this manœuvre closely threatened the enemy positions about Meijel and on the same day the town was occupied by troops of 8 Corps. On the right flank, troops closed on the perimeter defences of Roermond and cleared the villages on the left bank of the Meuse.

Once across the Zig Canal, Panningen was soon occupied. 8 Corps made a successful crossing of the Deurne Canal and thrust towards Sevenum, while other columns attacked south from the Venraij area. On 22 November both Sevenum and Horst were captured, and by the same date our troops had completed the clearance of the west bank of the river opposite Roermond.

At the end of the month the last enemy position west of the river in 8 and 12 Corps sectors was at Blerick. On 3 December a set piece attack was delivered against the strongly developed defences of this place. Flail tanks cut lanes through the wire protecting the anti-tank ditches across which assault bridges were launched. The lanes were then developed through the minefields while infantry followed up closely in Kangaroos. Once within the defences the infantry dismounted and quickly over-whelmed the enemy garrison. By nightfall the place had been cleared.

### SECOND ARMY OPERATIONS IN THE GEILENKIRCHEN SECTOR
### 18–24 November

30 Corps held the front between the River Wurm and the River Meuse, with 43 Division on the right and Guards Armoured Division on the left; on the immediate right of the Corps was 84 United States Infantry Division.

In conjunction with Ninth United States Army operations on the northern flank of the main American thrust to Cologne, it was arranged that 30 Corps should deliver an attack in the Geilenkirchen sector. 84 United States Division came under operational command of 30 Corps for this purpose, and on 18 November attacks were launched with the intention of capturing Geilenkirchen and working north along the valley of the Wurm.

Geilenkirchen itself was enveloped and captured, but after a few days further progress was halted. Heavy rain made the ground almost impassable to both tanks and wheeled vehicles. Our advance was running along, not through, the Siegfried Line and the reduction of its defences, though not difficult, was laborious; moreover, the enemy made strong counter attacks with two fresh divisions, 15 Panzer Grenadier and 10 SS, which were rushed to the sector. 30 Corps, therefore, reverted to the defensive, and 84 United States Division returned to command of Ninth United States Army on the night 23/24 November.

### UNITED STATES ARMY OPERATIONS DURING NOVEMBER 1944

After a series of postponements due to the exceptionally bad weather, Twelfth Army Group attack on the general axis Aachen–Cologne began on 16 November. After some extremely hard fighting in which both sides lost heavily, the American attacks were halted on positions overlooking the Roer valley. Progress was costly and hindered by the same difficulties which had beset 30 Corps further north; the weather was extremely bad, the ground was often impassable and the enemy produced considerable reinforcements. During the period 16 November–1 December no less than eleven infantry and five Panzer divisions were committed on the Roer valley front. In addition, in reserve between the Roer and the Rhine, the enemy had now formed up Sixth SS Panzer Army in an arc covering Cologne, and was considerably assisted by the floods in the Roer valley and his ability to control the flow of water from the system of dams higher up the river. General Bradley therefore decided that operations to force a crossing of the River Roer were impracticable until the dams were in his possession.

Further south, Third United States Army commenced its offensive towards the Saar on 8 November, and by the end of the month had captured the formidable defences of Metz and reached the line of the River Moselle. In the extreme south Sixth United States Army Group had advanced into Alsace-Lorraine. Seventh United States Army had captured Strasbourg and turned north towards Karlsruhe, while First French Army reached the Rhine between the Swiss frontier and Mulhouse. The enemy continued to hold a substantial bridgehead west of the Rhine in the Colmar area.


### REVIEW OF THE SITUATION IN EARLY DECEMBER

The weather throughout November had been exceptionally bad; not only had operations of the Allied Air Forces been considerably restricted, but progress on land in the flat waterlogged country had been extremely difficult. On 2 December the enemy breached the southern bank of the Neder Rijn west of Arnhem and inundated part of our bridgehead; the low lying ground to the south of Arnhem was quickly flooded as far as the railway running west from Elst, and Canadian Army was forced to withdraw to this line. Fortunately we retained a bridgehead adequate to cover the Waal bridges, but the possibility of attacking north to secure the high ground between Arnhem and Apeldoorn was now out of the question.

On the Allied front north of the Ardennes we were now 'tidy' along the line of the Rivers Roer and Meuse except for an enemy salient in the Heinsberg area, and virtually the only commitment remaining as a preliminary to major operations between the Rhine and the Meuse was the elimination of this pocket. I ordered Second Army to carry out the clearance of the Heinsberg area in early December, but eventually operations had to be postponed owing to the complete saturation of the countryside. Meanwhile 21 Army Group commenced regrouping for the Rhineland battle, and it was arranged that Ninth American Army would accept the commitment of the Heinsberg salient, receiving 7 British Armoured Division under command. This enabled me to speed up the regrouping, since I required Headquarters 30 Corps for the assault against the Reichswald Forest. While the Americans took over the right sector of 30 Corps, the balance of its commitments was transferred to 12 Corps and the plan was drawn up for concentrating Headquarters 30 Corps, Guards Armoured, 15, 43 and 53 Divisions, together with associated armoured brigades, in the Nijmegen bridgehead; the target date for the thrust towards Krefeld was 12 January, and by 16 December advance parties were on the move to their concentration areas in the north. While Canadian Army was preparing for this new thrust, Second Army under-took the study of the Rhine crossing and placed in hand the development of east–west routes up to the Meuse, which would later be developed across the Rhineland.

This was the situation when, on 16 December, the enemy launched his counter offensive in the Ardennes sector.

# CHAPTER FIFTEEN

# The Battle of the Ardennes

## THE ENEMY SITUATION, DECEMBER 1944

FOLLOWING the battle of Normandy the enemy was faced with two main problems: the re-formation of a front and the prevention of the Allied invasion of Germany.

During October and November the second preoccupation remained and accounted for the very bitter resistance to the American offensive in the Roer valley. The enemy also realized that the creation of an armoured strategic reserve was essential, because the rate of destruction of his resources in the winter battles, if allowed to continue, would result in the complete exhaustion of his armies by the spring, so that the Allies would be able to cross the Rhine and invade Germany with ease.

Benefiting from the autumn and winter weather which slowed down the pace of operations, the enemy began to refit his strategic reserve. Allied pressure, or the threat of it, first by 21 Army Group at Arnhem in September and October, and later by the Americans at Aachen in November and December, forced him to keep more than half of his total fifteen Panzer divisions in the west almost permanently engaged in battle. He did, however, manage to refit eight of them by December, including the bulk of the SS; these divisions were re-equipped to the scale of about one hundred tanks each, comprising the latest types of Panther and Tiger.

It will be remembered that late in August the enemy's armies fleeing north-east were rated at about the equivalent of twenty-three divisions; by mid-December the Germans had managed not only to re-form the front and limit the invasion of Germany to minor areas, but also to increase his field force to some seventy divisions. Even assuming that Allied operations continued with intensity throughout the winter, it was estimated that this force would increase to ninety divisions by 1 March.

## THE BATTLE OF THE ARDENNES

Such was the German military situation on the western front when for the second time during the campaign a reserve was to be pledged in a major gamble. Hitler himself ordered that his western armies were to be formed up for a last desperate attack, which was to surprise the Allies, cross the Meuse, and drive to Antwerp.

The operation was planned with great care and skill. A quiet, thinly held sector was selected for the attack and the concentration of troops, artillery and armour was carried out with a high degree of secrecy and concealment; the enemy was greatly assisted by the extremely bad weather which hindered satisfactory air reconnaissance.

The enemy plan was for Army Group 'B' to attack between Monschau and

Echternach with Sixth SS Panzer Army on the right and Fifth Panzer Army on the left, each including four Panzer divisions. They were to secure crossings over the Meuse between Liège and Givet, dropping off infantry divisions to picquet the flanks. No less than seventeen infantry, parachute and Panzer Grenadier divisions were to be committed behind the Panzer and SS spearheads.

Tactically the offensive, which began on 16 December, achieved complete surprise. It commenced with a heavy artillery barrage (the only one on such a scale fired by the Germans in the whole campaign) and the dropping of parties of parachutists along the projected route of advance. In addition, parties of saboteurs in civilian clothes and Allied uniforms infiltrated in jeeps in order to try and spread confusion behind the Allied lines.

By 18 December the enemy thrust had overrun 28 and 106 American Divisions and penetrated twenty miles to reach Stavelot and the road centres of Trois Ponts and Vielsalm, and there were indications of further attacks coming in north of Monschau directed on Eupen and Verviers. I learnt that the Supreme Commander had ordered the suspension of offensive action in the southern sectors, and had instructed Seventh Army to side-step to the north in order to release Third Army for counter attacks against the southern flank of the enemy penetration.

I was forced to consider the possible effects of the enemy's thrust upon the dispositions of 21 Army Group, for it has been seen that we were starting the process of transferring the bulk of our weight to the extreme northern flank. I therefore ordered the concentration for the Rhineland battle to stop and had plans prepared for switching British divisions from the Geilenkirchen sector to the west of the Meuse in case of any threat to our southern flank. I subsequently ordered the move of Guards Armoured and 43 Divisions from the area south-east of Maeseyck to the west, and moved 53 Division from Roermond to Turnhout. On 19 December I definitely abandoned the move of 30 Corps to the Canadian Army sector and ordered it to assemble in the general area Louvain–St Trond. This Corps was placed in command of Guards Armoured, 43, 51 and 53 Divisions together with three armoured brigades. The situation remained unpleasantly vague and I undertook emergency measures to get reconnaissance troops down to the line of the Meuse and to assist in forming effective cover parties for the Meuse bridges between Liège and Givet. Detachments of SAS troops and Tank Replacement Centre personnel were sent to the river in the Namur–Givet sector, while armoured cars of Second Army established patrol links between Liège and Namur. 29 Armoured Brigade, which was then re-equipping in western Belgium, was ordered to pick up the tanks it had recently discarded and concentrate by forced marches in the Namur area.

During 19 December enemy armour penetrated as far as Hotton, Marche and Laroche, and the gap in the Allied line appeared to extend from Durbuy to Bastogne. I could see little to prevent German armoured cars and reconnaissance elements bouncing the Meuse and advancing on Brussels; during the night, therefore, hastily formed road block detachments were posted round the capital. As 30 Corps moved with

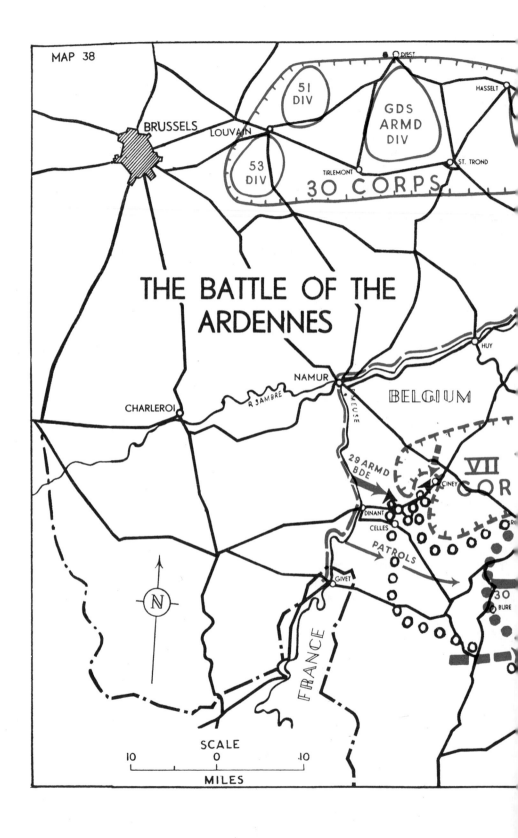

MAP 38

51 DIV

GDS ARMD DIV

HASSELT

BRUSSELS

LOUVAIN

TIRLEMONT

ST. TROND

53 DIV

30 CORPS

THE BATTLE OF THE
ARDENNES

HUY

NAMUR

BELGIUM

CHARLEROI

R. SAMBRE

MEUSE

29 ARMD BDE

CINEY

VII COR

DINANT

CELLES

PATROLS

GIVET

N

FRANCE

30

BURE

SCALE

10      0      10

MILES

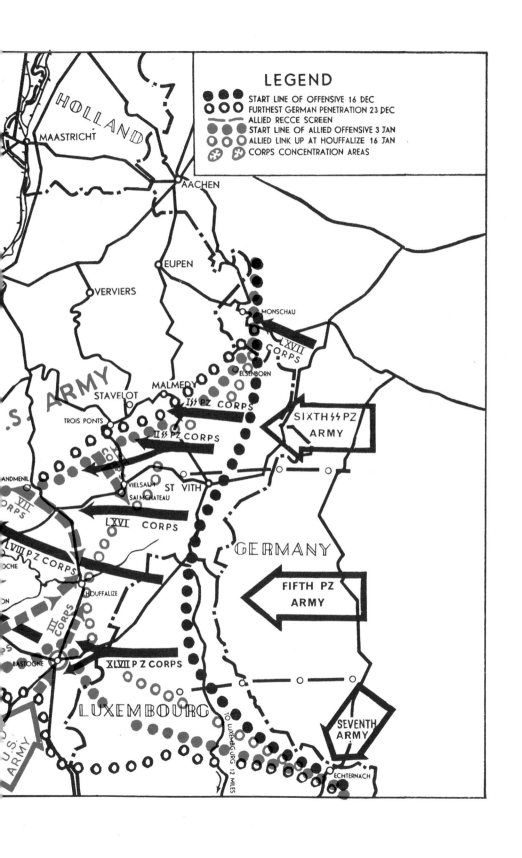

**LEGEND**

●●● START LINE OF OFFENSIVE 16 DEC
○○○ FURTHEST GERMAN PENETRATION 23 DEC
⌇⌇⌇ ALLIED RECCE SCREEN
◐◐◐ START LINE OF ALLIED OFFENSIVE 3 JAN
◐◐◐ ALLIED LINK UP AT HOUFFALIZE 16 JAN
⊛⊛ CORPS CONCENTRATION AREAS

HOLLAND

MAASTRICHT

AACHEN

EUPEN

VERVIERS

MONSCHAU

LXVII CORPS

U.S. ARMY

STAVELOT

MALMEDY

ELSENBORN

I SS PZ CORPS

TROIS PONTS

II SS PZ CORPS

SIXTH SS PZ ARMY

ANDMENIL

VIELSALM

ST VITH

SALMCHATEAU

VII CORPS

LXVI CORPS

GERMANY

LVIII PZ CORPS

ROCHE

HOUFFALIZE

FIFTH PZ ARMY

III CORPS

ON

BASTOGNE

XLVII PZ CORPS

LUXEMBOURG

TO LUXEMBOURG 12 MILES

SEVENTH ARMY

U.S. ARMY

ECHTERNACH

all possible speed into its new concentration area, and our detachments were assisting in the establishment of bridge guards between Liège and Givet, the enemy's opportunity of rushing the river diminished; once 30 Corps was in position we should be able to intervene, if required, in throwing back any hostile bridgeheads established over the Meuse.

Meanwhile, on the night of 19 December, General Eisenhower instructed me to take command on the following day of the American Armies (First and Ninth) north of the German salient; the depth of the enemy penetration had put these formations remote from the Twelfth United States Army Group axis and made their control by that Headquarters extremely difficult. I at once visited General Simpson (Ninth Army) and General Hodges (First Army). Clearly the first problem before us was to halt the enemy advance and oppose it with a firm front in conjunction with Twelfth Army Group to the south; this demanded certain regrouping, behind which we had 30 Corps ready to hold the line of the Meuse. The next process was to create a reserve corps in First United States Army available for offensive operations, and I decided to assemble VII American Corps under General Collins on the right flank of First Army with four divisions. Since these formations would have to be withdrawn from the battle, the process was obviously going to take a little time. The question arose of the possibility of employing British divisions south and east of the Meuse; this was a very difficult matter, because their administrative axes would run directly across the maintenance routes of both First and Ninth United States Armies, and it would therefore be extremely difficult to avoid congestion.

On 20 December the Supreme Commander instructed Sixth United States Army Group to extend its front to the north as far as Saarlautern and to remain on the defensive. Twelfth Army Group was to concentrate in the area Luxembourg–Bastogne in order to counter attack against the southern flank of von Rundstedt's salient, while the Armies under my command were to launch as soon as practicable a thrust against the northern shoulder of the salient.

American detachments holding out south-east of Vielsalm were drawn into reserve west of the town, and the assembly area selected for VII American Corps was north-west of Marche.

Meanwhile the German attacks continued with unabated fury, but almost from the outset the enemy plan miscarried, though the threat remained formidable. Sixth SS Panzer Army was attempting to breach the American line in the Malmedy–Stavelot sector using I SS Corps; it was then intended to push this formation through to Liège or to bring 2 SS Corps through the breach for the purpose. For a whole week I SS Corps spent itself in fruitless attempts to make a hole; finally, the frontal attack having failed on 22 December, 2 SS Corps was swung west to try and break through to Liège from the south via Durbuy. Meanwhile Fifth Panzer Army was heading west and north-west for the Meuse, by-passing Bastogne on the way. Although on 19 December there was still no strong Allied formation between Fifth Panzer Army and the Meuse, the German advance was too slow, for they should have seized crossing places over the

[354]

river at once. When they tried to do so later their dispersed spearheads were too weak, and were either cut off and destroyed or forced to regroup for properly organized attacks. A vital contribution to this slowing down of the enemy advance was the dogged resistance by isolated American groups at main nodal points, particularly St Vith and Bastogne, which severely congested enemy traffic by forcing it into lengthy detours and caused very considerable diversion of enemy resources.

As 2 SS Corps began to feel to the west in order to outflank First Army in the Hotton–Marche area, it began to come in contact with VII United States Corps forming up in its new area. The divisions of this Corps, intended as reserves, thus became engaged in the battle. Still further west the Germans came in contact with 29 British Armoured Brigade covering the Namur–Dinant sector. On 23 December enemy tanks were reported only twelve miles east of Dinant, and during the following two days armoured engagements in the general sector of Ciney took place between enemy spearheads and 2 United States Armoured Division and 29 British Armoured Brigade. The latter Allied formations made contact on 25 December in the area of Celles, where fighting took place only four miles from the river and considerable casualties were inflicted on the enemy.

By Christmas the enemy offensive had been sealed off within the general line Elsenhorn–Malmedy–Hotton–Marche–St Hubert–Bastogne, and all routes to the Meuse were blocked.

In the south, Third United States Army attacked towards Bastogne, where American troops, although surrounded, made a magnificent stand against tremendous enemy odds; General Patton's forces eventually relieved Bastogne on 26 December.

A factor of vital importance to the Allies was that a period of good weather commenced about 24 December and the great weight of the Allied Air Forces was deployed in checking the enemy advance; our aircraft did tremendous execution in the enemy salient and behind it, and this factor, together with the outstanding fighting qualities of the American troops, enabled the Allies gradually to turn the tide. It had not yet, however, been possible to form a reserve American corps available for offensive operations in First Army, and I now decided to commit British troops south and east of the Meuse in order to relieve VII United States Corps for the purpose. My plan was to employ 30 Corps on the right flank of First United States Army, taking over the sector Givet–Hotton. These reliefs were to be completed by 2 January so that VII United States Corps could thrust towards Houffalize on 3 January. Meanwhile Third United States Army continued its operations in the Bastogne sector and was widening its salient there. General Patton's thrust line was also directed on Houffalize, so that our respective offensives could join up and pinch out the head of the enemy salient.

After the clear weather over the Christmas period, which had proved so much to the advantage of the Allied Air Forces, the German Air Force made a decided attempt to neutralize our air effort by an all-out attack on the Allied airfields. Deploying the greatest concentration of aircraft employed in the campaign, a daring low level attack was carried out on 1 January against our main airfields in Belgium and Holland. These attacks succeeded in causing considerable losses to the Allies, but they were in no way comparable with those suffered by the enemy.

First United States Army launched the attack by VII Corps on 3 January. The enemy was well organized with dug-in tanks and anti-tank guns, and the weather was again bad, with visibility reduced to two hundred yards or less. Advances of two to three thousand yards were made, however, on the first day, after which heavy snowfall brought progress to a halt. The advance was resumed on 5 January, and two days later the Laroche–Vielsalm road was cut south-east of Grandmenil, thus denying the enemy his main northern supply route. This attack was a very great achievement on the part of VII United States Corps, for it was carried out in appalling weather against extremely bitter opposition. XVIII United States Airborne Corps supported the VII Corps attack on its left flank, and by 7 January 82 United States Airborne Division had reached the outskirts of Vielsalm and Salmchateau.

Meanwhile on the right of First Army, 30 British Corps attacked on 4 January on a front of two divisions. In the south 6 Airborne Division, which had been hurriedly brought over from the United Kingdom had some fierce fighting in and around Bure, but secured the area on 5 January, and on the left 53 Division moved forward in touch with VII American Corps and secured Grimbiermont and the high ground to the east on 7 January.

Following the failure of his repeated attacks launched from the northern side of the salient, the enemy tried to shift his main weight further west and south-west. Essential to this redisposition, however, was the capture of Bastogne and its road net. The dogged and indeed aggressive defence of Bastogne by the Americans continued to attract enemy divisions away from the northern sector until, by 6 January, there were no less than ten divisions, including three SS, fighting round the place. His failure to capture Bastogne was the overdue signal to the enemy that the Ardennes offensive must be called off. Sound appreciation would have told him that if the Meuse were not reached quickly, it would not be reached at all; obstinacy, and no doubt political pressure, made him keep up the attack for three weeks and pledge the whole of his strategic reserve in the effort.

The thrust towards Houffalize continued. In order to maintain the impetus of 30 Corps attacks, 51 Division was brought in to take the lead from 53 Division in an advance towards Champlon–Laroche. 30 Corps advance was to be taken up to the line of the River Ourthe. Laroche was captured on 10 January and meanwhile patrols of 6 Airborne Division reached St Hubert the following day, making contact with the left flank of Third United States Army. By 13 January, 51 Division was on the line of the Ourthe southwards from Laroche. East of the Ourthe XVIII United States Airborne Corps was attacking south-east from the Stavelot–Malmedy area towards St Vith, threatening the enemy communications at the base of his salient.

The enemy fought stubbornly and gave ground very slowly, but on 16 January First and Third United States Armies joined hands in the Houffalize and the hostile salient was reduced to a bulge. General Eisenhower now ordered First United States

Army to revert to General Bradley's command, while Ninth United States Army remained under my operational control.

I undertook the withdrawal of all British troops from the Ardennes with the greatest possible speed, in order to regroup for the battle of the Rhineland. Now was the opportunity to proceed with the utmost despatch to carry out our plans, in order to take full advantage of the enemy's failure.

### REFLECTIONS ON THE BATTLE OF THE ARDENNES

The enemy had been prevented from crossing the Meuse in the nick of time.

The German counter stroke had been mounted with skill, and the attempt to drive a wedge between the British and American forces and to strike at our main supply bases of Liège, Brussels and Antwerp had been a bold though desperate bid to upset the progress of our strategy and to turn the situation on the western front to the enemy's advantage. The ability of the Germans to continue the war depended on avoiding concurrent major offensives on both the eastern and western fronts. Their stringent resources demanded a policy of alternation, whereby one front was stabilized while they concentrated against the other.

By the Ardennes offensive the enemy had hoped to hit the Western Allies so hard that our plans would have been seriously retarded, and the German striking force could have been switched to the sore-pressed eastern front.

There was another reason for playing for time. Time was necessary for the development of production in the dispersed industries remaining in operation, and in the underground factories which were being speedily constructed. New weapons were on the way: jet-propelled aircraft and faster submarines. Efforts had also to be made to make good the losses suffered in the winter battles of attrition and to raise the standard of the depleted German infantry.

There may also have been political considerations prompting the Ardennes offensive; Hitler may well have hoped to secure some success to brighten the Christmas of the depressed German nation.

The enemy plan was the result of Hitler's personal intervention, and was the second occasion on our front in which he forced on his generals an undertaking which was beyond the capability of the resources they controlled. While a spoiling attack to delay our spring offensive was clearly a justifiable military proposition, the launching of a counter offensive was not. The enemy could not afford to risk his striking force in such a hazardous operation, because he had failed to win the air battle first (an essential preliminary to major offensive operations under modern conditions) and because he had not the resources in fuel to implement a plan of this scope. As he reached the limit of his penetration, the enemy was forced to abandon much equipment through lack of petrol and lubricants. Although he achieved some signal success in the initial stages, the enterprise was doomed to failure.

The battle of the Ardennes was won primarily by the staunch fighting qualities of

[357]

the American soldier; the enemy's subsequent confusion was completed by the intense air action which became possible as weather conditions improved. Sixth SS Panzer Army broke itself against the northern shoulder of the salient while Fifth Panzer Army wasted its time, first by waiting for the Sixth SS Army, and secondly by having to fight for road space. Regrouping of First and Ninth United States Armies, assisted by British formations, made possible the formation of a reserve American corps. While the might of our Air Forces came into play against the enemy, the action of the reserve corps, co-ordinated with the drive from the south of General Patton's troops, forced the enemy from the salient; Hitler's projected counter offensive ended in a tactical defeat, and the German Army in the west suffered a tremendous battering.

After his defeat in Normandy, the enemy had made a remarkable recovery. He had succeeded in forming and equipping new divisions, and had not only organized a coherent front on the rivers and canals of the Low Countries, and along the Siegfried Line, but had also built up a strong mobile striking force. By December this force was ready for action.

Clearly the employment of this striking force was a matter of vital importance to the enemy. With such tremendous issues at stake, Hitler should never have gambled it in a desperate venture, in which he had not the resources to ensure the prerequisite conditions for victory, and in which failure would inevitably cause tremendous losses which he could never again replace.

The launching of a counter offensive in the Ardennes was the second major German mistake in the campaign. It is estimated that the enemy lost some 120,000 men in the battle, together with 600 tanks and assault guns. The disruption of his communications by the Allied Air Forces resulted in tremendous damage to locomotives and rolling stock, and also caused very grave losses to the depleted German Air Force which tried to intercept our attacks.

The enemy had succeeded in wresting the initiative from us, and in forcing us to postpone our own offensive intentions. The Allies had been caught off balance by the enemy, and had suffered a tactical reverse. Had the quality of the German formations been of the same high standard as in the early war years, with junior leaders of great dash and initiative, the temporary effects of the counter stroke might well have been more grave; the enemy failed to exploit his success in the first vital days, and the fighting showed he was no match for the splendidly steady American troops.

The battle displayed many fine examples of Allied solidarity and team work. In particular, the passage of 30 British Corps across to the south flank of First United States Army, and its subsequent deployment east of the Meuse, was an operation of tremendous complications achieved without serious difficulty.

# CHAPTER SIXTEEN

## The Battle of the Rhineland

### ALLIED PLANS AFTER THE BATTLE OF THE ARDENNES

FOLLOWING the reduction of the enemy salient the American armies continued the bitter struggle to push the enemy back from the Siegfried Line defences, taking the fullest advantage of the enemy withdrawal and the heavy defeat which he had suffered.

Meanwhile the new Allied plan of campaign emerged. It was essential to strike quickly in order to exploit the enemy's reverse in the Ardennes, and my proposal to the Supreme Commander was that we should now revert to our plans for clearing up the area between the Rhine and the Meuse from Düsseldorf to Nijmegen and establish a bridgehead north of the Ruhr. This plan was accepted and it was agreed that Ninth United States Army should undertake the southern offensive from the Julich–Linnich area, and would be made up to twelve divisions. The Ninth Army was to be under my operational command for the battle.

This operation had been in my mind for many months, and I felt well pleased that at last we were in a position to begin what I believed to be the final phase of the campaign. Once the northern Rhineland was in Allied hands we could force our way across the Rhine and commence the isolation of the Ruhr. We should also gain the starting position necessary for mobile operations in the plains of northern Germany.

The provision of the required degree of strength for Ninth United States Army was destined to take time. So long as Twelfth Army Group offensive through the stump of the German salient continued to yield good dividends, American regrouping for the Rhineland battle was not feasible. Moreover First United States Army had to gain the Roer dams before Ninth Army could thrust across the River Roer, since control of the flood waters would have made it possible for the enemy to impede our operations. At the same time, further to the south, Sixth United States Army Group was being forced to react to German thrusts in the Colmar sector; the enemy had opened attacks on 31 December and had gained some local successes. The enemy was also active in the sector north of the Saar, and it was necessary to ensure the stability of the front in this area.

On 12 January the great Russian winter offensive began and this had obvious repercussions on the enemy; it seemed most probable that the priority of resources operating in favour of the western front would be switched to the east; it was important for us to take advantage of this fact.

In 21 Army Group, as soon as British formations could be released from the Ardennes, I pushed ahead with the plans for launching the thrust from the Nijmegen bridgehead. The operation was called 'Veritable'.

[359]

I issued orders for 'Veritable' on 21 January, giving a target date of 8 February, and at the same time suggested to the Supreme Commander that the complementary offensive by Ninth United States Army, called operation 'Grenade', should start as soon as possible after the British thrust.

The object of the battle of the Rhineland was to destroy all enemy forces between the Rhine and the Meuse from the Nijmegen bridgehead as far south as the general line Julich–Düsseldorf, and subsequently to line up along the west bank of the Rhine with the Ninth United States Army from Mors to inclusive Rees and Canadian Army from exclusive Rees to Nijmegen. After a most detailed study of the problem, the most suitable localities at which to make crossings of the Rhine itself had been found to be Rheinberg, Xanten and Rees.

In outline the task of First Canadian Army was to launch the attack south-eastwards from Nijmegen to the general line Geldern–Xanten. As the advance proceeded a firm flank would be established on the Rhine and plans made for bridging the river at Emmerich. During the battle, Canadian Army would remain responsible for the security of the Nijmegen bridgehead and of our northern flank along the Maas.

Second Army was to hold a firm front on the Meuse facing east and to assist the Canadian operations by every means possible. At this stage of planning I envisaged Second Army crossing the Meuse to secure Venlo as part of the 'Veritable' plan, though later this was cancelled because it proved unnecessary.

The task of Ninth United States Army was to launch its offensive across the River Roer from the Julich–Linnich sector, towards the Rhine between Düsseldorf and Mors. In the initial stages it had been agreed by the Supreme Commander that First United States Army would protect the right flank of the operation up to the River Erft, which would subsequently form the Ninth Army flank. The target date for 'Grenade' could not be fixed at this time, for reasons I have already indicated, but I ordered that preparations were to be made for the attack to take place as soon as possible after 8 February.

The whole of the offensive strength of 21 Army Group was to be employed in 'Veritable', and I intended that 12 Corps of Second Army would provide fresh divisions for First Canadian Army as the momentum of operations demanded.

At the time of issuing these orders I gave the armies a forecast of their subsequent roles. Second Army was to start planning for forcing the Rhine at Rheinberg, Xanten and Rees; the Rheinberg crossing, it was assumed, would become an American responsibility. First Canadian Army would eventually require to establish road and rail communications across the Neder Rijn at Arnhem, so that the capture of Arnhem and the bridging commitments there would be a likely future task for the Army.

### THE CLEARANCE OF THE ROERMOND TRIANGLE
#### 15–28 January

Before commencing the battle of the Rhineland there still remained a small commitment in the Roermond triangle. It will be remembered that operations had

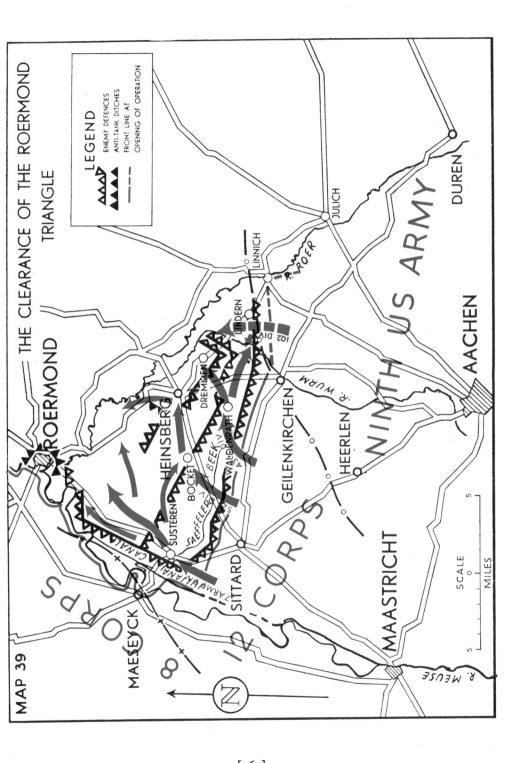

MAP 39

THE CLEARANCE OF THE ROERMOND TRIANGLE

LEGEND

ENEMY DEFENCES
ANTI-TANK DITCHES
FRONT LINE AT OPENING OF OPERATION

N

ROERMOND

HEINSBERG

DREMMEN

LINDERN

LINNICH

102 DIV

R. ROER

JULICH

DUREN

SUSTEREN

BOCKET

WALDENRATH

BEEK

SAEFFELEN

GEILENKIRCHEN

R. WURM

HEERLEN

AACHEN

NINTH US ARMY

MAESEYCK

SITTARD

JULIANA CANAL

7 ARMD

30 CORPS

12 CORPS

8 CORPS

MAASTRICHT

R. MEUSE

SCALE

5      0      5

MILES

been planned in December for clearing the enemy from the Heinsberg area. Bad weather had led to the postponement of these operations by 30 Corps, and subsequently the Ardennes counter offensive had prevented Ninth United States Army from carrying them out. As the Allies turned to the offensive in the Ardennes salient I decided to tackle this task with Second Army troops as soon as circumstances permitted, and on 10 January instructed Second Army to commence clearing the enemy salient on 15 January.

The enemy was holding an area bounded by the Rivers Roer, Wurm and Meuse. There was one important water obstacle in front of our forward positions, the Saeffeler Beek, and further west numerous minor streams which were likely to cause bridging problems. South-west of the River Roer the enemy had constructed three main lines of defence, and the town of Heinsberg itself was provided with very strong defences of the usual type. The enemy disposed two divisions on the front, but appeared to have no tactical reserves.

On 15 January 12 Corps commenced preliminary operations on the left flank in order to prepare approaches to the village of Susteren, and on the following day 7 Armoured Division began the main attack on the western flank. On 18 January an assault was launched in the centre sector in order to link up with armoured columns which were swinging in a left hook to get behind the enemy. The operations proved largely a matter for infantry as the going was so bad that tanks and special armour could give little effective support. On 20 January the high ground in the centre of the area at Bocket was secured and our troops closed in on the town of Heinsberg, which in spite of counter attacks was captured on 24 January. On the right flank, operations started on 20 January in conjunction with the left hand division of Ninth Army. In this area the enemy resistance was less spirited and the opposition was quickly cleaned up.

By 26 January 12 Corps had completed its task. The operation had in fact been a large scale methodical mopping-up operation carried out under the most difficult conditions. As a result the enemy suffered considerable losses, and apart from a small bridgehead south-west of Roermond, had now been pushed east of the Roer. The area was handed over to Ninth United States Army.

### PLANNING THE BATTLE OF THE RHINELAND

Very considerable study had been made for launching the northern thrust of the battle of the Rhineland, and indeed First Canadian Army was able to consider the problem and complete its plans while the Ardennes battle was being fought. The necessary maintenance resources were prepared and the improvement of communications necessary for major operations had proceeded with vigour. It is interesting to note that the tonnage off-loaded at Canadian Army roadheads during February reached the high figure of 343,800 tons of which 223,000 tons represented the build-up of stores for the offensive. 446 special freight trains moved the stores forward, in some cases to railheads within three miles of the front line.

Once therefore our formations could be concentrated, it was possible to undertake the operation without undue delays.

The uncertain factor remained the date of readiness of Ninth United States Army. While General Simpson and his staff were able to plan their part of the battle, it remained to be seen by what date the Army could be made up to its required strength for the operation: in view of the other commitments of Twelfth United States Army Group.

The weather remained an anxiety. The thaw was beginning and, apart from the floods, was playing havoc with our communications.

The concentration of 21 Army Group formations into First Canadian Army was a complicated process. 30 Corps had to be disengaged from the Ardennes and moved to the north, while other formations were fighting with 12 Corps in the Heinsberg salient until 26 January. The troops had to move into the Nijmegen bridgehead through the bottleneck of the bridges at Grave and Mook, and had to form up prior to the assault in an extremely limited area.

Elaborate arrangements were necessary in assembling the forces in order to mislead the enemy about our intentions, and steps were taken to give the impression that forthcoming operations were being mounted further to the west directed on Utrecht. Comprehensive camouflage schemes were devised to hide concentration of troops, artillery, and ammunition in the Nijmegen area and provision had to be made which would satisfy either normal ground conditions or snow.

South-east of Nijmegen the main features of the battle area were the Reichswald Forest, the flood plains of the River Meuse, the Niers and the Rhine, and the undulating and wooded country which lay between them. Owing to the excessive rainfall in December there was considerable flooding along the Rhine, particularly in the area of Emmerich, and the Maas floods extended to about a thousand yards on either side of the river. During January there was a drop in the water levels, but although the rivers receded to their normal channels the ground remained very saturated. A considerable amount of data had been collected regarding the effect on our communications both of artificial flooding and severe frosts; it was clear that the Rhine could be artificially flooded by breaching the winter dykes and we had to be prepared as far as possible to deal with such eventualities.

The enemy defences in the Canadian sector were organized in three main zones. West of the Reichswald Forest there was a belt of defences about two thousand yards deep, covered by an extensive anti-tank ditch and numerous field works in and around the villages. About three kilometres east of this forward position was the northern end of the Siegfried Line; some of its works had been constructed a number of years previously and were no longer evident on our air photographs, but a good deal of digging had been done in the recent months. The main belt of the line ran from the Nijmegen–Cleve road roughly south over the high ground in the Reichswald to the heavily defended town of Goch, whence it continued south to Geldern and thence along a slight lip which overlooked the valley of the Maas as far as Roermond. The northern portion of the belt was organized in great depth with a succession of trench systems stepped back to the high ground about Materborn. A further development in the last two months had been the construction of a further line east of the Reichswald from Cleve to Goch, thus making the forest a self-contained centre of resistance. The third defensive system was known to us as the Hochwald 'lay-back'. This was about ten kilometres east of the Siegfried Line, and ran from the Rhine opposite Rees to Geldern and thence away to the south.

In front of Ninth United States Army the natural obstacles of the Roer valley had been improved by the construction of a network of defences and minefields. There were also continuous trench systems along the east bank of the Meuse, with additional defences in areas such as Venlo and Roermond.

The Reichswald sector itself was controlled by 84 German Infantry Division with various reinforcements, including three battalions of parachutists. It was estimated that the enemy had nine divisions holding his front between Duren and Nijmegen, and it appeared that there might be three Panzer type and two parachute divisions available as a mobile reserve to deal with an Allied offensive on the north. Behind the enemy forward troops the two main routes were the road from Cleve to Xanten, and the railway from Cleve through Goch to Xanten; both depended on the bridges over the Rhine at Wesel, the nearest alternative being Homburg some fifteen miles to the south. There were no bridges over the Rhine between Wesel and Nijmegen, but we had observed a number of ferries along this stretch of the river which were kept under close attention by our Air Forces.

CANADIAN ARMY PLAN

First Canadian Army planned to launch the attack on a one corps front employing 30 Corps; as soon as a break-in had been achieved, and the front widened to permit the opening of additional maintenance routes, 2 Canadian Corps was to take over the left sector and the operations would be continued on a two corps front.

The formations available to 30 Corps comprised six infantry divisions, one armoured division, three armoured brigades, eleven regiments of specialized armour, five Groups Royal Artillery, and two anti-aircraft artillery brigades. The main features of the break-in operation were to be the development of a tremendous weight of artillery from well over a thousand guns, together with a comprehensive interdiction programme by the Allied Air Forces.

It is interesting to note that the strength of First Canadian Army was just under half a million men at the opening of the operation.

The initial assault was timed for 1030 hours on 8 February on a frontage of four infantry divisions, 51, 53 and 15 Divisions and 2 Canadian Division from right to left. In addition, 3 Canadian Division was to attack on the extreme northern flank later in the day, at a time when it would be possible to switch additional artillery support to the sector. The task of breaking through the Siegfried defences near Kranenburg, and of

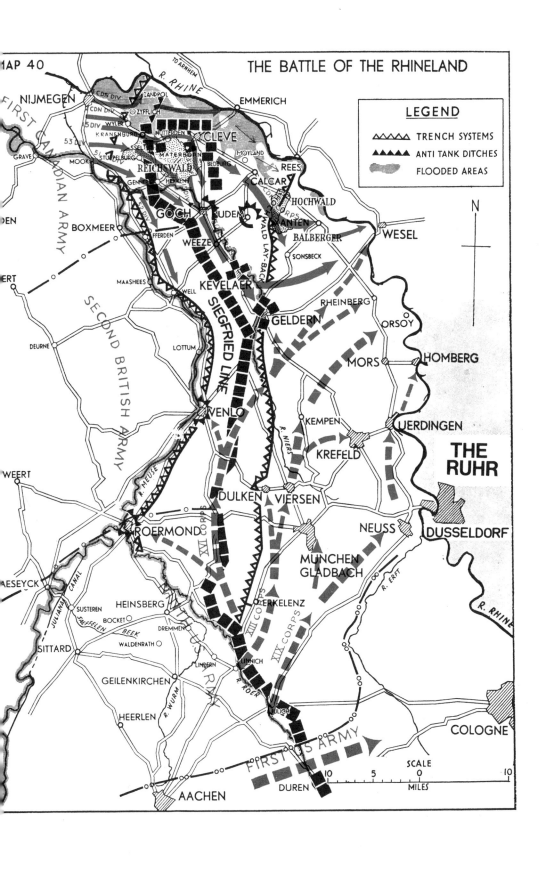

THE BATTLE OF THE RHINELAND

MAP 40

LEGEND

▵▵▵▵▵ TRENCH SYSTEMS
▴▴▴▴▴ ANTI TANK DITCHES
FLOODED AREAS

N

NIJMEGEN
TO ARNHEM
R. RHINE
EMMERICH
LANDPOL
CDN DIV
ZYFFLICH
CDN DIV
WYLER
15 DIV
KRANENBURG
NUTTERDEN
CLEVE
53 DIV
SSELT
MATERBORN
MOYLAND
RES
REICHSWALD
BEDBURG
CALCAR
HEKKENS
GENNEP
GOCH
UDEM
HOCHWALD
VANTEN
BALBERGER
WESEL
FIRST CANADIAN ARMY
GRAVE
MOOK
STUMPELBURG
BOXMEER
FFERDEN
WEEZE
SONSBECK
SECOND BRITISH ARMY
MAASHEES
WELL
KEVELAER
SIEGFRIED LINE
RHEINBERG
GELDERN
ORSOY
DEURNE
LOTTUM
MORS
HOMBERG
WEERT
VENLO
KEMPEN
UERDINGEN
R. NIERS
KREFELD
THE RUHR
R. MEUSE
DULKEN
VIERSEN
NEUSS
AESEYCK
ROERMOND
XXX CORPS
MUNCHEN GLADBACH
DUSSELDORF
JULIANA CANAL
SUSTEREN
HEINSBERG
BOCKET
BEEK
DREMMEN
ERKELENZ
XIII CORPS
XII CORPS
XIX CORPS
R. ERFT
R. RHINE
SITTARD
WALDENRATH
LINDERN
GEILENKIRCHEN
R. WURM
LINNICH
R. ROER
HEERLEN
JULICH
COLOGNE
FIRST US ARMY
SCALE
10    5    0    10
MILES
AACHEN
DUREN

opening the road to the high ground near Cleve, fell to 15 Division; it was then planned to pass 43 Division through to the Materborn area, whence it would swing round the east side of the Reichswald to capture the key centre of Goch in conjunction with 51 Division, which was to assault the town from the west. Immediately in rear of 43 Division Guards Armoured Division was to pass through the Materborn feature, turn south and seize the high ground north of Sonsbeck. Preparations were to be made to send a strong mobile column to seize the bridge at Wesel.

Extensive preliminary air operations were undertaken against railways, bridges and ferries serving the battle area and, during the night preceding the assault, Bomber Command delivered heavy raids on Cleve and Goch and on the main communication centres and billeting areas in the enemy rear.

### THE BATTLE OF THE RHINELAND: FIRST PHASE

At 0500 hours 8 February the artillery programme opened on the enemy defences and continued until 1000 hours, when the barrage proper started. In addition to this programme each division organized 'pepper pot' groups, which comprised the machine gun battalion and available divisional reserves of light anti-aircraft and anti-tank artillery, in order to saturate with fire the enemy defences on the immediate front and flanks of each divisional attack.

The infantry went forward at 1030 hours. The effects of our bombardment were very considerable, and in particular the counter battery measures largely neutralized the enemy artillery. Opposition to our advances was stiffest in the right sector against 51 Division, whose task was the capture of the high ground at the south-west corner of the Reichswald Forest. Here it appeared that the enemy had been recently reinforced as a result of prearranged reliefs. In the centre 53 Division secured the high ground on the north-west corner of the Forest and took some two hundred prisoners. Many mines were encountered and it was soon evident that the state of the ground was going to constitute a great problem to our future operations; the Churchill gun-tanks and bridge layers managed to keep up with the infantry, but flame throwers and flails got bogged down soon after crossing the start line. 15 Division was also hampered by extensive minefields and saturated ground, but by 1700 hours the village of Kranenburg had been taken and leading troops were approaching Frasselt. To the left rear of 15 Division, 2 Canadian Division secured Wyler by the early evening after some stiff fighting. At 1800 hours 3 Canadian Division in Buffaloes attacked across the floods north of the Nijmegen–Kranenburg road and were quickly in Zyfflich and Zandpol.

By midnight all formations had achieved the objectives set for the day. Over eleven hundred prisoners had been taken and our own casualties had not been severe. The bulk of the German 84 Division had been severely mauled, but air reconnaissance indicated that there was a general northward movement of enemy troops across the line of the road Geldern–Wesel.

Our main difficulties had been due to the extensive minefields and above all to the bad state of the ground; it was reported that the flood level in the area north of the Nijmegen–Cleve road had risen eighteen inches between 1300 hours and nightfall; the whole area was sodden, and in spite of the special provisions made for the creation of new tracks and the improvement of those existing, it was clear that we should continue to have grave difficulties in the maintenance of our communications.

During the night, operations continued assisted by 'movement light' and the leading divisions pressed forward to their further objectives. 43 Division, now concentrated in Nijmegen, was at one hour's notice to move from midday 9 February and Guards Armoured Division, concentrated near Tilburg, was also at one hour's notice to come forward.

Operations on 9 February went well against moderate opposition except on the extreme right, where 51 Division continued to meet stiff resistance. In the Reichswald Forest 53 Division cleared the Stuppelburg feature and the high ground southwest of Materborn, but ground conditions deteriorated so rapidly that the divisional axis completely gave way and had to be closed for repairs; meanwhile traffic for 53 Division had to use the 15 Division axis.

Starting at 0400 hours, 15 Division pierced the Nutterden defences of the Siegfried Line and by evening its leading troops were on the high ground at Materborn and patrols were in touch with strong enemy elements in the outskirts of Cleve. During the day, 43 Division was brought forward and reached Nutterden by midnight. North of the main road, 3 Canadian Division continued its water-borne operations in the floods, moving from one island village to another and capturing about six hundred prisoners. In some places amphibious patrols reached the banks of the Rhine.

Traffic conditions continued to deteriorate. It was apparent that the main Nijmegen–Kranenburg road would soon be completely under water, and, indeed, eighteen inches were reported on certain stretches at midday 9 February.

Away to the south, First United States Army was now threatening directly the Roer dams, as a result of which the Germans destroyed portions of the discharge valves of the Schwammanuel Dam. A volume of water was released which caused the River Roer to overflow its banks along the entire front of Ninth United States Army. It will be seen that I had intended to launch this Army on 10 February, but in view of these circumstances had to postpone the operation.

During the night 9/10 February there was fierce fighting in and round Cleve, where 43 Division was endeavouring to pass across the high ground and turn the north-east corner of the Reichswald. There was a number of German paratroop detachments in this area, and the delays imposed by our traffic difficulties had evidently given the enemy time to scrape together a number of units to oppose us. In the centre of the Reichswald the advance continued steadily, but to the south the enemy was still fighting desperately in the network of defences covering the road centres of Hekkens and Gennep. On 10 February the main Nijmegen–Cleve road was under more than two feet of water for a length of five miles; north of the road all operations had to be conducted in amphibious vehicles; south of the road the approaches to the

Reichswald and the tracks which ran through it had been severely churned by the traffic. South of the Reichswald there was a good road from Gennep to Goch, but here the enemy was quick to realize the importance of this sector and hung on in a series of well sited positions.

Meanwhile the Germans were quickly reinforcing the battle area; on 9 February a unit of 7 Parachute Division was identified, and, on the following day, units from two other reserve divisions, including 6 Parachute Division, had yielded prisoners. On 12 February the enemy committed 15 Panzer Grenadier Division and 116 Panzer Division.

In spite of the stiffening enemy resistance and the appalling difficulties of the ground, progress continued. Following a successful night assault across the flooded River Niers, 51 Division captured the village of Gennep; this was an important gain, as we intended to bridge the Meuse at this point in order to relieve the Grave bottleneck. Subsequently 51 Division reached the road centre of Hekkens where it joined elements of 53 Division. By 13 February 53 Division had cleared the entire area of the Reichswald after driving off, with heavy losses to both sides, a series of sharp counter attacks in the south-east corner of the Forest. Along the eastern face of the Reichswald, 43 Division, in its operations to roll up the German positions in the sector from north to south, secured Bedburg. The division was counter attacked a number of times by infantry supported by tanks. 15 Division mopped up Cleve and handed it over to 3 Canadian Division.

By 13 February the first phase of the operation had been completed. On the right we were well on our way to the key defences of Goch; the Reichswald Forest was completely in our hands; to the east we were converging on the Goch–Udem line; and meanwhile in the north a battalion of Canadians was on the west bank of the Rhine opposite Emmerich. Our main problem remained communications. The road from Beek to Kranenburg, a distance of five miles, was now under some four feet of water, and the supply and maintenance of all troops in the Cleve area had to be carried out by Dukws from a starting point near Beek.

The floods in the River Roer valley still made it impossible to launch the American assault from the south. Ninth United States Army was all 'teed-up' to launch Operation 'Grenade', and it was an extreme disappointment for us all that it should be forced to remain inactive until flood conditions improved. Meanwhile 'Veritable' had to continue alone, and against it the enemy was able to concentrate all his available reserves; it was therefore inevitable that progress was slower than had been hoped.

In order to maintain the maximum impetus, I ordered 11 Armoured and 52 Divisions to be transferred to Canadian Army from Second Army forthwith. An American reserve division relieved 52 Division on the Meuse front near Venlo. The difficulty was to deploy additional strength through the Reichswald Forest in view of the communications, but I wanted to make certain that General Crerar had at his disposal all the resources he could use for the battle. Although it had been planned to launch 'Veritable' and 'Grenade' almost concurrently, it was now to be hoped that the concentration of enemy reserves against Canadian Army would in fact greatly facilitate the progress of Ninth American Army when at length it could be launched.

Our troops continued their relentless pressure against the steadily increasing opposition; on 14 February we were faced by one Panzer, one Panzer Grenadier, four parachute and three infantry divisions; in particular the German parachute troops fought with fanatical obstinacy and ferocity and, however untenable their situation, hung on to the last man.

2 Canadian Corps took over the left sector of the front on 15 February and, the following day, 52 Division came into the line on the extreme right of 30 Corps. 30 Corps operations were directed on the two axes Gennep–Venlo and Goch–Geldern, while 2 Canadian Corps made for Udem and Calcar. 52 Division moved south from Gennep and took Afferden, but further progress became almost impossible owing to the floods. 51 Division closed in on the western approaches to Goch, and to the north and north-east 43 and 53 Divisions fought their way to the escarpment overlooking the town. 43 Division had withstood repeated counter attacks along the eastern face of the Reichswald, but had steadily rolled up the enemy's positions from the flank and had taken 2,300 prisoners in the process.

On 18 February, 15 Division began to pass through from the north, in order to lead the assault on Goch; the following day the German commander of the town surrendered, but it took nearly forty-eight hours before 15 and 51 Divisions had cleared Goch. On the left 2 Canadian Corps fought hard to secure the Udem–Calcar spur. An advance across the Goch–Calcar road towards Bocholt enabled us to outflank and capture Moyland, but efforts to turn the enemy out of Calcar were unavailing; he counter attacked strongly with the newly arrived Panzer Lehr Division and, indeed, gained some temporary success before being driven off. Another German infantry division (190) also joined the battle, bringing the total formations against us to eleven.

Meanwhile bridging operations had been undertaken at Gennep across the Meuse; by 15 February the bridge was nearly completed, but the approaches were two feet under water, and owing to the speed and height of the river the bridge was not finally opened to traffic until 20 February; it is interesting to note that this Bailey bridge was over 4,000 feet in length and was thus the longest we had so far constructed in this campaign.

With the capture of Goch and the progress we had made on the flanks, we were now through two of the three main defensive belts which the Germans had organized between the two rivers. In the north it remained to break through the last defensive system, the Hochwald 'lay-back', running along the high ground from opposite Rees to Geldern. 30 Corps was directed from the Goch area through Weeze and Kevelaar to Geldern, while 2 Canadian Corps was to deliver the main operation in the general area between Udem and Calcar through the Hochwald Forest to Xanten. 4 Canadian

Armoured, 11 Armoured and 3 Divisions were being brought into the battle, and regrouping took place in order to increase the strength available to 2 Canadian Corps for its new task.

## THE BATTLE OF THE RHINELAND:
## COMMENCEMENT OF THE SOUTHERN ATTACK

It has already been seen that the original plan was to launch the two converging thrusts for the battle of the Rhineland approximately simultaneously, but that it had not originally been possible to predict how quickly Ninth United States Army could be made up to the strength required for its task owing to other preoccupations in Twelfth United States Army Group.

In the last days of January, however, the Supreme Commander ordered the provision of additional formations to Ninth United States Army in order to complete it to the revised total of ten divisions. Since at this time we were planning to launch 'Grenade' on about 10 February, the American concentration in the north had to be completed with very great speed. It was in fact achieved remarkably quickly. Some of the United States divisions had to move over very long distances using appalling roads and tracks in the worst possible weather, but they got into position on time and gave an excellent example of the truly extraordinary mobility of American units when regrouping.

I have also mentioned how the plans for launching the Ninth Army thrust were delayed by the release of the Roer flood waters by the retreating Germans. Ninth Army stood ready, but suffered a period of great frustration awaiting the subsidence of the water.

On 17 February it was decided that the American attack would be able to start on 23 February providing we had no more heavy rain, and in fact at 0330 hours on that day General Simpson's troops assaulted across the River Roer with XIX Corps on the right and XIII Corps on the left.

Twelve hours after the crossing, sixteen battalions were on the east bank, Julich was clear of the enemy, and the lateral road to the north for some eight miles was in our hands. In spite of the great difficulty caused by floods and heavy shelling of the sites, seven heavy bridges and a number of light infantry assault bridges were thrown across the river within twenty-four hours. The casualties to American troops were light and 700 prisoners were taken on the first day.

Meanwhile on the right flank of Ninth Army, First American Army assaulted astride Duren.

The American formations advanced in fine style. The weather was fine and the ground was drying; on 24 February four divisions were across the river and were soon followed by armoured divisions; by 26 February the bridgehead was some twenty miles wide and ten miles deep, the town of Erkelenz had been captured and some 6,000 prisoners taken. Operations were developed on two main thrust lines. XIX Corps was directed on Neuss, Krefeld and Kempen, while XIII Corps was to pass west of München Gladbach towards Viersen and Dulken.

### THE BATTLE OF THE RHINELAND:
### THE LINK-UP BETWEEN FIRST CANADIAN AND
### NINTH AMERICAN ARMIES

On 26 February 2 Canadian Corps started its attack, directed ultimately on Xanten. Most of the enemy parachute troops were fighting in the sector and a desperate struggle took place on the Udem–Calcar ridge. Ground conditions were bad and much of the armour was bogged down, but our advance was pressed by day and by night; the enemy defences south of Calcar were finally breached and armoured troops drove on slowly to force a wedge between the Balberger and Hochwald Forests. By 3 March the greater part of these forests had been cleared and the armour was on the high ground to the south, round Sonsbeck.

As 2 Canadian Corps got under way the opposition further south began to loosen and 30 Corps started swinging south-east. In the centre of this corps front, 53 Division captured Weeze and pushed on down the road through Kevelaar towards Geldern. On the east bank of the Meuse, 52 Division, with a Commando brigade under command, reached Well, which was one of the sites selected for bridging operations over the river.

Meanwhile by 27 February, Ninth American Army had broken through the main enemy defences and the advance gathered further momentum. On 1 March XIX Corps secured München Gladbach, while on the right progress was rapid along the left bank of the River Erft towards Neuss. On the left flank, XVI Corps, which had now joined the operation, thrust north-west and entered Roermond and Venlo. Neuss was cleared on 2 March and the Rhine was reached in two places; at the same time XIII Corps, in the centre of the attack, captured Krefeld. Early on 3 March, the Americans were in Geldern, and 35 Division of XVI Corps made contact with 53 Division in the northern outskirts of the town.

### FINAL STAGES OF THE BATTLE OF THE RHINELAND

By 5 March the right and centre corps of Ninth Army had completed their tasks and were in possession of the left bank of the Rhine from Neuss inclusive as far north as Orsoy. XVI Corps was swinging south of the Venlo–Wesel road towards the Rhine at Rheinberg, in conjunction with 30 Corps which was turning east towards Wesel. By this time the enemy was concerned solely with holding us off from his shrinking bridgehead covering the crossings at Wesel; the key of his perimeter was the hinge about Xanten, where enemy parachute troops were fighting fanatically to hold back 2 Canadian Corps. On 8 March the Canadians launched a strong attack from the north-west against Xanten and secured most of the town despite the resistance. Two days later the enemy rearguards had retired across the river and blown the last remaining bridge at Wesel. Unfortunately the final days of the operation were very unfavourable for flying and hindered the Air Forces in their attempts to deal with the targets presented at the Wesel bottleneck.

### REFLECTIONS ON THE BATTLE OF THE RHINELAND

21 Army Group, with Ninth American Army, was now lined up along the west bank of the Rhine from Neuss to Nijmegen.

Although it had not been intended, the delay in mounting the southern attack of the battle had not in the end been to our disadvantage. When it could start the rapidity and violence of the Ninth Army thrust caught the enemy off balance; it relieved the pressure on the Canadian front, and by 1 March the enemy was threatened with encirclement and had no choice but to get as much as possible of his personnel and material back across the Rhine. The main features of the operation were the appalling weather conditions in the early stages, and the intense opposition of the enemy.

The operations along the Rhine plain north of the Reichswald were mainly conducted in various types of amphibious vehicles, without which equipment this flank could not have been cleared. In the central and southern sectors the mud and slush were indescribable; the heavily wooded areas were lacking in roads and tracks and the low lying meadows were either flooded or saturated.

The enemy parachute troops fought with a fanaticism unexcelled at any time in the war, and it is interesting to note that the Germans had available against Canadian Army some 700 mortars and over 1,000 guns of all types; the volume of fire from enemy weapons was the heaviest which had been met so far by British troops in the campaign.

We had employed the full concentration of our offensive resources for the task and had overwhelmed the resistance. The enemy had suffered yet another great defeat; Ninth Army took some 30,000 prisoners while, on the northern sector, 23,000 prisoners were counted. It was estimated that in killed and wounded the enemy lost nearly 40,000 men; eighteen German divisions and a large number of hastily formed battle groups had been severely mauled.

The Germans had committed the third major blunder of the campaign. Following the failure in the Ardennes, the only sound course open to the enemy was to stage a withdrawal back across the Rhine. His remaining resources might well have succeeded in causing us considerable delay on that barrier. But the tremendous importance of the Ruhr, battered as it was, and the impotence of his Air Force to act in its defence, led him to stand and fight west of the Rhine in the hope of masking that area.

After all that had gone before, the crippling losses sustained by the enemy in the Rhineland brought the end of the war to a matter of weeks. The Germans had not the manpower to raise new divisions, and in any case their industry could not have equipped fresh formations. Their remaining oil refineries and storage plants were being subjected to increasingly heavy air attacks, and their communications were rapidly being reduced to a state of chaos. Once we were across the Rhine the Wehrmacht would no longer have the tanks, transport or fuel necessary to compete with the Allied forces in battle.

# CHAPTER SEVENTEEN

# The Battle of the Rhine

### THE AMERICAN ARMIES CLOSE TO THE RHINE

WHILE the battle of the Rhineland was progressing in the north the American armies in the south were lining up on the Rhine.

On 7 March, following a swift break through, First United States Army secured intact the railway bridge at Remagen and immediately began forming a bridgehead on the east bank. The importance of this bridgehead to our subsequent operations cannot be over-estimated, as the enemy reaction to it was immediate and a considerable number of surviving enemy formations soon became committed in the sector.

Meanwhile, Third United States Army thrust to the Rhine at Coblenz and subsequently established a bridgehead south-west of the city over the River Moselle. On 15 March American troops thrust southwards from this bridgehead and eastwards from Trier while Seventh United States Army attacked northwards between the Rhine and Saarbrucken. While Seventh Army fought steadily through the Siegfried defences and pinned down the German troops, armoured columns of Third Army drove into the rear of the enemy positions. Resistance east of the Moselle crumbled, the Saar was enveloped, and the Rhine cities of Mainz and Worms were captured. By the third week in March the Allied armies had closed to the Rhine throughout its length.

### TRANSFER OF TROOPS FROM ITALY

In order to increase the weight of the Imperial forces on the Western Front, a decision was made to transfer additional troops from Italy to 21 Army Group. The despatch was arranged of Headquarters 1 Canadian Corps and Corps troops, with 1 Canadian, 5 Canadian Armoured, 1, 5 and 46 Divisions; 1 and 46 Divisions were not to be made available immediately, but the other formations were due to arrive in Belgium by April. The whole operation involved the transfer of a force the same size as the original assault forces for 'Overlord', and there was an extremely short time available for planning. Administrative and Movement staffs were despatched to Marseilles, through which port the force was to arrive, and a chain of transit camps was established across France. The movement started on 18 February and was completed in the second week of April. On 15 March Headquarters 1 Canadian Corps took over a sector on the River Maas, on our northern flank, with 49 Division under command, pending the arrival of its own formations.

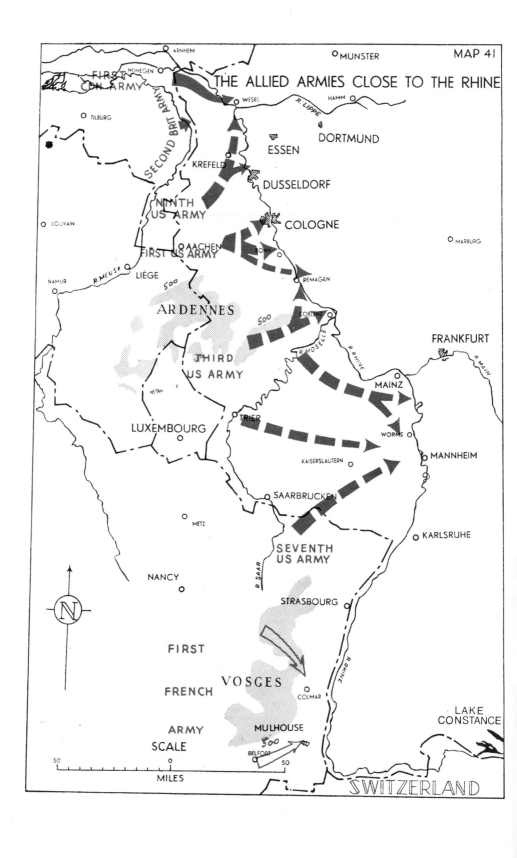

MAP 41

THE ALLIED ARMIES CLOSE TO THE RHINE

## ORDERS AND PREPARATIONS FOR THE BATTLE
### OF THE RHINE

On 9 March I issued orders for crossing the Rhine north of the Ruhr. My intention was to secure a bridgehead prior to developing operations to isolate the Ruhr and to thrust into the northern plains of Germany.

### *Outline Plan*

In outline, my plan was to cross the Rhine on a front of two armies between Rheinberg and Rees, using Ninth American Army on the right and Second Army on the left. The principal initial object was the important communications centre of Wesel. I intended that the bridgehead should extend to the south sufficiently far to cover Wesel from enemy ground action, and to the north to include bridge sites at Emmerich; the depth of the bridgehead was to be made sufficient to provide room to form up major forces for the drive to the east and north-east. I gave 24 March as target date for the operation. It will be recalled that the battle of the Rhineland was not completed until 10 March, so that the time available for preparing to assault across the greatest water obstacle in western Europe was extremely short. The all important factor was to follow up the enemy as quickly as possible, and we were able to achieve this speed of action mainly because of the foresight and preliminary planning that had been devoted to this battle for some months.

### *Some Planning Details*

The problem of forcing the Rhine had been studied throughout the winter months; a great deal of research was undertaken by the engineers to assess the likelihood and effects of flooding during our crossing operations. Early provision was made for reducing such risks by planning the construction of booms upstream from the crossing sites, for the replacement of certain floating bridges by pile bridges as soon as possible, and for making the bridges and their approaches flood-proof. I have mentioned that it had been concluded that suitable crossing places existed in the area of Rheinberg, Xanten and Rees. An assault across the river near Emmerich was not considered feasible; not only was there a number of minor waterways on the west bank of the river barring the approaches to bridge launching sites, but the high ground at Hoch Elten directly overlooked the whole area.

While the battle of the Rhineland was being fought, Second Army was directing the development of east-west communications, and as the progress of operations permitted, bridges over the Meuse were opened at Gennep, Well, Lottum and Venlo.

Plans were made weeks ahead for the assembly of the tremendous tonnage of administrative stores and requirements for the battle, and in particular of the immense quantity of bridging material of all kinds; a special engineer staff was set up to tackle the bridging of the Rhine.

The main maintenance build-up began when Second Army opened its roadhead between the Meuse and the Rhine about 8 March and continued at full intensity. A large proportion of the requirements had to be moved forward by road, and Second Army eventually disposed of a road lift of over 10,000 tons, exclusive of Corps transport and the bridging echelons. During the three weeks prior to the operation, 10,000 tons a day were delivered at railheads west of the Meuse.

By 23 March the roadhead had received 60,000 tons of ammunition and 30,000 tons of engineer stores alone. Other commodities accounted for some 28,000 tons, and were in addition to normal daily maintenance requirements. It was a fine achievement that these stocks were delivered into the restricted area concerned with such rapidity.

The movement problem was vast. In the week preceding the start of operations, operational moves in the Second Army area (as opposed to administrative movement) involved over 600 tanks, 4,000 tank transporters and 32,000 wheeled vehicles.

All available amphibious vehicles were collected, and in addition a flotilla of craft from the Royal Navy was transported by road across Belgium and southern Holland in order to take part in the battle.

It is important to notice the way in which planning for this battle was related to the grouping of forces in 21 Army Group. While the battle of the Rhineland was being fought by First Canadian Army, Second Army was holding a quiet sector of the line along the Meuse so that its Headquarters was free to concentrate on planning the Rhine crossing. General Dempsey was, indeed, charged not only with planning the Second Army operation, but also with assisting in any way possible the preliminary planning by Ninth American Army, which was engaged in the Rhineland battle. Towards the end of January, Headquarters 12 Corps was withdrawn into reserve in order to work out the highly complicated technique required for the actual assault crossing; considerable thought and study were given to this problem, and trials and practices were carried out on an appropriate stretch of the Meuse in order to perfect the battle drill which was subsequently adopted by the British assaulting Corps.

The fortnight between the end of the battle of the Rhineland and the start of the battle of the Rhine was a period of intense activity. Rapid regrouping of formations was carried out; 30 Corps returned to Second Army on 8 March and the sector on the Rhine from Wesel to inclusive Emmerich was taken over by 8 Corps, which was to provide the covering troops behind which the assaulting formations were to form up. As D-day approached, Second Army extended its front further to the west by taking under command 2 Canadian Corps; at the same time 12 and 30 Corps, which were to deliver the assault, gradually took up their positions and relieved 8 Corps. In the final line-up on the Rhine, Ninth American was disposed from Worringen, about twelve miles south of Düsseldorf, to the River Lippe just above Wesel; Second Army front extended from the Lippe to the Dutch frontier about eight miles west of Emmerich; from this area Canadian Army was responsible for our front to the North Sea.

Our final preparations were hidden by the creation of dense and continuous clouds of smoke along a front of some fifty miles; behind this screen the assaulting troops took station.

## Topography

The width of the Rhine on our front was between four and five hundred yards, but at high water it was liable to increase to between seven and twelve hundred yards. The mean velocity of the current was about three and a half knots. The river bed itself was composed of sand and gravel and was expected to give a good bearing surface for amphibious tanks and trestles. The course of the river was controlled by a highly developed system of dykes; the main dyke was generally sixty feet wide at the base and some ten to sixteen feet high, and formed a formidable obstacle. Although our operations in February had been severely handicapped by flooding, the waters were subsiding rapidly and the ground was drying remarkably quickly.

## The Enemy

Shortly before the battle, Kesselring became Commander-in-Chief West in place of von Rundstedt. The opposition facing us was largely provided from Army Group 'H' under Blaskowitz. The sector from near Krefeld to just west of Emmerich was the responsibility of First Parachute Army, while further west Twenty Fifth Army was disposed across north-west Holland to the sea. In the line between Cologne and Essen there were four infantry divisions along the river opposite Ninth American Army; between Essen and Emmerich there were four parachute divisions and three infantry divisions. In reserve, 47 Panzer Corps was in the area some fifteen miles north-east of Emmerich, with 116 Panzer and 15 Panzer Grenadier Divisions. It was estimated that local depots and training units could produce the equivalent of three weak divisions, and that the Volkssturm and other quasi-military organizations might find another thirty thousand men. Although Wesel and Rees had perimeter defences and an anti-tank ditch, the enemy defences in the main were only such as had been prepared in the short period since the end of the Rhineland battle. They had little depth and were mainly simple earthworks.

On the Ninth Army sector it was estimated that the enemy had deployed about fifty-five batteries, while some five hundred guns were believed available to oppose the British crossing. The enemy had deployed formidable anti-aircraft defences, as he had been able to call upon the extensive anti-aircraft layout of the Ruhr. It was appreciated that there were eighty heavy and two hundred and fifty light anti-aircraft guns in the Bocholt–Wesel–Emmerich triangle, and from their location it seemed clear that the enemy anticipated the use of airborne forces in our crossing operation.

## The Allied Forces

Ninth United States Army comprised XIII, XVI and XIX Corps with a total of three armoured and nine infantry divisions. In addition to 8, 12 and 30 Corps, Second Army included for the initial stages of the operation 2 Canadian Corps and XVIII United States Airborne Corps; the latter comprised 6 British and 17 American Airborne Divisions. The total forces in Second Army were four armoured, two airborne and eight infantry divisions, five independent armoured brigades, one

[377]

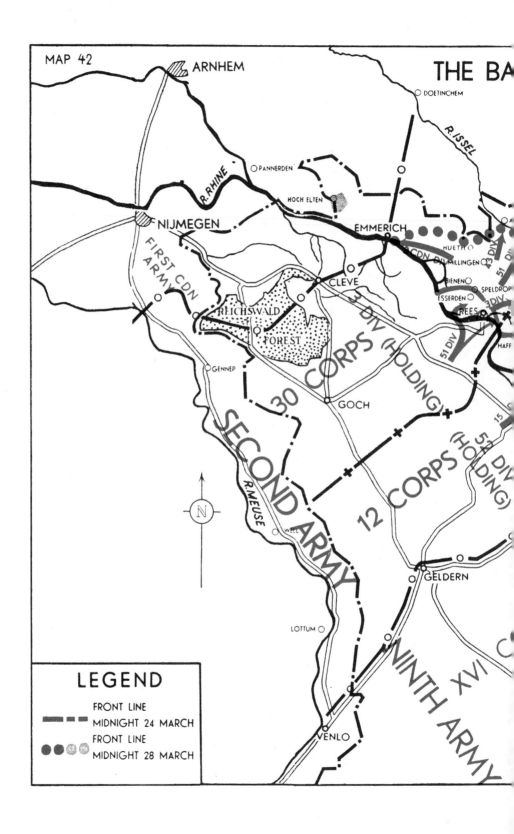

MAP 42

ARNHEM

THE BA

DOETINCHEM

R. ISSEL

R. RHINE

PANNERDEN

HOCH ELTEN

NIJMEGEN

EMMERICH

FIRST CDN ARMY

CDN DIV MILLINGEN

HUETH

3 DIV

51 DIV

CLEVE

BIENEN

SPELDROP

ESSERDEN

3 DIV

REICHSWALD

REES

3 DIV (HOLDING)

51 DIV

HAFF

FOREST

30 CORPS

GENNEP

SECOND ARMY

GOCH

12 CORPS (HOLDING)

52 DIV (HOLDING)

15 C

R. MEUSE

N

WELL

GELDERN

LOTTUM

NINTH ARMY

XVI C

VENLO

## LEGEND

——— FRONT LINE
▬ ▬ ▬ MIDNIGHT 24 MARCH
FRONT LINE
●●●◌◌ MIDNIGHT 28 MARCH

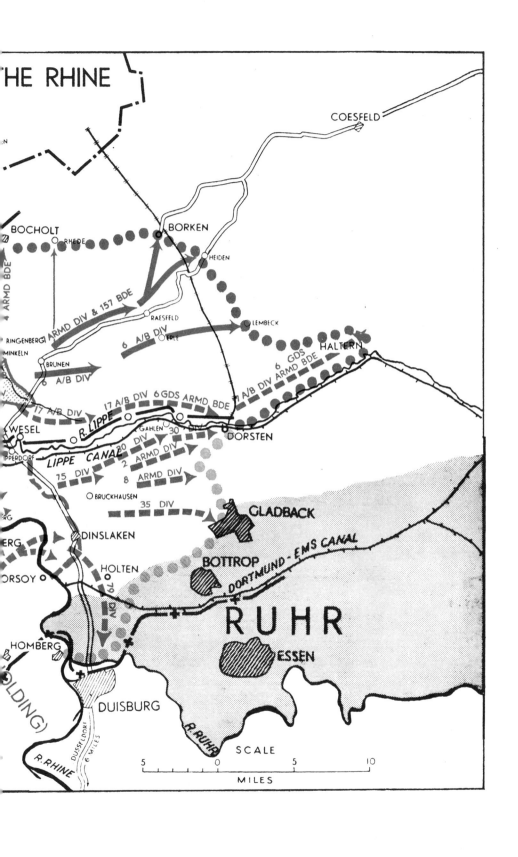

THE RHINE

COESFELD

BOCHOLT
RHEDE
BORKEN
HEIDEN
4 ARMD BDE
ARMD DIV & 157 BDE
RAESFELD
LEMBECK
6 A/B DIV
HALTERN
RINGENBERG
ERLE
6 GDS
ARMD BDE
MINKELN
BRUNEN
6
A/B DIV
A/B DIV
17 A/B DIV
17 A/B DIV   6 GDS ARMD BDE
R. LIPPE
WESEL
GAHLEN   30
DIV
DORSTEN
IPPERDORF
LIPPE CANAL
20
DIV
2  ARMD DIV
75  DIV
8  ARMD DIV
BRUCKHAUSEN
35  DIV
GLADBACK
ERG
DINSLAKEN
BOTTROP
DORTMUND - EMS CANAL
ERG
HOLTEN
79 DIV
ORSOY
RUHR
HOMBERG
ESSEN
OLDING)
DUISBURG
R. RUHR
DUSSELDORF
6 MILES
SCALE
R. R. HINE
5     0     5     10
MILES

Commando brigade and one independent infantry brigade. 79 Armoured Division was in support of the operation with all its resources of specialized armour and amphibious devices.

A tremendous weight of day and night heavy bombers, medium bombers and Allied Tactical Air Forces was made available in support of the operation.

### The Detailed Plan

The principle I laid down in planning the battle of the Rhine was that we should deliver our assault, and develop our subsequent operations, with the maximum weight and impetus at our disposal. The battle was to be delivered with such drive and strength that it would completely overwhelm the enemy and so lead us quickly to final victory in the campaign.

The object of the first phase of the operation was to secure a bridgehead on the general line Duisburg–Bottrop–Dorsten–Aalten–Doetinchem–Pannerden. The River Lippe was the boundary between the assaulting armies.

Ninth Army was to assault across the river south of Wesel, its principal task being to secure the right flank of the operation. The main bridging centre for this army was to be in the Rheinberg area.

Second Army was to deliver its assault north of the River Lippe. Its tasks were to capture the communication centre of Wesel, so that Ninth American Army could bridge the river at that place, and to secure the initial bridgehead from exclusive Dorsten to Pannerden. The main bridging centres of Second Army were to be at Wesel, Xanten and Rees. Formations of 2 Canadian Corps were to be passed over the Rees bridges at the appropriate time and to be employed in expanding the bridgehead north-westwards towards Doetinchem and Hoch Elten and in securing Emmerich.

The bridging of the Rhine at Emmerich was made the responsibility of First Canadian Army, and when this task had been carried out, 2 Canadian Corps was to revert to command of that army. In addition to this commitment, First Canadian Army was also made responsible for ensuring the absolute security of the Nijmegen bridgehead and of our northern flank from Emmerich to the sea. It was essential to ensure that we should not become unbalanced by enemy action against the Canadian Army sector.

The second phase of the operation involved the expansion of the bridgehead to the general line Hamm–Munster–Rheine–Almelo–Deventer–Apeldoorn–Otterloo–Renkum. The right boundary of Ninth Army was to run from the Rhine north of Duisburg to Dorsten thence eastwards along the River Lippe to Hamm. Its left boundary included Wesel, Raesfeld, Coesfeld and Munster. Between Second Army and Canadian Army the boundary was Emmerich–Doetinchem–Ruurlo–Borculo–Borne, all inclusive to Canadian Army. Ninth Army was to hold its bridgehead south of the River Lippe securely and pass a reserve corps through the right flank of Second Army to secure the line Hamm–Munster, forming a right flank on the River Lippe as it moved eastwards; this reserve corps was to come into the lead when we reached the general line of the railway between Dorsten and Borken. Second Army would then hand over to Ninth Army the area south of and including the road Wesel–Brunen–Raesfeld–Heiden.

Second Army was to secure a general line from Munster exclusive to Rheine and Hengelo. When Canadian Army took over the Emmerich bridgehead, and with it command of 2 Canadian Corps, it was to operate to the north to attack the Ijssel defences from the rear and to recapture Deventer and Zutphen. It was then to cross the Ijssel and capture Apeldoorn and the high ground between that place and Arnhem; Canadian Army was also to prepare to bridge the river at Arnhem and open up routes from Nijmegen northwards. A secure flank was to be formed facing west on some suitable line running north from the Neder Rijn about Renkum.

The tasks of XVIII United States Airborne Corps were to disrupt the hostile defences north of Wesel, to deepen the bridgehead, and to facilitate the crossing of the river by Second Army and its link-up with Ninth American Army. It was then to prepare for further offensive action to the east on orders from Second Army.

It was decided to drop the airborne troops east of the Rhine *after* the assault across the river had taken place. There were two main reasons for this decision: daylight was desirable for the employment of airborne troops and, secondly, it would be impossible to make full use of our artillery for the ground assault if airborne troops were dropped in the target area before we had crossed the river. In deciding the landing and dropping zones for the airborne forces, the principles employed were that they should drop within range of artillery sited on the west bank of the Rhine, in order to obtain immediately artillery support, and that the link-up with the ground troops should be effected on the first day of the operation.

For the airborne operation an elaborate counter-flak fire plan was built up. It was arranged that artillery would deal with enemy anti-aircraft guns within range, and that the Royal Air Force should undertake the neutralization of guns beyond this area which could engage the troop carriers and gliders. Very detailed arrangements were necessary for the control of artillery fire during the passage of the airborne fleets.

A great weight of artillery was disposed in support of the assault. XVI Corps, which was assaulting on the Ninth Army front, was supported by over six hundred field medium and heavy guns. Over thirteen hundred guns were available in support of 12 and 30 Corps.

There was a very great concentration of engineers for the operation; thirty-seven thousand Royal Engineers and Pioneers, and twenty-two thousand American engineers, were employed in the battle.

The assembly and passage over the river of troops and vehicles was controlled through a carefully planned organization known as the 'Bank Control Group'.

The Order of Battle and timings for the various assaults were as follows: 30 Corps: 51 Division 2100 hours 23 March; 12 Corps: 1 Commando Brigade 2200 hours 23 March and 15 Division 0200 hours 24 March; XVI United States Corps: 30 Division 0200 hours and 79 Division 0300 hours 24 March; XVIII United States Airborne Corps initially to drop at 1000 hours 24 March.

### PRELIMINARY AIR OPERATIONS

Although not directly related at the time to the operation of crossing the Rhine, the interdiction programme carried out by Bomber Command and Eighth United States Air Force, in order to isolate the Ruhr, was of direct assistance to our operation. The battlefield interdiction programme began on 10 March, and bombing attacks were carried out to isolate an area astride the Ruhr west of the general line Bonn–Siegen–Soest–Hamm–Munster–Rheine–Lingen–Zwolle.

During the three days prior to the operation, sustained bombing attacks were carried out with the object of reducing the enemy's capacity to fight, hindering his defensive preparations, and disrupting his communications. In the preliminary operations heavy bombers of the Royal Air Force flew over five thousand sorties and dropped nearly twenty-five thousand tons of bombs. The bombardment divisions of the Eighth and Ninth United States Air Forces flew over eleven thousand sorties and delivered twenty-four thousand five hundred tons of bombs.

The pre-arranged programme of air operations in support of the assault crossings included the establishment and maintenance of air superiority over the assault areas and dropping zones of the airborne troops; the neutralization of flak; the provision of fighter protection for the airborne forces; the provision of close support to the assault and airborne troops; and the prevention of enemy movement into and within the battle area.

### THE BATTLE OF THE RHINE:
### THE ESTABLISHMENT OF THE BRIDGEHEAD

At 1530 on 23 March I gave orders to launch the operation, as the weather was good. As the artillery programme reached its climax the assault waves of four battalions of 51 Division entered the river in their amphibious craft at 2100 hours 23 March. Seven minutes later a report was received that the first wave had arrived on the far bank. All crossings were successful; in the vicinity of the crossing sites the enemy was thinly disposed on the ground and his artillery had been neutralized by the counter battery bombardment. Good progress was made during the night and elements of the division rapidly approached the outskirts of Rees.

At 2200 hours 1 Commando Brigade began to cross the river about two miles west of Wesel and half-an-hour later was formed up just outside the town. Here they waited for fifteen minutes while two hundred Lancasters of Bomber Command dropped one thousand tons of bombs on the enemy defences, at a distance of only fifteen hundred yards from our leading troops.

The brigade advanced immediately the bombing ceased and, by 0300 hours, was entering the town. Fierce fighting took place, but the systematic elimination of the German garrison of Wesel went forward.

At 0200 hours the four leading battalions of 15 Division were water-borne, and made successful crossings in face of light opposition.

In the Ninth American Army sector, 30 Division of the left crossed north of the Ossenburg at 0200 hours with three regiments abreast, and an hour later 79 Division on the right crossed with two regiments up. The assaults were successful and casualties were light.

Our assault crossings had achieved success, and follow-up formations were soon beginning to pour across the river as the various ferries came into operation. The initial German reaction had been light, although the enemy achieved some measure of recovery on the left of the American landings and on the left sector of the British assault.

While the ground troops pushed on in the early hours of 24 March the airborne forces were forming up. 17 United States Airborne Division took off from bases in France, while 6 Airborne Division was lifted from England. Escorted by aircraft of Fighter Command and of the British and American Tactical Air Forces, the two mighty air fleets converged near Brussels and made for the Rhine. Over the bridgehead area an air umbrella was maintained by nine hundred fighters, while deeper into Germany fighter formations kept enemy aircraft away from the battle zone. A great weight of artillery fire from the west bank of the Rhine prepared the way for the airborne drop, and a few minutes before 1000 hours the ground troops saw the aircraft of the first parachute serial arrive. For the next three hours relays of aircraft came in to the dropping and landing zone areas in an immensely thrilling and inspiring demonstration of Allied air power; over seventeen hundred aircraft and thirteen hundred gliders were employed to deliver some fourteen thousand troops in the battle area. Our losses were comparatively light for an operation of this magnitude; under four per cent of the gliders were destroyed while the total losses in transport aircraft were fifty-five. Immediately following the glider landings, a re-supply mission was flown in very low by 250 Liberators of Eighth United States Air Force. The latter were met by heavy flak and fourteen were shot down, but eighty-five per cent of their supplies were accurately dropped.

On the ground the airborne forces met with varying resistance. In some areas opposition was negligible, but elsewhere troops came down on top of enemy positions and gun areas. 6 Airborne Division seized Hamminkeln and the bridges over the River Ijssel, and 17 Airborne Division took Diersfordt and the high wooded ground to the east and secured further crossings over the Ijssel. The Airborne Corps took 3,500 prisoners during the day and cleared all its objectives according to plan.

The arrival of the airborne divisions threw the enemy into confusion and accelerated the progress of the assault divisions. In the American sector Dinslaken was captured and the assault corps reached the general line of the Dinslaken–Wesel road. On the left, elements crossed the Lippe Canal near Lipperdorf about a mile short of Wesel.

1 Commando Brigade made contact with 17 Airborne Division in the Wesel area, having cleared the major part of the town. 15 Division captured Mehr and Haffen and established firm contact with 6 Airborne Division, but further north progress was not so rapid, as there was fierce fighting round the outskirts of Rees during the day.

Bridging and ferrying operations proceeded apace along the length of the river, except in the Rees area, where enemy parachute troops dominated the bridging sites. Alternatives had to be found for the bridges and ferries in order to avoid the heavy and accurate mortar and artillery fire directed on the crossings.

By nightfall Ninth American Army had the whole of 30 and 79 Divisions across the river and elements of two other infantry divisions were on their way. The Army had captured nearly 1,900 prisoners and was holding a bridgehead 4,000 to 6,000 yards in depth. In the Second Army sector 15 Division had secured a number of villages and repulsed several sharp counter attacks; 51 Division had captured Esserden and Speldrop and its leading elements were in the outskirts of Bienen where a brigade of 3 Canadian Division, under its command, was operating. The British divisions had been supported by regiments of DD tanks, whose appearance on the far bank had greatly disconcerted the enemy, their timely arrival in 15 Division area helping materially in dealing with the enemy counter attacks.

The weather had been most favourable for air operations and the resources of the Allied Air Forces were thrown into the battle; even air formations based in the Mediterranean area carried out missions associated with the battle.

### THE BATTLE OF THE RHINE:
### THE EXPANSION OF THE BRIDGEHEAD

During the night 24/25 March our positions were further strengthened and a heavy counter attack against the airborne troops north of Wesel was dealt with. Steady progress was maintained during 25 March. XVI American Corps completed the clearance of Dinslaken and its two assault divisions joined hands on the left. A firm junction had been effected with 1 Commando Brigade south of Wesel. In Wesel itself street fighting continued; the Commandos had by now taken 700 prisoners and were joined by units of 17 Airborne Division.

On the front of 12 Corps the advance of 15 Division continued and Bislich was captured. The division was reinforced by a brigade of 52 Division, while 53 Division began crossing the river over which a Class 40 bridge was now working. In 30 Corps sector, 43 Division crossed into the bridgehead and took station on the left. Meanwhile, except for one small pocket, Rees was cleared by 51 Division.

On the following day XVI American Corps made an advance of over six miles and captured Bruckhausen. The airborne divisions advanced steadily and on their left 52 Division captured Ringenberg. The bridgeheads of 15 and 51 Divisions were securely linked, and further left 43 Division with a brigade of 3 Canadian Division seized Millingen and Hueth. Early on 27 March, 79 American Division attacked to the south, captured Holten and reached the Dortmund–Ems Canal. In the centre of the American sector 35 Division came into the line and attacked to the east, while on the left 30 Division was meeting heavy opposition as it approached Gahlen. North of the Lippe River the airborne divisions made considerable progress, and enemy resistance on their front was progressively weakening; to add weight to their thrust an armoured brigade passed through the airborne sector at midnight 27 March.

12 and 30 Corps made progress, although on the left of Second Army's sector the four enemy parachute divisions were still fighting with all their usual tenacity and skill. 12 Corps troops pushed on to Raesfeld and Bocholt, while 30 Corps troops attacked north along the Rees–Ijsselburg road and were now meeting little opposition except from mines and artillery fire. 43 Division advanced in conformity, and on its left 3 Canadian Division took over the left sector of the Corps bridgehead. Except in the areas held by the German parachute troops, enemy opposition had now very largely disintegrated. On 28 March the Americans were in Gladbach and Gahlen while 6 Guards Armoured Brigade, carrying personnel of 17 American Airborne Division on their tanks, reached Dorsten and Haltern; 6 Airborne Division captured Erle and Lembeck. In the centre, Rhede was captured and an attack put in on Bocholt, while leading troops of 30 Corps reached the general line Haldern–Ijsselburg–Anholt after some stiff fighting and, on the extreme left, the Canadians were closing in on Emmerich and the high ground at Hoch Elten. At this stage 2 Canadian Corps became operational and took over the left sector.

8 Corps, which had been in reserve, was now activated and, with 11 Armoured Division, came up on the right of Second Army.

Conditions were now favourable for us to thrust out from our bridgehead.

### REFLECTIONS ON THE BATTLE OF THE RHINE

We had forced the River Rhine and were in possession of a springboard on the east bank from which to launch major operations into Germany.

Very great credit is due to the Armies for the speed with which this great undertaking was mounted and delivered, and to the Allied airborne and ground troops for the impetus and dash they displayed in the operation.

During March the enemy's losses in prisoners alone had so far averaged some 10,000 a day, and, with no fresh formations in reserve, it was clear that if he decided to continue the struggle, he had no option but to withdraw the remnants of his forces as best he might, with the hope of forming an improvised front further to the east. Meanwhile the mighty Russian Army was pressing on from the east: Hitler's Germany was faced with disaster.

# CHAPTER EIGHTEEN

## *The Advance to the Elbe*

### THE DEVELOPMENT OF OPERATIONS EAST OF THE RHINE

I MADE plans for the advance of 21 Army Group together with Ninth United States Army to the Elbe, with the object of establishing the United States forces on the river from Magdeburg to Wittenberge and Second Army from Wittenberge to Hamburg.

In the course of its advance Ninth Army would make contact with the forces of First United States Army, which were pushing north through Marburg from their Remagen bridgehead, and by this means the Ruhr would be encircled and its garrison cut off from the German forces in the east. It was intended to effect this junction in the area of Paderborn, but, if for any reason First Army were held up, I instructed General Simpson to push ahead to the Elbe, making his own arrangements for the security of his right flank. One Corps of the Army was to be detailed to hold the flank along the north of the Ruhr as far east as Paderborn, so that our lines of communication should be safeguarded, and the enemy forces which had retired into the built-up area south of the Lippe Canal would be contained, until we could conveniently dispose of them. To support its advance, Ninth Army was given, after 31 March, sole use of the Wesel bridge, which had previously been shared with Second Army.

Second Army's primary objective was the line of the Elbe from Wittenberge northwards to Hamburg, the left flank of the advance resting on the line Hengelo–Lingen–Bremen–Hamburg. There was a prospect that 30 Corps, operating on the left flank of the Army, might be delayed from breaking out of the bridgehead because of the continued opposition from the parachute divisions north of Rees. In this event, I intended to transfer 30 Corps to command of First Canadian Army, so that Second Army could concentrate all its attention on the task of driving to the Elbe. This regrouping did not, in the event, prove necessary.

Canadian Army was to open up a supply route through Arnhem, and to advance northwards to clear north-east Holland, the coastal belt to the north of Second Army's left boundary, and western Holland. It appeared that these operations would probably have to be carried out in the order in which I have given them.

When Second and Ninth Armies reached the Elbe, I anticipated that a temporary halt might be necessary in order that Ninth Army might assist in clearing the Ruhr, while Second Army might have to co-operate with the Canadians in reducing the enemy isolated west of the Elbe estuary. In order to ensure maximum support from the Air Forces, the Armies were instructed to pay special attention to the acquisition of airfields, particularly those in the Rheine and Munster areas.

[386]

MAP 43    THE DEVELOPMENT OF ALLIED OPERATIONS EAST OF THE RHINE

My plan of operations was similar in principle to those carried out by 21 Army Group in north-west France and Belgium during the preceding autumn. Just as in 1944 Second Army drove rapidly across the rear areas of the Pas de Calais cutting the enemy's east–west communications, while Canadian Army mopped up the enemy garrisons along the Channel coast, so in 1945 Second Army was ordered to strike straight for the Elbe across the east–west routes and to come in on Bremen and Hamburg with right hooks from the east, while Canadian Army cleaned up the coastal sectors.

Subsequently, however, the plan outlined above had to be modified. As a result of the general enemy situation, and particularly in view of the rapid American success following the seizure of the Remagen bridge, the Supreme Commander decided that the main Allied thrust east of the Rhine should be directed from the Kassel area through Erfurt towards Leipzig. By this means a junction was to be effected with the advancing Russian forces on or near the Elbe, and the remaining German forces cut in two. Subsequently, the formations of Twelfth Army Group were to be switched north or south, as the situation might dictate. General Eisenhower's orders provided that this thrust into Central Germany was to be initiated as soon as the encirclement of the Ruhr had been completed and the forces trapped therein reduced to an extent which rendered them no longer a menace to the security of our communications.

As a result of this plan, Ninth United States Army was reverted to command Twelfth Army Group on 4 April and formed the left wing element in the American offensive which began on that day.

The aim of 21 Army Group remained to reach the line of the Elbe in our sector, and to reduce the ports of Bremen and Hamburg. Now that the Allies would not be so relatively strong in the northern sector, it was to be anticipated that these tasks would take longer than I had previously hoped, and Second Army would require to watch for the security of its southern flank. I decided to establish an intermediate phase in our advance to the Elbe on the line of the Weser, Aller and Leine rivers. While Second Army advanced to this line, Canadian Army was to clear north-east Holland and the Emden–Wilhelmshaven peninsula.

### NINTH UNITED STATES ARMY OPERATIONS TO 4 APRIL

The operations of Ninth United States Army after the establishment of its Rhine bridgehead were characterized by great dash and speed. Enemy resistance was scattered and ineffective, and by 3 April, led by armoured divisions, XIII Corps on the left had reached the line of the Weser north-east of Herford, while XIX Corps, having established contact with First United States Army near Lippstadt and thus completed the encirclement of the Ruhr, pushed on to the east. On the right flank, XVI Corps forced its way southwards into the built up area of the Ruhr valley and subsequently operated with First United States Army in the reduction of the enemy trapped in the Ruhr pocket.

### THE ADVANCE OF SECOND ARMY TO THE ELBE

The main Second Army advances from the Rhine bridgehead were conducted by 8 Corps on the right, directed on Osnabruck, Celle and Uelzen, by 12 Corps in the centre, on Rheine, Nienburg and Luneburg, and by 30 Corps on the left, on Enschede, Bremen and Hamburg. It had also been intended, prior to the change in the overall Allied plan, to employ XVIII United States Airborne Corps on the right of 8 Corps, to capture Munster. This Corps, however, ceased to be operational on 30 March, and it was left to XIII Corps, under Ninth Army, to reduce Munster on 3 April. Of the British elements in XVIII Airborne Corps, 6 Airborne Division had passed to 8 Corps on 29 March, but 6 Guards Armoured Brigade remained attached to Ninth Army until 4 April, when it also reverted to 8 Corps.

The resistance to the advances of Second Army was lightest on the right flank in front of 8 Corps. Elsewhere it varied; in some areas the enemy succeeding in delaying our progress with hastily formed battle groups. Despite the general disintegration of his forces, however, the German skill in using demolitions to impede the pursuit was as marked as ever, and heavy burdens were imposed on our engineers as a consequence. The area between the Rhine and the Elbe was intersected by innumerable waterways, including such major obstacles as the Ems and Weser rivers and the Dortmund–Ems and the Ems–Weser canals; over five hundred bridges had to be constructed in the course of the advance.

8 Corps made rapid strides to reach the Dortmund–Ems canal, which was crossed without undue difficulty. Osnabruck was cleared, and by 5 April Minden and Stolzenau, on the Weser, were captured by 6 Airborne Division and 11 Armoured Division respectively, and bridgeheads over the river were seized in both areas. The Corps advanced north from the Weser on 7 April and within three days Celle had been captured by 15 Division and bridgeheads established over the Aller river. As the advance continued resistance stiffened in the area of Uelzen, where there was four days' hard fighting before the town was reduced on 18 April. At the same time Luneburg fell to 11 Armoured Division, which reached the Elbe opposite Lauenburg on the next day. By 24 April the west bank of the river had been cleared throughout the Corps sector.

12 Corps also had little difficulty in the early stages of its advance from the Rhine bridgehead, but resistance became firmer on the line of the Dortmund–Ems Canal. Bitter fighting took place for the airfields in the Rheine area, where troops from nearby Officer Cadet Schools held up the advance for some days. 7 Armoured Division cleared the area by 6 April, however, and then pushed eastwards to cross the Weser against light opposition. There was further resistance east of the river, where SS elements with 88 millimetre guns on railway mountings temporarily checked 53 Division at Rethem. Soltau was captured on 18 April and, on the next day, 7 Armoured Division cut the Bremen–Hamburg autobahn after a wide sweep to the north. The outskirts of Harburg, on the south bank of the Elbe opposite Hamburg, were entered on 23 April and 12 Corps closed to the river.

[389]

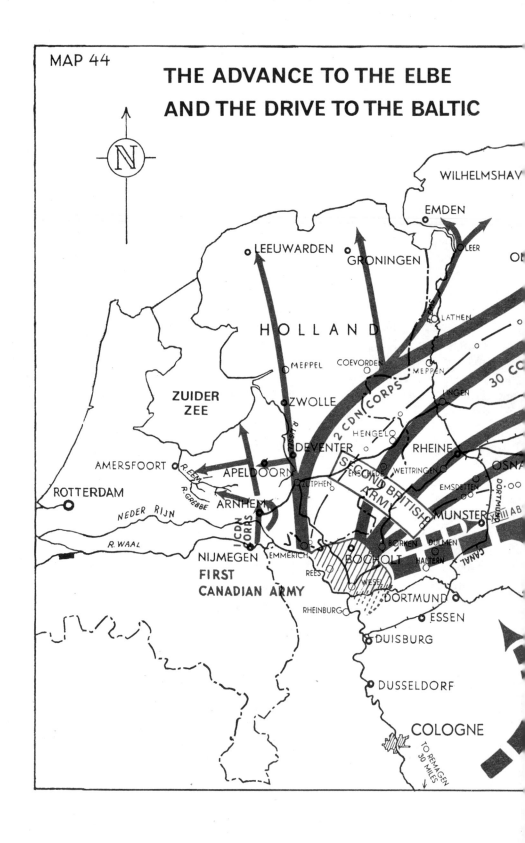

MAP 44

# THE ADVANCE TO THE ELBE
# AND THE DRIVE TO THE BALTIC

N

WILHELMSHAV

EMDEN

LEEUWARDEN          GRONINGEN          LEER

O

HOLLAND          LATHEN

MEPPEL     COEVORDEN          MEPPEN

ZUIDER     ZWOLLE          LINGEN          30 CO

ZEE          HENGELO          RHEINE

AMERSFOORT     APELDOORN     DEVENTER          OSNA

ROTTERDAM     ARNHEM     ZUTPHEN     ENSCHEDE     WETTRINGEN     EMSDETTEN     DORTMU

NEDER RIJN     R. GREBBE          MUNSTER     XIII AB

R. WAAL          BORKEN     DULMEN

NIJMEGEN     EMMERICH     BOCHOLT     HALTERN     CANAL

FIRST     REES     WESEL

CANADIAN ARMY     RHEINBURG     DORTMUND

DUISBURG

DUSSELDORF

COLOGNE

TO REMAGEN
30 MILES

SECOND BRITISH ARM

2 CDN CORPS

I CDN CORPS

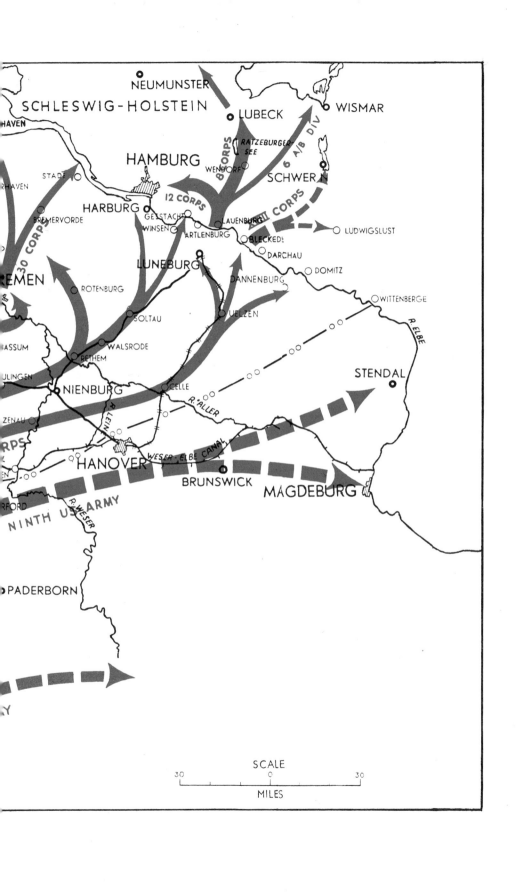

NEUMUNSTER

SCHLESWIG-HOLSTEIN

LUBECK

WISMAR

HAVEN

8 CORPS

RATZEBURGER-
SEE

6 A/B DIV

HAMBURG

WENDORF

SCHWERIN

STADE

12 CORPS

XVIII CORPS

HAVEN

HARBURG

GEESTACHT

LAUENBURG

BREMERVORDE

WINSEN

ARTLENBURG

LUDWIGSLUST

30 CORPS

BLECKEDE

DARCHAU

DOMITZ

LUNEBURG

DANNENBURG

BREMEN

ROTENBURG

WITTENBERGE

R. ELBE

SOLTAU

UELZEN

ASSUM

WALSRODE

STENDAL

RETHEM

ULINGEN

NIENBURG

CELLE

R. LEINE

R. ALLER

ZENAU

HANOVER

WESER-ELBE CANAL

BRUNSWICK

MAGDEBURG

RFORD

NINTH U.S. ARMY

R. WESER

PADERBORN

Y

SCALE

30          0          30

MILES

The 30 Corps advance met obstinate resistance by SS and parachute elements along the Dortmund–Ems Canal line near Lingen. It was not until 6 April that a further advance could be made following the clearance of the town by 3 Division. Opposition was encountered in some areas east of the Ems and stiffened considerably as the Corps closed in on Bremen, where the defence was considerably assisted by demolitions and widespread inundations. In these circumstances, the plan for the capture of Bremen was to deliver a twofold assault on the city, striking from front and rear simultaneously. A frontal holding attack against that part of the city west of the Weser was delivered by 3 Division while 43 and 52 Divisions, having crossed the Weser upstream, delivered a right hook from the east. By 19 April our forces were two miles south of the city on the near bank and ten miles south-east on the far bank, but it was not until the night of 24 April that the intervening ground had been secured. Once the attackers were within the city itself, however, resistance crumbled, and the chief impediment to progress lay in the debris caused by our own bombing. By 26 April the last pockets of resistance had been mopped up. With Bremen reduced, 30 Corps continued its operations beyond the Weser. Guards Armoured Division drove through Bremervorde to capture Stade and reached the Elbe estuary below Hamburg, while 51 Division was directed north towards the naval base of Cuxhaven, in order to complete the clearance of the peninsula between the two rivers.

### OPERATIONS OF FIRST CANADIAN ARMY

Under First Canadian Army, 2 Canadian Corps operated to the north of the Emmerich bridgehead while 1 Canadian Corps had the task of capturing Arnhem and opening the route to the north.

2 Canadian Corps reverted to Canadian Army as soon as Emmerich and the Hoch Elten feature had been captured. It then struck northwards to Doesburg and Zutphen, on the right bank of the Ijssel, and by 5 April had forced a crossing of the Twenthe Canal in face of strong resistance by parachute troops. From this point, 4 Canadian Armoured Division was directed north-east on the axis Meppen–Oldenburg, crossing the Ems in the Meppen–Lathen area on 8 April. The advance continued steadily towards Oldenburg but strong enemy counter attacks in front of the town slowed up progress. In the centre, 2 Canadian Division pushed on to the north and reached Groningen on 16 April and cleared the area beyond it up to the North Sea. In the course of this advance, the division joined up with the parties of Special Air Service troops dropped on the night of 7 April, east of the Zuider Zee, around Meppel. On the left flank, 3 Canadian Division took Deventer on 10 April and then held the line of the Ijssel River facing west. On 11 April, 1 Canadian Division, temporarily under command 2 Canadian Corps, attacked across the Ijssel towards Apeldoorn in conjunction with the operations of 1 Canadian Corps. Subsequently, 1 Canadian Division passed to command of the latter Corps and 3 Canadian Division moved on northwards to clear north-west Holland.

Meanwhile 1 Canadian Corps had opened its operation to clear Arnhem. By 5

April, the area between Nijmegen and the Neder Rijn was in our hands but, instead of attempting a frontal assault on Arnhem across the river, it was decided to seize the town by means of a right hook. While 5 Canadian Armoured Division and 1 Canadian Armoured Brigade occupied the enemy's attention south of the town, 49 Division made a surprise crossing of the Neder Rijn near its confluence with the Ijssel on the night of 12 April, and drove west to take Arnhem in rear two days later. 5 Canadian Armoured Division then crossed the river and struck north to seize the high ground between it and the Zuider Zee; the Apeldoorn–Amersfoort road was cut and the coast of the Zuider Zee reached on 18 April. Apeldoorn itself had been taken by 1 Canadian Division on the preceding day after a sharp battle with German paratroops.

Following these successes, 5 Canadian Armoured Division moved over to join 2 Canadian Corps in the task of reducing the enemy along the northern coastline, in which operations Polish Armoured Division had now been included. By 20 April, north-east Holland had been cleared except for a small area on the western shore of the Ems estuary. While 5 Canadian Armoured Division took over the country west of the Dutch–German frontier, 2 Canadian Corps was able to concentrate the remainder of its divisions east of the Ems to deal with the enemy between the river and the mouth of the Weser. As Bremen fell, 2 Canadian Corps was directed to seize Wilhelmshaven and Emden and to complete the reduction of the peninsula between the two rivers.

### RELIEF TO WESTERN HOLLAND

On the conclusion of the Arnhem operation and the isolation of the enemy by our thrust to the Zuider Zee, 1 Canadian Corps closed to the line of the Rivers Grebbe and Eem. I then instructed First Canadian Army to halt its offensive operations against 'Fortress Holland' and the position remained the same until the German garrison capitulated. Little use could have been served by a further advance at this stage. Although the enemy was completely cut off from any hope of relief or reinforcement, he was strongly entrenched behind a formidable barrier of artificial floods, and offensive operations would have required considerable resources, which were not at this stage available in this sector. The reduction of western Holland might also have caused even greater suffering to the civilian population, already reduced to desperate straits by lack of food and the ruthless inundation of their land.

A means of alleviating this civilian distress was, however, found when the German Civil Commissioner, Seyss-Inquart, approached the Allies with the offer of a truce which would permit the introduction of relief supplies. We readily agreed to take advantage of this opportunity and the movement of food stocks, medical supplies and other urgently required commodities was promptly initiated.

### AMERICAN OPERATIONS EAST OF THE RHINE

In spite of the increasing enemy forces that the Remagen bridgehead attracted, Twelfth United States Army Group expanded rapidly its territory east of the Rhine and began thrusting east and north-east in a drive which reached the Paderborn area by the end of March. Third American Army, which had eliminated the Saar triangle in conjunction with Sixth United States Army Group, crossed the Rhine astride Mainz in the last week of March and came up on the right of First Army.

By the middle of April First United States Army was within ten miles of Leipzig and General Patton's forces had reached Nuremberg and the Danube valley.

# CHAPTER NINETEEN

# The Drive to the Baltic

I T must be remembered that the Allies were not in great strength in the wide 21 Army Group sector east of the Rhine, and in view of this fact our advance to the Elbe had been conducted with creditable speed. It has been seen that, although the general enemy organization had largely disintegrated, there was some stiff fighting in certain areas, particularly on the Dortmund–Ems Canal, and our troops were faced with the usual problem of demolitions and mines.

Having lined up on the Elbe, it became the Supreme Commander's intention that 21 Army Group should advance to the Baltic and thus cut off Schleswig-Holstein and Denmark and proceed to seize the Kiel Canal and the north-west German ports. In order to give us some additional strength for this task, I was allotted XVIII United States Airborne Corps of three divisions.

On 22 April I issued instructions for the development of operations. My object was to capture Lubeck and Hamburg, seal off the Schleswig-Holstein peninsula and clear the area up to the Danish frontier. I envisaged the initial operations being carried out in two phases: first, the establishment of a bridgehead across the Elbe and secondly, a strong thrust northwards to the Baltic. A secure east flank north of the Elbe was to be formed by XVIII United States Airborne Corps on the general line Darchau–Schwerin–Wismar. As the operations of the Airborne Corps developed, 6 British Airborne Division would be added to it to help hold the flank position.

I anticipated that contact would be made very shortly with our Russian Allies and, to avoid misunderstandings, I directed that our troops would halt as and where they met the Russians and would be disposed in accordance with joint military requirements irrespective of the ultimate occupation zone boundaries.

In outline, the plan of Second Army was for 8 Corps to assault across the Elbe in the area of Lauenburg and to establish a bridgehead on the east bank about 15 miles wide and 8 miles deep. XVIII United States Corps was to establish a bridgehead on the right of 8 Corps sector, as it was estimated that any attempt to pass this Corps over the 8 Corps bridgehead would lead to congestion and delay in the carrying out of its task. Having secured a good bridgehead east of the river, 8 Corps was to develop a strong thrust northwards with all speed to capture Lubeck. Bridges were to be constructed across the river in the 8 Corps sector by 12 Corps: which would then cross the river and turn west to mask Hamburg, preparatory to an assault on the city.

The Elbe operation demanded very considerable tonnages of bridging, in addition to the normal administrative build-up. From the maintenance aspect, however, the advance to the Elbe had proved easier to support than the pursuit after Normandy,

MAP 45 1–15 APRIL
THE ADVANCE OF THE ALLIED ARMIES INTO GERMANY

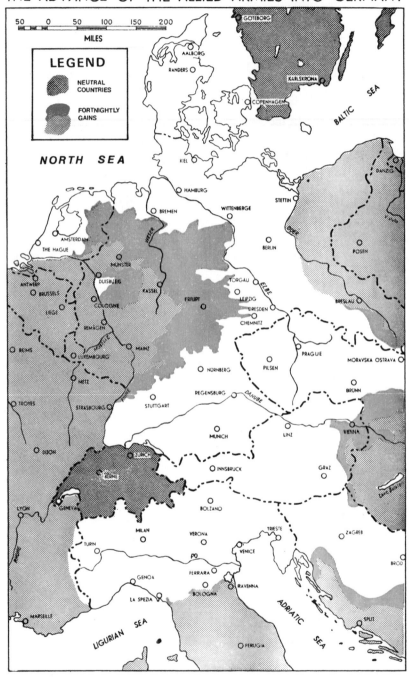

because of the well-developed bases in Belgium and the roadhead previously established near the Rhine.

Transport continued to be centralized, which gave great flexibility of allocation. To the extra 10,000 tons road lift which Second Army was allotted in March, a further 2,000 tons lift was added in April; at the end of the campaign Second Army had a transport lift from General Headquarters sources alone of 23,000 tons, which is the equivalent of seventy-six General Transport Companies.

Delivery of stores by air freight continued, but owing to the degree of centralization involved, the system was not flexible, and changes of priority could not be speedily made. Events showed that in a fast moving campaign completely centralized control of transport aircraft leads eventually to lack of economy and prevents improvisation, which is so essential under such conditions. I should like to mention here that returning aircraft did magnificent service in repatriating our released prisoners.

On 9 April, Second Army established a roadhead in the Rheine area and shortly afterwards near Sulingen. Forward delivery from Sulingen to the 8 Corps Field Maintenance Centre involved a carry of nearly 90 miles over extremely bad roads; the situation was eased, however, by opening a stretch of railway from Celle to a railhead near Luneburg.

While the administrative build-up was being completed, XVIII United States Corps carried out a remarkably rapid concentration, from points as far distant as the Ruhr and Cologne.

It was eventually found possible to launch the 8 Corps assault in the early hours of 29 April, while XVIII Corps was to make its crossing 24 hours later.

Next to the Rhine, the Elbe is the most important river in Germany. On the front of Second Army it was about 300–400 yards wide, with dykes similar in construction and appearance to those which existed in the Rhine valley. There was a number of ferries in the area, but only one bridge—a railway bridge at Lauenburg—and this had been destroyed by the enemy.

The German Army was now fast approaching disintegration, but it was estimated that there were some eight or nine battalions facing Second Army on the east bank of the Elbe. Almost the whole of the enemy artillery consisted of flak guns, some of which were mounted on railway trucks.

### THE LAST OPERATION

At 0200 hours on 29 April, 15 Division, with 1 Commando Brigade under command, attacked across the Elbe. The leading infantry were conveyed in amphibians, as in the Rhine crossing, and were assisted by the use of DD tanks, all of which reached the far bank without loss. The operation proceeded according to plan and a bridgehead was established during the day; opposition was generally light and over 1,300 prisoners were captured. The main trouble was caused by the shelling of the selected bridging sites, and some activity on the part of the German Air Force. We were now approaching the last group of airfields left to the Luftwaffe in Germany and, in the weather

## MAP 46   16 APRIL−1 MAY
## THE ADVANCE OF THE ALLIED ARMIES INTO GERMANY

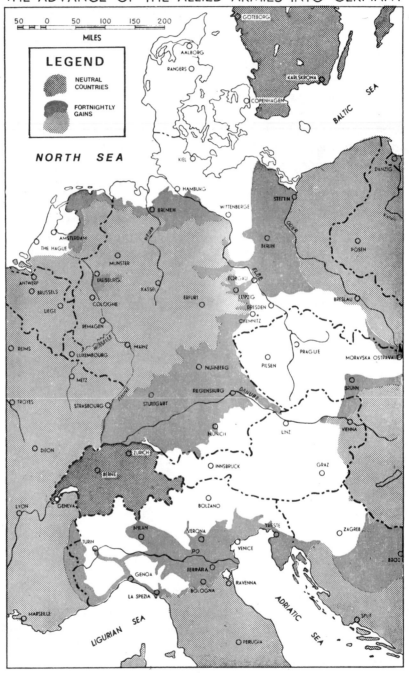

conditions which obtained, it was always possible for small numbers of enemy aircraft to approach under cover of clouds and take fleeting hostile action. The Royal Air Force provided the maximum amount of air cover, which included a number of our new jet-propelled fighters, and shot down thirteen enemy aircraft during the day.

On 30 April 82 United States Airborne Division attacked astride Bleckede in assault boats in the face of very light opposition. The construction of a heavy bridge was put in hand, and a bridgehead was quickly secured.

In the 8 Corps sector some regrouping took place to facilitate the development of operations. A Class 40 bridge was completed at Artlenburg and 6 Airborne Division began to cross the river, followed by 11 Armoured Division. Reconnaissance elements of 15 Division were some seven miles east of the river during the day.

On 1 May rapid progress was made by both the Allied Corps. On the right, 82 Airborne Division moved south-east along the bank of the river and 6 Airborne Division, which came under command of XVIII Corps at 1500 hours, advanced north for a distance of about eight miles. A Class 40 bridge was constructed at Darchau and 7 United States Armoured Division began to cross.

The advance from the 8 Corps bridgehead was led by 5 Division on the right and 11 Armoured Division on the left, directed on Lubeck. 11 Armoured Division advanced rapidly for fifteen miles and reached Wendorf, about half-way to Lubeck, with 5 Division making good progress on its right. Meanwhile, 15 Division, following the north bank of the river, had reached Geestacht, about sixteen miles short of Hamburg.

On 2 May 82 Airborne Division advanced further east and cleared a large area which included Dommitz. 7 United States Armoured Division made a swift advance of twenty miles and captured Ludwigslust while, further north, 8 Division captured Schwerin. 6 Airborne Division on the left made a forty miles advance against no opposition and occupied Wismar on the Baltic coast. A few hours after its arrival, Russian tanks appeared and made contact with our troops.

11 Armoured Division entered Lubeck without opposition after a drive of thirty miles, while 5 Division on the right continued along the west side of the Ratzeburger See.

In the meantime, the leading formations of 12 Corps had passed through the 8 Corps bridgehead with the task of capturing Hamburg, but this operation was no longer necessary as the German garrison commander came out to surrender the city unconditionally and our troops entered without opposition on 3 May.

The countryside north of the Elbe was now packed with a mass of German soldiery and refugees, fleeing from the Allied advance and from the Russians. It could now be said that the enemy had decided to abandon the fight and, apart from small groups of fanatics, nothing more than token resistance was to be expected from the German armed forces south of the Kiel Canal. I ordered a pause in our advance to be made on a line which would cover Lubeck and Hamburg, as German plenipotentiaries were on their way to surrender.

# CHAPTER TWENTY

## *The Surrender*

BEHIND the scenes those Germans who understood military arguments had for some time been trying to find a way to surrender. Once we had crossed the Rhine further resistance was obviously futile. But Hitler was deaf to military arguments. Moreover, those who were putting out feelers behind his back were anxious not so much to end the war as to buy us off in the west so that they could continue their losing battles in the east. This was the last round in their fight to avoid the two-front war the Germans had brought upon themselves.

The first approaches I heard of were made in March to the British Embassy in Stockholm, where the notion of a unilateral peace was rejected out of hand. Shortly afterwards we began to receive those hints from western Holland which I have already mentioned. Two meetings were held at the end of April with Russian, American and British representatives on our side to discuss feeding the Dutch. Beyond that, however, Seyss-Inquart would not or could not take a military decision while Blaskowitz, the military commander, refused to consider capitulation so long as any force continued to resist within Germany itself. We were able to start feeding the Dutch, but western Holland remained in German possession for another week.

Meanwhile, once again through Stockholm, had come the news that Field-Marshal von Busch was willing to come to terms with the British. General Lindemann in Denmark was also believed to be willing to capitulate. Again, however, it was not a straightforward matter. Von Busch was hoping to rescue his forces from the Soviet armies advancing rapidly towards their rear from the east. He let it be known that he would surrender, but not until we had reached the Baltic, where he would be cut off from the Russians and also, interestingly enough, from the possibility of SS reinforcements which might insist on the continuation of hostilities. In fact, the Germans fell into two categories: those like Hitler himself, who refused to consider giving up fighting at all, and those like Himmler and von Busch who hoped to do a deal which would divide the Allies.

Following the Second Army's assault across the Elbe on 29 April, Wolz, the German Commander in Hamburg, made contact with Major-General Lyne commanding 7 Armoured Division. On 2 May he had agreed to the local surrender of the city when it became known that his own superior commander, General Blumentritt, wished to surrender to Second Army. It was agreed that Blumentritt's delegation should come to General Dempsey's Tactical Headquarters next morning.

By now the situation was quite beyond German control. Hitler was dead (though we did not know it at the time) and Grand-Admiral Doenitz was trying in Schleswig-

Holstein to exercise command in his stead. He was prepared to end the war, but not to surrender to the Russians. He therefore ordered the armies retreating before the Russians to surrender to the Anglo-Americans. In the narrowing belt between the eastern and western fronts the confusion was most remarkable.

German willingness to surrender developed rapidly as the situation worsened, and instead of Blumentritt's delegation arriving at General Dempsey's Headquarters there appeared a much stronger team led by General-Admiral von Friedeberg, who was Doenitz's emissary, accompanied by General Kinzel, Busch's Chief of Staff. The delegation was empowered to discuss the surrender of the entire enemy forces in the north. Accordingly, they were sent on to my Tactical Headquarters on Luneburg Heath. Wolz, who had accompanied them, stayed behind to sign the surrender of Hamburg to Second Army.

When von Friedeberg arrived he told me that the German High Command wished to surrender to me the forces in the northern sectors, including those withdrawing through Mecklenberg before the Russian advance. He wished to save his soldiers from the Russians and asked my permission that civilian refugees should be allowed to pass through our lines into Schleswig-Holstein. I refused to accept the surrender of the German forces opposing the Russians, and explained that their capitulation should be negotiated with our Russian Allies. As far as the enemy on my own front was concerned I made it clear that I would only discuss the unconditional surrender of all forces— land, sea and air—still resisting in Holland, the Frisian Islands, Heligoland, Schleswig-Holstein, Denmark, and those parts of Germany west of the Elbe still in German possession. Unless I received their unconditional surrender I would order fighting to recommence: gladly. I then showed von Friedeberg a map of the current operational situation of which he was apparently not properly aware, and this helped to convince him of the hopelessness of the German position.

The delegation then explained that they had no power to agree to my demands; they were now prepared, however, to recommend their acceptance to Field-Marshal Keitel. Two members of the delegation left immediately by car to return to Keitel's Headquarters, while the others remained at my Tactical Headquarters on Luneburg Heath.

At 1800 hours on 4 May, von Friedeberg returned to my Headquarters, having obtained further instructions from Keitel and Doenitz. First I saw him privately in my office caravan where I told him that all I was interested to hear was whether he had brought back an answer 'Yes' or 'No' to my demand for unconditional surrender. On learning that the answer was in the affirmative, we adjourned to a tent nearby which had been prepared for the signing of the Instrument of Surrender.

The Instrument of Surrender was signed in my presence at 1820 hours on 4 May, and I received it under the powers conferred upon me for the purpose by the Supreme Commander. This document and the 'Cease Fire' order are reproduced.

The capitulation was to become effective at 0800 hours on 5 May. By its terms, the German Command agreed that all the forces under their control in Holland, north-west Germany (including the Frisian Islands, Heligoland and all other islands), Schleswig-Holstein and Denmark would lay down their arms and surrender unconditionally. The German Command would then carry out at once, and without argument or comment, any further orders which might be issued by the Allied Powers on any subject; and the decision of these Powers would be final were any question of interpretation of the terms to arise. It was understood that the Instrument signed at my Headquarters was to be superseded by any General Instrument of Surrender subsequently to be imposed relating to Germany and the German armed forces as a whole.

We had not long to wait for this final act, for by now the disintegration of the German ability to resist further had spread throughout all sectors of the fronts. The enemy had abandoned the struggle in Italy on 2 May, while the First and Nineteenth Armies, facing the Allied Sixth Army Group in Southern Germany and Austria, accepted the terms of capitulation on 5 May, 'cease fire' being ordered on the following day.

Von Friedeberg reported to General Eisenhower's Headquarters at Reims on 5 May. Even at this stage an attempt was made to obtain concessions, and to gain time in which to evacuate the maximum number of German troops before the Russian lines in order to surrender them to the Western Allies. The Supreme Commander, however, took firm measures to check this procrastination, and the Instrument of Surrender was signed by Colonel General Jodl, who had been taken to Reims on 6 May, at 0241 hours the next morning. It became effective at midnight 8/9 May. On 9 May Field-Marshal Keitel, for the German High Command, signed the formal ratification of surrender in Berlin.

Instrument of Surrender

of

All German armed forces in HOLLAND, in

northwest Germany including all islands,

and in DENMARK.

1. The German Command agrees to the surrender of all German armed forces in HOLLAND, in northwest GERMANY including the FRISIAN ISLANDS and HELIGOLAND and all other islands, in SCHLESWIG-HOLSTEIN, and in DENMARK, to the C.-in-C. 21 Army Group. This to include all naval ships in these areas. These forces to lay down their arms and to surrender unconditionally.

2. All hostilities on land, on sea, or in the air by German forces in the above areas to cease at 0800 hrs. British Double Summer Time on Saturday 5 May 1945.

3. The German command to carry out at once, and without argument or comment, all further orders that will be issued by the Allied Powers on any subject.

4. Disobedience of orders, or failure to comply with them, will be regarded as a breach of these surrender terms and will be dealt with by the Allied Powers in accordance with the accepted laws and usages of war.

5. This instrument of surrender is independent of, without prejudice to, and will be superseded by any general instrument of surrender imposed by or on behalf of the Allied Powers and applicable to Germany and the German armed forces as a whole.

6. This instrument of surrender is written in English and in German.

   The English version is the authentic text.

7. The decision of the Allied Powers will be final if any doubt or dispute arises as to the meaning or interpretation of the surrender terms.

_Friedeburg_

_Kinzel_

_Wagner_

_Pollex_

_Friedel_

B. L. Montgomery
Field. Marshal

4 am May 1945

1830 hrs

| FROM : EXFOR MAIN : | DATE-TOO |
| --- | --- |
| | 04 2050 B |

TO : FOR ACTION : FIRST CDN ARMY : SECOND BRIT ARMY :

L of C : GHQ AA TPS : 79 ARMD DIV :

EXFOR REAR :

FOR INFM : SECOND TAF : EXFOR TAC : 22 LIAISON HQ :

GO 411A SECRET . all offensive ops will cease from receipt this signal .
orders will be given to all tps to cease fire 0800 hrs tomorrow saturday
5 may . full terms of local German surrender arranged today for 21 ARMY GP
front follow . emphasise these provisions apply solely to 21 ARMY GP fronts
and are for the moment excl of DUNKIRK . ack

IN CIPHER if liable
to interception

DOP

EMERGENCY

~~~~~~~~~ BGS .

Copy to: All Branches Main HQ 21 Army Group
War Diary (2)

# CHAPTER TWENTY-ONE

## *'21 Army Group' becomes 'British Army of the Rhine'*

WITH the cessation of hostilities the task of 21 Army Group had been completed.

Formations were successively deployed within the British Zone to establish our Military Government, and set about their occupational duties. While the machinery of the Control Commission for Germany was being set up the Army was called upon to shoulder the responsibilities of government in an area as big as England and with a population of some twenty millions. Order had to be produced from chaos, and life in Germany, with all its attendant problems, restarted.

Meanwhile the status of 21 Army Group changed, and it was reorganized into an occupational force to which was given the title 'The British Army of the Rhine'.

The change in designation took place on 25 August 1945, and on this occasion I issued a special message to all ranks under my command, which is here reproduced.

### BRITISH ARMY OF THE RHINE

### PERSONAL MESSAGE
### FROM THE C-IN-C

*(To be read out to all Troops)*

1. On Saturday, 25 August 1945, the 21st Army Group will cease to exist and the British forces in north-west Europe will be known as 'The British Army of the Rhine'.

2. I cannot let this moment pass without a reference to the past achievements of 21 Army Group. This Group of Armies fought on the left or northern flank of the Allied Forces that invaded Normandy in June 1944; these forces liberated France, Belgium, Holland, Luxemburg and Denmark; they invaded Germany, and fought their way to the centre of that country where they joined hands with our Russian allies: and thus ended the German war.

   The Army Group completed its active operations by gathering as captives on the northern flank, in the space of a few days, upwards of two million of the once renowned German Army. The fame of the Army Group will long shine in history, and other generations besides our own will honour its deeds.

3. Officers and men of the Army Group are now scattered throughout the world; many are serving in other theatres; many have returned to civil life.

To all of you, wherever you may be, I send my best wishes and my grateful thanks for your loyal help and co-operation.

4. To those who still serve in Germany I would say that, though our name is changed, we still have the same task.

As a result of this war much of Europe has been destroyed, and the whole economic framework of the continent lies in ruins. We have a job to do which will call for all our energy and purpose; we have got to help to rebuild a new Europe out of the ruins of the old.

It is a gigantic task.

But we must face up to it with that same spirit of service to the common cause of freedom which has so strengthened us during the stress and strain of war.

Together we have achieved much in war; let us achieve even more in peace.

B. L. MONTGOMERY

*Field-Marshal*
*Commander-in-Chief*
*British Army of the Rhine*

25 August 1945

# INDEX

Printed in Great Britain by
T. and A. Constable Ltd., Hopetoun Street, Edinburgh